Political Prisoner

You can be indicted, arrested, convicted and sent to prison without committing a crime.

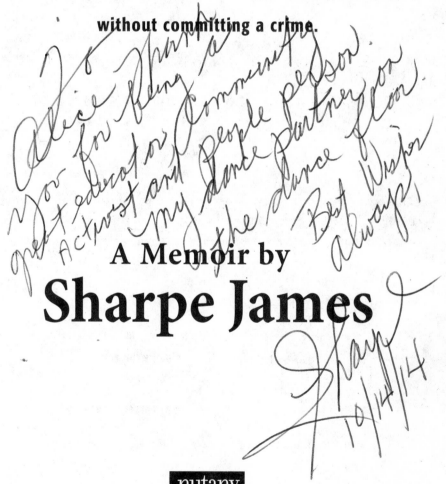

A Memoir by
Sharpe James

nutany
PUBLISHING COMPANY

**Printed in the
United States of America
Second Printing**

**Hard Cover: ISBN 978-0-9754719-5-1
Soft Cover: ISBN 978-0-9754719-6-8**

This memoir represents my effort to recreate events and conversations to the best of my recollection and knowledge and is my honest account of what has transpired; wherever possible legal and written documentation has been provided to substantiate my claims.

Cover photograph by Peter Murphy, Annandale, New Jersey
All other photographs provided by the author

Book Design and production by
Martin Maishman and NUTANY PUBLISHING COMPANY

PUBLISHED BY: NUTANY PUBLISHING COMPANY
NEWARK, NEW JERSEY

I dedicate this book to my loving mother,
Beulah Fluker James,
my wife, Mary Lou,
sons, John, Elliott and Kevin
and my exemplary chief of staff, Cheryl Johnson,
who were always there when I needed them.

I would also like to thank Patrice D. Johnson
for putting up with me while crafting the chapters prior
to my indictment and incarceration.

I LOVE YOU ALL DEARLY!

CONTENTS

CHAPTER ONE

Political Prisoner

"And God said, let us make man in our image,
after our likeness; and let them have
dominion over the fish of the sea, and
over the fowl of the air, and the cattle, and
over all the earth, and over every creeping thing
that creepth upon the earth." **Genesis 1:26**

O n the morning of September 14, 2008 I woke up early, showered, dressed, and called a cab to take me to Newark's Penn
Station. Mingling with the few who were traveling in the
wee hours of the morning on the Sabbath Day in the recently renovated
waiting room, I looked around and reflected on the transformation of
the station since my family first arrived in Newark by rail in the 1940s.

Penn Station was fairly new back then, having opened for the
first time in 1935. The station was more than fifty years old when I
became Mayor of Newark in 1986 and over the years it had become
"Squatter Station" as I often referred to it because of the number of
homeless people seeking shelter there. Whenever the opportunity
came my way I called for a new and improved Penn Station, one that
would approach the grandeur of Union Station in the nation's capital
where Bill Clinton had held one of his inaugural parties.

We were still not Union Station but a new and renovated Newark
Penn Station now boasted sand blasted bricks, cleaned stained glass windows,
a new open food court, polished brass rails, new benches in the waiting room,
improved video train scheduling, and new eateries including a McDonalds.

Newark was indebted to our now late U.S. Senator Frank Lautenberg whose home office in the Gateway One Office Tower overlooks the train station. It was Senator Lautenberg who fought for the federal dollars to make my dream of restoration come true.

At 6:30 a.m. I boarded the Amtrak train to Richmond, Virginia. From there I took a cab to the bus station and waited for four hours before boarding a Greyhound to Petersburg, Virginia. It was 7:30 p.m. when I arrived in Petersburg. Since I wasn't expected until the next morning, I decided to spend my last few hours as a free man relaxing, getting my mind off my predicament. The very next day I would become the property of the Bureau of Prisons (BOP), I would become a prisoner.

I checked into a nearby Ramada Inn at 8 p.m. I then decided to take in a movie at the local movie house. Sitting in the dark theater, munching on my last public hotdog, soda, popcorn and my favorite candy, Raisinets, I wondered what was going to happen to me and my family now. I was facing the unknown and the uncertain. I would no longer be in control of my life. I cannot tell you what the name of the movie was or what it was about. I was thinking about my wife, my sons, and wondering how they would manage without me. I had always been the breadwinner and head of the family.

My loving family had offered to drive me to Petersburg, as did my pastor, the Reverend Ron Christian, of Christian Love Baptist Church. I had refused their kind offers wanting to spare them the hardship of driving seven hours to and from Petersburg only for a tearful parting. Having sent three sons off to college, and later watched our oldest son, John, go off to serve his country in the Gulf war and later to Afghanistan, I wanted to spare them further hardship.

John's departure had been sad enough. He had almost been killed in Afghanistan when his military vehicle had hit a landmine, but miraculously he escaped death. We were very proud of him as we watched him receive the Purple Heart for bravery, an act of valor in defense of his country. We were so proud to be Americans that we had shed tears of happiness. My departure was quite different; I was on my way to a federal prison for an alleged crime I had not committed. "Stay home and prepare for the hard times ahead," I had said to my family before I left home on that dreadful morning. "There will be a lot of pain the family will have to face. Please help out and take care of your mother," I had said to my three sons.

On the morning of September 15, 2008 I checked out of the Ramada and took a cab to the Petersburg Federal Correction Center, arriving at 8 a.m. The cab parked in front of a sign, which read: "Welcome to Petersburg FCC." As I exited the cab, outside the main entrance, my mind reflected on some of the history of Petersburg that I had read the night before in a Ramada Inn magazine. I was standing near the same spot where General Robert E. Lee of the Confederate Army had fought his last great battle against overwhelming odds and was forced to retreat to Appomattox, Virginia.

Although there is a fitting monument nearby which clearly depicts this historical occasion, the beautiful southern landscape is now marred by unattractive, helter-skelter, drab looking, coarse, concrete structures and butler buildings along with the obligatory guard towers, razor wire and double chain-linked sensor fence. The sight made me think of an unfriendly concentration camp. I had been forewarned that many inmates never leave this facility alive, and no one could remember anyone ever escaping.

In recent years a large dormitory building had been added outside the fenced compound to host a Petersburg FCC camp program for non-violent inmates with less than ten years to serve. I was later told that many assigned to the medium and low security facilities dreamed of the day that they would be transferred to the camp program, which offered more personal freedom.

Looking at the facility from the outside I became a little concerned and uneasy. Gazing at the domino arrangement of the Petersburg FCC low and medium prison facilities, my worst fears emerged. Locked up and locked down I could be beaten, raped or even killed. I had heard stories of this happening. *Maybe the U.S. Attorney's office will get their death wish for me,* I thought. I took a deep breath, forgetting about history and beauty and started wondering about the next twenty-seven months ahead of me, and my pending appeal.

The fear of being confined behind bars in prison was becoming a reality, and it was staring me in the face. My worst fears had surfaced;

I was all alone in a frightful place. Suddenly, a hand touched my shoulder. Turning abruptly, I was face-to-face with a man in a brown khaki shirt and pants, wearing a tilted beige cap on his head. He wore a name-tag that read Petersburg FCC. "Can I help you?" he asked.

"I was due to report today," I said. "I'm Sharpe James #28791-050." He had a slight grin on his face. However, nothing about this place and facility was funny to me.

He followed my eyes looking east and west and with a pleasant voice said, "We have been waiting for you. I know what you are thinking; you don't have to worry," he said. "You are not on the prison side; you are on the camp side. See that large building over there without a fence, that's Petersburg FCC camp. You will be living there. Marion Barry, the former Mayor of Washington, DC stayed there." Starting to move, he said, "First, you have to go inside the Administrative building and be processed. Grab your bag and follow me."

Well, my rising headache and upset stomach began to fade when he said you will be on the camp side. What beautiful words to hear, "the camp side." *The U.S. Attorney and his staff will be bloody mad,* I said to myself. It was wonderful knowing that I was not going to be behind any razor wire fence, no bars, no cells, no armed guards; just a unit manager, case manager, counselors and security personnel in a dormitory-like setting.

On the morning of September 16, 2008 I woke up and found myself lying on a federal prison cot. I was a prisoner. *What am I doing here?* It took a few minutes before my brain started to register the events of the past twenty-four hours. Although I was on the camp side, and not confined to a cell, it was still prison. What was I going to do to pass the time? How would I get through this ordeal? It was here at Petersburg FCC facility, an overcrowded factory like structure, with a leaking roof, falling ceiling tiles, rows and rows of drab and cluttered bunk beds, poor ventilation, lighting and food, that I met a fellow prisoner who told me not to feel sorry for myself, but to have faith and encouraged me to start reading the Bible.

"Reading is the best way to escape this place," he said, noticing my surprised look. "Not escape physically," he added with a smile.

"But you can remove your mind from this place by immersing yourself into a book."

"What do you suggest I read?" I asked.

"You can start with the Bible," he said.

Sometime and somewhere that day I found a Bible and started reading it. It wasn't the first time I had picked up a Bible to read; actually my childhood had been steeped in religion. My mother is a strong religious woman rooted in the church. As children she would get my brother and me dressed on Sundays and drag us to church. As we grew up my brother and I became somewhat tardy and absent in attending church services.

Despite the reluctance of her sons to attend Sunday services, my mother continued to be a strong voice and advocate for the church and Lord Jesus. Her Bible was never more than ten feet away from her. She watched as our family church in Newark, Hopewell Baptist Church, first split only to later close the doors to one of them forever.

As a politician and father I again embraced religion as a family tradition, this time dragging my boys to church on Sundays. However my actual studying of the Bible would not fully evolve until I found myself in prison, abandoned by many of those whom I had helped in life, those who stopped communicating with me. I felt betrayed, angry, isolated and alone.

The more I read the Bible, the more it consoled me. I read the Bible before my 6 a.m. breakfast each morning. I read the Bible at the end of my fourteen cents an hour, eight-hour day job as an education tutor. I read the Bible after our 5 p.m. meal until the 10 p.m. lights out command, and then read some more with a pocket flashlight.

I soon stopped feeling sorry for myself. I was soon able to see beyond my darkest hours of despair and loneliness. I began to see visions of better tomorrows despite my present circumstances. I began to think of the future and not the past. I came to the stark naked reality; *I do not deserve this punishment. I am not a criminal, I am a political prisoner and I don't belong here.*

Reading the Bible helped me to relate to the fact that I was one more among many political prisoners, unjustly accused, indicted, and convicted. There was solace in knowing that I was not alone, not the only one who had been wrongfully incarcerated. By studying the Bible I learned that anger, jealousy, brutality and vengeful behavior occurred from the very beginning, in the Kingdom of God.

God created man in his own image of righteousness and good! Excessive abuse of power by man, a ruling class or an assumed authority was never ordained, perceived or planned. Unfortunately, the mandate of living in the image and words of the Lord is consistently violated. In Jesus' day man used the art of ridicule, indictment, arrest, unfair trials, imprisonment, torture, and even death to thwart those who would preach the gospel, defend their righteous kingdom, seek equality or simply speak the truth as Jesus, John the Baptist, or Prophet Jeremiah did. Today many of those in authority use the same tactics to get rid of people they deem a threat to their power.

The victim's title, office, position in life, family and power is thwarted for revenge or for personal and political gains. In such power plays the authority offers no justification for their clandestine action in denying one justice or even a fair trial. By so doing a political prisoner is created. A prisoner whose precious freedom, voice, leadership, vision or even protest has been interfered with, halted, or silenced forever. The political prisoner suffers mentally, physically and fiscally. He/she is subjected to humiliation, inhumane treatment and could even face possible death.

Unfortunately, this type of injustice is not so uncommon. It could happen to you, just as it happened to me. I learned that many politicians or want-to-be politicians will do and/or say anything to get elected or to move up in the political arena, anything to get more power, more money or both. They have no scruples and no conscience that hinders them. Being an honest man, and somewhat of a hard head, I found this out the hard way.

I should have remembered that playing the race card had become an invaluable tool in getting high powered Whites elected to public office. Even my good friend, a man who would have been elected to a third term in the White House, if our Constitution had allowed it, Bill Clinton, used it. He attacked Sistah Souljah in 1992 to sway conservative White voters.

I should have remembered that it was President George H. W. Bush who mentioned the name of Willie Horton, a convicted felon, at the 1988 Texas Republican convention to sway conservative White voters away from Michael Dukakis. In 1996 it was Governor Christine Todd Whitman, of New Jersey, appealing to conservative Whites. Dressing up in all white clothing and wearing Kevlar gloves, bringing to mind Michael Jackson, she patted down an African American male during a drug sweep in Camden, New Jersey, all the time smiling while being photographed to give the impression that she was tough on Black crime, in a crime plagued community.

If I had remembered this history, I would have been better prepared when U.S. Attorney Christopher Christie launched his campaign to make me his political poster boy; bringing down one of the perceived most powerful political African Americans in New Jersey, a democrat to boot, Sharpe James. He wanted to sway White conservatives to vote for him over Governor Jon Corzine in the 2009 race for control of the State House.

The fact that I had not committed any crime did not bother U.S. Attorney Chris Christie. The fact that he knew he could not prove his case in court, alleging that "Sharpe James steered property at a steeply discounted price" to a close personal friend, and that he had assisted her in obtaining said properties to the detriment of the city of Newark, (all charges rejected by witnesses and Federal District Court Judge William J. Martini— "You did not prove any corruption in this courtroom—I am aware that Ms. Riley did not receive any discounted prices for those properties") did not bother him.

Christie simply believed that, as in the past, if he stood a prominent African American politician before a mostly all White suburban jury and accused him of committing a crime, the likelihood of the jury rendering a guilty verdict, regardless of the evidence or testimony, was 99 percent in his favor. He had a better chance of winning a guilty verdict than he had of winning the governorship, and this bias action would enhance his GOP election bid.

What a feather in his cap my conviction would bring to him; Chris Christie taking down the recently retired Mayor of Newark, after having served a tenure of twenty years without a blemish on his record. A Black man who had bucked the establishment by helping to usher in Black political and economic power, and who had become mayor of the largest city in the state of New Jersey, a state that he was now seeking to control by becoming its governor.

Reading my Bible got me to thinking about Jesus, who went about Galilee teaching and preaching the gospel; and healing all manner of sickness and disease among the people *(Matthew 4: 23-24)*. Yet, Jesus was vilified, mocked, despised, smote and rejected for preaching the gospel *(Matthew27:28-30)*. I read that Jesus was taken from prison and judged, beaten, harassed, mocked and nailed to the cross between two thieves. *(Luke 22: 63-71; 23: 1-12, 26-32)* Jesus had done no wrong, committed no acts of violence, nor was there any deceit in his mouth; then, "At the last came two false witnesses," *(Isaiah 53: 3, 6, 9 Matthews)*.

I certainly know that I'm no saint, no Jesus by a long-shot, but I could relate to his innocence. I could truly say that I was innocent of the charges brought against me. Another big difference between me and Jesus is that he was quiet and without defense. He did not talk or argue with his persecutors. This was certainly not true of me. I cried foul every opportunity I could, and hired the best defense team I could find. No, I was not Jesus, but like with Jesus, false witnesses came to testify against me at my trial. Like Jesus, I was innocent of having committed any crime.

Lord Jesus was a political prisoner; he was crucified only to rise in three days. No earthly human being will ever be so exalted. Not even the great Houdini, or baseball Hall of Famer Ted Williams, whose families planned for their return, or those still searching and waiting for Elvis Presley to return, are so divine. So, with immortality out of the question, we must stop the violence against humanity, we can't undo it, no one is coming back.

Reading the Bible helped me to understand many of the things that were going on around me; it helped to put things into perspective for me, especially as it pertains to aggression. I remember an incident that occurred during my confinement. I'd been burning the midnight oil, or I should say the midnight flashlight, staying awake after the lights went out to read. I read that it was Prophet Habakkuk who recognized and spoke out against rising anger and violence. *(Habakkuk 1: 1-3)*

I'd always had a reputation for having a big mouth and I had come to realize that in prison your mouth could get you killed. I had been speaking with a fellow inmate, "Smiley," when he stood up and walked a few steps away to confront another inmate who had been talking loudly about him. "Hey man, leave me out of your conversation," Smiley had said. "You don't know "nothing" about me."

The other inmate responded with a few curse words and Smiley said, "Let's take it to the bathroom and resolve this (no witnesses, thus no discipline). Again the inmate responded with insults and obscenities. Like a flash of lightning, or a coiled snake, Smiley hurled every ounce of his 248 pounds at the other inmate, pummeling his head. He beat the inmate the full length of the hall until he was bleeding profusely from his head, face and neck. Bright red blood covered his white T-shirt. It was soaked in blood.

The beating continued until the unit manager came out of his office and put a stop to it. Smiley was the only one throwing punches. Smiley was immediately searched for weapons while the battered inmate was assisted to the unit manager's office to await emergency medical treatment. That night I stayed up well into the night, again, reading my Bible about violence.

I came to the conclusion that violence does not always come in physical form. Uncontrolled force is also an act of violence. Lucifer one of the highest angels as referenced by his name, "Bearer of light," wanted to be more powerful than God and had to be cast out into the earth. (*Revelation 12: 7-9; Isaiah 14: 12-13*)

It is not surprising to me that here on earth we witness the continued work of (Lucifer) Satan. It was in evidence when King Herod ordered the arrest and imprisonment of John the Baptist, whose only crime was preaching to the faithful, strengthening them in the words of the Lord. When a slovenly intoxicated King Herod, at his birthday party, highly pleased with the exotic dancing of his daughter said, "Ask of me whatsoever thou wilt, and I will give it to thee."

Herod's naive daughter went to consult with her conniving mother. She then returned and indirectly speaking for her mother, who was seeking revenge, asked for the head of John the Baptist. Having made a promise to his daughter, King Herod sent an executioner to the prison to behead John the Baptist. The head was presented to the King's daughter on a silver platter.

What was John the Baptist's crime? He was guilty of telling the truth. "It is not lawful for thee to have thy brother's wife. You are an adulterer," he had said to the king. John the Baptist had suffered the fate of a political prisoner. *(Mark 6: 16-28)*

King Herod still intoxicated with power and the excitement (entertainment) of having beheaded John the Baptist further abused his authority by killing Apostle James, the brother of John the Baptist. (Acts 12: 1-2) He was still not satisfied. He was filled with Satan's anger, hate, vengefulness, evil thoughts, and a desire to please others for political gains. King Herod ordered the arrest and imprisonment of Apostle Peter. His plan was to behead (for entertainment) Peter in the public square after Easter. Why Apostle Peter? It was to silence him. His perceived crime was in preaching the gospel and commanding the faithful to be baptized in the name of the Lord. Apostle Peter was a political prisoner. (Acts 12: 3-6)

I fell asleep that night thinking that I had something in common with John the Baptist and Apostle Peter. My head had been handed, on a platter, to US Attorney, Chris Christie. Not literally, of course, but I think that's what he wanted. He wanted me to rot the rest of my life away in prison. He was disappointed that I was only sentenced to twenty-seven months in prison, and probably angry when he figured out that my sentence would actually amount to eighteen months after time was taken off for good behavior, making me eligible for a six month stay in a half-way house in Newark. He threatened to appeal my sentencing. I asked myself "Does the man have a conscience?"

The old saying, "see no evil, hear no evil, and speak no evil" has become the prisoner's code of conduct. Snitchers work full time hoping to win FCC perks or reductions in their sentences. These despicable inmates would snitch on their mother or father and even lie for an early release. Being strong, independent and a respectful loner is your best meal ticket for a safe journey through prison. While I became a respectful loner, I also became an astute observer.

In building a case against me the U.S. Attorney in New Jersey presented seven false witnesses, (who are no better than snitchers) who lied after taking an oath to tell the whole truth, nothing but the truth so help me God. In a later chapter I speak more about these false witnesses. I asked myself over and over again, "What could make them lie?" Were they so unprincipled that they would lie under oath and help to put an innocent man in prison, or were they afraid to tell the truth? I opted to believe the latter, they were weak and afraid.

The BOP's first weapon against uncooperative inmates is to take away television, telephone and commissary privileges. For serious or violent violations of rules inmates are shipped to the "Hole" locked in a cell with built-in steel beds for two to three inmates; a mandatory toilet, sink and possibly a wall shower combination are the only other accommodations. In the worst scenario you could be sent to a minimum or maximum security facility and locked down.

Observing this practice of retaliation got me to thinking again about reasons witnesses lie under oath. Some of the witnesses that testified against me were government employees. What perks could they have received, what punishments could they have been threatened with? My own speculation was that it was the promise of a better job, a higher salary, or maybe the threat of loss of their job or the job of a relative. What skeletons were in their closets? The questions sent me back to my bible.

All too often as citizens we are scared to speak the truth. All too often we become accommodating out of fear of offending people or fear of retaliation. We tell them what they want to hear and not what they ought to hear. From reading the Bible I learned that Prophet Jeremiah had no such fears when facing threats of physical harm. He always spoke the words of the Lord. He always spoke the truth. For doing so he experienced personal suffering, had few friends and his life was constantly threatened for his perceived negative messages. The King even burned Jeremiah's writings.

When he was in the gate of Benjamin, a captain of the ward I'rijah took Jeremiah to the Princes. The Princes who were with Jeremiah smote (to inflict a heavy blow) him, he was placed in a dungeon before landing in a cistern, and then led to the palace prison. By continuing his calling as God's messenger, Prophet Jeremiah became a political prisoner. *(Jeremiah 11: 18-23; 37: 13-16; 38: 6-9)*

Tossing and turning on my uncomfortable prison cot at night, unable to sleep, bleary-eyed from straining to read, deafening silence broken up only by the staccato snoring of fellow prisoners, or a mental review of my thirty-eight, uninterrupted, years in public service, I tried to distinguish between the past and the present attitudes of office holders or public servants.

The term political prisoner should not be limited to only those who preach the gospel, face heresy charges, are labeled protestors and opponents, or those fighting for truth. One need not have to turn to the Old or New Testament to become acquainted with political prisoners. One need only study the recent careers, struggles, philosophy, trials and tribulations of those who have fought for freedom and justice; those who fought for equality.

My readings reinforced my knowledge that abuse of public office and its accompanying authority is nothing new. It is contagious, like a common cold or pneumonia. It simply spreads out and infects others like a plague. Only the time, location and characters change. The unwarranted horrible abuse remains the same.

I had to acknowledge that if abusing power and creating political prisoners occurred in biblical times, it should come as no surprise that this sinister practice would traverse time and reach the shores of the vast British Empire; and would later cross the great ocean to what is now known as the United States of America. To rescue me from the mundane daily prison life of sleeping, eating, working, recreation/exercise and watching television, I decided to add the reading of history books to my Bible studies; thus, bringing the world into my bunk space.

To satisfy my curiosity I went to the prison library and, from the limited collection available, took out history books and read about the powerful British Empire, the empire that eventually covered about a fourth of the world's land. Queen Victoria once proudly proclaimed, "The sun never sets on the flag of the British Empire." The expanding British Empire would eventually include Ireland, Scotland, Wales, Burma, Pakistan, Canada, New Zealand Newfoundland, Ceylon, Rhodesia, Ghana, Kenya, Malaysia, Nigeria, Sudan, New Guinea, Cyprus, Tobago, India and South Africa; and, oh yes, the American colonies.

It is my belief that under colonial rule the American Indians were reduced to political prisoners. Under colonial rule their best land was taken from them by acts of encroachment and they were placed on reservations that could not sustain them. Where is their justice? Thus, the more things change the more they remain the same.

Tracing the history of West Africa I noted that slave ships such as the "Henrietta Marie", the "Amistad" and many others, frequently raided the pristine, serene and natural beauty of its tranquil coast line. Strong African men and women were captured and reduced to being slaves, thus becoming political prisoners. A large percentage of them, 15-20 percent, died en route to the Americas, across the great ocean. Only the "Super" strong would survive. Where is their justice?

Leading the fight for India's independence from British control was Mohandas Karamchand Gandhi (1869-1948). The people called Gandhi, the Mahatma (Great Soul). He was searching for the truth. Gandhi was a small, frail, scholarly lawyer by profession, and lived a simple life. He believed it wrong to kill animals for food or to use their hides. Gandhi's method of protest against colonialism was using a non-violent resistance campaign. He used civil disobedience, strikes, lobbying, and the international press against the British Colonial Government. Ghandi was arrested many times and spent a total of seven years in prison for his political activities. He was a political prisoner.

After many wars with the Boers the British Empire included South Africa as one of its colonies. The Union of South Africa was formed in 1911. South Africa is the richest and most highly developed country in Africa. It produces more gold, gems, and diamonds than any other country. Unfortunately and tragically the Africans who make up 71 percent of the population, did not share in its wealth and quality of life. South Africa was one of the few countries in the world ruled by a racial minority (17 percent).

The most powerful opposition to this unjust system of apartheid in South Africa was the ANC (African National Congress) which emerged in the 1940s. Nelson Mandela would become its most influential and powerful leader. Mandela would be sentenced to jail in 1962 to silence him and end his powerful movement threatening to end racial injustice in South Africa. For this Mandela was sentenced to life in prison. He became a political prisoner, only to rise twenty seven years later and bring justice and equality to his suffering people.

At about the same time of Mandela's arrest in 1962, here in America, another mighty man of valor had surfaced by the name of Dr. Martin Luther King, Jr. King, the son of a preacher, whose father was the son of a preacher, emerged from a family of Christian soldiers marching to war against social injustices. His 1963 March on Washington, DC; and his "Letter from a Birmingham jail," shocked and inspired a nation regarding the evils of racism and segregation.

There have been many African American men and women of valor like Sojourner Truth, Harriet Tubman, Crispus Attucks, Mary McLeod Bethune, Frederick Douglas and Rosa Parks, just to name a few. These brave men and women fought against the dastardly acts of mob lynching and the evils of segregation. These early pioneers courageously fought for freedom and equality, for civil and voting rights and desegregation of schools. Many of them were arrested and placed in jails as political prisoners; some were even killed.

I personally believe that no mighty man of valor was more qualified, organized, prolific, articulate and courageous than Dr. Martin Luther King, Jr., who led the civil rights movement in America. In the eyes of those who wanted to thwart Black progress, deny us our constitutional rights, Dr. King was public enemy number one. He was targeted and hounded by then FBI Director, J. Edgar Hoover, who was obsessed over the thought of Dr. King becoming so highly respected and winning a Nobel Peace Prize in 1964.

My good friend and pastor, the late Reverend Dr. J. Wendell Mapson of Mount Calvary Baptist church in Newark, New Jersey invited Dr. King to Newark in 1968. Pastor Mapson opened his church doors for King at a time in his life when he had very few real friends. I will always be grateful for this visit because it afforded me an opportunity to meet Dr. King at my high school alma mater, South Side High School, now Malcolm X Shabazz, on March 27, 1968. One week later King would be insanely gunned down by James Earl Ray on April 4, 1968 while standing on a balcony of the Lorraine Motel in Memphis, Tennessee. Like Gandhi and Mandela, the Reverend Dr. Martin Luther King, Jr., was a political prisoner.

During my tenure as Mayor, it was President George W. Bush who asked for the head of President Saddam Hussein. It was the same President Bush who appointed Christopher Christie New Jersey's United States Attorney, a reward for Christie's fund raising activities for Bush. In addition to both being Republicans, they were both headhunters.

It was not surprising when *The Star-Ledger*, during my trial, reported that, Christie, at a staff party celebrating my political indictment and arrest, stated that, "At age 69 and with a twenty-year sentence facing him, Sharpe James will most likely die in prison." Following this statement Christie was witnessed receiving a standing ovation and giving high-fives to his office staff members. Christie didn't want justice. He wanted me to die in prison, that is, if he couldn't have my head on a platter.

It was alleged that Christie had abused professional ethics by using his office to run for governor of New Jersey in 2009. Then governor, Jon Corzine said that "I believe Christie may well have violated federal law by communicating with Karl Rove, former President George W. Bush's political adviser, while he was U.S. Attorney." It was also alleged that at that meeting Christie made known his ambition to run for governor.

To carry out his plan, Christie wanted my head. He wanted to silence the alleged most powerful African American Democrat in New Jersey prior to his run for governor. Christie wanted Sharpe James as a trophy to parade around his GOP conservative voters. At the 2007 League of Municipalities Convention in Atlantic City, Christie had bragged that he would win a conviction against me. He wanted to be governor at all cost. I was his sacrificial victim. Justice was not blind. I would become another one of his political prisoners.

I learned from reading the Bible and pragmatic experiences that those who imprisoned Jesus, John the Baptist, Mahatma Gandhi, Nelson Mandela and Dr. Martin Luther King, Jr. were all tyrants and bullies wielding power and seeking more power. To protect individual rights and freedom we must be aware of those in leadership positions who would abuse the power of their office, and take action to remove them.

Under no circumstances would I ever claim a place on the same pedestal as Apostle Paul, Prophet Jesus; or any of our modern day highly respected and renowned leaders in the persons of Gandhi, Mandela, Rosa Parks or Dr. Martin Luther King, Jr. These individuals are my heartfelt role models and heroes. They are leaders who cannot be cloned or duplicated in life. I strive only to learn from their sacrifices and suffering in becoming a better person.

While incarcerated I received so many letters from Newark residents and others who believed in my innocence. Those letters and the respect I received from the in-mates at Petersburg Correctional Center helped me to cope with a situation I had absolutely no control over. Against the demands of prison officials the in-mates referred to me as "Mr. Mayor." They were receptive to my instruction as a teacher and they were sympathetic to my circumstances. It was as though Christ himself had willed that the least of his people would give me the greatest encouragement during the storm that engulfed me.

Mr. Christie believes that he took twenty-seven months from my life, a small consolation for him considering that he wanted me to die in prison. I want to inform him that he didn't take those months from me; they were just another experience for me in the gift of a God given life. My life has been a marvelous one, serving the people that I love and living in the city that I love, Newark.

Following a history of social, economic, and political injustices towards African American residents, which culminated in the riots of 1967, I helped Newark to rise from the ashes of destruction. The following pages tell my story; the truth and nothing but the truth from a political prisoner. Although a jury of twelve individuals, not my peers, found me guilty of crimes I did not commit, you, the readers, will decide for yourselves.

CHAPTER TWO

A poor boy from Jacksonville, Florida

THE EARLY YEARS

Newark is my home, but I didn't start my life out there. We traveled many days, nights and miles before we finally found a one room, cold water flat on Howard Street, in the central ward of New Jersey's largest city.

I was born in Jacksonville, Florida in 1936 on unpaved, dusty, red clay Pippen Street. I never knew my father, Louis James, who died of pneumonia three months before I was born. My first name is the maiden name of my mother, Beulah Sharpe. So Sharpe James represents my mother and father's families coming together. Something like the John Fitzgerald Kennedy families coming together, only we were poor.

My earliest memories are those of growing up in a segregated South in a one family house on Pippen Street, with my brother Joseph, who is nine months older than me, my mother and her second husband, Willie Holmes.

The one thing I remember most about living on Pippen Street is that whenever we heard a police-car siren and saw lights flashing, we would always run to hide. Back then I didn't understand why we felt we should be running from the law. It was only as I got older and was stopped several times by the police myself, that I learned the police treated Blacks differently than Whites, and could be very brutal. The police were seen not as our friends, not as our protectors, but as invaders in our community; they were public enemy number one.

My happiest days were when we visited my mother's grandmother, Isabella Ladson, and my mother's Aunt Rose and Uncle Joe, who lived in a big house, with a porch wrapped halfway around it, on Caroline Street. They were always happy to see my brother and me, and they would shower us with loud and emotional praise and marvel at how fast we were growing up. They gave us plenty to eat and lots of attention.

Those memories have never escaped me. I went back to visit the old folks as much as I could, up until they died. They always greeted me with the same warmth and affection that I remembered: "Good gracious! Look at him!" "He's grown big!" "A fine young man! Wow!"

Southern people love to see you return home. It's almost as though you've been to the hospital and released. They're happy to see that you're alive. They talk to each other loudly; you'd think they were talking to 1,000 people in a stadium. They always greet you with a very warm handshake, a hug and a kiss.

You don't have that hospitality so much in the north. The feeling of family, of embracing, of saying hello was the strength of the south. It was this warm feeling, everyone eating together, staying together that I remember, and that I miss and have never found in the north. Here, all too often, people drop their head and eyes when passing each other. There is not as much eye contact in northern society.

Unfortunately, in our house on Pippen Street, my brother and I had to put up with an abusive stepfather. He was a veteran of World War II, who brought home many souvenir weapons from Germany—a German Lugar, a sword, and a bayonet. He felt that he had to demonstrate what a great soldier he had been by threatening us with them.

My stepfather had picked up phrases from the enemy in the war—the Germans, the Italians, the Japanese—and he would quote them. Their words became part of his regular vocabulary, fighting words like, "Banzai!" He would go around the house brandishing one of those weapons that he had proudly brought home, yelling, "I killed this one and took this weapon; I killed that one and took his gun." Then we became the enemy. He was fighting the war at home.

My stepfather also beat and bruised my mother. It was a frightening situation that we lived in. He and Mother would often be screaming, fighting, and complaining. My brother and I would run and hide. When I think back to those days, I believe drinking had to be part of his problem. He was an angry man.

Our Black military men, who had put their lives on the line for their country in World War II, came home and were reduced to living in segregated communities and couldn't find jobs. That would make the average person start drinking. It was the drinking and frustration that their families had to cope with once they came home. Frustration from the war and the segregated Army, frustration from being taught to be a killer, and yet probably ending up working in a kitchen, peeling potatoes or doing some other menial job.

Who do you take it out on? You take it out on your children; you take it out on your wife. That's the only outlet you have. Who else are you going to take it out on? That's what happened with my stepfather. He was a victim of the war. We won the war, but he lost a home.

One time my mother and stepfather were walking across a train trestle over a ditch. They got into an argument, and he pushed her off the trestle. She fell about one hundred feet. Miraculously she lived, but she ripped her whole arm. The injury left keloids the full length of her right arm. My mother, a very talented pianist, was never able to play the piano again.

Although my mother survived the fall, she decided that being alive wasn't enough. Next time it might not just be her arm, it might be her life. We had to get away from our stepfather.

Early one morning, in 1944, my mother woke my brother and me, telling us to be quiet and to follow her out of the house. We were sleepy and curious, "Where are we going, Mama?" we asked.

"I don't know, but we're leaving here," she said. "Shhh! Be quiet. Get your stuff on. Don't ask questions." We snuck out of the house with whatever we could carry in a bag.

Sometime later we arrived at the train tracks, and since there was no train station where we were, in rural Jacksonville, Mother stopped the train by setting a fire on the tracks. When the train stopped, we got on. My brother Joe and I were tired and hungry, but we were with our mother. We knew she would look after us and fight off all tormentors. She told us we were going to visit a relative, and that was reassuring.

My mother was the second oldest of five sisters. Aunt Willa Mae and Aunt Rose lived in Philadelphia. Aunt Rose subsequently mov to Lawnside, NJ, and after her husband Jack died, she moved back to Florida. We had often stayed with either of the two aunts in Philadelphia during the summer.

Our first stop after leaving Jacksonville was Philadelphia. It seemed to me that we rode on that train days to get there. We stayed with Aunt Rose for a few weeks and then moved to a subsidized, low-income row house.

After a while, we moved again to Newark, New Jersey. Our first home in Newark was on Howard Street in a one-room cold-water flat, with a large potbellied stove in the center of the room for heat and hot water. We took a bath by standing in a tub in the open room. There was an outhouse in the rear yard.

When one of the units in the rooming house caught on fire, we relocated to nearby Elizabeth to live with my father's younger brother, Uncle Jesse James. We all managed to live in a crowded, four-room apartment. Joseph and I attended George Washington School.

If anyone had personality in our family, it was Uncle Jesse, who drove a big Harley Davidson motorcycle, headed a motorcycle group in Elizabeth and Newark and was as flamboyant as Douglas Fairbanks, Jr. He was a real ladies' man. He probably fathered about 12 babies.

Even after Uncle Jesse was diagnosed with emphysema, he continued smoking. He smoked himself to death. Flamboyant to the bitter end, Uncle Jesse told me he had to have some vice while he was sick.

My father's other brother, Japan James, also lived in Elizabeth with his wife, on Magnolia Street. Uncle Japan was a brilliant engineer, the complete opposite of Uncle Jesse. Uncle Japan was a little eccentric. He invented things. I remember him putting a motor on his bicycle and riding it through town.

If my two uncles represented the two opposing poles of the James family, I would say I turned out to be more like Uncle Jesse, and my brother Joe, who became an engineer, took after Uncle Japan.

As for my mother, there was no stopping her when it came to drive ʾtion. After years of working as a domestic, she got a job as a short-ʾd eventually owned her own seafood restaurant in Elizabeth ʾe Streets. My mother was always a great cook and the ʾvided her an opportunity to show off her culinary talent.

I was only nine or ten years old at the time, but I got a chance to develop some culinary skills of my own. After school I would report to the restaurant to peel and cut potatoes for French fries and, occasionally, try my hand at cooking. My brother, Joe, who would reluctantly join in to help, was recalcitrant.

Eventually we moved back to Newark as soon as we were able to find an apartment. We were back on Howard Street again. Mother closed the restaurant, but continued to work in the restaurant business, becoming a top short-order cook at Woody's Seafood Market on Sherman Avenue in Newark. Although she was a single parent with two children, her frugality allowed her to save up enough money to buy a single-family house at 43 Emmet Street. Its cost of $4,000 seemed like $400,000 to us at the time. She paid cash.

Mother never believed in buying anything on credit or taking out loans. She inculcated her children with the same ethic. When I got my first teaching job and asked her to co-sign for a loan for a new car, she refused. "Look, Son, that's not the way we should do it," she said. "If God wanted you to have a car, he would have made a way. And I believe God is telling you to save enough money until you can qualify to buy a car in your name, with your credit, not mine."

My mother (who was born in Georgia and grew up in Florida) graduated from high school in Jacksonville. Her high school records, though, were destroyed in a fire. When she decided that she wanted to go into nursing, she applied for and received a high-school equivalency diploma from New Jersey in 1963, and with that she enrolled in a nursing program at Beth Israel Medical Center in Newark. She graduated from the program with honors in 1966 and went on to become an exemplary licensed practical nurse. My mother never accepted being poor and never used race as an excuse for not achieving.

In the south they always told us the north would be the "Promised Land", but it turned out to be the "Struggle Land." Our first winter here we had no idea what snow was. The first time I saw snow fall, I ran out and tried to catch it in a jar; I thought it was cotton. We danced and sang. We brought the jar of snow in the house and put it in the icebox. It was something new to us, like a toy. No book prepares you for this encounter. You have to be in it for the first time to really experience the thrill of snow.

We didn't have the proper clothes for cold weather. We wore sneakers all year. We had no other shoes. My first pair of shoes and my first suit would come in 1950, for graduation from Miller Street Elementary School.

When we lived on Howard Street, I went to Robert Treat School, which later became Marcus Garvey School. I had only one pair of lime-green work pants, one pair of sneakers and a few T-shirts that I washed by hand and hung near the stove to dry overnight. I wore those green pants to school every day, and my classmates teased me, calling me the "lemon-lime kid." My socks and sneakers were worn until they had holes in them. Yet, I never considered myself poor, because I thought everyone lived the same way.

In those days people judged you not by the brand of clothes you wore, but whether they were clean or dirty. People came to school every day wearing the same thing; that was not an issue. My mother saw to it that no matter where we were, we were clean and neat, and our home was organized. "You might be poor, but that's no excuse for being dirty. Our home is our castle," she would say.

My mother worked as a domestic both in Florida and in New Jersey. In the south, you either cleaned house or went to work in a factory; those were the primary occupations available to Black people after sharecropping ended. There were no public works jobs. We didn't drive buses. We didn't go out and sell insurance. Yet, it seemed that our life was better in the south.

We had our own house in Florida. Our family seemed well-to-do. In old photographs of my mother and her five sisters, they looked like the Pointer Sisters in their fashionable 1940s outfits. We left all of that behind when we fled north.

Whenever I complained to my mother about the holes in my sneakers and my socks and the teasing I was getting from the other kids or calling her attention to a sale that Sears & Roebuck's on Elizabeth Avenue was having on sneakers for $2.99, she would say that was way too much money; but she had a solution to my problem. She would walk into the kitchen, pull from the shelf a large jar that contained stiff cardboard tops from cereal boxes, and stuff two of them in my sneakers to cover the holes.

Well, they were still the same old sneakers, but at least I no longer felt the cold ground through the holes, and my schoolmates stopped making fun of me. I have often marveled at how different things were for my own children when they were going to school. Their closets were lined with designer clothes and dozens of brand-name sneakers. To be fashionable, kids their age were actually buying jeans with holes already in them. I wore holes in my pants too, but not by design.

After Mother purchased the house on Emmet Street, I attended Miller Street School, where I had a perfect attendance record upon graduation. I was never absent from school, because my mother was always working. When she worked as a domestic, and then as a cook, she'd drop me off early in the morning and would come to the playground to get me after work. In those days, if you didn't play in the playground, you could stay in the school gym. The school was a safe haven. No matter how many hours my mother had to spend scrubbing floors and cleaning kitchens, she knew she could come back to that school, because it was open to us for recreation.

I was the first kid to arrive at school every morning. The custodians would let me inside and offer me milk and Danish pastry. I would clean the erasers before classes began. I became a favorite with the teachers, going to the store for them and running the school film projectors. To me, school was an extended family, a home away from home. I was there all day. The teachers liked me, and I liked them. I did my schoolwork, I did my homework and, eventually, I earned and got good grades.

My first big disappointment in life was when the school announced which students would skip the second semester of the seventh grade and be promoted to the eighth. I cried because my name wasn't on the list. I thought that I should skip, too. My hard work would be rewarded later, though, in high school, when I made the honor roll in my senior year.

I was a good student, because my mother instilled discipline in both my brother and me; it didn't have to come from the teachers. My mother would constantly remind us that we couldn't go out to play until we did our homework. Now, Mama didn't actually sit down and go over the homework with us, but she set the rules.

If we ever brought a poor grade home, we would get a lecture. Good grades meant peace with Mama, and bad grades meant we stayed in the house longer, and she would be in our face about what we were doing in school. We got our report cards four times a year, and we had better make sure we brought something home that was worthwhile, and we had better not have had any absences.

Teachers were allowed to use discipline back then. If you didn't learn, they would threaten to keep you after school. They could smack you, too. They didn't worry about legal liability or parents coming in and beating them up. They focused on one thing only: learning. "You're not leaving 'til you finish your homework," they would say. And, "I'm taking you home after that." Teachers took a real interest in their pupils. Those days are long gone.

I used to be the class joker. My homeroom teacher at South Side High, Miss Hannah Curtis, although petite, took no nonsense from anyone. When I acted up, she would say, "Stop it, Sharpe! What do you want to be a clown when you grow up?" She challenged us to do our work and stay in school. She challenged us to be somebody; "Anyone can be a clown," she would say.

Throughout my years attending Newark's public schools, the student body was more than 50 percent White. All of my teachers were White. For a long time non-Newarkers held this false perception about the city's population, that it was overwhelmingly Black. In 1950, when I was 14, Newark's Black population was only 17 percent. (In 2002 Newark was 57 percent Black, and not 99 percent, as some people believed.) The ethnic Italians, Portuguese, Hispanics and Irish had never completely left Newark.

In school we all were family despite the differences in ethnicity. We loved each other. We were harmonious. There were no serious problems then. In the North Ward, perhaps, where residents tried to maintain a bastion for Whites only, there was some discord. In Vailsburg, where the Irish community tried to do the same thing, there were problems. But in the South and Central Wards the shrinking Jewish population got along with the growing Black one. Many of the churches you see in Newark today were once synagogues.

I don't remember any incidents of maltreatment in school because I was Black. In fact, the teachers would beat up on all of us

—Black and White—to get us to stay in school and do our homework. Teachers were teachers and students knew their place; you were supposed to learn. That's why, today, Sharpe James can read and write.

What impressed me most about Newark's schools was the access to extracurricular activities. We could go to school and have recreation afterwards, and we could pay $1 to learn how to play musical instruments after school. Newark's schools were far superior to what we, as African Americans, had been offered in the south.

Mr. Rip Rossi was one of my favorite teachers at Miller Street School. Every day he would see me on the playground after school. One day he approached me and said he was going to a basketball game at Madison Square Garden and asked if I would close up the playground for him. He said, "You come every day. You know the procedure. You know where the equipment is." He gave me all these keys and said, "When 9 o'clock comes take all the stuff in, turn off the lights, lock the gate and bring in the keys tomorrow."

I was so honored. Here was this man going to New York, trusting me, this young boy. Mr. Rossi later became athletic director and soccer coach at East Side High School. He became a top school official, and his trust in me at an early age sparked my interest in a career in sports.

Baseball was important in my development as an athlete. I grew up playing stickball with the other neighborhood kids. We played with a broomstick and a pink ball called a high bouncer. We would stand maybe 50 feet away and throw this pink high bouncer to the kid with the broomstick. And depending upon how far he hit the ball, he'd score a single, a double or a home run. We played the game all day.

When I went to high school and started playing baseball, with a white ball that was bigger than the pink ball, and a bat that was bigger than a broomstick, I thought I'd been given a gift from God. So, naturally, I became a great baseball player. I played baseball in high school for four years, and everyone thought that I would become a professional. I played for the Negro League's Newark Eagles in their final years, the famous Newark Eagles that sent more Blacks to the baseball Hall of Fame than any other team in the league.

I played center field and shortstop. I was a classic fielder, hitter and runner. I could do it all. I loved to show off, loved to do the Willie

Mays catch. Mr. Francis Delaney was one of my baseball coaches at South Side. He was tough, but fair. I'll never forget the baseball game we played at St. Benedict Field, where the pitcher had a no-hitter going, and the batter hit a ball right at me, playing center field. I started running at what seemed like 100 miles an hour. And then I put on the brakes, caught the ball on one bounce and threw it back to the second baseman, holding the runner to a single. The pitcher lost his no-hitter.

When I went into the locker room at the end of the game, all of my teammates said, "Sharpe, you should have dove for the ball, you should have tried to catch that ball." They were pissed off at me.

Hearing what my teammates were saying, the coach walked over and told me, "You did the right thing. If the ball had gotten past you we would have lost the game. You don't protect the no-hitter; you protect the game." By my thinking, if I had come in and tried to shoe-string it, and the ball ran past me 350 feet to center field, it would have been a home run. So, I played it safe, but I gave up the pitcher's no-hitter. We sacrificed the no-hitter for the overall goal of winning the game, one-to-nothing.

I never forgot that incident, because Coach Delaney could easily have sided with the group. He could easily have said nothing or spoken with me on the side. But he let everyone know that he thought I had made the right decision.

I thought that was wonderful. In a crisis situation, Coach Delaney demonstrated leadership. I always wanted to be able to do that, too. When someone is down, lift them up with the truth. Coach Delaney conducted himself like a businessman, wearing a suit and a tie every day. I learned a lot from him. He was a man's man and a role model; tough and demanding, but fair.

In high school I was an athlete, but not a personality, not a star. There were others who were dressers, they were the playboys. I was strictly a pure, raw athlete; I didn't have the clothes or the glamour. I was not a ladies' man. In fact, while in high school I saved up and bought myself a raggedy 1950 Ford convertible. It was yellow with black-and-white checkered seats and the top would not always go up or down. I became an instant hit with the girls, but they didn't get in my car. They wanted to, but I was obsessed with sports, not girls.

Sports took up all of my time. My life belonged to my coach. I was not a captain. I was just a good ball player. My teammates would argue about who was going to be captain of the team, I don't think they ever considered me, but everyone wanted Sharpe James to be on their team. That was more important to me.

I began saving for college while I was in high school. It was something my mother insisted on. I worked part-time jobs that would help pay for my tuition and enable me to buy books, since I received only a partial athletic scholarship. I did all sorts of things to earn money, including selling fruits and vegetables out of a wagon, delivering messages on bicycle for Western Union, changing tires, working in a factory that made plastic beads for necklaces, and selling children's furniture and toys.

Each job taught me a valuable lesson. My first job was on the fruit-and-vegetable wagon that rode through neighborhoods. I did an excellent job, but got fired and then rehired the same day. Why did my boss fire me? My first day on the job a guy came up to the wagon and said, "I want a dozen apples."

I grabbed a bag and picked up three, six, nine, twelve apples and said, "Here you are, sir." He paid me the money and went away.

The boss said, "Sharpe, you're fired."

"Why?" I asked. "What did I do wrong?"

He said, "You did everything wrong. Let me explain it to you. Never put 12 good apples in a bag. Pick up three good ones and hold them up in front of the man, put them in the bag. Now, while he sees the three good ones, you pick three bad apples. Then put six good ones in. Never give them 12 good apples or 12 good oranges. You always got to get rid of some of the bad ones with the 12. You got to have at least three bad ones in there."

It was like a game of three-card Monte. That was my first lesson in entrepreneurship; to cut your losses you unload on the public some bad with the good. It taught me never to buy 12 of anything unless I pick them myself.

I knew after working the job at the injection-mold plant, where the plastic beads were manufactured, that I would never work at another factory job again in my life. No matter how tired you got the machine never stopped its cycle. You'd spray the plastic into the machine, close the door, open it up again and shake the beads off.

It was such a monotonous and demanding job for such low pay. I'd get a 15-minute break, go outside and come back to do the same thing over and over again. On each break I felt like I was being born again. I told myself, "This is driving me crazy." I did learn endurance and responsibility from that job, though.

Luckily, I was able to find more interesting jobs. At one time I worked across the street from Miller Street School, on Frelinghuysen Avenue at Schwartz & Nagle, changing flat tires: car tires, van tires and truck tires. What a physical job that was! I had to use a machine to get the bolts off. The tires were bigger than me. I used to get so dirty; I had more dirt under my nails than in my backyard. And greasy! I could never get my hands clean with a job like that, but I enjoyed the physical challenge. I decided that whatever kind of work I chose to do in the future it would have to involve some physical activity.

When I was a senior in high school, to start me off in college, my high-school counselor sent me on an interview for a job at Tiny Town Juvenile Store on Lyons Avenue in the then-primarily Jewish, Weequahic Park neighborhood. The job was to set up toys and furniture for display and to help with deliveries. The owner was Morris Kaplan. His sister-in-law was Sally Bushberg, whose family owned the Bushberg Bros. Furniture Store in downtown Newark. I got the job.

Once I was reaching for a bicycle from a rear loft in the store. I accidentally placed my right hand under the fan for the ceiling gas heater and severely cut my pinky and ring fingers. Morris's sister, who just happened to be in the store that day, was a nurse. She bandaged up the fingers that were just barely hanging together by pieces of flesh, and rushed me up to Beth Israel Hospital. Today, because of her quick thinking and prompt action, I still have five functional fingers on my right hand.

After recovering from the accident, I returned to work at the store. I struck up a relationship with the Kaplan family that continued through the years. One day Morris Kaplan said to me, "Jimmy, (that was what they called me), why don't you take my daughter ice-skating?" I took his daughter, Wendy, ice-skating at the South

Mountain Arena during the mid 1950s. Years later, she became a first-rate, competitive skater.

The attendance at the arena back then was about 98% White, however, the fact that I was an excellent skater giving instructions to a novice drew little attention. Whenever the local folks would stare at me I would simply do a double or triple spin on the ice landing like a butterfly and in their eyes I instantly became a foreigner or White; certainly not a Black youth from the ghettos of Newark. Some of the young people would even ask if I was available to teach them.

I learned from those experiences that having unique skills made people look at you differently. One need only read the history of Jack Johnson, the first Black boxing champion who was idolized even in a racist society. Years later I would become the skating pro at the newly built Essex county ice skating rink in Newark's Branch Brook Park (1957).

Another time Morris went out to eat at Henry's Luncheonette on Bergen Street and said, "Sharpe, watch the store while I'm gone." While he was gone, a customer came into the store to buy a crib. Because I had listened to Morris selling cribs, I was able to give the customer all the information that he needed and make the sale. I was very proud of myself.

The hottest game for kids at the time was Scrabble. We used to hide the games under the counter to keep them from selling out too fast. Once when a VIP customer walked into the store and asked for Scrabble, not expecting us to have any, I reached under the counter and happily fulfilled his request. He must have taken the game to the park to play. I sold Scrabble games like hotcakes that day; it seemed everyone in nearby Weequahic Park came in wanting a Scrabble game.

When Morris came back from lunch, I told him I had sold a crib and several games of Scrabble. All he had to do was to ring up the sales. He was so impressed that I was able to talk to his customers and sell to them, that he promoted me to salesman. I eventually came to know the whole crib business and became a top buyer and salesman for Morris Kaplan at Tiny Town Juvenile Furniture Store.

I had not only won the respect of the Kaplan family and become a full member of the store; I had become a lifelong friend of the Kaplan family as well. I learned from that experience that Sharpe James, who had only been an athlete until the day he took over the store for an hour, could run his mouth and interact with people and was now accepted within Newark's Jewish business community.

In 1957, while attending college, I got a job as an ice-skating guard and instructor at Branch Brook Parks new, ice-skating rink, the first to open in Newark. I had taught myself to skate on the frozen lake in Weequahic Park. I'd found a pair of old ice skates that someone had thrown away. They were too big for me, so I put paper in the toes, and at the risk of falling through the ice, I taught myself how to stand up, keep my balance and skate. I became good enough to teach others and to become a member of the local Branch Brook Park Rink ice hockey team.

Growing up poor in Newark, we Black kids used to go around looking in the garbage to see what treasures we could find. Someone had thrown away an old wooden, rusty sled. I took steel wool and cleaned the blades, put new screws in it and rode that sled in the park. We could not afford to buy these things—they were luxuries as far as we were concerned—so we used our ingenuity to give new life to what others had discarded.

In the same trash that I found my first pair of ice skates, I found a pair of old skis. They looked odd to me, and I later learned that was because they were cross-country skis, which were extra long. I put them on and found some slopes in Weequahic Park. I knew that if I could go down a small slope and keep my balance, eventually I would find the tallest hill in Weequahic Park and ski down it, teaching myself how to turn and how to stop.

In later years I had the opportunity, with the proper equipment, to become an even better skier, and finally I just mastered the sport. Now, I can ski with the best of them and I can ice-skate with the best. Once I learn something, I'm able to master it, and I don't quit until I become proficient enough to compete.

I have passed my passion for these sports down to my sons. Two of them, John and Elliot both enjoy skiing, and John has won several downhill races.

I graduated from South Side High School with honors in 1954. I went on to attend Panzer College of Physical Education and Hygiene in New Jersey, which later became a part of Montclair State College. I received a Bachelor of Science degree in education from Panzer in 1958.

In college I continued running track. The school had no football team, but it did have a soccer team with a Russian coach. I had never played soccer before. But I was fast, and I could run, so I gave it a try. I got out there and although I couldn't control the ball in the beginning, I later became an All-American soccer player in college, All-American left center, and halfback.

I came to love the game of soccer and during the 1960's and 1970's, I would become a semiprofessional soccer player in the New Jersey League. I was the only Black on the team. Because of the space between my front teeth and my Afro (I used to wear braided Afros back then), people thought I was a foreigner "Who's the African you got?" they'd ask. It was Sharpe James from Newark.

As I was preparing to graduate from college, I was one credit short and looking for a course to take. My advisor, Dr. Hazel M. Wacker, directed me to a tennis class. Learning tennis in 1958 changed my life forever. I became a state tennis champion later on, and have never stopped playing the game.

I have played with tennis greats, like Arthur Ashe, Chris Evert, Ilie Nastase and Althea Gibson, and with seasoned amateurs like former New York City Mayor David Dinkins and former UN Ambassador and Atlanta Mayor Andrew Young (Young called himself the best tennis-playing mayor in the world until I embarrassed him 6-0, 6-0). While Andy had a great game, I had great speed and a determination to win.

In college, and then graduate school, my dream of becoming a professional baseball player was set aside. In college I quit the baseball team, because the coach chose my best friend and fiercest rival, Bobby Wolfarth, over me to play center field. I felt the coach was biased in Bobby's favor because he was White. I later came to see that I was wrong. My decision to quit the team was a poor one. Bobby was simply better than me. I had made a mistake.

My mother has always told me, "Don't ask or beg for anything. Just study hard, work hard, save a portion of your earnings, play by the rules, and good things will happen to you." Those words have followed me through my life, and to them I attribute whatever success I have achieved.

Shortly after college, in 1958, I was drafted into the Army. A group of us recruits, some of whom I'd known from Newark and some whom I had just made friends with, did not want to go into the service. We were, after all, college graduates. At first we thought we could get out it if we tried to fail the physical examination.

We were told to report to a recruitment center on Broad Street, where they stuck a tongue depressor down our throats and told us to cough loudly, which we struggled to do; then we were told to drop our pants and underwear. We had to stand there while civilians pulled on our testicles to determine if we had a hernia? My Hispanic friends, who were speaking English all day, pretended they couldn't speak English. Yet, to no one's surprise they announced all of us physically fit, ready to fight and die for our country.

I was in the Army now.

CHAPTER THREE

In the Army Now

I graduated from college in June, 1958. Four short months later, October 1958, I was drafted by the US Army. I had to report to Fort Dix, NJ for my induction. After that, I was a part of Company B, the 1st Battle Group, 30th Infantry, and 3rd Division. It was being whispered that we were to be secretly trained and sent to Germany.

Learning that we were to be part of a special unit made it a bit more exciting for me and my company, but when we asked questions about our assignment, no one would give us a straight answer. One morning our platoon sergeant woke us up and told us we were flying to Atlanta, Ga. This was my first airplane flight. It was scary flying on a military prop plane with the wings flapping like a bird. I still had no idea what I was going to be doing. From Atlanta we went to Fort Benning for basic and advanced infantry training.

Fort Benning was known to be one of the most demanding military training facilities in America. There were marches through the red-clay dirt in the morning in hot, desert-like conditions. Troops would wake up with snakes in their sleeping bags.

The town surrounding the base was no paradise either. Having left the South as a young boy, and not really knowing overt racism as I was growing up, I witnessed segregation for the first time on visits into town while on leave. My buddies and I would go into town and see Black folks living in what we called "ice houses," little shanties in segregated communities. We felt so bad; we wanted to donate money to the people living there. We came back to the post, thinking that if we had to go into hellholes like that, we'd just as soon stay on the base.

Finally, in May, 1959, we got the news that we had been waiting for: We would be traveling to Savannah to board the USNS Buckner, as part of Operation Gyroscope, an Army program in the 1950s that rotated whole units in and out of Germany to help keep peace during the Cold War. We were the 3rd Infantry Division, the "Rock of the Marne", and our mission was to "gyro" into Germany, replacing 5,000 troops already there, and to train for combat should tensions flare up between the NATO and Warsaw Pact nations. We were going to be the last Gyro group.

The next morning we took buses to Savannah and boarded the ship for our journey across the Atlantic. I had never been on a ship before, had never seen so many people together in such close quarters. We were sleeping in bunks, three in a row, and one on top of each other. We had to eat standing up, because there was not enough space for everyone to sit down. At night, on deck, we watched movies that were projected onto the undersides of inflatable life preservers.

Twelve days after setting sail from Savannah, we arrived in Bremerhaven, Germany. From there my unit made the 16-hour train ride to Schweinfurt, a major munitions-production center destroyed by the Allies in the Second World War. Schweinfurt was our training base before we went to the border between East and West Germany.

After 16 hours on the train we were hungry and tired. The train made one stop. At the station we saw local merchants with pushcarts, and we yelled out through the window, "Hey, comrade!" They just looked at us. We realized then that they didn't speak our language. It was the first time in my life that I had been in an environment where people didn't understand English. We called them names and acted as though we were in America and they had an obligation to know what we were saying.

We wanted to buy something to eat. We learned that there was something called a wiener schnitzel, much like a hamburger. We shouted out the window to one of the street vendors, "wiener schnitzel" and he started passing sandwiches to us through the windows. The vendor told us the price in German, but we didn't understand him, so we started throwing money out the windows. We didn't know whether it was too much or too little, but we were laughing and shouting, and he was shouting back at us. We were in a foreign country and couldn't speak the language, but we were being rude to the Germans, because they couldn't speak our language.

When we arrived at the barracks in Schweinfurt, I went up to my room and put my bag down. The soldier in the room said, "Welcome!" It turned out that he was also from Newark. I was replacing someone from Newark, NJ. He was so happy so to see me. His name was Ernie Monaco, and he later became a physical education teacher at Ann Street School in Newark, and a wrestling coach. I threw my bag on the bed, and said "It's nice to meet you." He grabbed his bag and said "Thank you," and ran out.

We had been in Schweinfurt about a week, going through the everyday routine, when we got our first pass to go into town. For someone who had never been outside of the United States before, it was a strange experience going out on the town in Schweinfurt. Trying to catch a cab, entering a business establishment everything was made more difficult due to the language barrier. Eventually we went to a local tavern, and that's when I made my first big mistake.

I was sitting with a group of my comrades, and bragging. I said, "I can speak German. I'm going to the Men's Room. See that door over there that says, Da Men?" I went rushing into the room, and there were 12 women in there that started beating me up, slapping me and screaming in their language. I ran out and said, "What's going on here?"

The owner of the tavern came over. Everybody was shouting at me. I said, "Why are you shouting? I was in the Men's Room." They said, "Damen is women. In German, damen is women." I learned that herren was men, and that you've got to be careful about language; words don't always mean what they seem.

Eventually, I learned to speak the language. By the time I left Germany, I had learned conversational German. I studied it in graduate school, but not really using it since then, I lost it.

The Germans who spoke English were the girls in the bars. They were friendly; they loved African Americans. They believed the myth of the Black male's extraordinary sexual prowess. They wanted to rub our heads, rub our skin. That created problems with the White soldiers. They were very jealous and angry about the affection German women were giving Black soldiers.

Whenever Black soldiers went anywhere off base in Germany, we traveled as a group, because there were a lot of confrontations along racial lines. The racism that existed in America carried over into the Army, into a foreign country, where women were seemingly drawn to and catered to African American soldiers. White soldiers from Alabama, Mississippi and even up North resented that. So, we traveled in our metropolitan-area pack for protection—not from the Germans, but from White American soldiers.

In Germany we went through what was called "cold-weather indoctrination." During the Korean War, Americans had died without ever firing their weapons because they were cold and because they were scared. The US Army would see to it that that never happened again. They put us up in Hohenfels and Grafenwoehr and taught us how to fight in the sub-zero weather.

Hohenfels and Grafenwoehr were U.S. Military training grounds about 70 miles apart. They were isolated uninhabited massive wooded and open areas of land where the army practiced open firing and sector firing (bullets crisscrossed each other to prevent any forward movement of enemy troops) as if in real combat. Once we fired in sectors not even a grasshopper could survive the torching of the land.

We had already learned how to fight at Fort Benning, Georgia. Now in Hohenfels and Grafenwoehr, under some of the most extreme weather conditions that a man could face, we were trained again so that we would not fear the cold, would not lose morale and become a competent fighting unit in 20-30 below-zero temperatures. We wore what appeared to be 60 pounds of protective clothing. Often, the ground was completely frozen. We were given enormous "Mickey Mouse boots", insulated boots that generate heat as you walk, to prevent our feet from becoming frost-bitten. The most important thing to remember was, don't get wet.

We were almost killed several times while being transported in a personnel carrier, a rubber-track carrier, where 10 or 12 men were seated, facing each other, with a driver in a seat that went up and down. Once, it lost traction and fell over a mountain 2,000 feet, with us inside. Tumbling down, I saw my life pass before my eyes. I thought the vehicle would hit ground and explode. But, the carrier went all the way down and landed upright in the water.

The driver drove us to shore, and we pried open the door and walked out. We had been harnessed inside for safety. I got out without a scratch and kissed the ground. We were all shocked at our good luck. The captain said, "It's made for that. It's built for land, water, and everything else." I fell in love with a personnel carrier that saved my life on the snowcapped mountains of Hohenfels, Germany.

During cold-weather combat training, I met the great rock-and-roll legend Elvis Presley. He was part of the 3rd Armored Division that supported our infantry. To see "The King", with a shaved head, in uniform, and yet still handsome, was surprising to me. In our chance meeting I told him Sam Cook was my favorite singer, and his, You Send Me, my favorite song. I asked Elvis to sing. Somewhat amused, he crooned three words, Love Me Tender, and we both laughed. I soon found out that he had applied to live off base.

Having recently lost his mother and still grieving, he would be able to spend off-duty time with his father and grandmother who were living in a house he had rented near his base. He also entertained several young ladies there. One of them, Priscilla Beaulieu, the 14-year-old stepdaughter of an American Air Force officer stationed in Germany, would later become his wife.

The officers expected me to be one of the leaders since I was a college graduate, had majored in physical education and I was in superb physical condition. Sergeant Andrews placed me in charge of drilling and marching my military platoon. I can still hear my cadence sound off, "One two, sound off, one two. I got a girl who lives in town, she won't give but her mother will, sound off, one two, sound off, one two."

The officers would talk to the troops from the New York area through me. If they saw eight or nine Blacks gathered together, which we naturally tended to do, because we were from the same metropolitan area, the officers would say, "Sharpe, break it up, now. We don't want no racism here."

Lt. Andrew Perkins, a Mississippian, would come over and yell at me: "What are you guys doing, scheming? Going to be a riot?" He never wanted to see Black soldiers congregating, and he held me responsible for that, because I was the leader of the group. Lt. Perkins never meant any disrespect. "To be successful a fighting unit needs to be integrated," he lectured, and he thought it was best we socialize the same way.

I was number one in physical fitness, number one in knowledge-training of warfare, number one in my classroom. I had temporary duty assignment (TDY), where I played on the company basketball team and on the company flag football team (Flag football is a type of football in which the advancement of the ball is stopped by removing a flag attached to the ball carrier's clothing). Our company team wore the blue-and-white patch of the 3rd Infantry Division, the same division that WW II Hero Audie Murphy fought in. I made the all-Army flag football team, where I played quarterback, and won all honors on the basketball team. In addition, I was an all-Army track star.

I enjoyed playing on those teams, because that was the only time enlisted men, noncommissioned officers and commissioned officers came together. On those company teams were captains, lieutenants and generals. Some of them had been all-American athletes in college.

My biggest rivalry was in track. Lt. Ray McKisson, the coach and captain of our track team, and I were the top half-mile runners. We pushed each other and competed against one another. He was a lieutenant, and I was a private. During the day he gave me orders, but at night we would train together as equals, run as equals and participate as equals because we were trying to get points for our division's team.

When Rome hosted the Olympics in 1960, I put in a request to try out. I would have been shipped back to the United States to train for the Olympics had not I suffered an injury in my final run in the USAREUR championships. I was running the 800 meter race, and I crossed the finish line to qualify in my heat. I felt a pain in my foot, but I thought if I just stuffed a piece of cotton in my shoe, the pain would go away. The next day I ran in one of the semifinals qualifying heats. I was getting ready for the championship finals. I told the coach not to worry about my foot. He said, "We'll get an x-ray when we go in."

The doctor took an x-ray and told me I had a splintered cuboids' bone. It happened on the second lap, but I ran a whole lap with it and finished the race. I was so competitive; I had to get into the finals. The minute the doctor told me I had a splintered cuboids' bone, I felt the pain mentally. I couldn't walk without limping. That day I did not run in the championship round. The coach said, "No, Sharpe. The Army can't be responsible." Because I didn't run in that 800-meter event, which I qualified for, I was out of the competition.

The treat of a lifetime came in the spring of 1960, prior to the track season, when I was given a two-week leave, and I decided to do what I, a poor boy, had often dreamed of. I decided to go to Garmisch-Partenkirchen, Germany, the site of the 1936 Winter Olympics. I went skating in Garmisch, and then I went skiing on Zugspitze, one of the great sites of the 1936 Olympics.

Not being satisfied with that, I went to Berchtesgaden, a town in the Bavarian Alps, and Eagle's Nest, where Hitler used to live. I wanted to see and actually stand in what were Hitler's private quarters, a place from where this madman tried to rule the world.

From the Bavarian Alps I went to Austria and descended into the salt mines, about a mile below ground, to see the different layers of ground. After coming up from the salt mines I went to visit the castles and homes of some of the great musicians like Beethoven and Mozart.

While on leave in Germany, I tried to experience the history that I had only read about in books. I went to Munich, to the famous centuries-old beer hall, Hofbrauhaus. I went to Nuremberg, where the Allied war-crimes trials took place, a beautiful city.

It is no lie that German trains run on time. On the second hand, that's when they pull out. Their technology was excellent. Passing through rural Germany, I saw many farm animals, lots of cows. I saw an Olympic size pool and an Olympic track-perfect. The Germans truly wanted to be a super race of people. I was amazed at the country's development since World War II. Although we dropped bombs on them, they managed to rebuild after the war and regain their status in the world.

My greatest achievement while stationed in Germany was earning the Expert Infantry Badge (EIB), the highest peacetime award one can earn in the infantry. I was one of 10 men (out of the 5,000 I was shipped over with) who passed the test for the EIB. The ten of us stood on the parade field in Munich, Germany in 1960 for the honors. As long as I live, I'll always remember that one of the ten was an African American boy from Newark, New Jersey. Brigadier General Elias C. Townsend pinned the badge on me.

To earn the Badge, we had to submit to a battery of tests over the course of several weeks. We had to demonstrate physical skills, comprehension and endurance. We had to run, jump and climb. We had to find our way out of the woods and mountains with just grid coordinates and a compass. We had to take weapons apart blindfolded and put them back together. We were tested for marksmanship. I became an expert in the Browning automatic and the M-12 rifle, and I was able to score almost perfect bulls eyes on the target. On the academic quiz I correctly answered all of the questions about military procedure.

The commissioned officers in my unit tried to persuade me to reenlist in the Army and go into Officer Candidate School (OCS) because of my discerned ability to lead and my ability to comprehend military procedures. They told me I should consider a career in the military; but, because I had already invested in an education, I decided not to re-enlist. I decided, instead, to apply to Springfield College in Massachusetts for a master's degree program.

The Army gave me an "early out" to go to school, on the condition that I serve two years in the National Guard. I opted to do just that while I was living in Springfield. By August, 1960 I was headed home on the USNS Maurice Rose. When we sailed into the harbor, past the Statue of Liberty, under the Verrazano Narrows (where one of the longest suspension bridges in the world was under construction), all of us were running and shouting, someone said, "Sharpe, Sharpe, we're not home, we're back in Germany. Look at those Volkswagens going down the highway!" The big ship began to list a little because all of us had moved to the side of the ship facing New York City. We were so happy to be home again.

Although we were happy to be home, we Black soldiers knew that we would be facing problems of discrimination on this side of the Atlantic. We came back to a nation that was undergoing drastic changes in race relations. We had heard about the student sit-ins across the South to desegregate Woolworth's lunch counters. Even in my native Jacksonville, I learned on my trip home, there was rioting when police brutally beat demonstrators taking part in a sit-in.

African American soldiers, once they came home from service overseas, often went back overseas to live. They were trying to recapture the life they led in another country, where they were treated better than they were in their native land. They felt that abroad they were somebody; at home they were just another Black stereotype.

In Germany I learned that people are basically the same during peace time, even when we didn't speak the same language. Though the communists in the East were our country's perceived enemy, there was a lot we had in common as individual human beings. While I was on guard duty one night, a soldier came across the border. I was about to fire at him, because he was trespassing. He came, hands up, a white flag on his bayonet, speaking broken English, and I wanted to shoot. I had my rifle and bayonet right in his gut. He wanted a cigarette. He asked me for coffee. He wanted to trade whatever he had for American cigarettes and coffee.

I don't believe this, I thought to myself. I didn't smoke in the service, so all I had to give him were ration cards, which he could not use. I told him, "No smoke; No coffee; Tomorrow maybe; Gute nacht." Back across the border he went, and sure enough, on another night he came across the border again. Finally, I gave him something, just to be diplomatic. I put some coffee and a pack of cigarettes on the ground. He took them and said, "Thank you, thank you."

Here we were, in a dispute, on opposing sides. We were not supposed to communicate. But he wanted American coffee and cigarettes. That was war. Hot or cold, there's always a time in war when soldiers become just human beings.

The peacekeeping assignment in Germany cost the lives of some of my friends, who were killed in training. They never made it back. In the training areas of Hohenfel and Grafenwoehr, while we were crawling around and firing for practice or throwing hand grenades, we often worried about the armored division troops that were firing practice rounds in our area. Some rounds exploded when we entered the artillery impact area.

Once a platoon member, while sitting in on a hand-grenade lesson in a concrete bunker in Hohenfels, was instructed to pull the pin and throw a hand grenade as far as possible out of the bunker and then to duck down. Instead, after pulling the pin he panicked, dropping the hand-grenade in the bunker. Luckily the supervising sergeant picked up the live grenade and tossed it out of the bunker, saving lives. War drills can be deadly.

Then there were those who were killed in friendly fire. At breakfast one morning, some of our troops started firing rounds on us during a practice exercise. Some troops died when trucks tumbled off the ice slicked mountains. These were written up simply as road accidents.

The worst incident occurring during that time was in Grafenwoehr, on September 2, 1960, shortly after I set sail for home. Stars and Stripes reported that 15 Americans were killed and 28 injured, when a large-caliber artillery shell was incorrectly fired and landed in the tent camp of the 3rd Reconnaissance Squadron, 12th Cavalry of the 3rd Armored Division

Although wartime casualties at enemy hands were widely publicized, death from friendly fire during peacetime was something of a military secret. I saw peacekeeping casualties firsthand, in Germany, when many of those who were with me in Fort Dix, Ft. Benning, and in Schweinfurt, did not come home.

All in all, my Army service was a great experience. I enjoyed the disciplined lifestyle, the opportunity to serve my country and still maintain my interest in athletics. I viewed the monthly pay, with free room and board, as a luxury. I simply banked all of my money and concentrated on being all spit and shine, the best soldier ever. Sightseeing in Europe while on leave and competing in sports against top athletes were thrills of a lifetime.

Four years later, I was teaching, earning a salary and gaining weight. I was seriously dating. In the military, I was a physical animal; all I did was train to be a soldier and an athlete. There was nothing else in my life. I was training for survival, thinking that someday, some fool was going to run across the East West German border and attack me.

I used to be out there on guard duty at night, and I'd hear all kinds of noises, and see all kinds of things. Some people who've lived all their lives in the city don't know what darkness is all about. They think darkness means the sun has gone down, but there are lights on all around. To be out in a field where there are no lights whatsoever, where it's overcast and you can't see the moon or your hand in front of your face, where you hear noises and you know that somebody is out there, is a frightening thing.

My thinking was that the only way one can prepare for such a thing is to try to become a superman. I was constantly thinking that I'd have to engage in hand-to-hand combat at any moment. I was always thinking that I was going to have to fight to the very end. So, I trained, trained, trained. Because I was skilled in track, I knew I could run. My attitude was that I could do anything; I could run and run, even through a wall if I had to.

After the Army, I lost that kamikaze mentality. Other things became more important, like dating and meeting the right woman. I received letters regularly from two young ladies from the States while I was overseas. However, when I returned home and sought to establish a real relationship, I found out both had gotten married.

I paid a visit to one of the women I had corresponded with and learned what a mistake it was to send unisex gifts to an alleged sweetheart. In Germany I had bought a Grundig radio and a Bavarian sweater at the Army-base PX—at a great discount—and proudly mailed them to this young lady. When I rang her doorbell, to my horror a man came to the door wearing the sweater! I guess she decided to keep her marriage a secret from me in order to keep the gifts flowing. I wanted to ask her to give the radio back. It was a painful lesson in betrayal.

Less painful was my transition from Germany to Springfield College in Massachusetts as a graduate assistant to the renowned Dr. Peter V. Karpovich, an acknowledged expert in sports medicine. It was now time to forget about weapons and muscles and put on my thinking cap for graduate school.

CHAPTER FOUR

Graduate School and Beyond

After transferring from duty overseas to National Guard duty back home in Newark, I searched for living accommodations in Springfield, Massachusetts, where I would be attending graduate school. I had graduated from Panzer College/Montclair State University, the number one physical education undergraduate school in America, so now I wanted to attend the number one graduate school in the country for physical education.

I had been told that Springfield College in Massachusetts was number one. Its mission was to educate the whole man, as stated in its logo: the trinity of mind, body and spirit. The Naismith Memorial Basketball Hall of Fame was located In Springfield as well.

I found a place to stay through my aunt Helen Mathis, who lived in Springfield. She directed me to Ms. Maybell Beam, who lived at 129 Eastern Avenue, within walking distance of the college. My aunt had told me that Ms. Beam was considering renting rooms to students.

"Maybell Beam, my name is Sharpe James. I'm just coming out of the military. You don't know me, but my aunt lives up here in Springfield," I said, when I called her on the phone. She told me to come on up and take a look.

Ms. Beam owned a one-family house on Eastern Avenue, and it would be just the two of us living there. To get to the room, I would have to have a key to the front door, giving me access to the whole house. After meeting me face-to-face, Ms. Beam trusted me enough to take me in. She became my biggest supporter while I lived in Springfield, my best friend and my surrogate mother. I got to know her family: her sons and daughters.

When I met her, Ms Beam was studying for a Post Office job. I watched her one day as she set up a file box and practiced alphabetizing. She fully prepared for the civil service test. She got the job, because she was a fighter, a strong lady. She kept an impeccable house. I lived there for a year and a half while getting my master's degree. After I became mayor, she would win recognition from Springfield College for allowing me to stay there.

I was at Springfield on a fellowship, as a teaching research assistant to the renowned Dr. Peter V. Karpovich, head of Springfield's exercise physiology lab. He had never hired a Black assistant before. I worked in the laboratory with him, and I helped teach physiology classes. Dr. Karpovich and his wife, Dr. Josephine Rathbone, who taught at Columbia University, were two of the founders of the American College of Sports Medicine in 1954.

Dr. Karpovich was doing research with Dr. Philip Gollnick, who was on loan to Springfield from Washington State University. I was their guinea pig. They put me on the treadmill and tested my reaction. They wanted to know what happened to the liver, what were the effects on the cholesterol level. I assisted in three of their studies. One, "Electro goniometric Study of Locomotion and Some Athletic Movements," received Springfield's department of physiology award.

One day Dr. Karpovich called me into his office. He introduced me to a doctoral candidate who was conducting a study on the bone structure of Black people and how it affected their ability to perform different types of physical activities. He said that he believed Black people couldn't swim, that they were sinkers, because their bone structure differed from that of Whites. For that reason, also, he said, Blacks excelled at running short distances, but did poorly in endurance runs.

Dr. Karpovich asked me, "What do you think of his study, Sharpe?"

"Well, Sir, quite frankly, I don't believe there is any difference between races. In fact, if you recall, an Ethiopian runner, Abebe Bikila, won the men's marathon race at the Rome Olympics in 1960 demonstrating that Africans, particularly East Africans, can run long distances. He set a new world record and won the gold medal." I said, and took a deep breath.

"During the same Olympic Games in 1960, a German runner, Armin Hary, proved that a White runner can beat Black runners in a sprint. He won the gold medal in the 100-meter race. So, clearly, no one can make the argument that the muscle and bone structure of the human body, especially the male body, varies according to race. My humble opinion is that your study is flawed and a waste of time. Research would not support your theory." After making my remarks, I left.

Later, Dr. Karpovich told me, "I just wanted you to tell him that, because that guy is nuts! You're a good assistant, Sharpe."

After that, Dr. Karpovich would ask me, "Are you free this weekend? Come to my house and cut the grass." When I wasn't busy, he would ask me to go out and clean his car. I went up to his summer home to trim the bushes. I did that better than anyone else, and he loved me.

No matter what Dr. Karpovich asked me to do, I would always tell people, nothing was going to stop me from getting my master's degree. I didn't hear him or see him when I was doing the work. All I knew was that I had a year-and-a-half to get my master's degree.

Dr. Karpovich and his wife were the ones who introduced me to Dr. Philip D. Gollnick. They told me they would recommend me for a full scholarship to study physical therapy at New York University.

For my undergraduate program at Panzer College I had completed my student teaching requirement in physical therapy at Kessler Institute in West Orange, New Jersey. The director was Dr. Potts, from Newark, New Jersey. At Kessler Institute I fell in love with physical therapy, and Dr. Potts encouraged me to pursue a career in it.

Dr. Karpovich and Dr. Rathbone filled out my application to NYU. Whatever they did, they got me accepted, with a scholarship. In two or three years, I would become Sharpe James, doctor of physical therapy.

The acceptance letter said that I first had to meet and obtain the approval of the chairman of NYU's department of education, Dr. Roscoe C. Brown. Dr. Brown, I learned, was a well-respected Black educator, who had taught courses on TV, not to mention serving as commander of the 100th Fighter Squadron of the 332nd Fighter Group—the famed Tuskegee Airmen—in World War II. He was the first pilot in the 15th Air Force Squadron to shoot down a German jet fighter.

Dr. Brown was also an alumnus of Springfield College. A Black man! Hallelujah! I thought I had it made. I had already made it pass a board of 35 White people and had the recommendations of Dr. Karpovich and Dr. Rathbone.

On the morning of our scheduled meeting I walked into Dr. Brown's office, and he asked me my name.

I said, "Sharpe James."

He said, "James Sharpe?"

"No, Sir. Sharpe James."

"You're sure it's not James Sharpe?"

"No, Sir. My name is Sharpe James."

He said, "I looked at your record, and it is outstanding, but you need more practical experience. You need to go out and do more teaching before you come into this program. I'm going to turn you down."

I said, "Dr. Brown, I don't want to go out and do any more teaching. I want to continue my education." He didn't budge. I hated him. Just the thought of a Black man destroying another qualified Black man's dream perturbed me.

Eventually, at the suggestion of Dr. Gollnick, I accepted a graduate research assistant position at Washington State University to study sports medicine. I had taught human anatomy in the lab and was a research assistant to Dr. Gollnick. I was disappointed that I wasn't going to be attending the program at NYU, but I accepted the decision. However, my first encounter with Dr. Roscoe C. Brown was not to be my last.

In 1972 while teaching at Essex County College, I was elected a representative of the Council of Higher Education of Newark (CHEN). The New Jersey Institute of Technology (NJIT), Newark Rutgers and the University of Medicine & Dentistry of NJ (UMDNJ) were considering a plan to merge shared services. To present the proposal I went to a meeting in New York City to explore the concept of colleges sharing resources conducted by Dr. Brown.

The meeting took place at New York University. After my arrival I entered the meeting room, sat down, and in walks Dr. Roscoe C. Brown. He said, "I want to go around the room and have everyone give their names and tell us something about themselves."

When my turn came I said, "My name is Sharpe James. I represent Essex County College, New Jersey Institute of Technology, Newark Rutgers and the UMDNJ, where there is a proposal to merge and share services, and there's been some resistance."

Dr. Brown said, "Are you sure your name is not James Sharpe?"

I said, "No, my name is Sharpe James."

He said, "Wait a minute! That's an unusual name. Have I heard that name before?"

I promptly stood up and said, "Dr. Brown, I'm the son-of-a-bitch who you denied a scholarship to ten years ago. That's the Sharpe James I am." He didn't look at me the rest of the meeting.

Now, fast forward to 1988, when I chaired Jesse Jackson's presidential campaign in Newark. Jesse called me and said, "Mayor, they're having a big fundraiser for me at Farleigh Dickinson University in Rutherford, NJ. I can't make it. Will you go up there and get the money from them? I'll have my finance chairman there; you can make the speech and hand the money over to him."

I said, "Fine. No problem. I'll be there."

Ten minutes later the phone rang. It was Jesse Jackson. "Sharpe, there's a problem. My finance chairman for the state of New Jersey is Dr. Roscoe C. Brown. Will there be any trouble? Is there something going on between the two of you?"

I said, "Jesse, it's all over. That's behind me. Tell Roscoe to give me a call." Dr. Brown immediately called me and said, "Sharpe, I'm not going to have a problem now, am I?"

I said, "Roscoe, it's no problem."

Although I was bitterly disappointed at being denied a scholarship to NYU, I decided to let bygones be bygones. I had suspected that the real reason Dr. Brown rejected my application was because he feared competition from another Black man. As it turned out, for whatever reason, his decision sent me down a path that ultimately led to my being able to confront him as an equal.

Perhaps as a consolation gift to myself I purchased a TR-4 Triumph sports car to make the long trip to Washington State. I drove four long days from Newark to Washington State University. Every bug along the western highway dove into my car at night and stained it from a light blue to a dark blue. I learned why so many cars heading east had that canvas mat over the front of their cars. Without it one could get killed from the kamikaze flying birds and animals drawn by car lights along pitch dark highways. I was lucky to arrive at WSU alive.

At Washington State I was under Dr. Gollnick's tutelage in sports medicine. He had returned to Washington after completing his research in Springfield. After I left Washington, and even after Dr. Gollnick died, his family continued to write me and we kept in touch.

At Springfield and at Washington State, the only Blacks the faculty came in contact with were jocks, on athletic scholarships. The professors loved Sharpe James, because I was an African American who did his job professionally and had personality. I could do the research and follow instructions. I was organized; I could read, write and think critically. My work was impeccable; and I had humor.

The faculty had not met many Black people who they felt were their equal. I was a graduate student, but I came to them, not with humility. I came to them as a competent individual. I didn't bow my head. I was untamed, free-spirited, and an athlete; but, I was smart and responsible. I didn't come to dance. I didn't come to have sex. I didn't come to marry their daughter. I came to do the work and still be Sharpe James from Newark, NJ. I think that shocked people. Maybe even the name Newark shocked them.

"Oh, you're different!" the White professors would say. I wasn't different. I didn't know what they meant by that. Different meaning what? Different meaning I was responsible? Different meaning I was intelligent? Different meaning that I was not an athletic jock?

Just about every Black male student at Washington State was on the football team. There might have been a half-percent of Blacks who wasn't there on scholarship (like the African girl I tried to date, who thought she was White and turned me down). Most of the Blacks were athletes who were there to win ball games. Kenneth Graham, my best friend at WSU, and Clarence Williams, both who later became NFL All-American football players, were star athletes. I was at WSU on an academic scholarship. Did I act like a football player? No. I acted like an academic scholar and did the work. I was still an athlete, though.

I'd get to work early in the lab, and I wouldn't leave until late. I knew every white mouse in the laboratory by name. I hated killing them and analyzing their blood and organs, but I had a job to do, and I did it. I passed all of my classes. Biochemistry, especially, was so difficult for me and caused me so much eye strain; I had to start wearing glasses. Truthfully, I messed up the lab several times.

There was a Nobel-prize winner teaching biochemistry. On the first day, taking attendance, he asked me, "Sharpe, are you in the right class?"

I said, "I beg your pardon?"

"Are you in the right class," he asked again?

At first I did not understand his question, and then I caught on. I was a Black man, sitting in his biochemistry class. He said he had never had an athlete take biochemistry before. I told him, "I'm not here as an athlete."

He said, "Every Black student at WSU is on a football scholarship." That was his bias belief. And that was a professor! He didn't believe that athletes should be in his class. He thought his reputation was being tarnished. After all, who would want to be in Pullman, Washington except a Black athlete? There was nothing in Pullman outside of the university. No place to party or go just to have fun.

I studied all the time. I had practically no social life. The most exciting thing that happened while I was there was when Louis Armstrong came to play on campus. Weekend fun was going to Seattle to see some Black folks.

My friends and I would drive three hours to get to Seattle just to see people who looked like us. We went to the World's Fair to see the Space Needle. Spokane was an hour's drive away, and there were some Black people there, but, Seattle was our vacation getaway spot to meet some real "soul" folks.

Sometimes I'd be working in the lab, and after I had completed my assignment I would go over to the window and watch the football team, cheerleaders and the band practice on the football field. In 1962, we had a football team that we thought was going to win the championship; Kenny Graham was on the team, so was Clarence Williams and that great unbelievable All American wide receiver with the glue hands, Hugh Campbell, was there.

I remembering walking over to Dr. Gollnick in the laboratory and saying, "Boy, the team really looks good." My remark startled him.

"Sharpe, it's a waste of time," Dr. Gollnick replied. "There is nothing but jocks out there. They should abolish the program," he said. "It's a waste of money that could be used for research." Every day he would say something to me, friendly, but condescending to the athletic program, the band, and the cheerleaders. They did not count in his mind and his world.

I was the bridge between the two worlds. I was the researcher-graduate assistant. However, because I was Sharpe James, inquisitive, friendly and with a sports background, I knew the football players. The football players were also happy that I was there, because I helped them with their homework.

A year into my studies at WSU the Dean of our department, Dr. Golden Romney, died. He was the brother of Michigan's Gov. George Romney and the uncle of future GOP presidential candidate, Mitt Romney. The university had to reassess our department. I told Dr. Gollnick, "Because of the death of Dr. Romney, and because of the uncertainty of my grant, I'm going back home." He looked surprised and hurt, but did not comment. My doctoral studies had come to a halt.

What it really was, I finally realized, was that I could not be in a world that clearly drew a line between sports and research. I loved and respected Dr. Gollnick, and I knew I had earned his respect, as well. But, he did not see any connection between athletics and research, even though I was the bridge. His family had been my extended family. Still Dr. Romney's death gave me an excuse to return to Newark and get on with my teaching and coaching career.

It was painful and tearful to tell the Gollnick family that I was quitting my doctoral studies and heading home. Yet, I felt relieved to let them know that I did not find happiness changing my personality from being a sports enthusiast, loquacious, back slapping and jovial individual to an impassive, monotonous, reserved and meticulous research laboratory worker. This was not to be a substitute for a planned career in physical therapy.

It was time to put the TR-4 Triumph sports car on the road again, this time traveling east for four rugged days and nights. Good bye WSU, Good bye Pullman, Spokane and Seattle. I will miss your raw beauty, your charm and challenges. Now I was looking forward to getting home and seeking opportunities that awaited me in my adopted city, Newark.

Here I come Newark!

CHAPTER FIVE

The Fight for UCC Area Board 9

My Initiation into Politics

The drive home from Washington State was still a long trip; however, I was better prepared for the hazards of the road this time. I had learned my lesson traveling west and my Triumph 4 was now sporting a tailor made canvas covering the front grill and hood. I was able to reach speeds of 115-130 miles per hour, with a keen eye on my radar screen probing for State Troopers, without worrying about having to paint my car once I got home. After traveling for three days on Highways 90 and 94 East I breathed a sigh of relief when I turned off Highway 80-East heading for the Oranges and Newark, New Jersey.

Once back in Newark I didn't have any trouble finding a job. I'd been a Newark teacher, teaching at Broadway Jr. High School, before I'd been drafted into the army. Having satisfied my military responsibility and furthered my academic credentials I didn't anticipate any problem returning to a teaching position in the city. So when I landed a job as the physical education teacher at the newly built Quitman Street elementary School I felt like I was back in my element, doing what it is that I liked to do.

My social life picked up considerably once I was back among my own people. I started dating a fellow teacher, Helen Barnes, from Vauxhall, New Jersey. Helen was a party girl; she had a great personality and was loved by the students as well as the faculty at Quitman. We had great times together attending sporting events, bar hopping and dancing the nights away at the fabulous Highest Peak Club, in Newark's West Ward.

Helen was a great dancer. She never missed a beat whether she was dancing on top of the bar, under the bar, or on the dance floor. She was 120 lbs. of fun and excitement. For a while I thought I was in love with her; so did most of our friends and family. They thought we would get married one day; so did I. That is until I got to know the "unapproachable Mary Lou Mattison."

I first noticed Mary, who was also a teacher at Quitman, as she stood on a stool, hanging up signs for her students. She was tall, slender and attractive. She was sporting a big afro at the time and she reminded me of Angela Davis. It was rumored by other male faculty members that Mary was antisocial and unapproachable.

Although I had many good times with Helen, Mary soon began to consume my thoughts and take up my time. It started with small talk in the school cafeteria and escalated when she eventually invited me to meet her cousin, whom she was living with on Eckert Avenue, in Newark. Dinner and movie dates followed. For a while I dated both Mary and Helen, the quiet one and the fireball. I knew I couldn't continue doing this much longer; I had to make a choice.

At twenty-eight years old I had begun to think about marriage and making a long term commitment. I knew I wanted a family and an active life as a teacher, an athlete, and a coach. I was becoming more active in my community, and without really knowing it at the time, I was being drawn into taking a more active part in bringing about real change in Newark. Who would be the better partner was the question I asked myself. Who would be home taking care of the children while I was out in the community?

I married the quiet one, Mary Lou Mattison, on Saturday, February 15, 1964. We didn't have much money so we decided on a small, non-pretentious wedding that took place at St. James A.M.E Church, in Newark. Reverend Blake presided at the ceremony. Afterwards we had a brown bag reception in the church basement. On Monday, we were both back to work at Quitman Street School. We had decided not to have a honeymoon; we couldn't afford to miss a pay check. The entire wedding cost us about seventy-five dollars.

Mary and I have been married for over forty-eight years and I can truthfully say we have never had a fight. I attribute this blessing to the words spoken by Reverend Blake to me and Mary before we got married, words that still ring out loudly in my mind. "Sharpe and Mary," he had said, "I never want you two to get angry at the same time. Sharpe when Mary is angry be quiet and understanding; Mary, when Sharpe is angry be quiet and understanding. When both of you are angry at the same time the pots will start flying. Remember my words," he had said. We have. Helen and I remained friends up until her death, and marrying Mary was the best decision I made in my life.

In the early 1960s African Americans in northern cities had little or no elected political power. Seeking opportunities to serve as board of education members, city council members, county elected officials and mayors only resulted in futile campaigns. Blacks lacked funding, organization and major-party support. In many elections a candidate had to receive a 50 percent-plus-one vote majority to win and avoid a runoff.

It was next to impossible for a member of a racial or ethnic minority to win an election under those circumstances. The White establishment would sometimes appoint a few African Americans that they knew they could control to fill offices left vacant due to resignations or death. African Americans were not necessarily guaranteed leadership in majority-Black districts or wards, however, because Whites would run, and win, in those areas, as well. Blacks had yet to achieve voting majorities.

Thus, in Newark one way for Blacks to gain and exercise some political clout was through the United Community Corporation, which administered federal antipoverty funds. Created by the Economic Opportunity Act of 1964, the UCC was mandated to fund neighborhood programs and to elect local community boards with neighborhood officers and a paid staff to address local concerns. The goal was to eradicate the conditions that bred poverty and discontent and to help the residents of Newark become more upwardly mobile and self-sufficient.

It was a program that would grow minority leadership and prepare them to assume municipal elected positions. Newark Mayor Kenneth Gibson, state assembly member George Richardson, Central Ward council members Jesse Allen and George Branch, council members-at-large Earl Harris, Donald Tucker and me, Sharpe James, were all products of UCC. We got involved at the grassroots level, with grassroots issues, and developed into polished politicians. We learned how to organize the community, to turn numerical power into political power, and to get the vote out. But it didn't happen overnight.

In my neighborhood, the South Ward, the established Jewish leadership, with South Ward councilman Lee Bernstein at its helm, directed all of the antipoverty funds to their hand-picked staff and selected programs, leaving the rising African American population in the South Ward without a voice. There was no interest, on the part of those who held power, in letting the budding, and increasingly militant, Black leadership get its hands on federal dollars.

Bernstein was one of three Newark council members who, in 1965, had made up a special committee that issued a report attacking the UCC for paying "outsiders" high salaries. The fact of the matter was that some of Newark's politicians resented their lack of control over the antipoverty agency. As Dean C. Willard Heckel of Rutgers Law School, then-president of the UCC, put it, "Certain members of the City Council feel threatened by the new leadership that is coming forward as the poor assume responsibilities."

By mandate, the UCC Area Board, which consisted of eight members, was supposed to hold annual elections for officers and report to the community. Bernstein, along with his friends and cronies, who controlled UCC Area Board 9 of the South Ward, ignored all of the mandates. They set up their own organization. They held no meetings, issued no reports, and developed no programs. Theirs was a closed society, and they took the position of to hell with the community.

By the end of 1965 Blacks in the South Ward were demanding that Area Board 9 be held accountable, that it hold a meeting and call an election. Blacks were demanding that they be part of the federal program. Certainly, it was this type of attitude that helped stoke the Black rage that spilled over into the riot of 1967.

According to the constitution of Area Board 9, elections for new officers were to be held in October of each year. The president at that time, Anthony Defino, had not held a public meeting in more than a year. One day, during a meeting at the Area Board 9 community center on Osborne Terrace, a group of people from the South Ward said to me, "Sharpe, why don't you go to Lee Bernstein's headquarters at 555 Elizabeth Avenue? You're a teacher, you're an athlete. Go in there and tell Lee Bernstein he hasn't held any meetings, and the bylaws of UCC say you must hold an annual meeting to elect officers. He has been taking government money. No meetings, no report. We don't know what's going on. Go in there and tell him that."

I guess they figured a coach is a tough guy, so let the coach go in there and talk, let the coach go and do this on behalf of the community. I lived in the community. I was active with Boy Scouts and Girl Scouts, and whenever a community concern developed, residents would just gravitate to me. Everybody else was scared to go.

That same day I rode over to 555 Elizabeth Avenue with a couple of my neighbors. Bernstein's office was set up in the luxurious apartment building complete with indoor swimming pool. When I knocked on the door, the door opened and I was allowed to come in to make my presentation. Bernstein, along with several other White people, was sitting in the room.

I said, "Councilman Bernstein, my name is Sharpe James. I'm a teacher in Newark, and the community asked me to come here and ask you about this antipoverty program. I know you've got an office, and I know you've got all these people paid at the desk, but the rules say you've got to have an election. The rules say that local people are supposed to be involved. We don't know what's going on. When are you going to have a meeting?"

After I finished speaking, one of the men, a police officer, pulled a gun and said, "Nigger, we'll shoot you for coming in here. Do you know that? Don't ever come in here again telling us about rules and regulations. We do what we want to do. Do you understand?"

I put my hands up and said, "Wait a minute. Don't get crazy now." There I was in an office, surrounded by White men, with a gun drawn on me, thinking that I wanted to fight, thinking that I wanted to shout, scream and curse them out. But instead I realized that I was married and that I was an educator, so I held my emotions in, turned around and said, "Thank you very much," and I left.

There were about a dozen people, waiting on the sidewalk for me to come out. I said, "You folks must be crazy! They're killers in there.

They were serious." We knew then that Bernstein's people were not going to give up anything voluntarily. Many of my neighbors were now feeling a sense of hopelessness, powerlessness and of being disrespected. This was still the situation in the summer of 1967, when Newark exploded in a riot.

The lack of electoral power was a source of great frustration for Newark's Black population in the mid 1960s. Under the 1954 charter that reestablished Newark's city council-mayor form of government, there had been only two mayors. Leo P. Carlin, a former teamster union official, was the first under the new charter. He served two terms, and was defeated by seven-term Congressman Hugh J. Addonizio in 1962.

Addonizio was a liberal Democrat who came to City Hall by forming an alliance of Italians and Blacks to wrest control of the city government from the Irish. But as Newark's Black population continued to grow (from 34 percent in 1960 to 54 percent by 1970), it began to demand an even greater voice in the running of the city.

Blacks had been relegated to the poorest neighborhoods through racist redlining practices on the part of banks and insurance companies. About a third of Newark housing, at the time, was substandard.

The city's police force was a source of great conflict between Blacks and the Addonizio administration. Most of the policemen were White, while most of those arrested were Black. I never saw Black and White policemen together in a patrol car, so even within the force itself, there was racial tension. Black officers were continuously passed over for promotions.

The city's Black residents complained of the aggressive, confrontational attitude of White policemen patrolling Black neighborhoods. With no civilian review board, however, Blacks were faced with limited means of redressing police brutality complaints.

On top of that, the city was hemorrhaging for money as spending for services increased. People came to Newark to work and do business during the day, so they had to have public transportation, clean streets, as well as police and fire protection. With the reduction of home ownership in the city and a mass exodus of middle-class Whites to the suburbs, revenues from property taxes declined. Vacant lots dotted the city's landscape and stood waiting for development.

As usual, Black neighborhoods were last in the delivery of municipal services. There was less money for schools, which were about 70 percent Black at the time. The high school dropout and unemployment rates among Black youth were well above the city average. Fifteen percent of Newark's Black population was without jobs.

This was the situation in the summer of 1967, when Newark exploded in a riot.

The Riot of 1967

Blacks felt they had little say in the way Newark's government was run. It was only through the federal antipoverty programs that Lyndon Johnson introduced as part of his "Great Society", that we were able to empower ourselves and gain a foothold in the political system. Black political activists were starting to spread the idea of Black Power.

Two issues led to confrontations between the city's Black population and the administration prior to the riots. One was the mayor's nomination of a White man, with only a high-school education, over a Black man, the city's budget director, who held a master's degree in accounting, to succeed the retiring Board of Education secretary.

The other issue was the designation of 150 acres of land in the Central Ward, where most of the city's public high-rise housing was located, as the site for the construction of the New Jersey College of Medicine and Dentistry. This would displace some 3,500 Blacks in one more urban renewal project initiated by Addonizio that was forcing people from their homes and, perhaps, out of the city altogether. Naturally, some Blacks saw this as an attempt to erode their political power.

So, emotions were at fever pitch on Wednesday, July 12, 1967 in the midst of a heat wave, when a 41-year old Black cab driver, John W. Smith, was stopped by two White police officers in the center of the city's Black Central Ward. Smith had been tailgating the slow-moving patrol car in front of him and then tried to pass it. The police cut him off and ordered him out of his cab and then tried to arrest him. Smith objected to the arrest. The officers claimed he began to resist and had to be subdued. Smith said he was beaten for no reason, and then dragged from the patrol car into the Fourth Precinct station in the Central Ward.

Across the street from the precinct, at the Hayes Homes housing project, residents watched angrily. A call went out to Oliver Lofton, a prominent civil rights attorney, who at the time was Newark's director of legal services, to come and represent Smith. By the time Lofton arrived at the precinct, an angry crowd of about 200 people had gathered.

A rumor began circulating among the crowd and on cab radios throughout the city that Smith had died in police custody. He had not, but Lofton said he sustained lacerations to his head when the police dragged him by his heels from the patrol car into the precinct. Smith's head was bumping on the steps, and that's what the people in Hayes Homes saw. Afterward, police officials had agreed to take him to a hospital for medical treatment.

Lofton went outside the precinct to explain to the crowd what was happening. He got on top of a car with a bullhorn and started to talk. He, along with other community leaders, including Timothy Still, president of the United Community Corporation (UCC), and Robert Curvin of the Congress of Racial Equality (CORE), were trying to organize the crowd to march to police headquarters downtown, but they couldn't get the crowd to budge; they just weren't ready to do that. They were not ready to walk away from the situation at the Fourth Precinct.

With police officers lined up outside the precinct, and the crowd, ten to fifteen feet away from them, all hell broke loose. Some that were present said the police officers started it when they began to charge the crowd. Others said the residents were arming themselves with rocks, sticks, bricks and anything else they could find to throw at police. Once it started, that was it. People started venting their anger, and chaos ensued thereafter.

Although police finally managed to disperse the protesters by 4 a.m. the next day—after 25 people were arrested and significant damage had been done to the precinct—the anger, violence, arson and looting continued for four more days.

On Thursday, Mayor Addonizio met with Black community leaders and agreed to transfer the officers who had arrested Smith and seek a federal investigation into the police brutality allegations. But that night Blacks again gathered in front of the Fourth Precinct and threw rocks, stones, bottles, sticks and metal at Black leaders who tried to explain the mayor's position.

During this time, other Blacks began to rip iron gratings from storefronts along Springfield Avenue, the wide commercial block that runs from the suburbs through the heart of the Central Ward into Newark's downtown. As police tried to contain the looting and violence in the Central Ward, where it had began, Blacks in other parts of the city started their own protests. Some police officers were issued shotguns, and the entire 1,400-member force was put on 12-hour emergency shifts.

At 2 a.m. on Friday, Addonizio asked Gov. Richard Hughes to call in the national and state police. Hughes, who mobilized 2,600 National Guardsmen and 300 state police troopers, recalled years later what Addonizio had told him: "The town is burning," he had said. "Nothing will be left." By Friday night 14 people were dead.

The National Guard, young soldiers mostly, were afraid of their own shadows. They did not know how to deal with the situation, and that led to the ominous turn of events. The guardsmen, almost all of them White and from suburban or rural areas, had no city maps. Coordination among the city and state officials and the guardsmen was nonexistent.

After the arrival of state police and guardsmen, nearly two-thirds of the city was occupied by troops and tanks. Reports of snipers led to police and National Guard firing wildly into the air.

By the end of the fourth day, Saturday night, 220 stores had been looted along Springfield Avenue, and seven more people had died. Four more were killed Sunday night and the 26th person died after being wounded by a fire bomb. One of the dead was a ten-year-old boy. Property damage totaled 15 million-1967 dollars.

Meetings with Black leaders, the mayor and governor continued throughout the rioting, but it was not until Monday, the sixth day that the troops were withdrawn.

Although the arrest of taxi-driver John Smith has often been cited as the incident that sparked Newark's riot, the governor's Select Commission on Civil Disorders concluded "Neither the arrest of Mr. Smith nor any other single factor could explain the events that followed. There is no full or logical explanation for mass violence such as Newark experienced."

The looting was an excuse for some African Americans, who had little respect for the law before the Smith incident, to demonstrate lawlessness in the guise of political protest. Their actions were not justifiable, but they were understandable. The Black community had been provoked.

During the unrest, I was one of the community leaders trying to calm people down, trying to tell them that violence was not the way to go. We needed to organize. We needed voter registration. We needed voter education.

As for Smith, he was convicted of assaulting one of the arresting officers, and found not guilty of assaulting the other. Lofton appealed the conviction, all the way up to the U.S. Supreme Court, and Smith never served a day in prison. The reason being that New Jersey grand juries were chosen from all-White Rotary and Kiwanis clubs. Smith could not get a jury of his peers, Lofton argued. And from that case, the whole grand jury system in the state of New Jersey was overhauled.

Later in that same July month, Newark was the site of the first National Conference on Black Power, attended by more than 1,000 delegates from hundreds of organizations across the country and some of the most vocal Black activists of the day: H. Rap Brown of the Student Nonviolent Coordinating Committee (SNCC); Jesse Jackson of the Southern Christian Leadership Conference (SCLC); James Farmer of CORE; professor Maulana Ron Karenga; playwright and poet Amiri Baraka and actor Ossie Davis.

Although the setting of the conference had been chosen prior to the riots, it was perfect timing. The month's events lent an even greater urgency to the call for Black power. James Farmer announced a recall campaign against the Addonizio administration, however, that never got off the ground. Over the next two years Newark's Black community leaders would mount a serious challenge to the entire White political establishment. It was time for solidarity. It was time for a change.

After the riots, with Newark now a scarred city, we returned to unfinished business at UCC. Members of the Area Board signed a petition to call a special meeting for the election of new officers. Defino and all Area Board 9 members were notified well in advance of the November 30, 1967 date, the place, the time and the purpose of the special meeting, but Defino ignored the information. Despite this, more than 70 Area Board 9 members, including Newark's Human Rights executive director Harold Hodes and Dean Harrison of the UCC's community action department, braved seven inches of snow and freezing temperatures to show up for the meeting. After officers had been constitutionally elected for the 1967-1968 year, with me being chosen as interim president, Defino called another meeting for December where another election would take place that would surely be rigged in favor of his team.

"Is this legal?" I posed the question to Timothy Still, UCC's president, in a letter dated December 2, 1967. "At this time I seek your help in the transfer of Area Board 9 records, functions and responsibilities to the new slate of officers," I wrote. As far as I was concerned, Defino had abrogated his authority by failing to hold meetings and elections on the constitutionally designated dates.

UCC responded by establishing a board of inquiry, chaired by Charles Mabray, in January, 1968. The UCC executive committee would work with Area Board 9 for the development of a new constitution, that would be "fair and equitable," and elections would be conducted fairly, in accordance with the new constitution.

The board of inquiry held its first meeting in mid-January to address the issues I had outlined in my correspondences to Still. My recommendations went to UCC's executive committee, headed by executive director Dr. L. Sylvester Odom. Having heard my complaints, Odom decided to convene a meeting to hear from the other side. My supporters showed up, but Bernstein and his supporters did not. As a consequence, Odom declared Area Board 9 in default of UCC by-laws and ordered a new election.

At its regular meeting in February, the committee agreed to adopt the recommendations of the board of inquiry, with some minor changes. Only those who were residents of the South Ward and members of Area Board 9 would be allowed to vote in the election. Voting machines would be used for all elections. The ballot would contain one line for accepting or rejecting the UCC constitution, two lines representing the slate of officers, one from each side, and one line for write-in votes. The election would be held in the Area Board 9 offices at 315 Osborne Terrace on March 14, 1968 (pushed back from the original date of March 7).

Each side had to submit a slate of officers by mid-February. Bernstein's slate was the same list of cronies who had been running the Area Board for years. My slate, "We the People", consisted of all the Jewish and Black block leaders and was headed by "Sharpe James for President." We were concerned about neighborhood deterioration under Bernstein and the abuse of federal dollars earmarked for the poor. I put out flyers with a Black-and-White-handshake logo: "We the People," and "Kick Bernstein Out."

Prior to the election there were many complaints, arguments, meetings and conferences that had to be mediated by the UCC central office. Each side had its designated challengers. We learned that Bernstein's side was padding its membership lists with police officers and fire department personnel who lived outside of Newark, which we felt would unfairly tip the vote in their favor. We were trying to create a bona fide list of active members of UCC Area Board 9, who would be committed to vote, as opposed to a bogus list of members, favoring Bernstein and his slate. When I took our complaints to Timothy Still, he said, "Go get some members yourself!"

Because he was councilman of the South Ward, and because he knew a lot of police officers and firemen, Bernstein tried to intimidate us. The police posted at the entrance of Area Board 9 were not our friends. The word was out that those who were behind in child support or had outstanding traffic tickets better not show up to vote on Election Day, or they might get arrested. A lot of Black folk won't come out under those conditions, and for this reason I wanted UCC to cancel the planned election and accept the November 30 election results.

Charles Mabray, a most respected gentleman, was the person at UCC who took all my abuse; he was the hearing officer. Timothy Still, UCC's President, gave us the guidelines. Still was a former boxer well known for wearing a black-and-gold Duker's Athletic Club jacket and a black hat. He was probably 60 then, 6-foot-3, a heavyweight. He was tough, street smart, and everybody liked him. Years later, Larry Hazzard, who became New Jersey's athletic commissioner, would say this about Still: "He was the community activist in the housing projects. He took all the kids on the street, put us in a gym, and taught us how to box. If Timothy Still hadn't died, for my money, he would have been the first Black mayor of Newark."

A meeting was held three weeks before the election at UCC's executive office to draw for ballot lines. There were about two dozen people in the room, from both sides. "You mean we've got to have an election?" I asked, Still. My supporters thought we were the winners anyway. The other side had been in violation for so long. "You should kick them out," I told Still. "They spent all the money. They didn't do right. You're telling us we've got to go into an election with thieves?"

"There is going to be an election," Still said.

I angrily responded, "Well, that's wrong! There shouldn't be an election. You and Dr. Odom should kick them out and declare us the winners."

"No," Still said, "I can't do that."

I screamed back, "We're going to draw ballots with these thieves? We're going to see who is going to be on Line A and B? That's ridiculous! They control everything."

Still looked around the room with a stern demeanor, he leaned over to me and said under his breath, "Sharpe, let me tell you one more time, there's going to be a fair election, but you will be on Line A." I couldn't believe what I had heard.

Each slate of officers was placed in its own plastic capsule. The capsules looked the same, and nobody knew which was which. The capsules were then sealed, and put in a drum. The drum was rotated. Still called someone from the audience to reach in and draw the first capsule. The names in that capsule would be on Line A. Sure enough, "We the People" slate was in the first capsule drawn.

What had Still been telling me? This was how Newark's Democratic machine worked. No one could ever say that drawings were rigged, and that there was cheating going on. But, when the "man with the golden arm" reached in to draw a slate of officers, the machine's slate was going to be on Line A.

On election day, March 14, we had Big Apple, a huge man, a longshoreman who had previously worked in a slaughterhouse, knocking out horses when a gun didn't kill them right away, and Herb Calloway, a street fighter and Little League Baseball organizer, who always entered Area Board 9 with a baseball bat, outside to ensure that the people who came to vote could do so, without being intimidated by off-duty police officers supporting Lee Bernstein. "We the People," represented on Line A, won against Bernstein's slate, headed by Harold Hodes. The election was certified in April 1968. This was the beginning of my life as an elected official.

Tragically, one of my first duties as president of UCC Area Board 9, also known as the Weequahic Opportunity Center, was to attend the funeral of Rev. Martin Luther King, Jr. in Atlanta. King was assassinated on April 4, 1968 in Memphis. Once again, there were riots in major Black urban areas. Newark, though, had learned its lesson: You don't go downtown and try to burn down Prudential; the police will shoot you. We had to get political power; that's what had been missing.

People from all over Newark and surrounding areas held a peaceful march through the Central Ward in the days following the assassination. Even Amiri Baraka, who had been arrested, and later convicted, on charges of inciting a riot during the summer of 1967, met with the mayor and community leaders, Black and White, to seek peaceful, political alternatives to violence. Of course, there were those who wanted to riot in Newark, and I felt compelled to stand before them and say that there was a better way than committing violence, and that way was to organize. We had to start off with voter registration. But we soon learned that voter registration was not enough. We had to educate Black voters and motivate them to vote by showing them that it was possible for Black political candidates to be victorious in an election.

The Area Board 9 office stayed open 24 hours a day in the immediate aftermath of King's death. We formed a special patrol to canvass the area and deal with possible acts of violence and looting. We also created a Youth Patrol Program to quell neighborhood disturbances, and the group won personal praise from Mayor Addonizio.

I changed the name of UCC Area Board 9 to the Dr. Martin Luther King, Jr. Center in honor of our fallen hero. Throughout the rest of 1968 we set up programs to meet the community's needs. We held food and clothing drives for people who became homeless as a result of fires. We offered them temporary shelter.

We made education, employment and recreation for the neighborhood's youth our priorities. Helping students obtain financial aid and scholarships for college, and introducing the Youth Employment

Service (YES) to the city of Newark, was among the many other youth-oriented projects we initiated. Young people came in and told me their skills, and told me what they could do. People from the community would just have to call me, and I would match these kids up with someone who needed a job done. "You need a painter? All right, who were the young people who could paint?"

People would come to the center and ask us how they could get involved. People in the community needed guidance; they needed leadership. We were there for them. We would go to The Center after a full day's work at our regular jobs and stay, burning the midnight oil, toiling and laboring for the people. There was no pay involved. We did it for love of community.

One of the reasons Black people felt free to loot stores owned by White merchants downtown and on Springfield Avenue during the rioting, was that the White merchants were notorious for price gouging, tipping scales, and selling goods of inferior quality to Blacks. Most stores in downtown Newark had a policy of no returns and no refunds, claiming that customers would often soil or damage the merchandise themselves, and the store owner, in turn, would be unable to send the item back to the manufacturer.

In late 1968 a woman named Elaine Blackwell came to see me with a complaint. She said that she had bought an electric stove from Bernstein (of no relation to Councilman Lee Bernstein) Furniture Store on Springfield Avenue. After she brought it home, she discovered that she couldn't use it because it required a 220-volt electrical outlet, which she didn't have. She had told this to the salesman. I said, "Come with me," and we went to speak with the store owner.

I said to the owner, "This lady came in to make a purchase. She told you that she didn't have a 220-volt electrical outlet. You sold her the stove anyway. Here it is, still in the box; it hasn't been used. What's the big idea?"

"Our policy is no refund, no exchanges," the store owner said.

I said, "Now, listen to me. She told you up front that she didn't have a 220-volt outlet. She gets home, she opens the box, and the directions say it needs 220 volts. I think what you did was wrong."

"Sorry, we don't make any refunds."

I went ballistic in the store and cursed the owner out. He called the police. When they came, they listened to his complaint about my threatening and harassing him. When I asked for an opportunity to make my case, one officer barked, "Shut up! You are nobody. Get out of the store!" He grabbed my arm. I shook off his grip and asked him not to pull on me. "Okay, you're resisting arrest, too," he countered. For the first time in my life I was carted off to a police station and thrown in jail. I had been a model student, a model teacher. Now I was in jail, charged with creating a disturbance.

As I entered the precinct house, I noticed a man, weighing about 450 pounds, sitting in a chair in the room. I had to walk around him when the police brought me in. I soon learned that his name was John Love and that he was a lawyer. When the precinct commander asked me if I had a lawyer, and I said that I didn't need one, because I didn't do anything wrong, he directed me to John Love. I said, "Okay, let me see him."

Love walked into the cell and sat down. There was very little room in the cell before Attorney Love walked in, now there was absolutely no room in the cell. I said, "Mr. Love, I don't know why I need you, because I didn't do shit, and they're trying to rob this poor woman out of her money." He started talking about plea bargaining. I said, "I'm not making any plea bargain. I didn't do anything wrong. I'm not pleading guilty to something I did not do."

Love said, "If you go to court, you could lose, go to jail, or pay a fine."

"I am not plea-bargaining," I insisted. "The lady is right, I'm right, and I don't give a shit what those people say. I'm not going to plea-bargain."

Love got me out on bail and continued to try to persuade me to plea-bargain, and I continued to tell him no. In the meantime I did some research on him.

My sources told me that John Love sat in courtrooms, sat in jailhouses, knowing Black people were going to get arrested. He would tell defendants to plea-bargain. They'd pay him $500. They'd walk out of jail, but with a police record for life, often for something they did not do. That was not the kind of lawyer I wanted. I got back to Love and said, "John, I know what your history is. I'm not going to plea-bargain. I'm ready to go to trial."

Area Board 9 members wrote letters to the store owner, threatening him with a boycott if he did not drop the phony charges. They wrote letters to the police saying their action was wrong. And they wrote letters to Newark Municipal Court in my support. Eventually the storeowner dropped the charges against me. The prosecuting attorney was never able to produce any witnesses against me. The arrest remained on my record, but I learned I could beat a lawyer like John Love. I used to think of him as the defender of the damned.

My arrest for fighting for that lady was my first encounter with overt discrimination. It opened my eyes to the need for someone to be a voice for the voiceless, for someone to be a fighter.

I did not seek reelection for president of Area Board 9 in March, 1969. By then I had become of Athletics and Physical Education and Recreation Department Chairman at Essex County College. Before that I had worked as a teacher at West Side High School. I couldn't teach full time, coach full time, and be at the Area Board full time.

Coaching was time-consuming. I had to be like a father to the track team members. I picked them up, drove them home, fed them and saw to it that they got to each meet. While coaching I had to travel during the day, and practice the team during the day, all the time.

In 1968 I coached the championship cross-country and track teams at ECC. I was spending my evenings at the Area Board. I also became a father to my own child for the first time, when my son John was born July 19, 1968. I decided it was best to pass the baton to other leadership within the UCC organization. We had brought the Area Board back to the community. The battle had been won. Community programs had been established, and UCC was now functioning for everyone in the community. I believed in those programs that had been established, and I thought others should be given a chance to lead. These were not salaried positions. I didn't believe that people should stay in them forever.

Moreover, the success of the UCC in creating Black leadership had led to a backlash among White city officials nationwide. They felt threatened by the Black community's new sense of empowerment. The fact that federal money was going straight to community programs, run by community activists, meant that the ability to hand out patronage jobs was out of the control of local politicians. So, Washington was pressured to limit the power of community organizers within antipoverty agencies.

Congress responded in late 1967 with the Green Amendment (introduced by Rep. Edith Green, D-OR, an opponent of community action programs), which stipulated that local elected officials had the authority to designate the official antipoverty agency for their areas. Only agencies receiving such official recognition could receive federal funds.

The Quie Amendment of 1967 (introduced by Rep. Albert Quie, R-MN), required that one-third of antipoverty agency boards of directors be composed of elected officials, another one-third be composed of private sector representatives, and the remaining one-third, a minority, be representatives from the community.

Even though I ended my official relationship with the UCC, I will always recognize its value in bringing together an army of highly dedicated grassroots citizens, seeking to improve the quality of life for all and especially the citizens of Newark. The United Community Corporation (UCC) was a pioneer in developing programs for the poor that the rest of the nation would emulate.

UCC organized early-childhood programs such as Newark Pre-School Council which ran the nation's first year-round Head Start program for four-year-olds. Early in its development UCC recognized the obstacles Spanish-speaking families faced when obtaining services. In 1967, UCC funded the Field Orientation Center for Underprivileged Spanish-speaking residents (FOCUS) to help 6,000 Spanish-speaking Newark residents learn English, train for and find jobs, obtain housing and gain access to health and social services.

These programs are still in existence more than 30 years later, empowering Newark's Black and Latino communities. I felt a sense of pride in being a part of these upward social initiatives.

Now it was time to move on to other challenges.

CHAPTER SIX

The Black and Puerto Rican Convention
(1968-1969)

"One Man, One Vote"

"In 1842 Henry Shoemaker was a hired hand on a farm in Indiana. Suddenly he remembered it was Election Day, and he had forgotten to vote. He never knew he was setting in motion that his one vote would make the difference between war (with Mexico) and peace and to give statehood to Texas."

— *The Importance of a Single Vote Harry S. New*

When Mary and I first got married, we were working school-teachers. We had been married for five years without any children. Mary had one very disappointing miscarriage; however, we both kept going. Our jobs as teachers kept us busy and the community work never stopped. After the miscarriage we began to wonder why Mary wasn't getting pregnant. Then all of a sudden, she's pregnant.

In 1968 our first son, John, was born. Becoming a father changed my life forever. I became mellower. I looked forward to coming home at the end of the day to my wife and son. My family was first priority in my life, but my love for community and my passion to rebuild my city never ceased.

The South Ward was a very progressive neighborhood where some of the city's most prestigious residents lived. Legendary attorney, Joseph Cohen, was my neighbor on Wilbur Avenue. Donald Payne, another neighbor, became the first African American South Ward Democratic

Chairman. It was at their urging that I ran for and was elected as 39th District Leader of the Essex County Democratic committee, of the South Ward in Newark, a position I held from 1970-2007.

After the birth of my son, I took a leave of absence from my job at West Side High School to become athletic director at the new Essex County College (ECC), a two-year community college, which would be admitting its first full-time students in temporary quarters in downtown Newark. It was my responsibility to develop a sports program from scratch.

The school had no facilities—no gym, no lockers, and there was a shortage of uniforms and equipment. As much as I hated to have to do it to Mary, I brought home the team's dirty uniforms, which she washed along with our clothes, until the school signed a contract with a cleaner. Despite our handicap, ECC was able to produce championship teams in basketball, soccer, golf and baseball in our first year. We called ourselves "Champions without facilities."

After stepping down as president of UCC Area Board 9 in 1969, I was elected president of the Weequahic Community Council. The group received no federal dollars and had no programs to speak of. There were just regular meetings at the Osborne Terrace Library to discuss community concerns, and to provide moral leadership. Where UCC demanded programs and had a budget, office, and paid staff there was no budget, office or staff for The Weequahic Community Council. We were governed by creativity, energy and consensus building.

In the South Ward, under the leadership of the newly formed South Ward Democratic Organization, a recall campaign had been organized against South Ward Councilman Lee Bernstein. Bernstein was planning to run for an at-large seat on the city Council for the 1970 upcoming election. He was fully aware that he could not get reelected to the South Ward Councilman position now that the South Ward was predominantly Black.

Rather than wait for the 1970 election, The South Ward Democratic Organization decided to recall Bernstein as a ward councilman to prevent him from even seeking a run as an at-large candidate. Abyssinian Baptist pastor, The Rev. Horace P. Sharper, was selected to run against Bernstein in a special recall election. On June 17, 1969, in the first and the only successful-recall election in Newark's history, Sharper defeated Bernstein by a vote of almost 4 to 1. We were learning fast.

With UCC and the South Ward battles behind me, I was now able to focus on my teaching and coaching career. I had gained some visibility as ECC's athletic director, and as a community leader. That summer I got a call from Dr. David N. Alloway, the director of the National Summer Youth Sports Program at Montclair State College. He said that the college had some funds for a program for disadvantaged kids and that the money would have to be returned to the federal government unless they could enlist enough children who met the government's criteria for being poor. The city of Montclair didn't have them. "Do you think you can come up with a program?" he asked.

I said, "I've got a great idea. Why don't I run a program where I bring kids from Newark up to Montclair State College on a bus every day? They can tour the campus, receive classroom instruction, and then use the facilities for swimming, basketball and track. You divide the program into an academic and a sports portion," *What a great thing,* I was thinking. *City kids having an opportunity to spend the day in the campus atmosphere of Montclair State College!*

The plan was to gather 50 kids in the morning, put them on a bus and take them to Montclair. We would give them academic instruction, lunch, recreation and then bring them back home. Officials at the college liked the plan, but there was a problem.

Wally Choice, the great all-American athlete at Montclair, got wind that Sharpe James of Newark was going to bring city kids to the college. He was a teacher in the recreation program at Montclair State as well as a Montclair resident. I guess he figured, *Why should a Newarker get that money?*

Dr. Alloway called to warn me that if I brought Newark kids up on a bus, Choice was going to be there to chase us back home. I told Dr. Alloway not to worry about us.

On the first day of the program I got all of my kids together and went and purchased 50 Louisville Slugger baseball bats, the biggest bats I could find; they looked like tree trunks. I told the kids, "We're going to participate in a program that's going to benefit youth. Montclair wants us to do this; they're going to give us the money. If anyone gets in your way, smack them with the bat! I'll smack the first person."

When the bus pulled up at Montclair State, just as promised, Wally Choice was there to meet it with some mean looking demonstrators. The door to the bus opened, and 50 Black kids with Sharpe James got off with Louisville Sluggers in our hands. Choice did a 180-degree turn and walked away. The program was one of the best summer youth programs ever, and Wally Choice and I became good friends. We both wanted to help our youth. Dr. Alloway later wrote a letter praising me for "An exceptional demonstration of professionalism of the highest order," despite the program's late start and the "many and unusual problems" it had faced.

The program continued for a couple of more years with Roslyn Lightfoot, a college classmate of mine, who would later become athletic director at ECC, following me. When I later became mayor of Newark, I hired her, first as manager for the city's Division of Recreation and Cultural Affairs, and then as Director of Newark's Symphony Hall.

Meanwhile, the street talk in Newark was all about the upcoming Black and Puerto Rican Convention. Once the convention delegates chose their candidates, anyone else who presented themselves as a candidate, in theory, would get his head bashed, get spit on, shamed, or discouraged from running. Everyone was urged to get behind the selected candidates in order to win. The community was encouraged to vote; voter education, registration, and an election-day get-out-the-vote (GOTV) campaign were organized.

Initially, I had no personal interest in attending the convention. I was not going to be one of the 2,000-3,000 people participating in this procedure, listening to political speeches. I would be coaching or teaching somewhere instead. I'd be with my son somewhere, or playing tennis as usual.

George Richardson, a mayoral hopeful, decided that he would not attend the convention because he believed it was rigged in favor of Ken Gibson, who had first made his bid for mayor in 1966. When Richardson announced his boycott of the convention, the Rev. Horace P. Sharper, the incumbent and obvious choice for South Ward Councilman, decided that he, too, would boycott the convention. Richardson and Sharper were inseparable friends.

There was no candidate to represent the South Ward. Who could the organizers get to represent the team and win strong support? That was the question. And then someone said, "Go and get that big-mouth coach, Sharpe James." Ruth McClain, a labor specialist, who had been deputy director of Mayor Addonizio's Office of Total Employment and Manpower (TEAM), came knocking on my door to inform me of Richardson's and Sharper's departure from the convention. She asked me if I would be interested in joining the Community Choice Team as the candidate for South Ward councilman.

My first questions were: "How much time will I have to give to this, and will I get paid?" I wasn't really interested in the salary. I never knew what Bernstein earned. I never knew what kind of staff he had. I didn't know if it was a full-time or a part-time job. I had to think; did I really want this? I had a job. How would this impact on my teaching and coaching job?

As the convention date approached, the Community Choice Team was still without a full ticket. I thought long and hard. I spoke to my wife, Mary. Finally, I felt, as a community activist, that I could not say no. I said "Yes." In the words of Robert Frost, "I choose the path least traveled." I did it out of my love for the community and my passion for service to the community that I loved. After making my decision I went to the library to study. I wanted and needed to know the history of Newark, and the facts leading up to and creating a hue and cry for this convention.

New Jersey historian, John Cunningham, had written that Newark has always had a changing form of government. Growing tired and suspicious of their commission form of government in the 1950s the citizens formed a study commission to explore other options.

The Commission rejected the old form, and declared "the government of the City of Newark could be strengthened, made more transparent, responsive and accountable to the people; and its operation could be made more economical and efficient under a Mayor-Council Plan C of the Optional Municipal Charter (Faulkner Act) Law."

Following the commission's report, "Plan C," providing for a nonpartisan mayor and a nine-member city council, was overwhelmingly approved by the voters of Newark on November 3, 1953, and took effect on July 1, 1954. Under this form of government the duly elected members of the city council served as legislators and the mayor as the chief executive (administrative duties) officer. It was viewed as a check and balance form of government whereas the mayor's department heads had to be approved by the members of the city council.

The newly approved form of government led to the election of the first Irish mayor, Leo P. Carlin who served from 1954-1962, and the first Italian mayor Hugh J. Addonizio who served from 1962-1970. While the Irish and Italians fought for control of city hall, the city's majority population (African Americans) felt left out, powerless, and lacking in social, political and economic opportunities.

In the 1966 mayoral election Addonizio had easily defeated the first serious African American candidate for mayor, an engineer by profession, Kenneth A, Gibson. Why did this happen?

The African American community was disorganized, divided and politically impotent. Many were not registered to vote and many who were registered to vote did not vote. Like in South Africa, a racial minority ruled the 50% plus majority. In Newark, the shifting of political power between the Irish and Italians never once addressed the basic needs of its majority population; who for the most part were jobless and living in substandard housing.

Something had to be done to gain political power commensurate with our voting numbers, thus a hue and cry of "one man one vote" rang out throughout the community. A spark was needed. It didn't take long. The rebellion or "The riots of 1967" as some refer to it, was the spark that was needed to ignite the community into political action.

Following the rebellion leaders from the Black community emerged and decided that the minority community needed to control who would run for office, and the number of minority candidates running for office; all too often minority candidates would split votes allowing a single non minority candidate to win by gaining 50% plus one vote.

To bring about change three totally different community activists came together to explore political options: Willie Wright, who worked for the Newark Housing Authority was tall, skinny, muscularly built, and with a full facial beard. He wore overalls and was tough both physically and in appearance. Willie simply scared people and had his equally intimidating sons and a personal army of supporters. He was someone you could not ignore.

On the other hand, George Richardson had Hollywood good looks, a head of curly hair, perfect teeth and a smiling personality. George could sell snow balls to Eskimos. George was our Black Clark Gable. He had been elected to the state assembly. He was all spit and shine, a polished individual. George wanted to be Newark's first Black mayor. His last minute decision to boycott the convention had opened the door for me to become a councilman.

The third community leader was dashiki wearing poet-play-wright, Leroi Jones, (who later changed his name to Amiri Baraka) who was a Black Power advocate; and at times sounded like a socialist. Small in size and feigning quietness he was a rabble rousing instigator and agitator for change. Amiri's verbal assaults were lethal and libelous. He always won the war of words.

While other community leaders joined in the discussion none bore more weight than the big three distinct personalities, Wright, Richardson, and Jones/Baraka. The singular goal was to elect minority candidates to public office. The African American and Hispanic communities were tired of being a majority in population and a minority in political power. We needed political power and we needed it now.

The committee picked Charles Scott, the same "Big Apple" that had helped us gain control of UCC Area Board 9, as one of the official enforcers. "Big Apple" worked at Port Newark as a longshore-man; it was said that he could pull a cargo ship in by himself. His presence was frightening, especially his beefy Black penetrating eyes. He was not a gentle giant.

Newark residents loved to tell the story of a police officer coming to arrest "Big Apple" for an alleged traffic violation. "Big Apple" was standing on his porch with his customary nine inch Cuban cigar protruding from his lips. The police officer approached him and a heated argument developed over an alleged parking ticket.

Voices were raised and the officer drew his gun. "Big Apple's" neighbors were screaming and scrambling. "Big Apple" looked down at the skinny police officer and said, "Son you better put that toy down, it ain't gonna hurt me, it ain't going through me, but I'm fixing to hurt you real bad."

The crowd roared with approval as "Big Apple" approached the officer. The officer surrounded by a hostile group and the advancing "Big Apple" looked surprised and confused. He began sweating profusely, his face turned red; he scratched his head, and nervously put his gun back in his holster, turned and ran to his police vehicle never to be seen again.

Big Apple unfazed by the police officer was blowing smoke rings and chewing on his Cuban cigar. With a smile on his face he shouted to the crowd, "Where did the cop go?" He received a roar of joyful laughter in response.

The Black and Puerto Rican Convention took place over three days, November 14-16, 1969, at Clinton Place Junior High School (later renamed University High School). Attorney Raymond A. Brown gave the opening keynote address. He touched on the need for Black unity as an essential ingredient in the 1970 elections, but he also spoke of the need for coalition politics that would permit "Blacks, Puerto Ricans and White people of good will to work together toward the achievement of intelligent and progressive city government."

Brown, who was perhaps New Jersey's most skilled criminal lawyer, won standing ovations again and again from the audience of almost 1000 as he denounced the corruption of the Addonizio administration, and described what a conscious Black citizenry must do about it. The theme of the convention became "We shall overcome in May 1970."

Incumbent and former Congressman, Hugh J. Addonizio, although he had a 64-count indictment standing over him, had refused to resign and would put up a strong fight. It was a slugfest from the beginning to the end.

Actor Ossie Davis followed Brown to the podium and had the audience responding with "Ahh-hahs" and "Amens," as he spoke of Newark's potential and the coming of full political representation for the Blacks and Puerto Rican communities. At the end of Davis's speech one energetic senior citizen kept applauding and dancing around in front of the stage for several minutes after most of the audience had cheered itself hoarse.

On the second day of the convention, Saturday, workshops began at 9:45 a.m. The topics covered included, city finance, city boards and commissions; city land and housing, law enforcement, health, welfare, education, economic development and youth.

Mayor Richard Hatcher of Gary, Indiana, addressed the general body, criticizing President Richard Nixon's economic policies. Afterwards, some 300 delegates voted on proposals for improvements in those areas discussed during the workshops. In a 12-page platform, the convention called for abolishing the post of city police director (held by Dominick Spina, who had been in charge during the 1967 riot) and creating a civilian review board, among several other recommendations.

At the convention's closing session, delegates dominated candidates for the Community Choice ticket. Ken Gibson was the unopposed choice for mayor. Other contenders for mayor were George Richardson and Harry Wheeler, a former Newark school teacher who did not take part in the convention, but who were considering an independent run for the mayoral seat.

Each of the candidates had to go out on stage and tell everybody who they were and what they were all about. I had come up with an idea for a "Little City Hall," which I had borrowed from Cleveland's Mayor, Carl Stokes. I decided that rather than just walk out and say, "Look at Sharpe James," I would give the audience something else to focus on.

When it was finally my turn to walk out on the stage before more than 1000 delegates and tell them why they should they select me as South Ward Councilman, a part of the Black and Puerto Rican Convention Community's Choice Team, I was ready. Being a political novice I thought I had to do something different.

I walked out on the stage with this little model of a house that I had built out of cardboard and painted white with a red door and window trim. I said, "If I get elected, you won't have to come downtown to 920 Broad Street, City Hall, for your services and complaints. You can visit my Little City Hall on Bergen Street. I'm going to bring government to the people. I'm going to bring government to the ward." People in the audience started screaming and stomping their feet. "It's time to rid the community of political prostitutes, stooges, puppets and political pawns," I told them. "It's time for a change."

When I went backstage I said to Earl Harris, who was running for one of the at-large seats on the City Council, "Earl they like me. Isn't this fantastic? I don't know anything about politics, but did you hear that noise out there? They like me."

"No, Sharpe, that's not why they're screaming and clapping and jumping up and down. They've never seen anyone with an Afro hairdo, black-and-white Thom McCann shoes, green checkered pants, and a checkered pink shirt. They thought you were Bozo the clown out there! That's why they're screaming. That's why they're shouting. You belong in the circus baby," Earl had said to me.

He hurt my feelings and he didn't care; it was the real Earl Harris. I kept a picture of me on that day, in that getup, at my South Ward Little City Hall, because it reminded me of my humble beginnings in politics. I didn't dress right, didn't look right, and didn't act right, but, I had the right motivation and the right ideas. I loved people, loved my city and wanted to make it a better place for all.

The convention delegates chose a ticket with Ken Gibson as its choice for mayor, three Blacks for councilmen at large, (Earl Harris, C. Theodore Pinckney and Donald Tucker) and one Puerto Rican (Ramon Aneses). Aneses was chosen by acclamation before the voting on machines took place, to ensure that Puerto Ricans, who were only 10 percent of the participants, would have at least one candidate on the ballot. Three Black men, Dennis A. Westbrooks, Al Oliver and Sharpe James were the candidates selected for the Central, East, and South Wards respectively.

The convention did not select candidates for the North and West wards. The thinking was that only an Italian candidate could win in the predominantly White-Italian North and incumbent Michael Bottone had a lock on the Irish vote in the West. We decided not to spread ourselves too thin. Let's put our marbles where we can win was the calculated business decision.

With the Community's Choice slate complete, the most spirited, heated, arm twisting and racially divided election in the history of Newark began. The show of Black and Puerto Rican solidarity on display at the convention soon gave way to hostility and division among the Community Choice team and Black candidates who chose to run independently.

Even with my endorsement of the Black and Puerto Rican Convention, I ended up running against five people for the South Ward council seat, including the Reverend Sharper. Another contender was community activist Carl Dawson, who later changed his name to Carl Sharif. Much later Sharif would run Cory Booker's smear and fear campaign in the 2002 mayoral election. Carl probably ran for every office there was in the City of Newark, at one time or another.

Two of Dawson's very close friends approached me one day during the campaign. One of them, Sandra King, would later join the staff of Channel 12 New Jersey Network, the other was Gwen McClendon, a teacher at Weequahic High School. They said, "We want to meet with you. We represent Carl Dawson, and we don't think you should run for office."

"Why not?" I said.

"You're not handsome enough; and with that hairdo, the way you dress, and that gap between your teeth, you're not going to win. You should drop out now. Carl is going to run an image campaign and win. He's far better looking, more articulate, and we like him. Sharpe, you are wasting your time and money. Don't run!"

I said, "No, ladies. Thank you for coming to me. Thank you for bringing this message from Carl, but I plan to run, and I plan to win."

Supporters of George Richardson were publicly charging the Black and Puerto Rican convention with being racist and with deceiving voters into believing that there was only one Black choice for mayor.

Richardson had walked away from the convention, saying it was rigged for Ken Gibson. The third Black candidate, Newark school teacher Harry Wheeler, simply told voters I'm the best candidate and I should be selected to run for mayor. Everyone in the Black community agreed that Wheeler was the intellect of the group, had worked as an organizer with Mayor Addonizio and knew government. Harry was a community activist and highly skilled orator.

There was some truth in the statement that the convention was rigged for Ken to win; not by deceit or trickery, but as a sentimental choice. There was no way that Gibson could have out debated Richardson or Wheeler. No way did Ken Gibson have the charisma of Richardson or Wheeler. However, he would have won the nomination of the Black and

Puerto Rican convention with an open ballot, where delegates would vote by a show of hands, instead of on voting machines. That is why Richardson was demanding a closed ballot among other things.

Participants at the convention did not forget that Gibson had had the courage to run in 1966, and the feeling was that the convention should support him in 1970. Gibson had the most organized campaign working behind-the-scenes gathering votes at the convention. Key Black leaders at the time were pro Gibson. George Richardson on the other hand, had been defrocked as a state senator. The state democratic party threw him out for being a disruptive force. He had no real local base organization.

Also, Richardson was viewed as being too political. More people feared how they would fit into a Richardson administration as opposed to a Gibson administration. They felt more comfortable with Gibson, who was more predictable than Richardson.

Gibson had the backing of Amiri Baraka, who had established the New Ark Fund to raise money for the campaign. But Gibson also had a White campaign director, Daniel Armet, and was able to attract the support of national Black political and entertainment figures. It was clear that Richardson and Wheeler were outgunned.

Eventually, on the eve of the May 12th election, Wheeler withdrew from the race and endorsed Gibson. Wheeler feared that the risk of another four years of Addonizio as mayor was too great to split the Black vote.

George Richardson was still an angry man. He believed that he was the political leader of our community. He had won a state position. He had led the successful recall of South Ward councilman Lee Bernstein. Richardson had been out there longer than Gibson. "I'm more qualified than Gibson," George had said.

Initially George had the odds as a convention favorite because of his high visibility and prior service as a state assemblyman. He would have won the nomination if it hadn't already been decided in Gibson's favor.

At age 38, Gibson had a quiet demeanor. He was an engineer, non-threatening. He was the turn-the-cheek candidate. He would not offend anyone. A nice clean guy image, Gibson was someone whom the White establishment would feel comfortable with. Ken would be the choice of the convention; George Richardson would simply sulk and not run for mayor. Later George would organize a United Freedom Party line of candidates, to take votes away from the Democratic Party, until they invited him back.

For my South Ward campaign, I had to take all the energy I had as a coach, all the energy I had as a teacher, all the skills I had as a community organizer in Area Board 9 and the Weequahic Community Council and go out and press the flesh, kiss the babies and organize a team of supporters.

In the beginning it wasn't easy because I hadn't done it before. But the same traits that brought me success in my previous efforts clearly worked in the South Ward, as I garnered support from an army of people in the community. I faced fifteen other candidates but my three biggest challengers were: the Rev. Horace P. Sharper, Leon Ewing, who had been appointed by Addonizio to take the place of a deceased at-large council member, and community activist Carl Sharif, now running for the South Ward seat thinking that he could not win a citywide election.

It became a knock-em-down, pick-em-up, knock-em-down-again-type campaign. There was name calling, intimidation, pushing, shoving, fist fights and a charge of voter fraud throughout the campaign. Carl's brother, Clyde Dawson, walked into our Bergen Street headquarters and pulled a gun on me, because we accused his workers of pulling my signs down. When my staff showed no fear and wanted to physically throw them out, they nervously retreated. Throughout the campaign, the streets of Newark were tainted with blood.

The White minority population was not going to surrender their hard earned political power. It was reported that the dead had been registered to vote in the North and East wards. At our request, federal marshals were called in to observe voting on Election Day. History was in the making. All eyes were on the City of Newark. Everyone was guessing the outcome.

On May 12, 1970 when the smoke finally cleared after days, weeks, and months of street by street, building by building, door to door non-stop campaigning and a spirited GOTV effort on Election Day, great news came. Exhausted cries of hallelujah, hallelujah spilled out into the streets after the polls had closed and the votes were counted.

The Black and Puerto Rican "Community's Choice Team" had placed four (Ken Gibson, Earl Harris, Dennis A. Westbrooks and myself) of its eight candidates in a June 16th run-off election. With this news the next thirty days generated even more excitement, more volunteers and more donations. The community turned out in record numbers, almost eighty percent of registered voters, cast their ballots.

On June 16, 1970 Ken Gibson won the election by 12,000 votes, becoming Newark's first Black mayor, and the first Black big-city mayor in the northeast. The support of a defeated White mayoral candidate, Newark's former fire chief, John Caulfield, certainly helped Gibson in White enclaves such Vailsburg and the Ironbound. There was a heavier voter turnout for the runoff than there had been for the first round in May, so our get-out-the-vote drives in the Black community seemed to payoff, as well. In fact, this was the largest voter turnout for a runoff election in Newark's history.

The Community Choice candidates all won their respective run-off races. Although Earl Harris' at-large victory was a narrow one, Dennis Westbrooks and I won by large margins in the Central and South Wards. Westbrooks defeated Newark's first African American elected at-large official, Irvine Turner, by almost 6-to 1, and I beat Leon Ewing who had called me a drug dealer in a desperate attempt for votes, by more than 2-1.

At the Terrace Ballroom in Newark's Symphony Hall, where thousands of Gibson's supporters had been waiting on election night for the results, shouts and cheers of jubilation had erupted when we learned that Gibson had won. Early on, the crowd had been anxious about a possible defeat. Addonizio's core White supporters remained enthusiastic about their candidate, despite his legal troubles. They were coming out strong to vote.

When Gibson was trailing in votes a longtime friend, supporter and confidant, Pearl Beatty had told the curious press, who saw that Addonizio was winning, "Just wait until the returns come in from the South and Centrals wards," she had said. "Just wait!"

Gibson was winning large pluralities in the South and Central Wards, his base of Black support. He was even picking up White liberal votes with the help of Caulfield in the West Ward and community activist and political power-broker Steve Adubato in the North Ward. Still, everyone at the Terrace Ballroom was on pins and needles until Gibson's tough-guy, loud-talking strategist and street enforcer John Harvard entered the room and yelled, "We won! Addonizio lost! Hallelujah! We got city hall!"

Back at the Terrace Room the crowd joined in singing, "Happy days are here again." It was like New Year's Eve, with the music blasting, hats being thrown up in the air, champagne and beer raining down, balloons and tinsel falling and sirens wailing in the street.

The Gibson campaign's trademark, Gibson Girls, with their Black-and-gold sexy blouses, short skirts, hats and "Gibson for Mayor" sashes, were hugging and kissing everyone in sight. It was time for the Black people of Newark to celebrate. We now had a mayor of our own. At last we were somebody. We were free of the chains that held us back. Addonizio was now history.

Citizens were dancing in the streets at the four corners, where Newark began its history in 1666, Broad and Market Streets. They, reportedly, were tying up traffic with car horns blaring, creating a gridlock, before marching to the steps of City Hall. "It now belongs to us, hallelujah, hallelujah," was the roar from the overflow crowd of voters, supporters, campaign workers, curiosity seekers and reporters. Newark was basking in the limelight. Now, like Cleveland and Gary, Indiana, Newark had made history and national news by electing an African American mayor.

I now had new responsibilities in my life. Friends debated whether to call me Teacher, Coach, Athlete, Sharpe or Councilman James. I wondered how I was going to manage being a husband, father, teacher, coach, athlete and a councilman. My plate was full, but I was "fired up and ready to go." Now I had to live up to my campaign promises as South Ward Councilman; promises made should be promises kept.

The 1970 Black and Puerto Rican Convention had been a huge success. It was the greatest show ever of African American and Puerto Rican solidarity in Newark. In one of the closing speeches comedian Dick Gregory said, "They [Whites] have always given us the power to elect, but never the power to select. We've got to get the Black brothers and sisters out of the ghetto and into City Hall."

The winds of change were blowing. Ken Gibson was now our mayor. Gibson made a pledge of unity: "We're going to appeal to every voter in this city; every voter," he had said. In our unity there was strength. We were a force to be recognized.

CHAPTER SEVEN

South Ward Councilman and Councilman-At-Large
(1970-1986)

When I became a Newark councilman, the first thing I had to do was discard my Thom McCann shoes, my checkered green pants and my checkered pink shirt. I went to a blazer and gray pants, solid black shoes and a haircut. I was trying to assume a more business-like appearance. The renegade, militant look and the I-don't-care attitude, of clothes-don't-make-the-person, all had to be cast away in favor of a more acceptable business-like dress.

So, "change" became my mantra. Change in my dress. Change in my behavior. Change in my militant attitude. I had to learn the art of compromise. As an athlete and a coach, I thought of only victory or defeat, at all cost. In the political arena, I had to learn that the art of compromise was a test of one's stewardship, that my success would no longer be determined by winning or losing on an issue, but by whether I could galvanize enough support from my colleagues and have others carry my political platform to fruition, as opposed to just doing it myself.

The years 1970 through 1974 were difficult times in the Newark City Council. The council consisted of six Whites and three Blacks. Although we came to office in a historical election, three against six meant nothing. Any progressive legislation that we three would propose for the benefit of the city, anything that looked like it would benefit the African American community would go down in terrible defeat, 6-3. The majority on the council even held Mayor Gibson hostage. They questioned his appointments and the changes he tried to make. All the dreams he had envisioned, all the promises he had made, he could throw out the window, because he could not get a majority vote from the six solid-White votes aligned against him and the three Black members on the council.

The person who controlled the City Council was East Ward Councilman, Lou Turco. Turco was the most political person on the City Council. He always thought that he should be mayor, because he considered himself to be a political genius. In fact, he was the first ward councilman to serve as council president. The council president was usually one of the four at-large members, because they were elected citywide. At-large councilman Anthony Guiliano, who was the overall top vote-getter in the 1970 council races, with 44,807 votes, made his bid for the presidency.

Turco, the only incumbent ward councilman, had gotten more votes (7,850) in the election than any previous East Ward councilman. He thought that the unwritten rule determining council presidency should be abandoned and that the title should go to him. We sat there in awe as he put forth his argument, and because of his persuasiveness, eloquence and political savvy as ward councilman, he became president of the City Council.

Turco was clever and handsome, with an olive complexion that became even darker with his frequent trips to Puerto Rico. In fact, he won because he looked off-White on the campaign flyers he distributed in the African American parts of the East Ward. He lightened the photo for the White constituents. You had to love him; he was a 24-hour politician.

It was Turco who was responsible for securing the two White votes needed to finally confirm Edward Kerr as the city's first Black police director, after a White-majority vote initially rejected him. Once he got a piece of whatever it was he wanted from the city, Turco was interested in seeing the city move forward during a very difficult transition period.

From the North Ward we had Frank Megaro. He was handicapped. As a child, he dove into a pool and suffered a concussion. For the rest of his life he sustained some paralysis. He struggled to walk and didn't have full movement of his limbs. He was under tremendous pressure because he was such a nice guy. The pressure was coming from the African American community which was flexing its power, and the

Italian community, which was trying to hold onto its power—and he tried to be neutral. He was always the person in the middle who the other council members tried to lobby because they felt he was an approachable moderate. (This characteristic would often cause him great anguish. In fact, some years later, as a member of the New Jersey State Assembly, he reportedly absented himself during a critical vote on the issue of police and firemen residency by hiding in a closet.)

Michael Bottone was councilman from the West Ward. He replaced Frank Addonizio, who was under indictment with Mayor Hugh Addonizio. Bottone was in a ward that was seeing the greatest change in demographics, from Irish to African American plurality. He was in a constant controversial situation in the ward, and he would soon be challenged daily by Vietnam veteran, later West Ward Councilman and future State Senator Ronald Rice, recently returned from the Vietnam War.

Earl Harris, councilman-at-large, was probably the most popular, the most visible, the most active Black politician, other than George Richardson, on the scene at the time. With his gray hair, he was known as "The Silver Fox." He had been an Essex County freeholder. He had been one of the biggest elected official voices in fighting for the location of Essex County College in Newark, rather than Verona. He had, in essence, replaced Calvin West, one of two previous Black council members— along with Irvine Turner—under indictment with Mayor Addonizio.

Harris was an experienced politician. He always had that ready handshake when you walked up to him. He would extend his hand like a gun. He'd give you that big, pearly-white-toothy smile and a hug. He was always very handsomely dressed and well tanned from sailing on his yacht. He was a Black man who made no apologies for living the good life.

I once said to my wife, "Mary, how come when you see Earl Harris you get all excited, you get tickled? What is it?" She said, "He always shakes my hand. He always says hello. And he always kisses me. I can't say that for Ken Gibson, who hides behind his bodyguards, and, in fact, I can't even say that about you." I never asked that question again. The Silver Fox was a smoothie. He had no problem dealing with anyone. He could cut a deal with the devil.

Dennis A. Westbrooks, born in Pittsburgh, Pa., was a newcomer to Newark, a newcomer to politics. Once elected, he became Amiri

Baraka's personal representative on the council. It was not uncommon at council meetings for Baraka to approach me and say, "Sharpe, come over here and talk to me. Vote this way." Sometimes I couldn't go along with him, but he always found a sympathetic ear in Central Ward councilmen, Dennis A. Westbrooks, who was replacing a legend, Irvine Turner, the first Black elected to Newark's city council. Turner had suffered a stroke, which affected his speech. He was almost incoherent when Westbrooks ran against him, and won.

Westbrooks would clash with at-large councilmen Guiliano and Ralph Villani, two Italians who represented the old establishment. Villani had become Newark's first Italian-American mayor in 1949 under the commission form of government and was first elected councilman-at-large in 1962. He had been debilitated by a stroke. When Westbrooks would launch into one of his tirades on the council floor, Villani would punch me and say, "Sharpe, Sharpe, get him to shut up!" Halfway through the meeting Villani would have to stand up because of his illness. He couldn't sit for prolonged periods. Like Irvine Turner, he had become practically incoherent.

At-large council member Michael Bontempo had this big, booming, boisterous voice. He had been a former police officer, and he spent all of his time on the council screaming at Westbrooks, who would be writing all these community-issue reforms and would bring Baraka's viewpoints front and center. Bontempo would say, "Goddamit, I don't give a shit!" He would just pound his fist and use the toughest street language. Bontempo was against anything that resembled progress for the African American community.

I was a people person, an educator from the South Ward, which was basically a tree-lined, homeowners' ward, thus I was tolerated. I was viewed as a peacemaker, someone who wanted to bring people together, someone the old guard could talk to.

Westbrooks was considered the biggest troublemaker on the council. He would frequently go off to the side and get information from Baraka, who was always disrupting meetings with his demands. The rest of the council would be in an uproar, trying to silence Westbrooks, who was probably the first city councilman to use the filibuster to hold up a vote.

Between Botempo cursing Westbrooks out and wanting to fight, Villani tapping me on my shoulder and saying, "Tell him to shut up, Sharpe!" and Giuiliano being boisterous (although not obscene), the council meetings became a circus.

Among the many things I learned about politics is that elected officials often say one thing and do another. There'd be times when council members would say publicly that they were for an issue, but then, these same council members wanted the rest of us to vote the measure down. I thought that was the height of deceit.

Turco, for example, was against a proposal to build new housing in the heavily Portuguese and Hispanic East Ward. Ward council members are supposed to be the first and final voice of activities for their ward. Turco didn't take kindly to the construction of any mixed-use development or housing that might lead to an influx of other ethnic groups to the East Ward. He would lecture the city council behind closed doors to vote the proposal down: "I'm the ward councilman," he'd say to us. "I'm going to stand up and support the measure. It's the right thing to say publicly, but, privately, I want the council to vote it down." We voted it down.

I learned early that candidates running for city council, who had platforms that advocated for the people's needs, and had spoken about saving money for the taxpayers, changed their thinking once they got in office. The ideas they spoke of before their election went out the window. They soon became concerned with what they could get out of the government.

The only reason council members were able to get cars from the city is because Earl Harris, elected with me, didn't have a car. And, he wanted a car. Up until then a car went only to the council president. There was one old Cadillac waiting for that person. Harris said, "I don't care about the council president. I care about me. I want a damn car."

Then, of course, it became a practice that would manifest itself over and over again: In order to satisfy the needs of one council member, who didn't have a car and wanted a car, the City of Newark had to purchase nine cars, one for each council member.

Everything we didn't have, we had to multiply it by nine. Someone said, "I want another staff person." Well, we would have to add nine new staff people. When I first became a member of the council in 1970, each council member had two aides; each aide received a salary of $12,000 a year. When I left the council in 1986 each council member received a salary of $86,000 and had five aides. Each councilman had a car and a private office, as opposed to all of us sharing a common area with partitions between us. Everyone had his own private quarters now. Everyone had his own office equipment. Excessiveness became the order of the day, and the cost of government began to go up.

No other city in America paid its council members the salary and perks that Newark council members were receiving at taxpayers' expense. Still not satisfied, council members continued to add to their perks and abused council expense accounts daily. Newark's City Council was getting way out of control.

I became an enemy of the council when I did not accept a car initially. I became an enemy when I would not travel with the council to every conference that was available to us, especially during the winter months. Council members would take a travel book and look up the various conventions across the United States, in warm climates, of course. They would then take the list of conventions, throw them up in the air, and whatever page hit the floor first, they'd say "That's where we're going." It was a big joke to the council members that they could travel anywhere at any time.

The conventions that were organized by groups like the National League of Cities and the County Association were about issues to improve the quality of life in our cities, and issues about government. They were organized by government agencies that served elected officials. They were legitimate. But when council members started going to a cooking conference because it was in Hawaii or a meeting of journalists in San Juan, Puerto Rico that had nothing to do with any of the issues council members dealt with, that was just a junket. Nevertheless, off they would go.

Once at a conference, council members partied day and night. Any meetings that had to do with business were not attended. It was not uncommon for male council members to be in the company of female companions or entire staffs going sightseeing on these trips, paid for by a public unaware of the fiscal abuse taking place under the guise of "conferences."

On one occasion, Earl Harris and the entire City Council flew to San Francisco for a National League of Cities Conference in 1977. We already had reservations at a hotel, but when we got there and got out of our cabs, Earl Harris looked at the hotel and said, "This is not the hotel for us. I don't like this hotel. It's beneath our dignity." The hotel was probably a four-star hotel. Earl wanted us to cancel the reservation to this hotel and go to whatever the most expensive hotel in San Francisco was.

In fact, Councilwoman Marie Villani, who had taken over the at-large seat of her husband, Ralph Villani, when he died in office in 1973, said, "I want to go to the St. Francis." Of course the St. Francis was a luxury hotel. Marie looked like Marilyn Monroe in *Gentleman Prefer Blondes,* with her jewelry and fur. She had gone one up on Earl.

All of this luxury was at taxpayers' expense. If council members ran out of stamps, we'd budget $500 for stamps, then $1,000 for stamps, and then $5,000. There was never an end. The nine council members were never satisfied. I didn't want a car. All of my expenses were below what was expected of a council member. I didn't abuse travel. I spoke out against excesses by the council and the administration. Most of the time, when the council went on trips, I would stay home and be of service to my constituents.

This was partly because I was still active at Essex County College as a professor and athletic director. So I didn't travel as much. I didn't feel a need to abuse the expense accounts. Later, it became a matter of principle with me. It offended me that individuals who campaigned to get into office, especially African Americans who had talked about all the vices of previous administrations and councils, would turn around and then do the very same thing.

To be an effective councilman, though, I had to compromise. I had to temper my criticism of the other council members to get them to support my proposals. There was one clear message: If you attacked the council, even if it was a legitimate attack, even if it was about abuses that should be corrected, even if it warranted a criminal investigation, the council would gang up on you, and you wouldn't get their votes for anything—not even a wastepaper basket or pencils. Like the policeman's "code of blue," the council had its own code: "We'll band together against anyone who wants to attack this institution or who attacks our perks," was their mantra.

Once, a council member billed the city to pay an auto mechanic friend for replacing the engine of a new council car. I criticized this expense as totally irresponsible. At the next council meeting the "council of the whole" voted against every request I made. I wanted to ask if a motor was really put in the car, but realized I could be lynched for raising the question. The same council member once drove the car to Miami and then billed the city for flight tickets.

When I became a councilman, the job was considered part-time, and, in 1970, the salary of $12,000 was low enough for it to be part time. Later, Earl Harris and others would say, "I'm a CEO, and I want to be paid like one, with all the perks," and council members lobbied to get a CEO salary—$86,000—five staff persons, a car, unlimited gas and unlimited meals, making for a very attractive full-part-time job.

I had to balance running between the college and the community and, for the most part, was able to do that. Often they were the same constituents. The student would be a community person; the community person would be a student, because Essex was a community college, and most of the students were from Newark.

I put more time into council work than I did at the college. At the college I was committed for only 13 hours a week. I would teach three hours a day, and end up spending eight or nine hours a day doing council work. Wherever I went, I bore the title councilman. During this time African Americans were excited to have access to an elected official; never before had there been so many Black elected officials in the city of Newark.

I taught 13 hours a week and had five hours office time for counseling. That was 18 hours a week, maybe four hours a day commitment at the college. The balance of my day and beyond—nighttime—would be spent doing constituency work. If I went to a store, someone would come up and say, "I'm looking for you." If I went to a restaurant, people would take a seat at my table and end up eating with me.

Once I went into a Popeye's restaurant in neighboring Hillside. I was sitting at a table with three pieces of chicken and French fries in front of me when one of my constituents came up and said, "Excuse me, can I sit down with you?" When he finished, I had no more chicken on my plate. Everything was gone, and he just kept on talking. He even had the gall to try to order his food at my table to continue the conversation.

During the altar call on Sundays the pastor would encourage, "Those who want to come to the altar for prayer, to come forward. "I knew, as a politician that I needed prayer now more than at any time in my life. I would get up and go to the altar, kneel down, place my hand on the rail, and someone would, invariably, tap me on the shoulder. I'd be thinking this person was going to give me some spiritual advice. But it was always, "Can you help me with a job? Can you help me with housing? I've been looking for you."

I could never turn anyone away, because I believed what I always told people, "No one put a gun to my head and said, 'Be councilman.'" I made the choice, and I knew my responsibility. That responsibility was to serve my constituents as best I could. Their problems were now my problems.

No matter where I was, in school, walking the streets, or playing tennis, I could never get away from people making demands on me. I was in a championship tennis match in Weequahic Park once, getting ready to serve match point, and somebody yelled out, "Hey, Sharpe, I need a job. Can you help me out?" I was unnerved for the rest of the tournament. Because of the distraction I lost my concentration and ultimately the match. I had been playing excellent up to that point.

Before I got elected, I played tennis every day, seven days a week. I had won many tournaments. After I got elected to the city council, my mind could not stay as focused on the game. I'd be playing and thinking about someone needing housing, someone needing a job, or what could be done about that vacant lot, that abandoned building. I would reflect back on a disagreement, of which there were many, that I had with a constituent. People wanted quick-fix solutions to complex problems, and I couldn't give them that.

I now had the hardest time freeing my mind of all the daily problems people would bring to me. Sleep did not come easily. Before, I easily slipped into Delta sleep as soon as my head hit the pillow. Now, I was dreaming, constantly waking up and answering questions that people had brought to my attention during the day. I had to learn how to balance addressing all of the issues and complaints and emotions of my constituents with my personal life. I had to learn how to adjust, or it would kill me.

During my early days as a council member, I still entertained the idea of furthering my academic studies and taking on more responsibilities as a college professor or administrator. I took courses at Columbia and Rutgers in preparation for a doctorate. However, as my community and elected responsibilities increased, I found myself unable to keep up with the rigorous schedule of attending classes and turning in assignments. I, therefore, decided to put my formal course work on hold. I didn't want to half-step in the classroom. I was now more politician than educator.

I decided that Sharpe James, the athlete, was no longer going to play physical sports. I was going to play the intellectual sport of politics. I would use my experience and instincts as a coach to come up with a plan to solve the problems of the South Ward and to deal with the many issues my constituents brought to me. I would map out strategies, get my staff involved and coach them toward resolutions. No more playing tennis, no more running track and jogging, no more going to the health spa. My constituents' complaints became my sport. My aides became my assistant coaches, and we were all part of a team.

Harold Edwards was the first aide I hired. His mother, Ella Edwards, had been active with me on Area Board 9 and had asked me to give her son a job. When I learned that he was also looking for an affordable apartment, I allowed him to move upstairs at our Little City Hall and pay $200 a month for five rooms. He played loud music and wore military dress with boots. I thought he was a member of the Black Panthers and that he would never last on the job. I gave him two weeks to fire himself.

Harold proved me wrong. He accepted and followed every assignment to perfection and had ideas on how to address the many issues we faced. He was a workaholic, arriving at the job early and leaving late. But most important to me was his letter-writing. I was always impressed by the fact that whenever I wrote a letter to Mayor Addonizio or to U.S. Rep. Peter Rodino of New Jersey, I received a prompt and well-written response, regardless of the content. I promised myself that I would respond in the same manner to every letter that came to my desk.

When I read a previously filed letter to a constituent and thought what a good job I had done in responding, I realized that Harold had written the letter and knew from that day on he had a bright and rewarding future. Harold would later become president of his own public relations company, Amistad Communications; the Newark Municipal Council became one of his clients.

Cheryl Johnson came on board as my chief of staff in 1974. One of a family of 12 children, Cheryl grew up in public housing. She was the first Black to be hired in Newark's Office of the City Clerk, and I had observed her outstanding secretarial skills (including her ability to take shorthand as fast as one talked) when she worked there. In 1972 I asked her to come to work for me. She politely told me she would consider my offer if I got reelected.

Well, I did, and Cheryl took the job. She became the most valuable person to me outside my family. She was able to fashion a polished, productive and caring staff from whomever I had hired under her. She would take time to review and correct every staff correspondence to make sure that it conformed to her standard of professionalism, taking each staffer aside to explain how he or she could have done something better.

Though slim and youthful in appearance, Cheryl was affectionately called "Mother" by her crew. On Fridays, she would take them out after work for happy hour. It was only then that Mother Cheryl would let go of her all-business demeanor, sip her favorite red wine and flash a big smile. She saved my behind many times and quite literally saved the life of another staffer when, on one of the fundraising cruises I had established as mayor. A group decided to take a ride on an inflatable raft pulled by a speedboat. The staffer—a woman who couldn't swim—fell off and lost her life jacket. Cheryl, the only strong swimmer on the raft, found the sinking woman and lifted her to safety.

After I hired Cheryl, she enrolled at Rutgers University graduating with honors in accounting. She became my campaign treasurer, guarding the checkbook to make sure there were no bogus entries and no violations of campaign funding laws, which she knew by heart. She prepared financial reports that were second to none and would put any CPA in the city to shame.

I started issuing report cards in 1970. I was the only elected official in Newark who, every year, would evaluate himself with a report card. I designed it so that it would look just like the one I used to get in school, right down to the manila envelope. I guess that was the teacher in me.

In public office I always had realistic goals, and worked like a dog to achieve those goals. Every year I brought back my report card that said, "This is what I promised. This is what I did." I didn't make 50 promises. I made eight that were doable. I might have tried some that weren't doable, but I never raised anybody's expectations about their outcome.

As I had promised when I was a candidate for South Ward councilman, I opened a Little City Hall. "You don't have to come downtown to City Hall. You can come to 1072 Bergen Street and there will be a staff person to assist you," I had pledged. "You don't have to drive downtown and try to find parking. I'm coming to you. I'm bringing City Hall to you, my constituents." How proud I was that I was the first councilman in Newark to open an office exclusively for that purpose, and how proud I was that that Little City Hall was still there at 1072 Bergen St. more than 30 years later.

Within one month after taking office in 1970, I walked next door from 1072 Bergen St. to the then-First Jersey National Bank and told the bank officer, "I want to buy that building to open up my Little City Hall. Is it for sale?" "Yes," he told me, "but you have to go to Jersey City to apply."

The banker I was talking to was Thomas Stanton, the bank's chief executive officer; he told me the building cost $14,000. He asked me how much I had for a down payment. I told him I had nothing. "We don't give 100 percent mortgages," he told me. "What are you going to do with the building?"

"I'm going to help people. I'm going to open up a Little City Hall. I'm going to help the community. I'm going to hold community meetings. People who have complaints can bring them there. I'll write them up; then I'll take them downtown and try to get them acted on. I'm going to try to improve the quality of life in my ward." Stanton looked at me and said, "Are you serious?" I said, "Yes." And so, for the first time in its history, First Jersey National Bank granted a no-down-payment, full mortgage for $14,000 for 1072 Bergen St.

One day a week my staff and I would drive through the South Ward and pick out things that we saw were wrong so we could bring them to the attention of City Hall. We didn't wait for people to complain to us. The entire staff of five people would get into two cars, and armed with pads and pencils, we'd go down every street. We'd take the horizontal streets one week, the vertical streets the next, and then send our findings to the Gibson administration. We colored in on a map the streets we had covered, and did that until we had been through the entire ward.

I represented a neighborhood of homeowners, and quality of life was my utmost concern. During my 12-year tenure as South Ward councilman not one new liquor license was ever approved for the ward. Any store or restaurant owner in Newark who wanted a liquor license had to apply to the Police Department. A police officer was assigned to each ward of the city to take applications and review them. The officer would ask the ward councilman for his opinion. The officer assigned to the South Ward knew my opinion: no new liquor licenses in my ward. Forget about it, it wasn't happening.

I introduced several quality-of-life ordinances that benefited every ward in the city. Even the White council members felt obligated to support them. My voting record on ordinances was nearly identical to that of the North Ward council member, because we both represented tree-lined neighborhoods of property owners—Forest Hill, Weequahic— having the same interests, and the same needs.

My office got a New York City developer to come to the South Ward to renovate two houses on Willoughby Street with private funds. There was an orphanage, St. Peter's, at the corner of Leslie Street and Lyons Avenue with a vacant lot. Herb Calloway, a community activist who was a Little League volunteer and had been playing on the lot, went to the orphanage with a proposal to create a quality Little League field in the South Ward. At first the orphanage turned down the proposal, but I talked it over with the clergy there, and they finally agreed to sell the land to the City of Newark. That lot became St. Peter's Park, with a state-of-the-art Little League baseball field, a recreation center, and a swimming pool. This gave the South Ward a new identity.

When Newark Beth Israel Medical Center, which had been in the South Ward for more than 70 years, wanted to expand its facilities in the 1970s, many residents thought that, once again, plans were being made by people outside of the community to push Blacks out. Lester

Bornstein had become Beth Israel's executive director in 1967, and his plans for the hospital's expansion had placed him on a collision course with the growing Black middle-class in the surrounding Weequahic neighborhood, which was once predominantly Jewish. One meeting at the Area Board with Bornstein, to discuss the community's concerns, turned violent when some of those present started shouting ethnic slurs at him and one person threw a brick.

At the time, Beth Israel wanted to build a new patient-care unit and a parking garage. In 1970 the outgoing City Council had approved construction of the unit, but the problem of the garage was left for the incoming council members. Many residents of the South Ward feared that the garage would bring increased vehicular traffic to the area.

There was a vacant lot in front of Stewart's Restaurant on Lyons Avenue and Clinton Place, which was designated as the site for the new George Washington Carver School. The hospital wanted to use the lot for temporary parking while its buildings were going up. I proposed that we fill in this gravel lot, which had piles of trash, stagnant pools of water and rats, and let people from the hospital park their cars there. The hospital could then build its garage and new unit on the other site at Osborne Terrace, between Lyons and Lehigh Avenues, and return the lot to us for the school when construction was through.

I was called a traitor and a sellout, but I believed that the community needed both, a quality school and a health facility. The Central Ward had lost St. Barnabas Hospital to Livingston because the community fought efforts to expand. Not everyone in Newark could get to St. Barnabas. My wife, Mary, had miscarried when her water broke and we couldn't make it to the hospital in the snow.

Some in the community—particularly Gibson supporter Roslyn Alexander, one of the most vocal demonstrators against the hospital's expansion—believed that the hospital would never give the lot back, and that Bornstein and the rest of the hospital administrators were trying to trick the Black community. As it turned out, the hospital completed its construction, returned the cleaned-up lot to the community, and we built the beautiful George Washington Carver School.

Beth Israel invested $250 million into their new medical center and remained in Newark as a quality healthcare provider making it a win-win situation. Bornstein, who retired from the hospital in 1996, and I decided to become friends. We created a neighborhood partnership, and Beth Israel Hospital and the South Ward saw their greatest economic growth during our tenure.

Some years later, as I was walking out of a meeting next door to Beth Israel, I ran into Roslyn Alexander, who was standing on the sidewalk in tears. She told me her husband had collapsed at home and was in Beth Israel, receiving excellent care. I gave her a hug, and knew then that I had made the right decision siding with the hospital on expansion. Back then she had called me a "Jew-lover," a traitor, and she hadn't cared about saving the hospital. Now, the hospital that she didn't want in our community was saving her husband's life.

Councilman-At-Large
(1982-1986)

Once again the more things changed, the more they remained the same. I began to think about my future. I had been South Ward councilman for twelve years (1970-82). I had been the first ward councilman to run unopposed in 1978. And, by being fiercely independent, a maverick on the council, serving and taking on issues for citizens in every ward of the city, Sharpe James became a household name. I was known as a person who would stop on the street and talk with you, a person to go to for help and a person who would help you find a job.

I was behaving like a councilman-at-large. Councilman-at–large Donald Tucker, kept reminding me that I was only a ward councilman, and should butt out of citywide matters. He felt my citywide visibility would hurt his fundraising efforts. We often clashed over territorial issues.

As a councilman-at-large, Tucker, wanted to change the name of Elizabeth Avenue to Dr. Martin Luther King, Jr. Boulevard. As the South Ward councilman, where Elizabeth Avenue was located, I reminded Tucker of its historical significance in being the road used by George Washington en route to Trenton, as well as the fiscal hardship that would be incurred by legally changing the name of the Weequahic Park row of apartment buildings, home to thousands of tenants. I suggested an alternative street to honor Dr. King. Councilman Tucker, being belligerent, would not accept a compromise. It simply had to be his way.

We battled with petitions before the full council trying to win a majority vote. Tucker argued that as a councilman-at-large his voice should carry more weight. I argued that the city council was an equal body and each councilman represented one vote, and no one council person carried more weight than the others.

The city council is made up of five ward council members and four at-large members. The four ward council members sided with me. I had won a bruising territorial battle. While I saw no need to celebrate, historical Elizabeth Avenue is still Elizabeth Avenue, and we honored Dr. King by changing High Street to Dr. Martin Luther King Boulevard. Because of this unnecessary fight I decided to run for councilman-at-large, knowing that no ward councilman had ever been elected at-large. Councilman Donald Tucker, wearing a huge smile, saw my decision as the political end of a meddling Sharpe James.

Councilman-at-Large Tucker again became angry when Mayor Gibson called a meeting and asked him and candidate Dr. Ralph T. Grant, Jr., to team with me or "you guys might lose." Reluctantly, we formed a James, Tucker and Grant team. Their personal belief, however, was that I would lose and they would win. It was a team in name and literature only. No one trusted the other guy.

Matters grew worse when a May 1982 *Star-Ledger* headline read, "James Top Vote Getter with 29,000 votes." I was the top vote getter in the at-large race over three incumbents, including Councilman Donald Tucker, who immediately cried foul and wanted a recount. My gamble had paid off, and I was the first ward councilman in the history of Newark to be elected at-large.

As the top vote getter, I reminded the council that in 1970 East Ward Councilman Louis Turco had demanded that he be selected President of the City Council based on having the highest percentage of votes. As the highest vote getter in the most difficult at-large race citywide, I asked to be selected Council President.

Upon learning of my request, Councilman Tucker immediately wrote a six page legal size document on yellow paper saying, "To hell with most votes, it's who can get the most votes from the nine member city council." He was furious and on fire as he went to each member seeking their vote. I calmly followed him and again called upon the rule of the council member receiving the most votes being named Council President.

The council was split and became paranoid in choosing between Tucker and me. They liked both of us for our work ethics on behalf of the citizens of Newark. There was even talk of making us both President and/or splitting the four year term; two years apiece. Again, Tucker would not budge, it was all or none.

With our spirited and heated fight continuing, Mayor Gibson stepped in and used his influence and promise of patronage to create five votes for councilman-at-large Dr. Ralph T. Grant, Jr., his choice for Council President. Gibson felt that he might be held hostage or be giving a future rival a platform, if Tucker or I became Council President. Ralph, with his snappy dressing and elocution was just happy to be Council President. He would pose no threat to Ken.

Tragically, the two most knowledgeable workaholics, and most respected members on the city council cancelled each other out of this leadership position. It reminded me of Marlon Brando and Montgomery Cliff, both fighting to be recognized as the best dramatic actor of their time. Little did I know, at the time, that Councilman Tucker and I would battle to be the voice of Newark until his untimely death in 2006.

Donald Tucker and I had a strong love/hate relationship. He read everything. I read everything. We kept a step ahead of the other members of the city council and they respected our positions based on our review of data presented to members of council. Outsiders often had us pegged wrong. We fought over issues. We fought over what's best for Newark. We never fought each other.

Years later when I was mayor, the council's designated White attorney, Leonard Berkeley, also a personal friend of Councilman Tucker's, was angry that I was revealing to the council that he had overcharged the city in attorney fees. He immediately, in a loud and boisterous voice, demanded that I be removed from the Council's Pre-Meeting Conference Room. Berkeley resented what I was saying and wanted to speak to the members of the council privately. I was boiling and ready to blow my top at this out-of-towner demanding that the mayor be asked to leave the room. I was about ready to punch him in his mouth. As a known supporter and friend of Donald Tucker, I knew he was playing to the council and the alleged split between Tucker and me.

However, unexpectedly and most shocking to everyone in the room, Councilman Tucker jumped up, flung his chair back against the wall, with anger in his face, revealing 250 pounds of body language, approached a frail and shaking 125 pound Berkeley, screaming at the top of his lungs, "Don't you ever order my mayor out of any room, do you hear me? I will throw your ass out first. Show some respect," Tucker said. The room went completely silent and a red-faced Berkeley quietly took a seat. I continued with my message to the members of the city council.

It's the same old story all over again, never try to break up a husband and wife fight, or, as an outsider, get between two councilpersons that love Newark. Leonard Berkeley, although a personal friend of Councilman Tucker, was not a Newarker.

CHAPTER EIGHT

A Sharpe Change

I was at Earl Harris' campaign headquarters on Park Place when he announced his candidacy for mayor in February, 1982. I was there out of curiosity; having served with the legend, Ken Gibson, and having been elected on the same ticket as both Ken and Earl. Now, twelve years later Harris was saying that he was going to make City Hall more professional and improve the delivery of municipal services. "We're going to change the way they do business at City Hall," he had barked before a loud and boisterous crowd of his supporters. "Ken must go!"

Earl's campaign was troubled from the outset by serious negatives within the Black community. For one, he supported the use of police dogs to fight crime in Newark. Failing to recognize the passions that this issue aroused within a community that feared and hated police dogs from the time they were used in the South to attack civil rights marchers, was uncharacteristic of this great political strategist. Moreover, two White former members of the City Council and White militant Anthony Imperiale had championed the use of the K-9 force; and the Black community certainly was not buying anything pushed by the race-baiting Anthony Imperiale, who had referred to our great and honored civil rights leader, Dr. Martin Luther King, Jr., as "Dr. Martin Luther Coon."

Earl's second mistake, and perhaps the more serious one, was his decision to take the solid support he had had among Black voters for granted, and campaign almost exclusively in the predominantly White North and East Wards with their respective White leaders. Behind his back, Earl was called a "White nigger." While his strategy delivered a convincing win over Gibson in the North and East Wards and a slim margin of victory in the West Ward, it was his brothers and sisters kicking his butt three to one in the Black South and Central Wards that sealed his narrow defeat. By losing his bread-and-butter Black base in those two wards, Earl became the first mayoral candidate to win three of the five wards only to lose the race.

Also, Earl scared people because he had stated in belligerent and obscene language what he was going to do to the Gibson people. He talked about "kicking ass" and "getting a bus and sweeping all of the dead weight out of City Hall." He said that "Bodies are going to fly!" People were saying, we know what we got in Ken Gibson, but God forbid, we don't know what we're going to get in Earl Harris. He acts like a mad man sometimes. They did not take kindly to anyone running against Gibson by attacking his character, his work force and his programs, because he was still the first African American elected mayor of a major northeast city. Earl Harris should have—because it was expected of him—run against Ken in a dignified manner and treated him with the ultimate respect.

With two popular local heavyweights in the race, the community expected a debate on the issues, not personal attacks. Even Ken started saying, after giving the worst speech he could give, exciting no one in the room, displaying no humor, "I'm telling you, you know what you've got, but you don't know what you're going to get." This simple statement would wake up and win the crowd over. It was his life preserver.

Thus, it is my opinion that Earl Harris lost—Ken Gibson did not win—in 1982. Harris' defeat taught me, halfway through 1982 to 1984, when I was thinking about running for mayor, and in 1985, when I had made up my mind to run, the first thing I had to do was to be serious, professional, respectful, focused and to look and act like a mayor. When the people saw Ken's deadpan demeanor, some had said it was because he was carrying the weight of the city on his shoulders, and he was serious. He was working hard on their behalf. His critics said he was merely disinterested and sleeping on the job.

I had to make sure that Sharpe James dressed like a mayor, looked like a mayor, and that he, too, was viewed as serious, with the weight of the city on him. When the mayoral campaign started in 1986, this is exactly what the people saw in this challenger to Ken Gibson. I was not going to make the same mistakes Earl Harris had made. I was not going to lose. Ken Gibson would have to beat me, not win by default.

In 1985, when Gibson made a second run for the governor's seat against the Republican incumbent Tom Kean, he had had four years to rebut what Newark's voters were saying in 1981. But, conditions in the city were worse now. If that weren't true, his friend and confidante, Earl Harris, would not have run against him in 1982. If it had not been for the deteriorating conditions in the city which drew national attention, Phil Donahue, the Chicago-based talk-show host, would not have had the audacity to say on national television in 1983 that U.S. officials would never take foreign visitors to Newark if they wanted to show the country in its best light. Although favored to win in the polls, Ken Gibson garnered just 26 percent of the vote in the 1985 Democratic gubernatorial primary.

Gibson thought everything was all right. He was in a state of denial. He could not be talked to. He would not compromise nor listen to anyone. He was an engineer who was dogmatic and stubborn in his way and unreachable. Many felt that he used his bodyguards, not to protect his life, but to insulate him from constituents who wanted to approach him and ask questions of him or even shake his hand.

Gibson would go to a party, sit at the end of the table, separated by bodyguards, and for one, two or three hours never talk to anyone. He had an annual picnic up at Suntan Lake, in Riverdale. Everybody would go. More than 3,000 supporters would navigate their way to this isolated camp ground. Disapprovingly, Gibson would come late, towards the end of the event. He would drive up, come out at the command post and wave to the crowd, say hello and then he'd be gone from his own picnic. He didn't come to participate, have fun and get to know his constituents; he came only as an obligation. Running Newark had become a laborious job for Gibson. His performance was being called into question. He had lost his enthusiasm and was simply going through the motions.

In running for governor Gibson was sending a message that he wanted out; he wanted to get away from Newark. He wanted to get away from the hands-on operation of New Jersey's largest city as its CEO and to get to where he would have surrogates and cabinet members carry out his mandate. He viewed becoming governor as political relief, an escape from Newark. Reporter after reporter challenged Gibson on Newark's quality of life, especially since more than a quarter billion dollars in federal and state funds, spearheaded by a friendly president, Jimmy Carter, and New Jersey Democratic Congressman, Peter Rodino, had not measurably ameliorated the city's plight. Newspapers displayed pictures of dilapidated public high-rises—abandoned Columbus Homes, depopulated Hayes Homes, depopulated Archbishop Walsh Homes, depopulated Stella Wright Homes.

Contrary to what Gibson had promised in his 1970 campaign, "Wherever American cities are going, Newark will get there first," Newark was still at the starting block, while other cities like Baltimore, Chicago, Boston, Indianapolis and Cleveland were on the move, experiencing economic growth after having similarly suffered decades of distress. People saw little change in quality of life in Newark. If anything, they saw signs of deterioration.

People in Newark were saying, "Here we are, the largest city in New Jersey, and we can't go to the movies." There was no family entertainment in the city; no movie theaters, no roller-skating rinks, no shopping malls, and very little in the way of safe, decent and affordable housing. The feelings of hopelessness and despair that was experienced in 1967, before the riots, were resurfacing. The city was not functioning. It was unable to deliver municipal services in a timely fashion. The city's streets and vacant lots were strewn with garbage. Police officers were being laid off every year, while the people were clamoring, asking for more safety in the city. Even when the City Council placed funds in the budget to hire more police, Gibson stubbornly refused to do so.

Gibson's characteristic response was, "See that lot over there? I had the National Guard come and clean it last week. Now, it's dirty again." Gibson always answered a criticism with an explanation. He made a good point, but he never took responsibility for the city's ills. He never said; All right, no matter how it got dirty, no matter who did it, I'm going to do something tomorrow. Instead, he was always defensive. On the eve of his fifth run for office, he told a television interviewer, "We have poor sections, but what would you expect the city of Newark to do? We don't put money in people's pockets. The city doesn't do that; I didn't create the problem of teenage pregnancy. I certainly didn't father those children."

I, too, began to find fault with the promise and realities of the administration, which now had a pro-Gibson council. As council members, we were constantly reminded by the mayor that we were legislators and not administrators. He advised us to stick to our turf and let him manage the city on a day-to-day basis. Yet, the opinion of the majority of the city council was that those selected by Gibson to run the city simply lacked the experience, vision and creativity to propose meaningful solutions to the myriad of problems we faced.

It appeared that the "Peter Principle" had finally caught up with a significant number of Gibson supporters who had moved from the campaign army directly into high-level managerial positions, often without proper credentials or experience. These supporters may have excelled at handing out campaign literature, knocking on doors, licking stamps, operating telephone banks and guarding the polls on Election Day, but that didn't necessarily mean they had the basic skills or aptitude to become administrators, let alone supervise personnel.

The worst place to reward political favors was at the Board of Education, because it would affect our children's education. Yet, Gibson asked the state commissioner of education to waive the educational requirements so that Newark's business administrator, Alonzo Kittrell—who had been a staunch Gibson campaign supporter—could be appointed superintendent of Newark's public schools. And the commissioner did it because of Gibson's statewide clout.

When Carl Stokes won the election in 1967 to become the first Black mayor of Cleveland, Ohio, he called all of his supporters together and said, "Congratulations! You can have all of the barbecue you can eat and all of the soda and beer you can drink. And, by the way, tomorrow, if you want a job, you can apply over there at my transition office. Please bring your résumé." Gibson did it another way. Far too many members of his victorious army marched right into City Hall and received key administrative jobs, whether they were qualified or not.

As the initial euphoria of electing Newark's first Black mayor subsided, and Newark's constituents began demanding greater accountability from the Gibson administration, the mayor remained unflappable, weighing each crisis with the cold, analytical eye of an engineer. An incident, highlighting this trait, occurred in March, 1976, when North

Ward Councilman Anthony Carrino and State Senator Anthony Imperiale, angered by the assignment of a new police commander to the North Ward, led a crowd of White demonstrators to the mayor's office. Demanding an immediate audience with Gibson, they kicked in his office door, while Gibson remained at his desk and continued eating. Apparently unfazed, Gibson granted them an audience with him in the council chambers. Reportedly, one of the demonstrators dropped a gun on the floor.

Observers debated whether Gibson should have been congratulated for keeping a highly volatile situation under control, or whether he should have had Carrino and the others shot on the spot by his bodyguards for unlawful breaking and entering or, at least, removed from the premises and told to schedule a meeting. The way I saw it, he gave in to mob rule at City Hall.

I realized that I had to make a decision. I could choose to remain councilman-at-large for as long as my constituents wanted me; taking on more legislative responsibility; and earning a decent salary while continuing to hold a part-time teaching job, yet limited in my ability to improve the quality of life in Newark. Or, I could do something about it by getting in the race to become the city's chief executive officer. Agonizing over the decision, I chose the latter.

The latter had many pitfalls and minefields, because Gibson had a 97 percent recognition factor, name and visibility. Gibson also had a legion of 5,000 people in the municipal workforce. Gibson had money and could easily raise more money from the business community. Notwithstanding all those advantages, which created tremendous odds for anyone even thinking of running against Gibson, I decided to put my career on the line. Either I was going to move out of Newark or be part of the change needed in Newark. To be part of that change I felt I had to run for mayor.

By this time Mary and I had a vested interest in Newark. We had purchased a larger four-bedroom house across the street from the first little house we had purchased in 1967. Our family had also grown; we now had three sons to care for. Elliott, our middle son, was born in 1972, and our youngest son, Kevin, was born in 1978. If the conditions of the city did not improve, rather than see my family's investment in our home and the neighborhood continue to decline, I would pack up my bags and go to the suburbs to live and raise my family. I would give up my seat on the city council. If I couldn't help turn Newark around, then I would move on, rather than be identified with a failing city. I would be a suburbanite, and I would be happy, I told myself. But rather than curse the darkness, I chose to light a candle. I would run for mayor to bring about the changes that I had been dreaming of for Newark. That was my choice. No one thought I could win. "Gibson is unbeatable," many said.

Even after the violence of the street struck home in a frightening incident in December 1985, I still believed that Newark was worth fighting for. I was not in Newark at the time. I was at the National League of Cities meeting in Seattle, when Donald Tucker came up to me and yelled out in front of everybody in the NLC conference room, "Sharpe, call home! Your son, John got shot!" I immediately booked a five-hour red-eye flight home, but was unable to sleep thinking of the horror that awaited me.

On a Saturday morning, December 5, the day that the Elizabeth Avenue Presbyterian Church had opened its doors for the first time in 20 years, John was standing at the bus stop in front of the church, wearing his brand-new leather bomber jacket. He was waiting for a downtown bus to St. Benedict's School to participate in a chess tournament. Five individuals approached John and demanded his jacket. When he refused, they beat him and fired five shots, striking him in the leg, abdomen and thigh. They took his jacket and left him for dead.

Hearing voices in the church basement, John crawled about 100 feet toward the voices and fell down the steps, banging against the door. The church parishioners opened the door, and there was this young man bleeding from his wounds. Someone took a white tablecloth and tried to stop the bleeding. An ambulance was called. At the hospital John was given only first aid, because he was under eighteen he needed parental consent to be operated on. Mary had gone shopping in New York that day and could not be reached. So, one of the church members pretended to be John's mother in order for him to undergo immediate surgery.

At UMDNJ, where emergency medical services took John, Leroy Smith, director of EMS, stayed with him for two straight days. Dr. E. Wyman Garret, a celebrated community activist who had trained minority doctors at that hospital, delayed his vacation to treat my son.

He called every head doctor in the hospital and would not allow any interns to operate on John. I believed that because of his efforts and that of Leroy Smith my son survived and had a full recovery—although one bullet could not be removed from his right leg. There it remains, setting off metal detectors every time John goes through airport security.

I couldn't believe that anything like this could ever happen in the South Ward. I was living in a class-A residential neighborhood. There had never been incidents of this nature against anyone that I could remember. I had been called a bad father by my sons for so many years, because I would not succumb to buying them the things that other boys had—the leather jackets, the jewelry, or designer clothes. It was in a moment of weakness that I went to New York City's Orchard Street and purchased three bomber jackets for all three boys. Immediately after that incident I would prohibit my sons from ever wearing their leather jackets again.

The police issued an all-out alert to apprehend the assailants in this case. I had to demand that the police department treat this case like any other. I did not want the people of Newark to get the impression that because John was the son of an elected official, the police were making extraordinary efforts to solve the case. Still, the opinion prevailed that the police were going out of their way, leaving no stone unturned to catch the individuals who performed this dastardly act.

In a short span of time the police caught the perpetrators. This led to another saga that was probably as shocking as my son's being shot. Judge Betty Lester, who was also my neighbor, called Mary and me before her, and asked us to sign plea-bargaining papers for the five who had shot my son. I felt that it was the most absurd request that I had ever received in my whole life. These people shot and thought they had killed my son for his jacket. Miraculously, he lived. But now we were supposed to accept a plea bargain? That would be a slap on the wrist. Mary and I never signed the papers. We vociferously protested. We refused to go to court, and I never knew what the fate of those five individuals was, nor would I recognize any of them if they walked past me on the street.

I came away from that episode thinking that the court system treated Black-on-Black crime too lightly and often excused it. If you stole a TV or car in Newark, it was a misdemeanor. If you stole a TV or car in Milburn, it was a felony and you'd go to jail. After the attack on my son I took up the issue of selective judicial sentencing. I called the presiding Essex County Superior Court judge, and made a complaint. I brought representatives from the community before the judge to voice our outrage. We talked about recidivism; we talked about the wheel of crime. The judicial system was letting too many criminals walk the streets, and the sentencing was all wrong. Yet, it seemed that no one was listening or seemed to care. It was just our tough luck!

I announced my candidacy for mayor at the end of January, 1986, after Gibson announced his plans to run for a fifth term. I filed officially on March 19, the third challenger to Gibson to do so after the Reverend Oliver Brown, a school board member, and Dennis Knight, a substitute teacher and political novice. There were rumors going around that Gibson had asked the other two candidates to run in order to split the anti-Gibson votes. My decision to oppose the mayor led to anger, hostility and division in Newark. For the first time two of Newark's most popular elected officials, with the same constituents were facing off against each other. For 16 years the voters of Newark supported us both, now, husbands and wives and voting-age sons and daughters were split over their choice for mayor. It would become the most heated election in the history of Newark.

Delores Lewis, who had graduated from high school with me, had been a loyal Gibson/James supporter all along. Now she had to choose between Gibson, the man she was working for as a fiscal officer in policy and development—the man who signed her paycheck—and Sharpe James, her high-school classmate, and the councilman she had voted for for 16 years. Mamie Hale, of Brown and Hale Architects, was a strong James supporter; her husband strongly backed Gibson. Lionel Robinson was an activist in the Sharpe James camp, while his grandmother was an active member of the Ken Gibson Association.

To win this election I had to do what had once been unthinkable for me. I had to criticize our first Black mayor, who would always be a hero to me. I had to score him on ignoring neighborhood economic development while catering to downtown businesses; on having no vision for a better Newark; and on squandering millions of federal dollars on poorly planned municipal programs.

I ran on a platform of public safety and fiscal stability as my highest priorities. I would hire more policemen and bring about safety in our city. During this time the police were on strike and instigating a fear campaign by handing out leaflets on Broad and Market Streets, warning residents and visitors that Newark was not a safe place. Although the City Council had appropriated the money, Gibson wouldn't hire more cops; rather, he laid them off. He argued that there were cities larger than Newark with fewer police officers and that Newark's police budget was bloated. He even took the council to court to prove that only he had the right to hire police, notwithstanding any action by the municipal body.

I took the position that I would never lay off hundreds of police officers the way Gibson had done, especially in the face of rising crime. I would create an environment that people would want to live in, work in, and visit in comfort. I was going to create new tax revenues by making Newark, once again, a destination for businesses, a destination for people to relocate. My whole focus was to get people coming back to the city of Newark to invest.

The number-one movie while I was running for mayor was *Out of Africa,* and I once stood up in front of a group and said, "What a tragedy that you have to go out of Newark to see *Out of Africa!* When I become mayor, we're going to find a way to open movie theaters in our downtown area." I also talked about building a new roller-skating rink. Newark needed more places for families and young people to go for recreation and enjoyment.

I believed what Donald McNaughton, CEO and chairman of Prudential, said, that the criteria for a viable city is not just mortar and bricks, but being able to go out to night clubs and movie theaters. It's what you do after work or in your leisure time. In Newark we would bring that about, as well. I called upon the voters to make Newark a destination city once again, a place people want to come to work, to live, to visit—not a ghost town after work.

I talked about housing and sharing in the American dream. Gibson had built only one house between 1980 and 1985. Public housing in Newark was among the worst in America. On a visit to Montreal, Canada in 1985, Mayor Jean Drapeau said to me, "Where's public housing?"

I couldn't point to it, and he said, "We don't build poor housing; we build housing for the poor." I said, "When I get back to Newark, if I ever get a chance to be mayor, I'm going to do that."

Gibson's supporters, fearing loss of their jobs, had vowed to destroy anyone who would challenge him. The mayor himself would declare at every public gathering, "If you are thin-skinned, have skeletons in your closet, beat your wife, write bad checks, sell used cars, have a family member working for the city or you are not prepared for a war, I would suggest that you not run for mayor of Newark," to which his supporters would laugh and hoot uproariously. I learned the hard way that he was not kidding when his supporters tore down $20,000 worth of campaign posters that I put up around the city. They defaced $15,000 worth of my first citywide billboards. During working hours municipal employees with municipal equipment could be seen removing my campaign signs as they put up Gibson's.

Then, in the eleventh hour, having lost thousands of dollars and hundreds of hours in campaign work that was to no avail, Abdul Khadir Muhammad from the Mosque of Islam on Broad Street came to see me. He said, "Councilman James, I understand you're having problems getting your advertising up and keeping it up. I want to help. I've watched your career as a councilman, and we would like to be supportive. I respect Ken Gibson, and I admire him, but I'm here to help you."

At the time, I thought it was a crazy overture, however, I went out and purchased another $30,000 worth of campaign placards and signs and gave them to him. The next morning when I went out, all over the city the new posters were up with big black-and-white letters that read: "Newark Needs a Sharpe Change" (a slogan dreamed up by my recently hired New York campaign consultants, Tony Harrison and Don Cherry). I thought the posters would be gone the next day, but when I went out the following morning, they were still up. I called Muhammad in and said, "Brother Muhammad, you put the signs up, and they're still there. What happened to Ken Gibson's gang out there pulling all my signs down and destroying them with spray paint?"

He said that he had met them the previous night and assured them that out of respect for the Mayor, he and his crew would not pull down Gibson's posters. However, if they insisted on tearing down

Sharpe James's signs, the Muslims would be willing to stay out all night to retaliate. After that there was no more tearing down of posters. This gave me an opportunity to mount a campaign, to be visible, to get my message out. While he supported me, Muhammad never disrespected Gibson. He simply believed in fairness.

During the campaign my house was firebombed, and the police refused to investigate the incident. When a carload of Gibson supporters fired a weapon at me and tried to force me off the road, I used the police radio in my city council car to call for help. The police director, Charles Knox, a Gibson appointee, issued the order over the air that no police officer was to respond, suggesting that my call could be a prank. Before it was over, I had received every kind of verbal abuse and threat imaginable. Gibson's camp called it good old politics, but I called it criminal behavior.

"I can't control all of my supporters. This is politics; workers on both sides get excited," Gibson said. "I am not aware of anyone in my camp doing anything wrong. You have to be tough to run for mayor; it's not for the weak at heart." He dismissed my complaint as sour grapes. I felt I had no other recourse than to ask the New Jersey attorney general and the state police to come to Newark and monitor the May 13 election, out of concern for the safety of my family and supporters. To my surprise—and to Gibson's dismay—their response was "Yes."

Yet, even with all the fireworks of the campaign, Ken and I were very respectful toward each other during six mayoral candidate debates and any chance meetings that we had. We continued to act the part of being members of the same Community Choice team, who worked closely together for 16 years. That tended to defuse the almost insurmountable tension in the community and among family members. Neither of us wanted to win at the expense of the city, no matter how bitter our supporters were.

After the polls closed on Election Day, the campaign workers ran through the streets of Newark, reporting their tallies. After many conflicting stories of who won and who lost, thousands of citizens gathered at both Gibson and James' headquarters, waiting for a victory or concession speech or some news. Newark had not seen this much excitement since Gibson beat Addonizio in 1970.

With four candidates in the race, it was likely that no one would receive a 50-percent-plus-one vote and there would be a run-off election in two weeks. Gibson would probably win then, political observers predicted, because he would still have some campaign funds left, while I would be flat broke.

Those predictions proved wrong. Gibson had prepared his victory speech, but he would not get to deliver it that night. Cheers of joy from my supporters and gasps of disappointment from Gibson's filled the air when the newspapers rolled off the presses that night: "James beat Gibson on the first ballot." I had received 56 percent of the votes cast to Gibson's 40 percent, and I had swept all five wards. I had won the senior citizens vote over Ken. His dating a White woman, Camille, who he later married, divided his stronghold among senior citizens. There was no need for a run-off election.

I was happy and humbled that the citizens of Newark were giving me this chance to lead their city. With so many people calling to congratulate me—including Senator Kennedy, the Rev. Jesse Jackson, and even my landlady from my Springfield College days, Maybell Beam, I kept thinking over and over again, I must keep my promise for a "Sharpe change."

Gibson had ushered in an era of political reform and honesty, following a corrupt administration. He ended the notion that there was a price tag on Newark City Hall. Although he had his own brush with scandal, when in 1982 he and Earl Harris were tried for allegedly giving a no-show job to former councilman-at-large Michael Bontempo at the Newark-owned watershed, it didn't weaken Gibson's standing in the African American community. However it did, no doubt, raise a red flag among Whites that maybe Gibson was lining his pockets with city funds, too. (Harris was found not guilty, and the prosecutor eventually dropped all charges against Gibson and Bontempo.)

Gibson, the honest engineer born in Enterprise, Alabama, brought hope that Newark's revitalization would be fashioned by African Americans, Whites and Latinos, working together. Yet, his 16-year term was probably like 32 years to him because of his struggles with the council, which from 1970 to 1978 was controlled by Whites. It wasn't until his third term that Blacks gained the majority. So, for many years he had to deal with a majority White, racially divided council, and he had to deal with a still racially divided community.

Having been a councilman myself for sixteen years—not to mention a college administrator for twelve—I felt I was better equipped to confront the council than Gibson had been. He had never served in public office before being elected mayor. I knew how the council worked, and I was sure that I would achieve some things that Gibson could not. We—the city and the council—had burned Gibson out. He had to bear the weight of being the first African American mayor of a major Northeast city, and that took a terrible toll on him physically, mentally and emotionally.

I commend Ken Gibson for being able to withstand the pressure and all the tribulation for as long as he did, and running for a fifth term. Some said it was not Gibson, but the people around him who were trying to protect their jobs, who sought his reelection. During the mayoral debates Gibson had with me and the two other challengers, I was his principal opponent, and he lost to me each time. It was as though he was walking into a situation that was uncomfortable for him, and knowing that I'd run my mouth, he graciously lost. He had name recognition; he was the mayor. I had everything to gain and nothing to lose by showing people that I could beat up on him. He had nothing to gain, and, yet, he showed up at all of the debates and let me come away a winner—a clear indication to me that his heart wasn't in the race.

Gibson had created in Newark the spiritual atmosphere for change. He had given the city some renewed stability, but he was not the person to bring about the necessary changes. He was not a hands-on, do-this, get-it-done mayor. Some people who have the best ideas and best plans may not be the ones to implement them. In the words of a Gibson loyalist, at-large councilman, and then-council president Ralph Grant, Jr.: Ken Gibson mixed the mortar, but he got tired. Sharpe James would now lay the bricks. I would never forget that Ken Gibson opened the door for me to become mayor. Without Ken there would be no Sharpe. He is my hero. He is still my mayor.

CHAPTER 9

Newark's Cheerleader

On July 1, 1986 I was sworn in as Newark's 35th mayor at Newark Symphony Hall. My sons, John, Elliot, and Kevin, my brother, Joseph, and my mother attended the swearing in ceremony. My wife, Mary, held the Bible during the ceremony. My college president, Dr. Margaret C. Brown, 90-plus years-old, was there too, looking like an aerobic exercise instructor, jumping up and down, shouting "That's my boy!"

My family was at the Inauguration, because they felt their attendance was obligatory. They couldn't wait to leave. They were apolitical. I had an apolitical family. My boys were not political. My wife was certainly not political; they feared politics, thinking somehow it would put them under attack. I'd never tried to force politics on them. Eight-year-old Kevin kept tugging at my jacket, asking, "Daddy, when can we leave?"

My brother, Joseph, the NJIT graduate, was a scientist. He never attended a political meeting in his life. Mary hated politicians. She wouldn't allow them to smoke or drink in her presence. She believed that now that I was mayor it would mean opening up our family, our house, our block for more scrutiny. It was an invasion of our privacy, which she had guarded so well as a Southern woman.

Mary had begged me not to run for mayor. She tolerated my being a councilman. On the council, you could get lost. But being mayor, not only could you not get lost, but the buck stopped with you, as Harry Truman had said. On the City Council there were so many opportunities for chicanery. You could make back-room deals and have eight people vote the way you wanted them to vote, while you voted the opposite. Yet there's only one mayor who takes the blame for every-thing; he's responsible for the decline or growth of the city.

Politics had a different meaning for me. I was driven by the very people who supported me in the Black and Puerto Rican Convention to become an elected official. They had asked me to serve the community, and I was going to do just that. Newark had taken a poor boy off the streets, gave him an education, gave him opportunities, and now I wanted to give something back. If Newark could make me into something, I had an obligation to reach out to as many youths as possible to guide and encourage them to go on to higher education, and, even more, to join mainstream American life. If I could do it, so could they.

As an athlete I could handle the public demands, the long hours, the time, the confrontations. To me it all seemed exciting because I was competitive, and I loved helping people. A certain amount of pride and team work went into giving back to the city.

This would be the first time in 25 years that I would not be teaching, instead, devoting full time to public office. I had to hit the ground running and know that I was running in the right direction, with the right programs. I could not count on having 16 years to fulfill my promises to clean up the city, combat crime and create employment opportunities as Mayor Gibson had. I could not rely on the mere symbolism of being Newark's first Black mayor. The citizens of Newark would not be so forgiving of me. They expected me to solve all of Newark's problems overnight. I realized that I needed support from the City Council, the business community, community-based organizations, the clergy and the citizens of Newark to turn campaign promises into concrete programs that would help the city.

Once I was sworn in as Mayor, I immediately focused my attention on the selection of the City Council president. My choice was South Ward Councilman, Donald Payne. I could depend on Payne to be fair and an objective supporter of administrative decisions that would move the city forward. I advised every member of the Council that he was my choice.

But now, as Mayor, I was an outsider looking in. I had lost the clout I had as a 16-year member of the Council. Councilman-at-large

Donald Tucker, who had been my constant foe since he was elected in 1974, was busy trying to line up five votes himself. He argued that he should be awarded the presidency because he had been the top vote-getter in the 1986 at-large race, the same argument I tried to make in 1982, when I was the at-large candidate with the most votes, which he had derided in a six-page thesis. "Damn most votes! It's who can lobby five votes from council members first," he had said back then.

The thought of Tucker becoming council president almost gave me a heart attack. Large and portly, now armed with a degree from Goddard College, paid for by the City of Newark, Tucker was still, loud and confrontational. Tucker, however, was extremely knowledgeable of political issues and governing procedures—he read everything—and was a warrior-in-waiting.

Fearing that my administration could be held hostage by a council with Donald Tucker as president, I decided to align myself with a coalition of White, Hispanic and Black members of the council who were supporting Henry Martinez as the first Hispanic council president. Hank was no choir boy—he was known to hang out with some disreputable characters in the East Ward—and posed a potential threat, because he was not a team player. I thought; better to live with a menace than to be condemned to hell with Donald Tucker serving as City Council President. Martinez won in a 6-0 roll-call vote, with Tucker, Ron Rice, and, to my surprise, Donald Payne not voting.

With that fight over, I informed the newly sworn-in council that I would be appointing an acting Business Administrator, Milan Johnson, on loan for free from Prudential Insurance Company, and would forward, for their approval, the names of my department directors. I named Police Lieutenant Louis E. Greenleaf, a 19-year veteran of the force, to replace Police Commissioner Charles Knox, and Claude M. Coleman, a 22-year veteran of the police department and its then-legal adviser, as Fire Director, replacing John P. Caulfield, who had held the post for 27 years. Glenn A. Grant, an assistant Corporation Counsel, was chosen to head the office of Corporation Counsel. Arturo Lopez, director of International admissions at Rutgers University, was named director of the Department of General Services, the first Hispanic to head a major city department. I proposed a new Department of

Development and a Department of Land Use Control, which the council enacted immediately into law.

I decided early on that I would need a professional Business Administrator, chosen for his management skills rather than for his politics. I wanted someone who would focus on the real issues and needs of the city. I conducted a nationwide search to find the best possible person to fill this position. In the meantime, the very competent, Milan Johnson easily won my respect and that of the council and citizens of Newark during his brief tenure. Our first task was to expand our revenue collection, pay our bills and balance the municipal budget. We could, then, move to hire more police officers, address healthcare issues, build affordable housing, improve our recreational and cultural offerings, and create jobs through economic development.

For the Sharpe Change to become a reality, I had to become a "cheerleader." In my first days in office I tried to corral the energy of the city's work force and citizens by getting everyone to work together as a team. As head cheerleader, I would promote the many positive aspects of the city by using a salesmanship approach.

The new James administration, in its first month, committed $300,000 from my campaign funds to conduct a management productivity study by a 55-member independent task force, headed by the auditing company Coopers & Lybrand. My transition team chairman, Gustav Heningburg, (a Black consultant who had served in the same capacity for Gibson in 1970) would guide the effort, while Milan Johnson would be the liaison between the task force and city government officials. The goal was to determine the city's strengths, weaknesses, and to develop a plan of action.

Ken Gibson graciously assisted in the transition. He introduced me to the city's Chamber of Commerce leadership and, in June, a month after the election, he took me to the U.S. Conference of Mayors meeting in Puerto Rico and presented me as Newark's mayor elect. Whatever humiliation he might have felt introducing the person who had defeated him, he didn't show it and was all smiles. He would drop by City Hall and answer any questions that I might have. He also warned me of many things not to do in office, such as seeing developers and other businessmen one-on-one, where it could be their word against mine in potential conflicting situations. Gibson told me that I should have an observer present, at all times, when I meet with contractors. He made his records available to me, and held out the olive branch of cooperation.

Gibson's eleventh-hour appointment to fill a vacancy on the Newark Housing Authority, however, would rob me of the opportunity to exert my influence over this powerful body. I was to be sworn in at noontime on July 1, 1986. I was excited about the prospect of appointing members to the Newark Housing Authority so that we could begin implementing my program of imploding abandoned public high-rises and constructing new townhouses. Gibson waited until that morning to appoint Ralph L. McNeal to the Housing Authority.

The council rammed the appointment through. I later went to New Jersey Superior Court to challenge it, charging that Gibson had no right to make appointments on the day I took over City Hall. The judge, though, was sympathetic to the outgoing mayor and dismissed my case. That meant I would have to live with the appointment for four years. Hell, if Gibson's commissioners built only one house in five years, I certainly didn't want them on the Housing Authority Board. Gibson's appointment that day meant that I could not expect the immediate support I was seeking for my radical new housing implosion program.

Admittedly, Gibson did what all mayors try to do when leaving office. They try to stack the house with their people so that they can go back for favors or stymie the incoming mayor's proposals. By leaving their people entrenched, some outgoing mayors can have greater influence than a sitting mayor. An out-of-office mayor with all his board members and commissioners in place still has power.

The next step in bringing about a Sharpe Change was identifying the true leaders in the private sector. Establishing a relationship with them was very critical. I knew my city well, and the top corporate leaders—five in number—had previously organized themselves as the board of trustees of an organization called Renaissance Newark, Inc. I met with Robert Van Fossan of Mutual Benefit Life Insurance Company, Robert Winters of Prudential Insurance Company, Robert Ferguson of First Fidelity Bancorp, E. James Ferland of Public Service Electric and Gas Company (PSE&G) and Anton Campanella of New Jersey Bell.

They constituted the largest taxpaying, property owners, and employers in the City of Newark.

Our informal meetings led to several goals conferences. Two of these conferences were structured to identify our separate and common concerns and problems. The meetings at Prudential headquarters were intense. I was the heavyweight facing my opponent at the weigh-in. Both sides tried to demonstrate toughness without being disrespectful. It was no secret that the business community, although no friend of Gibson, had strongly supported him for reelection. I was an unknown outsider, a hot-shot councilman in the view of some of these CEOs.

Van Fossan went so far as to phone Gustav Heningburg, to ask, "Who is this guy, Sharpe, who just got elected?" Somewhat taken aback, Heningburg replied, "One thing you should know about him, he cheats at tennis." To that Van Fossan had laughed and said, "Well, hell, Gus, I can live with that kind of mayor." Van Fossan turned out to be one of the best corporate partners any mayor could wish for.

The corporate group focused on mutual concerns for improved police protection, a cleaner and more beautiful city, improving the quality of education (the business community had complained of the lack of a knowledgeable and skilled workforce) and changing the negative image of Newark.

Once these issues were before us, and on paper, we saw quite simply that the major problems were common to us all; the priorities were the same to us all, and the magnitude of the challenge easily outstripped the resources and abilities of any one of us to bring about a resolution. We therefore concluded that we needed to work together. We needed to share resources, and we needed a commitment to cement that relationship.

As Mayor, I would recommend to the City Council several measures to formalize the partnership by ensuring adequate and timely sharing of information, planning, and input into decisions. The measures proposed by me, unanimously supported by the corporate leaders, and unanimously approved by the City Council were:

1. The creation of the position of Deputy Mayor for Economic Development to advise, recommend, and implement the development agenda of the Administration and to serve as a liaison with the business community-
2. The establishment of the City Commercial Development Advisory Council—the major economic policy group in the city—which would be comprised of ten members, five each from the public and private sectors and
3. The appointment of a City Commerce Commission, whose membership would be comprised of the working heads of all city and city-related agencies involved in the development area.

The individual chosen for the Deputy Mayor for Economic Development would have to be well-versed in development, understand and appreciate the inner-workings of the private sector, and be able to relate effectively with corporate leaders, while at the same time be experienced, knowledgeable, and sensitive to the workings of the public sector. We jointly found such an individual, Everett Shaw, who was hired and paid by the corporate leaders as president of Renaissance Newark, Inc., and appointed by me as the city's Deputy Mayor for Economic Development at a salary of $1 per year.

Subsequently, Shaw was named chairman of the city's development team (the Development Department staff, the Mayor, Business Administrator, Corporation Counsel, and the Director of the Newark Housing Authority) as well as the city's Commerce Commission. In November 1986, a draft of The Cooper & Lybrand report, "Financial and Productivity Management Review," came out. The report made 693 recommendations for change. It found that there was "no citywide system for planning or achieving objectives; no information base for planning and managing resources; no system for planning or monitoring productivity improvements."

After a thorough reading, review, discussions, heated debates and consensus-seeking on the report's findings, I proposed, and the council readily enacted, the most sweeping reorganization of local government since the adoption of the city's present charter in 1954. Many agencies were consolidated, shifted, or even eliminated, while others were created.

We created new Departments of Development and Land Use Control. We transferred the Division of City Planning to Development to provide a more effective linkage between the City's plan for growth and the City's development agenda. We added The Division of Tax Abatement and Special Taxes to the Department of Finance to better manage the growing financial and administrative requirements of tax-abated projects, as well as parking, payroll and hotel taxes. The Department of Health and Human Services was restructured to reflect an increased emphasis not only on health care, but also on social services and recreational activities. The Office of Citizens Services was created to provide citizens with a convenient, single point of contact with the municipal government concerning complaints or inquiries, and to provide a quick referral mechanism to the appropriate agency. It was an ambitious attempt to adapt Newark's government to the needs of the late 20th century.

Just in time to implement the changes, our nationwide search for a business administrator produced a young multitalented professional, Richard Monteilh, who had worked under two mayors, including Andrew Young of Atlanta, Georgia. Monteilh was willing to relocate to Newark, and did so in January, 1987 bringing energy, vision and leadership to the office.

At his first confrontation with the members of the Newark Municipal Council, this cultured, Southern individual was rudely challenged and cursed out by Donald Tucker. Monteilh had never faced this type of situation before, and asked me what he should do. I told him to curse back and don't be intimidated. Well, he must have listened closely, because he developed the sharpest tongue in the James Administration. At times he even scared Tucker himself. The council fought Monteilh, but he got the job done.

Our Administration had inherited a city with a $30 million budget deficit. The Cooper's & Lybrand audit had discovered $30 million in uncollected municipal summonses. Traffic and other violators in Newark simply wouldn't pay their tickets. They assumed that the records would be misplaced or lost and that they would never hear from the city. So, they simply tore up their tickets and threw them away. Some violators owed as much as $5,000 in outstanding municipal fines.

We started the police scofflaw program to collect outstanding fines. Police officers, with summonses in hand fanned, out into the neighborhoods, knocking on doors at 8 in the evening hoping to catch folks watching prime-time television, and presented them with a warrant for their arrest if they did not pay their outstanding fines immediately. We had to compete with the Cosby Show, but we won, and much needed dollars began to flow into the city coffers.

We made it easy for violators to pay-up by attaching a self-mailer to summonses placed on automobiles for nonmoving violations. All one had to do was tear off the form and just drop it in the mail with a check; no court appearance needed. That way we were able to receive thousands of payments and had to open a post office lock-box system to handle the large volume of mail. We served notice that we would go out of town to catch violators, as well. One scofflaw who had fled from Newark to Miami was arrested on the ninth hole of his favorite golf course. His golf clubs were confiscated for collateral.

The collection rate for fines doubled. We followed the scofflaw program with a vigorous water-turn-off policy to similarly force delinquent water users to settle their outstanding debts. We were moving to run the city as a business. I was no longer a politician seeking votes by saying yes to everything. I now viewed myself as a CEO running a corporation; held accountable to a board of directors. The days of seeking photo opportunities with victims of violence or their grieving relatives were over. No more just kissing babies and shaking hands. The people of Newark demanded a city that functioned, a city that delivered municipal services in a timely and professional manner.

One of the primary tasks of the newly created Departments of Development and of Land Use Control was to build and renovate houses at a record pace. We were going to make the American dream of home ownership a reality to an increasing number of Newarkers. The average rate of home ownership in urban cities across the country was about 46 percent in 1986. Newark was lagging way behind at about a dismal 14 percent. I found this to be intolerable and an indictment against the 16-year administration of Ken Gibson.

K. Hovnanian Enterprises of Red Bank, one of New Jersey's great builders, had been negotiating with the City Council to build housing in Newark. Just prior to my election they had obtained a large parcel of land in the University Heights area of the city, but had learned from its engineers that the site was contaminated, and that it would cost $13 million to clean. They suggested bringing in clean soil the size of three football fields. K. Hovnanian asked the city to finance the cleanup. I thought the request was outrageous and turned it down.

I called upon the New Jersey Institute of Technology (NJIT), one of the top engineering colleges in the country, located in Newark, to help by investigating the site. Three weeks later six engineers from the college came to my office and told me they could solve the problem. I asked them how much it would cost. They told me about $200,000. *Were they crazy?* How could their cleanup estimate be so low?

They had found that some of the homes on the site had oil tanks in the ground. All they had to do was to identify those homes and pluck the tanks out. It would cost nowhere near the $13 million that K. Hovnanian had cited. There was no need to encapsulate— to pour concrete over the contaminated site and construct on top of it—the engineers said. The city could immediately go into the ground and start building.

With this NJIT assessment, the housing program seemed affordable. Newark gave the developers the green light to build 1,400 townhouses, a club house, tennis courts and a pool that would rival any suburban development. The development would be known as Society Hill at University Heights. About 12 percent of the units would be designated for low-moderate-income families. Quality housing would take the place of taverns, abandoned buildings and other eyesores in the heart of the Central Ward, where the riots had started two decades before.

Newark's homeless problem, consisting of between 5,000 and 8,000 people, was exacerbated during this time when New York's Mayor Ed Koch began sending large numbers of homeless New Yorkers to Newark. Our hotels and motels were overcrowded and the disturbances created by the growing number of homeless people were putting a strain on our police force, not to mention other city services. I called Mayor Koch to ask him to stop exporting his homeless problem to Newark. He insisted, however, that those people had a right to live here. "Sharpe, people don't need a visa to move to Newark," he quipped. "What's your problem?"

The issue erupted into a media war between the two of us, ending with Channel 9 in Secaucus setting up bleacher seats for 500 in its studio, and inviting Mayor Koch and me to debate live for one hour on its news program. Knowing that Mayor Koch and I were alumni from South Side High School in Newark (class of 1941 and 1954, respectively), I went to our alma mater and asked for a copy of Ed's yearbook photo, and blew it up to about 3-by-3 feet. During the introductions I produced the picture, and a horrified Ed Koch screamed, "What happened to my hair?" In high school he had a full head of curly dark hair, in contrast to the two thin patches on each side with a clear highway down the middle that he now had atop his head. Having broken the ice, what was to be a debate, instead turned into a lecture to the audience by both of us on the problems of the homeless and some possible solutions.

In addition to homelessness there were numerous other problems that the new James Administration had to address immediately. The incidence of AIDS was on the rise in Essex County, with Newark's problem being greater than that of any of the surrounding towns. The federal government created an Essex County AIDS Council and sent all of the money to Newark so that it would coordinate AIDS education, prevention and treatment programs throughout all of the cities in Essex and Union counties.

Members of the AIDS Council fought like cats and dogs over which municipality was going to get how much money. In the end, after all the fighting, very little funding was released and some money had to be returned to the federal government. All the while, AIDS victims were suffering, and I was taking a beating in the press, because I had no answer to the problem.

I fired my Director of Health and Human Services, Bobi Ruffin, and with a new director, Catherine Cuomo-Cecere, in place, we eventually brought in a young woman, Maria Irizarry, to get the AIDS Council to work as a group. Irizarry, as AIDS coordinator, immediately pulled the group together, gained its respect and confidence, and was able to get more funding to the Council, and come up with a distribution plan.

Later on, Irizarry would come to be recognized as an AIDS and HIV expert in New Jersey.

Newark had an alarmingly high infant mortality rate, and that was because health care for parents was inadequate. Those who needed treatment most were less likely to go to healthcare centers to receive it. We needed a program that would bring health services to the neighborhoods. We started a Visiting Nurse Program, and with a big, old mobile unit, put immunization services on wheels. The unit would pull up in the courtyard of housing projects, set up tables, start playing music, give out free lollipops and balloons, and invite parents to bring their children out for immunization. It became an instant success.

Another serious issue we had to deal with was lead poisoning. Newark was the third oldest major city in America, behind Boston and New York, and because of our old housing structure many homes had been painted with lead paint. When the paint began to peel, very young children picked it up and put it in their mouths. We had a serious epidemic of lead poisoning in Newark and insufficient local funds to treat it. We didn't have enough certified lead inspectors to go into homes. But we came up with the idea of a "lead safe house;" a renovated lead-free house owned by the city. Here we would temporarily place families with children suffering with lead poisoning, while the city cleaned up the contaminated residence. We could not renovate units fast enough to meet the demand, and had to turn to the federal government for additional funds.

Methadone centers became the big issue in our fight against drug usage. There was a row of Methadone Clinics on Saybrook Place, which would later become the site of the proposed $200 million New Jersey Performing Arts Center (NJPAC). I deplored the fact that so many of these clinics, where heroin addicts would receive the methadone in their mouths, then go out and sell it by spitting it into somebody else's mouth, were so close to the downtown area.

Newark residents always opposed the locations of the methadone centers, because drug addicts tended to loiter near them. My administration recognized the plague of heroin addiction and the need for these facilities, but we wanted to make sure we placed them in industrial areas, where there would be the least exposure to homeowners, children, and residents.

I was tired of Newark being the dumping ground for every county and state social-care facility. When I learned that the State was considering building an arts center in New Jersey to compete with the concert halls in New York, I established a task force to lobby for building the center in Newark. The task force included Richard Monteilh; Everett Shaw; my new Director of Development, Harold Lucas; Director of Newark Economic Development Corporation (NEDC), Al Faiella, and me.

Our task force went to Washington to seek a grant from Jack Kemp, the hard-nosed Secretary of Housing and Urban Development. He turned us away, chiding us for fighting for an arts center in Newark, when, he thought, we should be focusing on the homeless and AIDS. I told him he was wrong. The lights of Broadway didn't dim during the depression. We could save souls and still build a better city; the challenge was to do both.

Back home, I asked Governor Tom Kean, "What about some positive things in Newark? We house all the evil things that no community wants. How about selecting Newark to build the arts center?"

"We have to conduct a study, to determine the best location for the arts center," he told me. He hired Carl Shaver to carry out the study. Shaver had previously consulted on the selection of the site for New York's Lincoln Center, in a predominantly Black and Puerto Rican neighborhood known as San Juan Hill. Several months after being hired for the New Jersey project, Shaver revealed in a big press conference, with the governor, the choice of Newark as the site for NJPAC. After the announcement I, who had been standing nearby, yelled to Kean, "Governor, I told you that six months ago—for free. Now you're paying this guy $300,000 in consultancy fees?"

Kean answered, "Sharpe, I'm not going to let them erect just a building in Newark. People won't come. You've got to have an area, like in New York, where you can sit outdoors on a patio with a water fountain. We've got to have an area where people will feel safe, an area that people will want to visit." That's why the NJPAC area was designated at 12 acres—to expand and have other support structures.

Yet, site selection did not lead to the immediate groundbreaking for the arts center. The doubters and nay sayers went to work bashing Newark. Public funding for the project was always subject to political whims, but the millionaire philanthropist Ray Chambers, of Morristown, who graduated from Newark's West Side High School and who was a co-founder of Wesray Capital Corporation, stepped up to the plate with Robert Van Fossan. They agreed to underwrite a $26 million letter of credit needed to begin the project.

James Rouse, the internationally known developer of Boston's Faneuil Hall Market, Baltimore's Inner Harbor and New York's South Street Seaport, among others, unveiled a drawing of the proposed arts center after the funding was announced. He said it was the broadest showing of private support he had seen during his entire development career.

Chambers and Van Fossan, along with P. Roy Vagelos, CEO of Merck Pharmaceutical until his retirement in 1994, raised $60 million, the largest private contribution for a public facility in the history of New Jersey. It took all of their skills and courage to motivate three governors—two Republicans and a Democrat—to bring this project to fruition. Tom Kean provided the impetus. He had the vision and the desire to bring the arts center to Newark. Then there was Jim Florio, who didn't see any need for an arts center. We had to work on him. Twice we took him to New York City to see a play. He started nodding and falling asleep, and I thought we were going to lose the project under him, but he continued the funding. When Christine Todd Whitman was elected, we reached an impasse over whether the state would provide funds to purchase the steel for construction, but we got over that obstacle and the center was finally underway.

At one of the executive board meetings with Vagelos and Chambers, Vagelos was told that there wasn't any money for a parking garage. He said, "Do you think we could paint the roads yellow, all around the PAC from the New Jersey Turnpike and from the Garden State Parkway and Route 280?" He was worried that suburban patrons to NJPAC might get lost after exiting the parkway, turnpike or Route 280, and might end up on one of Newark's mean streets. To avoid this, why not paint the roads from these major arteries yellow and safely deliver suburbanites to the Emerald City of NJPAC?

The room of CEOs was silent at his suggestion. I said, "Did I hear you correctly? You must have seen that movie *Bonfire of the Vanities,* where a White couple got lost in the South Bronx and found themselves in the neighborhoods, fearing that the Black and Hispanic people and gangs were going to attack them. That's insulting, Mr. Vagelos. We're not going to do that. People in Newark aren't going to mug and rob anybody." The silence continued.

"Let me tell you a story," I said. "I used to listen to a radio program, hosted by Gene Shepherd on WOR. He said that his worst fear, when he was in Mississippi, was that he would run out of gas on a back road, and he would look up and see a carload of Blacks approaching. Well, he said his worse fear did come true. He said, 'That happened. I got a flat tire on this abandoned road and had no spare. I looked up and two carloads of Blacks were approaching. I was scared. They stopped and asked me what was wrong. Then they got out and changed my tire and got me on my way. Racial fear can sometimes distort our reasoning.'"

Looking around the room at the CEOs, I said, "That's where we are right now. I'm of the opinion that White people have these fears, and they're not going to come to Newark if they have to park on the streets; and we're not going to paint the roads yellow. But we do need parking." I suggested that Newark lease the Military Park garage to the arts center. The private group came up with a $10 million budget to renovate it, and the garage became an integral part of NJPAC where one could buy coffee or tea and pay for one's parking in a well-lit, air-conditioned, people-friendly facility.

Of course a Sharpe Change did not come about without a fight. You would think that the people of Newark, needing everything, would welcome a change for the better. Not so. Newark could have been a hell hole, the worst city in America, and yet when there was talk about progress, there were those who refused to let go of the past. Convincing them to do so was a painful process.

In the end, when those same individuals saw the progress, they got amnesia and would come up to me to say, "Congratulations, we did it." You have to have courage and belief in your convictions in order to go forward, against the odds, against popular opinion to get things done. It can be a lonely job.

Harold Lucas, a Newark lawyer with previous development experience in Atlantic City, would initiate a $5 billion economic development renaissance. It would change Newark's dying downtown into a vibrant and growing metropolis that would soon see a state-of-the-art performing arts center and a new minor league baseball stadium. International Discount Telecommunications (IDT), MBNA, Verizon, Cogswell Realty Group would all join Newark's downtown landscape with new corporate headquarters. We introduced plans to build neighborhood movie theaters, a little league ball field, and a roller skating rink. We planned to develop our waterfront and to build a rail link from downtown to the airport.

Some citizens began complaining that everything was happening downtown and nothing was happening in the neighborhoods. They failed to realize that a vibrant downtown would serve the entire population and create jobs as well. My administration's response was to build and rehabilitate housing in every ward and neighborhood. We challenged the Newark Housing Authority, to which I eventually was able to appoint commissioners, to tear down abandoned high-rises and replace them with new townhouses.

Like the city of St. Louis, which in 1976 tore down the 2,740-unit Pruitt Igoe Housing Projects—a symbol of the failure of high-rise public housing in the United States—Newark would rid itself of these towering hellholes. I initiated the biggest implosion program in the history of this nation, by bringing down more than 50 high-rise buildings, completely changing the landscape of Newark, N.J.

Councilman Tucker had argued against the program, saying that we would be destroying homes for the poor. But some of the buildings had been empty for more than twenty years. What homes were we destroying? The Lower-Income Housing Coalition, spearheaded by Tucker, took us to court. A judge ruled that we could not tear down a unit without a plan to build a new one; the "one-for-one" rule. This started a massive building of townhouses in Newark addressing the court's mandate.

With the construction of Society Hill and the movie theater, two long-standing neighborhood businesses, Fit Rite and Nole Locksmith, fought against relocation. They fought the city in court for two-and-a-half years while we were assembling the land. After the costly fight, the court decided that the city had the right to condemn the property, assess it, and put the money in the bank at fair-market value.

The city kept its word to help Fit Rite and Nole Locksmith relocate. We put Nole on Elizabeth Avenue and Fit Rite, a clothing store, on Springfield Avenue. After relocation, the owners were making more money than they had ever made in their lives.

Pearl Coles, a community activist, who lived in public housing, had vociferously opposed the construction of the movie theater. "Damn you, Sharpe!" she had said. "We ain't going to let you build no movie theater. We ain't going to let you tear down these houses. We ain't going to let you relocate these people."

We built the movie theater, and on opening night, with all the movie stars coming and free popcorn, the person who had the most hot dogs, the most popcorn, the most soda, who came up to me and gave me the biggest kiss was Pearl Coles. She said, "Sharpe, boy you really outdid yourself! This is a great movie theater!" My mind flashed back to this lady threatening me, with all her name-calling. *Someone has to lead, because people are against change,* I thought. But, once it happens, and people see the benefits of it, they then fall in line. Sharpe James was the "relocation mayor." I relocated 12 churches, more than 5,000 people and a countless number of businesses. There was not one gripe after it was all done. During the process, I had been vilified.

Over the years I would have to fight the City Council over granting tax abatements. A majority of the members of the Council supported tax abatements, accepting my philosophy that it was better to grant a tax abatement to a developer who would take a vacant lot and turn it into a tax-generating property rather than let the lot remain vacant, generating no revenue for the city.

Council member Donald Tucker, who was chairman of the council tax abatement committee—and later on Bessie Walker and Gayle Chaneyfield Jenkins —would debate tax abatements. They would demand that each applicant come before the Council and subject the applicant to intense questioning, and then demand concessions, such as hiring Newark residents for the projects in order to gain their vote. In this way members of the Council used tax abatement as a tool for gaining personal political favor—because they thought they were granting something of value—rather than creating a tax ratable.

At this time Newark had a bad image. We had to dangle carrots to get investors to come to the city. Tax abatement was one of those carrots. We were desperate. We needed services. We needed the facilities. We needed a better image, but we would have to bend in order to get it.

Many property owners were opposed to tax abatements because they thought those getting the abatements would pay less taxes; but this is not how it works. People who get tax abatements do not pay less than existing property owners, but they do not pay any more. In other, words a homeowner or business putting up brand new construction, would ordinarily pay significantly more in taxes than the homeowner or business owner next door, because the current fair-market value of the property would be much greater.

Legally, you couldn't get an abatement if you didn't apply before the beginning of construction. Twice I had to go to Superior Court to have the law bent so that individuals who were paying $10,000 in taxes for condominiums in Newark—because they were on the books at fair-market value—could pay a tax-abated amount. All of the major developers of housing in Newark applied for tax abatements. If they hadn't done so, the cost of a house would be confiscatory, and a lot of houses would have gone unsold.

After Newark had been under the gun for so many years, it was to be expected that most of those who made the applications for tax abatements were companies from outside the city. Many of those investors who were fueling Newark's renaissance were not based in the city. Yes, outsiders would benefit, and many in Newark weren't happy about that. In exchange, though, Newark would benefit from the services, the new housing, new stores and strip shopping malls that they brought. They get a tax benefit, but we get a new image. It was a tradeoff that we could not turn down. You can't be dying of cancer and then want to debate the cure. We were changing the landscape of Newark. We were making Newark a destination city, "Newark was on a roll."

I felt that all of my cheerleading was for the good of Newark, because it put the city in the national spotlight. I welcomed every opportunity—big and small—to promote the interests of the city. This required a good sense of humor, such as when the Fashion Foundation of America took note of my transformation from a councilman in tennis shorts and sneakers to a nattily suited mayor, and, in 1987, named me one of America's "Ten Best Dressed Men" in Civic Affairs. This put me in the same league as Arnold Schwarzenegger and Ronald Reagan, and invited comparisons with San Francisco's stylish Mayor, the incomparable Willie Brown.

Of greater weight were the awards presented to me and the city of Newark in 1991 by the National Civic League in San Antonio, Texas, The U.S. Conference of Mayors, and Waste Management of North America Inc., at the Conference's annual convention in San Diego. Receiving the National Civic League's All-America City Award and the U.S. Conference of Mayors' City Livability Award were testament to the success of Newark's initiative of bringing business, government and residents together to solve community problems.

That year in San Diego the U.S. Conference of Mayors also selected me to serve on its 10-member board of trustees. The board helped mayors across the country solve problems in their cities, and as a member I would be able to guide other local officials whose cities suffered ills similar to those of Newark. Newark was now in the national spotlight for its renaissance. *The Star-Ledger* editorial was correct, "Newark is on a Roll."

CHAPTER TEN

Other Political Affiliations

The two most prestigious organizations representing local government are the National League of Cities (NLC), founded in December 1924 and representing more than 18,000 cities, villages and towns, and the United States Conference of Mayors (USCM), founded in 1932, representing 1,139 cities in the United States with populations of 30,000 or more. Both organizations seek to improve and strengthen local government through research, information sharing, development of an effective national urban/suburban policy, and to lobby the federal government on behalf of local government.

I joined the United States Conference of Mayors in 1986, and was a member of the Executive Board until my retirement in 2006. I chaired many committees and studies on the issues of unfunded mandates, the importance of the arts and recreation, recycling and challenges facing a local and global economy.

On our United States Conference of Mayors trade mission to Japan in 1998, I used my municipal expertise on the disposal of garbage (Newark had explored a landfill, transfer station and a new $350 million Resource Recovery Plant) to convince Japanese officials to build a resource recovery plant in Tokyo without fear of community environmental concerns, and to produce and sell electricity as a byproduct.

I had joined the NLC in 1970. It was made up of councilmen, aldermen and other categories of local elected officials, and represented 17,000 municipalities. Most elected officials who got involved in these organizations did so because they were looking for a junket, a chance to travel, go to parties, play golf or tennis, but they never wanted to attend meetings or join committees, much less chair committees, because that would mean work. I had a proven record of being an activist in the NLC, active on the committees, and actively involved in writing and amending resolutions that were brought to the policy floor. I was a sought after speaker at state league meetings as well, because I had a no-nonsense approach to good government.

President Of The National League Of Cities

Electing me president was the League's way of recognizing the work I had done for the organization as a member of various committees. I was a workaholic in the NLC. That's how I got to the top. Yet, it did not come without a fight from another councilman from Spokane, Washington, who felt he should be selected. After a fierce floor fight among delegates, I was elected second vice president at the end of 1991, the first New Jersey elected official since the early 1930s, this automatically placed me in the line of succession for vice president the next year, and the presidency the year after that.

In December 1993 I became president of the National League of Cities, which would propel me to the position of spokesman for urban America. I accepted the position, and traveled throughout the USA giving speeches before state leagues on how to improve the quality of life in our cities. As I traveled the length and breadth of the nation, I learned the best practices in America for addressing urban problems. I brought them home to Newark. I believe that the renaissance that took place in Newark, beginning in the 1990s, was a direct result of my having visited so many other cities and seeing firsthand what others were doing to solve their problems. I became much wiser, and more knowledgeable on what worked and what didn't work.

I led the fight against unfunded mandates by the federal and state governments. The federal government was requiring that municipalities end ocean dumping, cut down on lead violations, build new water filtration plants, as well as make other environmental and structural improvements. For example, Washington required Newark and other cities to test their drinking water for a pesticide that was found only in Hawaiian pineapples. I argued that since Newark didn't grow pineapples, we shouldn't have to spend money for a testing program. "If you mandate, send a check," was our rallying cry.

We addressed issues of privatization, which meant contracting out municipal services such as sanitation, data processing and street sweeping to reduce the public payroll. These initiatives were implemented in Newark and other cities and saved the city a great deal of money. Of course, there had to be sensitivity in the decision making if these actions resulted in the layoff of local residents who would become jobless. It was a balancing act between human misery and saving municipal dollars.

There was an arm of the NLC that gave technical assistance to cities. Because of my presidency, Newark would become the training ground of new ideas and technology. Later, people began to see and hear about the renaissance in Newark and became curious about my leadership, "How was I able to turn Newark around?" was a question that everyone asked. Nelson Mandela would even call from South Africa.

Another benefit of NLC leadership was that I now had Congress and the President's ear on urban issues. I had been a Bill Clinton supporter since he was Governor of Arkansas, and making a bid for the White House in 1992. I was an honorary co-chairman of the New Jersey Clinton/Gore campaign and had made trips to Arkansas in support of the Governor.

In March, 1994, just after I announced my candidacy for re-election, I went to Washington, D.C. to support Clinton's plan to consolidate more than 150 federal job training programs, operating throughout 24 agencies, into one agency. Clinton's proposal would end the fragmentation that shuttled unemployed and underemployed workers back and forth with little hope of any real employment.

I spent the second week in March presiding over the NLC convention, where we drew up a five-point agenda, calling for: passage of anticrime legislation that would create programs for prevention and enforcement; improving jobs-creation programs; putting an end to unfunded federal mandates, economic development and infrastructure improvement. The President agreed with the general thrust of the NLC agenda and asked for our help in passing his national crime legislation. In April three other mayors and I were back at the White House to rally support for the bill.

From the White House Rose Garden, I spoke to about two thousand law enforcement officers and officials from around the nation, urging them to lobby and get behind the passage of the crime bill that would place 100,000 police officers on duty in urban cities to stem violence and crime, it was an idea whose time had come. "Let's not lose another life due to congress's inactivity," I challenged them. At the end of my NLC presidency, President Clinton would thank me and other League members for our support in getting the "toughest and smartest crime bill in the history of our nation" passed.

Back at home, in Newark, I was facing three challengers in the upcoming mayoral election. None of them had ever held an elected office, and none of them was able to raise a sizeable war chest as I was. Still, Dr. Colleen Walton, a podiatrist, Ras Baraka, a school teacher and son of poet/play writer Amiri Baraka and William Payne, head of a non-profit youth mentoring program and the brother of U.S. Representative Donald Payne, all wanted my job.

Dr. Colleen Walton was a highly visible, very loud critic of my administration, although she offered no new ideas on how to improve the city. On one occasion she stood before a powerful group of senior citizens and said, "When I get elected I won't be like Mayor James buying you popcorn, hotdogs, and soda or taking you on trips to buy your votes."

Before Dr. Walton could finish her thought the most respected member in the senior group, Ms. Louise Epperson, jumped out of her seat with a snarl on her face and shouted, "How dare you come in this room and criticize the mayor for caring about us, you should be telling us what you're going to give us, not what you plan to take away from us." The other seniors in the room roared their approval. The next day I visited the site bringing more popcorn, hotdogs, and soda and took the group to Yankee Stadium to a ballgame. After that day, Dr. Walton's campaign for mayor was on mouth-to mouth resuscitation and did not survive.

Ras Baraka took a different approach. He used his youthful appearance and theatrical training to lecture to his supporters that it was time for a change and that poor people should share the wealth of the middle class. Little did Mr. Baraka know, that the middle class was not willing to give up their life style or their perks to help any perceived lower class, nor would poor people come out in support of his candidacy and be a get-out-the-vote (GOTV) factor on Election Day. He was whistling in the dark and simply running a trial balloon.

The debonair William Payne, the brother of my good friend, the late congressman of the 10th congressional district, Donald Payne, was the intellect and egotistical maniac running against me. He was in love with himself and knew everything and everybody. Payne suffered with diarrhea of the mouth. He could have been a formidable foe.

Payne's boisterous campaign rhetoric centered on how bad I was doing as mayor, and how bad the city was doing, and how he would save all of us if elected. Once, I asked his audience three questions. "If I'm doing so bad, and the city is so bad, why did he move from his tree lined suburban home in neighboring Maplewood, New Jersey to run for mayor? Why did Mr. Payne's company, Urban Data Systems, on Frelinghuysen Avenue in Newark, using federal funds, go bankrupt? If he couldn't save his own company how can he save Newark?" Payne had no answers. He had been exposed.

All three of my opponents were on the attack like a pack of wolves. I was running on the slogan, "Let's Continue the Progress," emphasizing the growth in new housing, neighborhood revitalization, crime and auto theft reduction, favorable bond ratings, and downtown commercial development that had created jobs. My opponents proved a valuable lesson I learned in politics that you have to bring something to the table, you have to offer the citizens something and just mere rhetoric will not work.

I was taking advantage of President Bill Clinton's crime bill to hire more police officers, utilizing federal funds. While other mayors were hesitant, I was on the telephone begging President Clinton to send more money to Newark, which he did. I never answered the question of how do you pay for them once you run out of federal dollars? "I will cross that bridge when we get there," was my comment to the members of my cabinet and the city council.

To my surprise, my mortal enemy, *The Star-Ledger,* New Jersey's leading newspaper, endorsed my re-election in its Friday editorial before the voting on Tuesday, May 10th. Expectedly, the citizens of Newark voiced their approval of my record in office by giving me a 23,000 vote or 64% percent majority win.

My leadership continued at the local and national levels. I had created a renaissance in New Jersey's largest city. I had been reelected, and yes, the investigation of my personal and campaign funds continued. The issuance of subpoenas continued. I remained a controversial figure despite my success in improving the quality of life and opportunities in Newark. I was too independent and un-bossed. I was too pro Newark. For these reasons, the media treated me as marked man. I was frustrated, but I would not bend.

State Senator
29th Legislative District

In 1971, just a year shy of her 50th birthday, and in a raucous town election, former Essex County Freeholder Wynona Lipman of Montclair, New Jersey, became the first African American woman elected to the New Jersey State Senate, and for most of her career the only woman in the Senate. A graduate of Talladega College in Alabama, Atlanta University, and Columbia University where she earned her PhD; she also received a Fulbright Fellowship to study at the Sorbonne in Paris. A French major while at Talladega, Lipman had served as a French professor at Morehouse College.

At this time New Jersey was being challenged to find a redistricting plan that would comply with the U.S. Supreme Court decision mandating "one man, one vote." Under the new plan Lipman's safe suburban legislative district was eliminated, and another was carved out where a minority candidate could win within the boundaries of Newark and Hillside, New Jersey.

Thus, to be re-elected, Lipman had to move from tree lined suburban Montclair, where she had lived for more than two decades, to the inner city of Newark, where the scars of the 1967 riots were still visible. Whether the reasons were political, social, or because of a troubled marriage, her Caucasian husband, Matthew Lipman, refused to relocate to Newark. One thing is certain; the move made Lipman's entry into Newark politics more palpable.

For residency purposes, Lipman moved into a luxury high rise apartment, with an indoor swimming pool, at 555 Elizabeth Avenue. Although initially called a "carpetbagger;" her captivating smile and warmth captured the hearts of her new constituents. In 1973 she won re-election as State Senator in the newly created 29th Legislative District.

For the next 26 years Lipman would serve on the state senate budget and appropriations committee fighting for women's rights, minorities and children. In a quiet and dignified manner she was a nonstop workaholic for the 29th district in Trenton and in Newark.

Serving as her South Ward Councilman, I quickly learned to respect, work with and love State Senator Wynona Lipman. She was always a lady and she never bullied anyone or abused her leadership position. Fortunately, God has a master plan for us all, and our most courageous and legendary State Senator died May 9, 1999 after a battle with cancer.

"Let the work I've done speak for me" is the best description for Wynona Lipman. Before the family could give her a well deserved home going celebration, there was a hue and cry in her district to fill her unexpired term. Who would the Democratic Party select? Who would carry on her legacy and best represent the 29th Legislative District? This was the challenge facing party officials.

Almost immediately, the name of Newark Councilman-at-large Donald Tucker surfaced, and he was actively pursuing support from party officials. Other interested candidates, including then Assemblyman, Willie Brown, were fearful of opposing the powerful, highly vociferous and vindictive Donald Tucker. Tucker appeared to have had a lock on being selected as Lipman's replacement.

Initially I had no interest in serving as a dual office holder; my plate was full being mayor of Newark. Some of my key advisors began warning me, though, that the selection of Donald Tucker, my nemesis on the city council, would arm him with "senatorial courtesy," and could hold me and my programs in hostage. "He could block appointments and demand perks in voting for officials that the city needs at the state, county and local levels," was the argument. More than one person said, "Look how unresponsive he has been serving on the Passaic Valley Sewerage Commission; the only people getting jobs are members of his family." After a few more similar salvos from members of the community, I reluctantly became a candidate to replace my idol, the Honorable Dr. Wynona Lipman.

I petitioned the Democratic Party to appoint me, and In June, 1999, I was appointed to the New Jersey Senate to fill out the unexpired term of Senator Wynona Lipman. In November I was elected to the position; re-elected for a full-term in November 2001 and in 2003 representing part of Newark in Essex County and all of the Township of Hillside in Union County.

Because the 29th district was 56% Hispanic in 2003 my former aide, deputy mayor and then Councilman-at-Large Luis Quintana decided to challenge me claiming, "I don't see anything that he's done that's of importance to the constituency." He lost the Newark vote and my margin of victory in Hillside was 8 to 1 to win the 2003 democratic primary and later the general election over two Republican opponents. To the dismay of Councilman Quintana it confirmed that I had the support of all ethnic groups.

My first bills in 1999 as State Senator-Senate Bill #2030 dated June 24, 1999, and Senate Bill #2001-were to "end dual office-holding" in the State of New Jersey. My fellow colleagues in the Senate laughed. "Hey Sharpe, the press might hate you for being a dual officeholder, but I might become one someday; your bill is dead on arrival," stated Senator Diane B. Allen from the 7th Legislative District. Through the Grace of God, I served as State Senator for the 29th legislative district from 1999 until my retirement in 2008.

CHAPTER ELEVEN

Overnight Guest at the White House

"To Dream the Impossible Dream"

As a United States soldier in Europe, elected official and as a world traveler, I have been blessed to be able to visit some of the world's most beautiful, historical and treasured places of interest. Some of the sites and places that I have visited, and will never forget are: the U.S. Arizona Memorial in Hawaii, the Eiffel Tower in Paris, Buckingham Palace in London, the Great Wall and Forbidden City in China, the tragic and man's inhumanity to man concentration camps in Germany, market places in Ghana, the inhumane Slave Port of no return on Gore Island, in Gambia, West Africa, the Hiroshima Museum in Japan; and beautiful cities such as Barcelona, Athens, Sydney, Hong Kong, Tokyo, San Juan, Rio de Janeiro, Munich, Johannesburg and Cape Town in South Africa.

Just thinking of some of these places make my eyes water and my heart race as my mind wrestles with their natural beauty, cultural history, tribulations, and their progress and future challenges. They serve as a reminder of the good, bad and ugly of ancient and modern civilizations. Interestingly enough while we yearn to study the old world, those from the old world want to study the new world. They want to visit and see the richest and most powerful nation on the planet earth, the United States of America.

Oftentimes a visitor's first stop in America is the nation's capitol city, Washington D.C. They want to see our monuments. On many of my trips to Washington D.C., I have seen people lined up for tours of the Washington, Lincoln, Jefferson and Vietnam memorials; some hoping to be lucky enough to visit the White House. I have been one of the lucky ones.

I have visited the White House several times representing the United States Conference of Mayors and the National League of Cities, especially as President of the NLC. Although all of these visits have been memorable, the most memorable have been when I was a participant in meetings with the President and members of his cabinet. I have always considered each of these occasions to be an exciting and intriguing adventure.

Upon entering the White House one must go through the most thorough security procedure imaginable. Security staff will enter your social security number and driver's license into the White House data base learning all there is to know about you. Whether or not you pay your taxes, what accounts you may be delinquent on; your fiscal profile and whether or not you have made threats against anyone will all be revealed. White House Security will be able to determine if you are a dangerous person or a mental risk factor.

I found the White House to be a misleading fortress, and yet so impressive, so beautiful; reminiscent of the lyrics to the song, "See the pyramids along the Nile." Both are mysterious, historical, massive, breathtaking and imposing manmade structures. I never grew tired of visiting the White House representing local government. I was always overwhelmed with the knowledge that I was visiting the residence of the United States President and his family. The structure has 132 grand rooms situated in the middle of a beautifully landscaped 18 acre plot at 1600 Pennsylvania Avenue.

The first floor of the White House is for official business and viewing by the general public. The second floor consists of the private living quarters of the President and his family. Interestingly, while slaves labored with the bricks, mortar, concrete, steel, lumber and exquisite marble to build the White House, once built African Americans were denied entry unless in some bootblack or other menial house servant role. To me this conjures up an image reminiscent of "Nanny," assisting Scarlet O'Hara in the widely acclaimed movie, *Gone with the Wind*.

There existed a quiet understanding among noble men and women of the time, especially from the south, that African Americans were not welcomed in the White House. Fortunately, there were some notable exceptions to this quiet rule or gentleman understanding. During its first century in existence, Frederick Douglass, a free Black man, orator, editor and staunch abolitionist met with President Abraham Lincoln in the White House on three different occasions.

In 1864 when Douglass visited the White House on "Open House Day," celebrating the President's second inaugural, he was initially turned away by the guards; apparently on standing orders that Blacks were to be excluded. Douglas sent the President his business card before departing, and President Lincoln immediately sent for him. Reportedly, President Lincoln asked Douglas how he had liked his inaugural speech, adding, "There is no man in the country whose opinion I value more than yours."

"Mr. Lincoln," Douglas reportedly answered, "That was a sacred effort."

It is also rumored that Lincoln invited Sojourner Truth to the White House the following year to discuss emancipation and presidential policies. Thirty seven years later, in 1901, President Theodore Roosevelt was widely criticized for inviting the most influential Black leader and educator of his time, Booker T. Washington, to the White House for a private dinner. Roosevelt was told "It was not the proper thing to do."

The civil rights era opened the doors for many African Americans and visiting Africans to be invited to the White for various functions. It is believed that the first African American guests invited to sleep in the White House were Sammy Davis, Jr. and his wife, Altovise, in 1973, as guests of President Richard Nixon. They were followed by African American singer, Pearl Bailey, in 1974, a personal friend and overnight guest of First Lady Betty Ford. However, the real termination of White House policy of exclusion, or limiting the number of African Americans as guests to the White House, occurred in the 90s during the Presidency of Bill Clinton.

"Bill" and Hillary Rodham Clinton would place a "welcome mat" at the front door of the White House. He jokingly called it "public housing." Celebrities, politicians, contributors, religious leaders, philanthropists, professionals and just plain ordinary people might receive an invitation to the White House on the President's gold seal stationary. I am sure that many of these invitations were laminated for safekeeping or framed and put on prominent display in the homes of many recipients as a lifelong memento of having been a guest at the White House. That's what I did with mine.

My presidency of the National League of Cities and holding press conferences at the National Press Club in Washington; attending State League Meetings; and being a spokesman for urban America had placed me on the White House Guest List for its annual Christmas Party, hosted by President Clinton and First Lady Hillary Clinton. It was known to be an exciting event and hundreds of elected officials were invited, on various evenings, to bring in the holiday with the first family, and to take a memorable holiday photo with Bill and Hillary.

The food, desert, entertainment and liquor at this event was not bad either, all top shelf. The Clintons knew how to throw a party. How could I ever forget "free" Johnny Walker Red, Chivas Regal and Hennessey served at the White House? I would be the first to bet that if the constitution had allowed for a third term, Bill Clinton would have won in a landslide.

At one of these annual group gatherings at the White House, rumors were flying all around that some supporters had made $100,000 contributions to the Democratic National Committee for the privilege of staying overnight at the White House. A radio commentator had started the rumor on air, whispering, as if he was being discreet, "Just between us, if you want to stay at the White House, bring your checkbook." This had given some the notion that sleeping in the White House, as a guest of the Clintons, came with a price tag.

You can imagine my surprise and complete disbelief when I was told by a White House staff person to expect an invitation from President Bill Clinton and First Lady, Hillary, to be their overnight guest at the White House on Friday, March 11, 1994. I was reluctant to repeat this to others for fear of being embarrassed. I had a mental flashback to the whispered rumor that *only those who had contributed $100,000 or more to the Democratic National Committee would be considered as overnight guests at the White House.* I knew someone was playing a joke on me; there had been many during my tenure in office. Nevertheless, I checked my schedule to confirm that the second week in March 1994, the NLC was holding its convention in Washington. Now, leading up to it, my wife, Mary, and I might spend the most memorable weekend of our lives as overnight guests at the White House.

I couldn't believe that Mary and I would receive an invitation to spend the night at the White House. I knew that we didn't have $100,000 to give to the Democratic National Committee. I knew that we would probably be the poorest people who ever slept in the White House as guests of President Clinton. I thought maybe this was all a dream. *The staff member must have given me the wrong information. This is just another prank. I will just keep quiet, wait and see. This crude joke will go away.*

However, it didn't go away. First, there was a telephone call from a White House Presidential assistant to my municipal office in Newark, extending the invitation. My executive secretary, Ms. Deborah Moore, received the call and behaved as though she had just won the New Jersey Lottery; she was so excited. The office erupted in near hysteria. Of course, I immediately replied, yes, to the invitation. The White House Assistant said that a formal invitation would follow in the mail.

Sitting in a chair in my office, and staring at the wall, I thought of my childhood days living in a one room cold water flat on Howard Street, with a pot bellied stove smack in the center of the room and an outhouse in the backyard; having only one pair of pants, sneakers and socks with holes in them, and more often hungry than not. That was a long time ago, but some things are never forgotten. Some things are meant to be remembered to remind you of where you've been and how far you've come. Now, I was being graciously offered an invitation for an overnight stay at the White House. I was excited and terrified at the same time.

I wondered how I would break the news to Mary, my non-political wife. "Thank you, but no thank you" was her routine response to every political invitation. I also reflected that her childhood experience in South Carolina had been no different from mine. We both shared a humble upbringing, and had never dreamed of ever visiting the White House. It was not a mind set for poor Blacks like us. Now I wondered if I had made a mistake accepting the invitation, which was clearly for husband and wife. My customary, solo political appearance would not be acceptable.

Mary hated politics and wasn't particularly fond of politicians. Her upbringing had been in a family that did not trust the political system. Our marriage and my subsequent election to public office did little to change her thinking. While accepting my newly elected position and duties, she never accepted a role in the campaign, the elected office, or had any involvement with the army of people who interacted in a political office. Her favorite comments were, "I didn't get elected you did," and "I am not your secretary. Get an answering machine. I don't have to entertain your political folks; take care of your business at the office not in our home."

Mary limited any obligatory political husband and wife appearances to a bare minimum. Without any thought of compromising, she was totally uncomfortable with anyone drinking, swearing, and talking loud or smoking in her presence. Only because she was my wife did she tolerate my elected position. She continuously asked me, "When are you going to quit? You can't win in politics, you only survive."

Upon arriving home that evening, I calmly told Mary that we had been invited to the White House as guests of the first family and that I had accepted for both of us. I waited for the response, dreading the prospect of being placed in the embarrassing position of having to call the White House and offer our regrets.

"Really?" Mary asked. "You mean to say that we have been invited to the White House?"

"That's right," I said. Then all hell broke loose. Mary, started rambling "Oh, no. What will I wear? I need a new gown. That means new shoes, too," Mary rattled on and on. Then she began to pace the floor; "My hair! I have to get my hair done and nails, too. I need to make an appointment. Sharpe, you just can't wear anything to the White House," she had said.

Mary suddenly became lost in excitement and a world of things she had to do. It was one of the few times that a politically motivated social event brought utter joy to my wife. To her, a stay at the White House was not political, but a once-in-a-lifetime opportunity to experience the place where so much of America's history had been made. Mary told me after it was all over that she had kept a diary of our visit to the White House, something she had never done before; she never wanted to forget our visit.

From this experience, I learned that life's most treasured memories sometimes come from events that are unplanned and unexpected. Our White House invitation meant so much to us. We didn't know how to plan for or what we would do at the White House. We could only wait and see. We were giddy with anticipation, like two high school kids preparing for our senior prom, not knowing what to expect.

On the evening of March 11th, Secret Service Agents met Mary and me at the Washington Hilton Tower Hotel to drive us to the White House. We arrived there around 5:30 p.m. and were taken by executive staff members from the first floor, where groups were touring the public areas of the White House, to the President's living quarters on the second floor. It was pointed out to us that the White House has eight guest rooms; only two share the second floor with the first family's bedrooms.

With the passes that were issued to us, distinguishing guests from public tourists, we had access to the section of the White House that was referred to simply as the President's Living Quarters. We were told that we could visit any room on the second floor with the exception of the closed President's suite, reserved for him and his family. An escort guided us to the elevator that would take us to the second floor.

Mary and I were assigned use of the prestigious Lincoln Bedroom and study, and bath which was located at the opposite end of the hall from the President's bedroom. The room is jokingly referred to as the bedroom Lincoln "never" slept in and rightfully so. Lincoln did use the room, but not as a bedroom. He used the room as an office during his stay at the White House. It is kept in the same state as it was in 1863. To sleep on the same floor as the President and all the previous presidents made the occasion even more memorable.

On our way to the Lincoln bedroom, where our luggage had been delivered, we decided to poke around a little bit; We looked into Chelsea's bedroom, which was located just outside of the President's private suite, and the President's study. We couldn't believe that we had a free rein in the President's home. Mary and I agreed that Chelsea's room was not unlike any other teenage girl's room, warm and charming. We could sense real family love, sharing, and caring by the pictures and personal effects in her room. Like most young ladies her age, there were wonderful dolls and stuffed animals galore.

Strolling around on the second floor, I was afraid to walk on the spotless, simply immaculate, light beige carpeting with my black shoes. It was like no one had ever walked on the carpet before, and I knew this was not possible. Everything was immaculate, clean, fresh, and in perfect order. It was simply breathtaking; a fairytale environment.

Mary and I found the view from the balconies and windows just as breathtaking. We could see the monuments, ponds, gardens and flowers all adding to the charm and beauty of the home. Even the wallpaper was exquisite, adorned with historical prints and landscapes. I was told that every President had made some change to the White House that reflected his own personality or needs; John F. Kennedy had added a swimming pool, Bill Clinton a jogging track.

Once in the "Lincoln bedroom" where Lincoln had signed the Emancipation Proclamation, Mary and I carefully explored the room, touching and inspecting every item. We had been told that all of the bedrooms had working fireplaces. A button on the wall was to be pressed if we needed any assistance with anything. We still could not believe that we were really in the White House. I sat down at the desk and started writing a speech, inspired by the thought of writing on Lincoln's desk, in Lincoln's room (I would later learn that the desk, which was originally in Lincoln's summer home, was not, in fact, the one on which he had signed the Emancipation Proclamation).

The Clintons hosted a reception in the Yellow Oval Room, where guests got to mingle with each other before dinner: former Governor William Winter and his wife, Elise, of Jackson, Mississippi; Philanthropists Millard and Linda Fuller of Habitat for Humanity International, in Americus, Georgia; the Rev. James G. Lumpkin, Sr. and his wife, Jean, from North Little Rock, Arkansas, with their daughter, Mickey, and her husband, and the Rev. Anthony Mangun of Alexandria, Louisiana, were among the prestigious guests. The President and the First Lady arrived and moved about the room, warmly greeting everyone.

Following the reception we enjoyed a buffet dinner in the State Dining Room. The beautifully decorated table had sumptuous offerings of shrimp, roast beef, turkey, salmon, chicken, ham, salads and dessert choices that could rival any of those ever served at the, now closed, but once world famous Mama Leone's Restaurant in New York City.

After dinner we were led downstairs to the family movie theater, located under the East Terrace, between the east wing and the main building, to watch the made-for-cable biblical movie "Abraham." First Lady, Hillary, graciously served soft drinks, candy and popcorn. She was the perfect hostess.

Before retiring for the evening the overnight guests gathered on the second floor, to listen to Mickey Mangum play the piano and sing, and Millar Fuller recite a poem. At the end of the evening we all stood in a circle and held hands while the Rev. James Lumpkin led us in prayer I was very impressed that the Clinton's started and ended each activity with a prayer. It didn't take the presence of the Reverend Jesse Jackson or the Evangelist, Billy Graham, prayer was a part of the Clinton's personal recognition of the importance of God, and I thought it was wonderful.

After the closing prayer, the guests started to move toward their respective rooms, engaging in conversation along the way. President and Mrs. Clinton walked with the group, chatting away with their guests. Once on the second floor, Mrs. Clinton headed for her quarters, while the President walked guests to their rooms, turning off lights in the hallway along the way. Mary and I lingered a little, not wanting the evening to end. Governor William Winter and his wife Elise were assigned to the Queen's bedroom, directly across from our room. The other four couples were assigned to guest rooms on the third floor. Finally, all of the goodnights had been said and we retired to the Lincoln bedroom.

With all of the excitement of being in the White House, and sleeping in the Lincoln bedroom I was prepared to stay awake all night from anxiety. However, after a brief debate of whether the mattress was stuffed with feathers or cotton, both Mary and I fell sound asleep. It had been a long and memorable day and neither of us had realized how exhausted we were.

Upon rising the next morning the overnight guests had breakfast in the beautiful sunny glass enclosed solarium on the third floor of the White House. The walk to the solarium revealed a beautiful, personal, pictorial biography of the first family on the walls. The President greeted us in the solarium already prepared for his regular morning jog. Before departing everyone extended best wishes to each other. The President and the First Lady were warm, hospitable, and congenial throughout the visit. They were real down to earth people. I never felt their title or power only their warmth and sincerity.

I later learned that our invite had nothing to do with my title as president of the National League of Cities, or being the Mayor of New Jersey's largest city, Newark. I was invited because of the friendship that had developed between me and the Clintons when I joined others to travel to Little Rock, Arkansas, shared breakfast in a local diner and gave political support to someone who, like me, stayed under attack.

The Clintons were just like regular people, they really made us feel welcome in their home. There is a real sense of family about them. They were just Bill and Hillary. It was clear to me that although they remembered the big things in life, the Clintons, also, never forgot the little things.

Under Bill and Hillary's tenure, the White House was referred to as "public housing." It belonged to the citizens of the United States of America, and everyone was welcome. They demonstrated a "Yawl come back" attitude, without any pomp and circumstance. Mary and I will never forget our overnight stay at the White House. Bill and Hillary Clinton know how to make people feel comfortable, and right at home. Mary and I signed their guest book for 1994. Our visit was now official.

CHAPTER TWELVE

Political Collaborations

I t's funny how some little things that happen in life can have a profound effect on you, sometimes without you even knowing it. This brings to mind two life experiences that were rather troubling for me. The first occurred at my alma mater, South Side High School. Clowning around in my science class one day saying, "I'm going to blow this laboratory up," to the roaring laughter of my classmates, my teacher, Dr. Rectenwald, kept me after class and asked me to fill a basin with water. He then asked me to rapidly stir both hands in the water. I splashed freely making a big mess like a baby sitting in a tub of bath water.

After removing my hands, Dr. Rectenwald asked, "What do you notice about the water?" I answered, "Nothing." Dr. Rectenwald said, "You're right. Just as the water, after being disrupted, returned to a peaceful tranquility after you removed your hands, no trace of your involvement. That's how your life as a class clown will be remembered; no traces, no involvement, no history, and no making waves. Is that what you want out of a precious God-given life," he asked?

His remarks caught me by surprise. I was ready for a shouting match, more detention or even a fight. I was not ready for someone caring about me. "Sharpe," he gleamed, "I suggest that you find ways to be remembered in life. Find ways to make yourself and your family proud. I don't want a clown in my class," he said. From that day on I became a South Side High honor roll student.

The second incident occurred many years later while I was a soldier in Schweinfurt, Germany. I was being reprimanded by my southern army platoon leader, Lieutenant Andrew Perkins, for not giving him a timely salute acknowledging his presence and respecting his rank.

He called me to attention, came nose to nose with me, eyeball to eyeball and said, "Sharpe, you need to remember that you are saluting the uniform and the rank, not necessarily the man in the uniform. Do you get that?" He went on to say, "I don't give a hill of beans whether you like me or not, but you will honor the rank and the uniform. You will honor the men and women who spilled their blood wearing this uniform, do you understand?" Emphatically, I shouted, "Yes Sir! Yes Sir!"

Decades later, as a Mayor and State Senator, those two incidents with their cerebral message are deeply entrenched in my mind. They guide my thinking and dictate my day-to- day actions on how I treat others. My position has presented a real challenge on how to deal with the inherent power of the office.

Many people believe that with success come power, influence and sometimes unwanted attention. I always remember the monkey theory, *the higher you climb in life, the more your ass is exposed.* As chief executive officer for the largest city in the state of New Jersey, vice chairman of the State Senate Budget and Appropriations Committee, presiding over a budget more than $30 billion, past President of the National League of Cities (NLC), Trustee for the United States Conference of Mayors (USCM), Board of Directors for the International City/County Management Association (ICMA), Vice President of the New Jersey Conference of Mayors, Executive Board Member of the New Jersey League of Municipalities, a college professor/administrator and an athlete, I have encountered countless people seeking my assistance to advance their personal, political and/or business agenda.

I had no political or social relationship with many of the people seeking my assistance. Most of them were not even acquaintances. Often the people seeking "access" contacted me by appointmet, e-mail, letter or telephone. Sometimes they simply walked into my office unannounced. They represented an illustrious list of elected, non-elected officials and philanthropists. People like Nelson Mandela; Ronald Reagan, Rev. Al Sharpton, Robert Kennedy, Jimmy Carter; George Bush; Rev. Jesse Jackson, Sr.; Bill Bradley; Jim Florio; the first African American at the stock exchange, Travis Bell; the Rev. Dr. Leon Sullivan with his "Sullivan Principles" for South Africa, as an alternative to complete disinvestment; Philanthropists, Ray Chambers, Doris Duke and many others.

I knew it was simply a case of saluting the office and title, not necessarily the man in the office. I had no illusions about this. Once out of office the letters will cease and your telephone rings less and your car does not move when you are sitting in the back seat.

Still, when requests did not conflict with my personal goals and philosophy, or that of the Sharpe James administration, I would bend over backwards to communicate, cooperate, and provide these people with some level of assistance. It had to be a mutual agenda for improving the quality of life and opportunities in Newark as well, though. The ideas or plans had to be positive or make sense.

Fortunately, in these cases one's personality precedes him. My desire to improve the quality of life in Newark was public knowledge. My goal was to address acute poverty, create jobs, promote public safety, build affordable housing, provide adequate health care, and to address a failing educational system. I wore the "Scarlet Letter" for the power-less, faceless, and indigenous population. I was a people person. I could never forget that I was selected (at the historical 1970 Black & Puerto Rican Convention) and elected by the citizens of Newark.

Moreover, I was haunted by Matthews' 25:40 ecclesiastical mandate: "What you do for the least of my people, you do for me." I saw helping others as a way of creating a domino effect in promoting public service. Truthfully, by helping others I believed I was, in actuality, helping my city. In order to better serve my constituents I needed to create and interact with supporters at the local, county, state, and federal levels of government and business. To be successful, I had to recognize our shrinking boundaries and operate within the framework of a local and global economy. It was extremely important to identify foreign supporters through existing International Sister City programs.

The James administration placed a high priority on creating and strengthening governmental, public and private partnerships. This initiative led to changing the image and quality of life in Newark. Unlike former Mayor Gibson, who was somewhat reluctant to seek outside advice, I did not believe that Newark's problems could be solved from within our own boundaries. I was never too smart or too proud to seek outside help.

Following are some of the leaders I sought to collaborate with in moving Newark from urban blight to urban bright. It was not about personalities, it was about a mutually beneficial political agenda; sometimes it worked and sometimes it did not. My philosophy was to err on the side of trying to collaborate as opposed to becoming a micromanagement maniac.

Bill Bradley For United States Senate -1978

Bill Bradley had it all. He was tall. Women found him handsome. He had a brilliant mind, was a star athlete and rich. He was elected to the United States Senate in his first bid and was predicted to become President one day. Unfortunately, Bill Bradley lost it all. *For the emperor has no clothes.*

In 1978, I received a telephone call from retired Baltimore Colts and New York Jets Pro football great, Johnny Sample, who was now my nemesis on the tennis court. He said that Bill Bradley, a great friend of his, who had participated in summer basketball leagues to assist minority students, wanted to meet with me. "Bill hung around and mixed well with the students," Sample had said

"Sharpe, he's really a nice guy. We call him 'Dollar Bill.' He will be calling you," Sample said. Shortly thereafter, I did receive a call from Bill Bradley, and he asked if I would join him for lunch at the Treat Restaurant on Park Place in Newark. Quite frankly, the only thing I knew about Bill Bradley was that he had played basketball for the New York Knicks. I knew nothing about his outstanding performance at Princeton University or in Tokyo as a member of our 1964 gold-winning U.S. Olympic basketball team. I didn't even remember how he looked, nor did I know if I would like him personally.

I arrived at the Treat restaurant early and took a seat where I could see everyone entering the restaurant. I had decided that the first really tall, White guy that walked in would have to be Bill Bradley. So after a parade of 5 to 6 footers had entered and left, the door opened and this 6'5" slim and businesslike White guy walked in. I immediately walked up to him, extended my hand and said, "Hi Bill, welcome to Newark," as if I had known him all my life.

"Sharpe, thank you for agreeing to meet with me," Bill said as he extended his hand, giving me a warm smile. We took a table near the window overlooking beautiful Military Park. Over tuna sandwiches, Bill told me that then-Essex County Democratic Chairman, Harry Lerner, had denied his request to be the party's nominee for U.S. senator from New Jersey, to oppose the Republican incumbent, Clifford Case.

"In fact," Bradley said, "Lerner insulted me by suggesting that in the eyes of the public, I am still nothing but a tall, rich White jock, running around in short pants and not electable." Bradley then said that he had heard that Sharpe James was a campaign workaholic, very visible, loyal and persuasive. He wanted me to join his campaign organization and sell Bill Bradley to the public.

I sat there at the table with Bill staring at me with penetrating, owlish, focused steel brown eyes waiting for an answer. He did not move but sat rigid like a statue. "Bill," I said, "if Johnny Sample says you are a great guy, you got my vote; Johnny is a tough guy to please. I'm on board."

A more relaxed Bill, now wearing a broad smile on his face, extended his hand for a handshake. "Thank you, and remember you can always count on me," he said. "I value your friendship more than just a campaign."

Of course, I would support him and get people I knew to support him, but there was a price I had to pay. At that time Gov. Brendan Byrne had nominated me to become a board member of the New Jersey Sports and Exhibition Authority (NJSEA). Gov. Byrne, hearing about my meeting with Bradley, called me down to the governor's mansion and told me that it would not be wise for me to support Bill Bradley against the party's choice, Richard Leone. If I did, I could not expect my name to advance to the State Senate to be considered for membership on the board of the NJSEA. I was given an ultimatum; I had to drop my support of Bill Bradley or my nomination was in trouble.

Essex County Democratic Chairman Harry Lerner also-called and said, "Sharpe, I hope it's not true that you are supporting that basketball jock Bill Bradley over the party's choice; he certainly can't win but you could lose," he said. "We are not playing basketball, we are playing politics," he said. "Remember, Bill Bradley is just a basketball player, they come and go every year, jocks are a dime a dozen," he roared.

Thus, when I agreed to help Bill Bradley, my invites for tennis matches with Gov. Byrne soon ended, and my pending appointment to the NJSEA was placed in the wastepaper basket. Gov. Byrne made it clear to me that I was playing on the wrong team. The Democratic Party had put the squeeze on me. I could play on only one team, "the Democratic line team."

I had made my choice. I would continue to support Bill Bradley, even if it meant my name would be dropped from consideration for board membership of the NJSEA; and that I would receive fewer, if any, favors from the Democratic Party. I felt that Bradley's qualifications, his vision for a better New Jersey, and his attractiveness as a candidate—especially when compared to the party's nominee, Leone, or, on the Republican side, Clifford Case and his challenger Jeffrey Bell—were far superior, and that he warranted a chance to run.

There was something about Bradley—a brilliant Rhodes Scholar, an athlete, and yet, he was like the man next door. When I first got in his humble, nondescript car, with banana peels, old apple cores, old clothes and other objects strewn about the car seats and floor, front and back, I knew Bill Bradley was our common candidate, the guy you could go next door and borrow a cup of sugar from.

Bill Bradley had Johnny Sample, Bill Russell, Willis Reed, and Earl (the Pearl) Monroe speak highly of him. He was always viewed as the "All-American Guy," the team player, the guy who would run down on the fast break and rather than try to make the basket, would pass it off for an uncontested lay-up, the ultimate in teamwork. He didn't care whether he scored; he wanted the team to win. His 1976 book, *Life on the Run,* made the best-seller list, and moved him toward a career in politics. I saw Newark, New Jersey and America winning with Bill Bradley as our United States Senator.

Since Bradley was an unknown political entity, politically, we put photographs of him with local politicians and celebrities on flyers with his platform message. Palm cards featured me and Moe Layton—a graduate of Newark's Weequahic High School and professional basketball player with the Phoenix Suns—with Dollar Bill Bradley in the middle. We went statewide with that flyer, which always had the same message, but carried a different picture according to the locality. In that way we were able to gain recognition for Bradley and galvanize local support statewide.

Bradley proved to be a tireless campaigner. He campaigned as though he were making a fast break on the basketball court. He went everywhere, smiled, shook hands and autographed everything. One thing Bill Bradley could do was walk. And he would walk. The fact that he was a basketball player created a great deal of excitement among the public, something that became evident to me the first time that we met at the Treat Restaurant in downtown Newark.

At one campaign stop a woman, wearing a halter top, came running up to Bill with a felt-tip pen in her hand. She pulled down her blouse and asked him to autograph her breast. Embarrassed, he nervously took the pen and wrote, "Bill" on her left breast. I said to myself, "This, is going to be an exciting campaign."

Although Bradley was the underdog, he beat Leone in the primary, getting 61 percent of the votes. His chance of winning was good against the lesser-known, Jeffrey Bell, who had defeated Senator Case in the Republican primary. We were cocky and ready for an all-out fight. We were ready to give the opponent a New York Knicks fast break and a slam-dunk.

Bradley's platform was a liberal one. He had one main issue: cutting taxes. Bradley also supported passage of the Equal Rights Amendment and the right for women to have abortions, and he was against capital punishment. He won the race against Jeffrey Bell with 56 percent of the votes, becoming the youngest Senator at age 35.

From the basketball court to the U.S. Senate chambers on his first try for public office—not bad. After the election I went looking for Essex County Democratic Chairman, Harry Lerner; I wanted to tell him face-to-face that the "White Jock" had won.

After the campaign was all over, I was proud that I had helped Bill Bradley become a U.S. Senator. He selected Newark for his victory party. Standing in front of the same restaurant, in Newark's Military Park, where we had first met, and with over 5,000 supporters and well-wishers, he thanked me personally by calling me from the crowd to come up and join him, Earl Monroe, Dave DeBusschere and other dignitaries on the makeshift stage. The stage looked like it would collapse at any moment. When Bradley introduced me, he said, "I want those on this stage who were with me from the beginning to be recognized. Thank you, Sharpe. And I will be there for you," he said.

Bill Bradley rewarded me by opening a satellite office in Newark. His main office was in Union, right off Route 22, serving the entire state of New Jersey, but, his only urban office was in Newark, utilizing my Little City Hall at 1072 Bergen Street with the staff that I had selected for him. The first minority person Bill hired was Yvette Richardson, one of my former council aides. We opened all his mail, read all his correspondence and gave him recommendations on how to best service the urban community. He sought my advice on the recruitment and hiring of minorities and other state and national issues. NBA star Willis Reed and I were often invited to his home in Denver, New Jersey, for dinner with him and his wife, a professor at Montclair State University.

Once Bill was elected to the U.S. Senate; and once he began hobnobbing in the nation's capitol with the powerful, rich and famous he was no longer comfortable operating in an urban environment, even on a limited basis. It did not take long before I noticed a change in him. The cozy relationship that he had with Black professional athletes and celebrities did not transfer to a rapport with the average Black citizen, with whom he seemed rather aloof.

Bradley soon became even less likely to listen to local politicians. The smiling, jovial, handshaking "Dollar Bill" morphed into an academician concerned more with passing his and Senator Dick Gephardt's 1983 "fair tax" bill and issues on the environment. He had no time or interest in welfare issues, crime, drugs or other urban problems. He wanted to improve the universe not cities and neighborhoods. These were not glamorous issues that required scholarly answers.

I was not surprised when Bill Bradley decided to close his South Ward neighborhood office on Bergen Street. Subsequently, he became predictably slow in hiring minorities for his Senate staff. The closing of his Newark office was the first signal of a changing relationship between Bradley and me. The next was in 1983, when he ignored the pleas of Democratic Party officials to go to Chicago to help Harold Washington become the city's first Black mayor. I received a telephone call from Sen. Ted Kennedy, asking me to speak to Bradley about supporting Harold. "Sharpe, can't you talk to him," Ted asked in a pleading voice.

I arranged a breakfast meeting with Bradley at the Hilton Hotel Bentley's restaurant in downtown Newark. "Bill, I got a call from

Senator Kennedy," I said. "He told me that you are the only leading Democrat who will not go to Chicago to help Harold Washington in his run for mayor."

"So what," Bill replied. "What's the big issue," he asked?

"The party believes that he is highly-qualified, and could be elected the first Black mayor of Chicago," I replied. "It's about history," I said.

Bill put his fork down, wiped his mouth with his napkin and looking me dead in the eyes, said, "Sharpe it's a local issue. I don't get involved in local matters. Let's change the subject."

"Local," I shouted back at him. "It's not a local issue. Ted and the party believe he can change the quality of life in Chicago overnight and clean up its image," I stared him down. "You've got to be a part of this effort. Your presence could make a difference."

I impressed upon Bill that this was a national issue: Chicago, with the problems it had had in the past, Dr. Martin Luther King's coming North and saying that what he saw in Mississippi and Alabama didn't measure up to what he experienced in Chicago. I told Bradley that he was being laughed at on the streets of New Jersey; people thought he was too squeaky clean. They were calling him "Mr. Lysol," antiseptic, and here was an opportunity to prove them wrong.

I was unrelenting in letting Bill know that he was making a mistake. I had begun to question Bradley's posture as a remote intellectual in the Senate and his reluctance to become involved in community affairs. I warned him of the possibility of losing minority votes if he did not show his support for Harold Washington.

Bill looking somewhat angrily at me remained silent for awhile. Finally he said, "Sharpe, I still don't see why all the fuss about my going to Chicago." His response was cold.

"You are missing the boat," I said. "People in New Jersey and elsewhere want to see, feel and touch the real Bill Bradley, the one they saw racing down the court making lay ups; the real New York Knicks Bradley. They don't care about how many books you write, they want you to be more visible."

"Stop it, stop it," Bill said still chewing his scrambled eggs. "I don't agree, but if it will make you, Ted and the party happy I will go, but don't blame me if Washington loses," he said.

Reluctantly, Bradley reconsidered and went to Chicago. Harold Washington won, and not only did Bradley come back at the end of that campaign and talk about Mayor Harold Washington's victory, he took full credit for it. Suddenly it became something to add to his resume; a topic for banquet speeches. He put aside his fair tax and Olympic speeches. Almost overnight he had become Mr. Civil Rights. "Bill now had jungle fever!"

But "Dollar Bill" was never a civil rights leader. We would soon find ourselves at odds with each other again. He was expected to win big in his reelection bid for the Senate in 1990, and then announce his candidacy for President in 1992. But he blew it.

First, in the 1990 campaign Bradley's opponent, then-unknown former Morris County Freeholder, Christine Todd Whitman, a presumed GOP sacrificial lamb, repeatedly challenged Bradley to defend then-Governor Jim Florio's record tax hike, the hottest topic of the day. The State GOP made this tax hike a major campaign issue.

Bradley simply refused to defend or question Florio's tax hike. He apparently considered himself too big and too important to dwell on state party politics. He ignored the questions and rambled on about issues he deemed important. Even my nonpolitical wife, Mary, kept asking me, "Why doesn't Bradley answer the questions? He's making her look good," she had said.

Meanwhile, Whitman never missed an opportunity to give a passionate, clear and detailed analysis on the hardships resulting from the Florio tax package. She came off as attractive, articulate, charismatic and knowledgeable. While Bill was somewhere on cloud nine planning his run for the presidency in two years.

At the same time, Bradley turned his back on the minority community, which he had always supported and which supported him. Even though he was invisible in minority circles and never championed urban issues of welfare, crime, drugs and housing, he was still our beloved "Dollar Bill." He began to take the minority community for granted and decided that, even with a 12 million dollar campaign war chest, he would not open up a campaign headquarters in the state's largest city-or any other New Jersey urban community.

In his 1990 Senate race Bill decided to go after suburban Whites with zeal worthy of a presidential campaign. He was testing his suburban popularity. He was testing his run for President. The $12 million dollars did not deliver the knockout White suburban votes as Bradley had expected. They went to Whitman.

Even though Bradley outspent Whitman twelve to one, and even with the advantage of name recognition and incumbency, Bradley barely won with a slim margin of 70,000 votes, or three percent. Those 70,000 votes came from the minority communities that he had totally ignored. He won through the back door. Whitman in losing was a winner and would carry her momentum to become the first female governor of New Jersey in 1994.

Perhaps one reason Bradley decided to retire from the Senate in 1996 was that he really saw politics as an academic adventure divorced from everyday life issues and political compromises. Bill was never a great speaker. He was too academic, too abstract, monotonous and boring. He put people to sleep. He enjoyed writing and interpreting his Olympic play (How the Russians did not know that he knew a little Russian) on the courts rather than dealing with real people and real issues.

I also recall that Bradley alienated himself from the state Democratic Party by being unapproachable and aloof in the appointments he made to the courts and in his choice for United States Attorney. Every county chairman was angry at him for making unilateral decisions. Essex County Democratic Chairman, Tom Giblin, once asked me to speak to Bill Bradley about a pending appointment.

"This guy is nuts and doesn't listen to anyone. Can't you tell him that he is part of the Democratic Party? We have to live with his appointees. Sharpe, tell him to come down from the clouds," Giblin had pleaded. Unfortunately, the pleas fell upon deaf ears. Bradley never did come down from the clouds and most of the time remained isolated from the rest of the party.

While having lunch at the New Jersey Performing Arts Center with former United States Senator Robert Torricelli, a guest brought up the subject of Bill Bradley, asking "What's Bill Bradley doing now since leaving politics?" Senator Torricelli dropped his head, then started shaking his head and said, "You know I could never figure that guy out. Bill was a strange individual, you could never figure out where he was coming from, he was a loner. I tried to communicate with him and failed. I wish him all the luck in the world," Bob had said.

I don't think Bradley was ever happy as a U.S. senator. He didn't like fundraising and grew tired of handshaking and smiling. Nonetheless, on December 3, 1998 he was the luncheon keynote speaker at the National Congress of Cities conference in Kansas City, Missouri. Backstage, prior to his speech, he asked to speak with me, a past president of this largest organization of local elected officials. "Sharpe, I need your help. I am going to run for President in 2000. I think the time is ripe," he said. It was obvious that he expected the same resounding yes I had given him twenty-two years ago when he ran for U.S. Senator.

I had never gotten over the fact that as a Senator Bill Bradley had not taken a stand on pressing urban issues, such as racial profiling. Instead he became an academic recluse, divorced from real people and the real world. On the other hand, Vice President Al Gore, who was also expected to run for president in 2000, was viewed as an important player in creating the urban agenda established under President Bill Clinton's administration. The Clinton/Gore administration had established itself as a partner with Newark in attacking major urban problems such as fighting crime, creation of jobs, more affordable housing and health care.

I advised Bradley that I was going to support Vice President Al Gore. "He's the party's choice," I told him. I could only wish him good luck. Bill was speechless and turned beet red. He looked hurt. He never spoke to me again.

The next week at a press conference in Newark, at the New Community Corporation (NCC), with only a handful of selected supporters and his family in attendance, Bradley announced what everyone had been expecting for a long time: the kickoff of the Bill Bradley for President Campaign was on.

Thus, when the Democratic candidates debated at the Apollo Theater in February 2000, Gore turned the focus on me, when the question of racial profiling and Bradley's inaction came up. At the press conference, I was asked to come on stage and talk about what Bill Bradley knew about racial profiling. I told the truth about Bill's apathy regarding local and urban issues. Sitting with the Republican leadership, at their invitation, was none other than Cory Booker who wanted to be mayor of Newark. He followed me to the podium and voiced his support for Bradley.

Guess who came to Newark to walk the streets in support of Cory Booker during the 2002 mayoral campaign between me and Booker? Bill Bradley. This was payback for my telling the truth and supporting Al Gore and for Booker's loyalty to Bradley. When the Democratic primary smoke cleared Al Gore was the party's choice to run for President in 2000.

Bradley had lost to Al Gore in the primary. I had lost Bill Bradley as a friend. "The emperor (Bill Bradley) has no clothes."

Ted Kennedy For President -1980

Ted Kennedy's 1980 campaign for President had started poorly. He failed to inspire the nation when announcing his candidacy and his CBS interview with Roger Mudd had been a disaster. He had no subsequent idea of why he wanted to be President, other than the fact that he was born a Kennedy. He also proved that he was not his brother, John Fitzgerald Kennedy.

Furthermore, the tragedy at Chappaquiddick still hung over Ted like a scarlet letter. He was viewed as a playboy. Still, with this baggage he wanted to rescue the nation from what many Americans believed to be an incompetent President, Jimmy Carter. Ted promised to make America better. He was willing to take the risk. I was willing to support him. I answered his call.

In April 1980 the South Ward Democratic organization called a meeting with Mayor Ken Gibson to clarify who we were going to support for President. Gibson said that he was going to announce that the City of Newark was supporting Jimmy Carter for reelection, and most of the South Ward, indeed most of Newark, went along with Gibson. But many, like me, felt Kennedy offered a better urban program.

Mayor Gibson, sitting at the head of the table shook his head. "I, and my people, am going to support Jimmy Carter. I had dinner with him, I like him," he had said. Ken did not allow for any other discussion or comments, he just kept shaking his head defiantly.

Ken Gibson bragged to us that he had been a house guest of Jimmy Carter's, and that Jimmy Carter was a folksy politician. It is true that Carter's homespun quality had helped him win Black support (particularly in the South) in 1976, and without it he would not have won the presidency. Carter had been good for the city. His administration developed the nation's first comprehensive urban policy. Under the Department of Housing and Urban Development's various programs, it targeted federal funds to provide aid for the urban poor. Federal funds flowed into Newark. National politicians viewed Gibson, a former president of the U.S. Conference of Mayors, as a spokesman for urban America, and they catered to him.

Despite the fact that certain localities, like Newark, had received an influx of federal money in the months the preceding 1980 election, the Carter Administration had begun gutting domestic programs to balance the budget, while preserving military expenditures. Black unemployment was double the national rate, and inflation was high, at 13 percent.

Kennedy's voting record in the Senate was consistently liberal; he supported spending for social programs at higher levels than the Carter Administration proposed. Besides, Ted always had that Kennedy mystique about him. Other than the Rev. Dr. Martin Luther King, Jr., Ted Kennedy was probably the most eloquent speaker I'd ever heard on civil rights, human rights, and overall, the dignity of man. Kennedy spoke with compassion, as opposed to Carter's matter-of-fact Southern drawl. With Carter there was no grabbing, hugging or engaging you.

Ken Gibson continued to insist on our support for Carter. I left the South Ward meeting angry and completely disillusioned. My first break with Gibson, my mentor, would come when I decided that I would oppose his choice for President and form a coalition for Ted Kennedy. Along with county freeholders, Jerry Greco and Pat Sebold, I co-chaired the Essex County Committee for Ted Kennedy in 1980 while I was councilman-at-large.

Kennedy's son, Ted, Jr., sister-in-law Ethel, Robert Kennedy's widow, and the Rev. Ralph Abernathy paid a visit to Newark in the summer of 1980. I gave them a hearty welcome and an endorsement at my Little City Hall on Bergen Street. My staff had cleaned up the street, cleaned up the office, cleaned up everything. Unfortunately, we overlooked an important detail. Ted, Jr. said he had to use the bathroom. After a few minutes the law enforcement agent accompanying the Kennedy entourage came up to me and whispered, "Mr. James is there any toilet tissue in the office?" I learned a valuable lesson from that experience; when preparing for guests, "It's still the little things in life that count."

I was taking them on a tour of the University of Medicine and Dentistry facilities. We had started down the street in my car, I was driving Ethel, Ted, Jr. and the Rev. Abernathy when a Black policeman, Officer Stewart (we had graduated from high school together), pulled up on a motorcycle and said, "Sharpe, where are you going?"

"I have Ethel Kennedy, the Rev. Abernathy and Ted Kennedy, Jr. with me," I said. "We're going to UMDNJ to tour the facilities."

"Oh, fine," he said. "Follow me." He moved to the front and turned on his siren and lights.

Ethel turned to me and said, "Isn't that nice that he's going to give you a police escort?"

The Rev. Abernathy, with all the elegance of an Academy Award winner, said, "Oh, no, darling. He's not doing it for the Councilman; he's doing it for the Kennedys." Abernathy had such class and wit.

Later in the campaign Ted Kennedy, himself, visited Newark. Understandably, given Newark's reputation and the Kennedy family history, Ted Kennedy was fearful for his life. We chose Springfield Avenue, one of the primary streets affected by the riots of 1967, for the major walk with the candidate. Sharpshooters were perched all over the rooftops. Helicopters were flying overhead. Kennedy wore a bulletproof vest. Prior to seeing him put it on, I had never known how uncomfortable the vest was. It made Kennedy appear larger, and it made him sweat profusely.

As we were walking down Springfield Avenue I saw that the Secret Service were prepared to knock down and kill anybody to protect their charges. They told the crowds, "Stay behind the barricades," as Kennedy walked the length of Springfield Avenue shaking hands along the way. Anyone who went past the barricade got pushed to the ground by the Secret Service and removed—no debate. I said to myself, *I'd like to have all these guys on my football team;* they were brutal. But, then, their job was to save lives, not win popularity contests. I admired their courage and professionalism.

I never sought to run anyone else's campaign. People came and asked me, based on the recommendations of others. I never had the heart to turn anybody down. Bill Bradley had asked for my endorsement after my commitment to Al Gore for President. I never asked for money in exchange for my help. I had my own built-in, little dedicated army. That, I felt was the key thing. Jimmy Carter called me at home on the telephone and asked for my support in 1980 based on the South Ward's contribution to his victory in 1976.

If I had not been committed to Kennedy, I probably would have agreed to work for Carter again. I liked him as a person, but I thought he had a tendency to micromanage, and unlike Kennedy, he appeared ready to trade the liberal ideals of the Democratic Party for a policy of fiscal conservatism.

As a result of my efforts on behalf of big-name politicians, I became more widely known. With the Kennedy campaign, I was all over the county, but I was also traveling the state. I came to develop a cadre of support in other cities and other towns, especially urban communities throughout New Jersey.

At the Essex County Democratic meeting to choose delegates for the Democratic National Convention in New York, Gibson's supporters had rented the first two rooms of the Grand Ballroom at the Robert Treat Hotel. My contingent of Kennedy supporters could fill only the third and last room, the Crystal room. To walk to it we had to share a common space with Gibson's people, who harassed us and tried to intimidate us. Gibson had maybe 1,000 people packed into two ballrooms. We had about 300 Kennedy loyalists.

The message that I gave to my people was, "Let's go out and show that it's not going to be by might, but by right, that we win for Ted Kennedy." I tried to boost their morale and told them, "Despite the insults, the hostility we received coming into this room today, we're going to win."

We went out of that meeting so enraged at the insults and harassment from Gibson's Carter delegates that we went to work in the trenches of Essex County. In the New Jersey Democratic primary we beat Carter and Gibson in Essex County two-to-one. If ever there was a victory that showed me that force doesn't necessarily translate into votes, it was in this primary, where Gibson tried to use his muscle to get people to support his choice.

I served as a Kennedy delegate whip (a delegate selected to motivate other delegates to follow the party platform) at the national convention in New York. Not only did I suffer insults in Newark, but once in Madison Square Garden, the Gibson people tried to intimidate the Kennedy delegates, who were in the minority. We were fighting for proportional seating, and they wanted to give us the worst seats. I was seated next to N.J. State Sen. Wynona Lipman, a Carter supporter, and we fought the whole time. We fought over viewing space, standing space, and who would use the mike to speak.

The press accused me of being disrespectful to Senator Lipman. Nothing could be further from the truth. It was just the normal heat and tussle of a convention.

Carter won the nomination, but lost in the general election to Ronald Reagan in a landslide. The highlight of that convention was the great Kennedy keynote address, sometimes referred to as "The Dream Shall Never Die" speech. In it he chided the Republican Party for attempting to portray itself as friend of the common man, and then, proceeded to attack the GOP's record, quoting nominee Reagan's most callous remarks concerning unemployment insurance, aid to cash-strapped cities, social security and the environment.

Even today, I can still see "Teddy" in my mind, and hear his memorable, profound and heart-stirring speech. It had brought tears to the eyes of many among the standing room only Madison Square Garden delegates; both Democrats and Republicans alike were touched by his speech:

"The commitment I seek is not to worn-out views but to old values that will never wear out," he told the convention audience. "Programs may sometimes become obsolete, but the ideal of fairness always endures. Circumstances may change, but the work of compassion must continue: (a) The poor may be out of political fashion, but they are not without human needs; (b) Someday, long after this convention, long after the signs come down and the bands stop playing, may it be said of our campaign, that we kept the faith."

He concluded with the line:

"For all those whose cares have been our concern, the work goes on, the cause endures, the hope still lives, and the dream shall never die."

I will always remember Ted as one of my eloquent heroes who had the courage to speak out for the poor, the voiceless and for a better America. He wanted everyone to enjoy life as he did.

Reverend Jesse Jackson For President - 1988
Donald Payne For Congressman -1988

By the end of my first year in office, the citizens of Newark were beginning to see tangible evidence of Newark's rebirth. The streets were cleaner. Citizens' telephone calls and letters were being answered. People were able to get City Hall to respond more quickly to their needs.

In 1987 my program of demolishing high-rise public housing projects was underway, starting with Scudder and Columbus Homes, soon to be replaced with new, safe and affordable townhouses. Continental Airlines signed a 25-year, $225 million lease with the Port Authority of New York and New Jersey for a new terminal at Newark International Airport after the company bought People Express Airline. Continental Airlines would become the number-one job provider for Newark and the surrounding region and, also, one of Newark's best private partners.

I had continued solidifying my political partnerships, as well. Jesse Jackson announced his candidacy for President in late 1987. I wholeheartedly endorsed him. When he made his first run for President in 1984, won Newark in the primary, so he knew that he could count on our support once again. He asked me to be the chairman of his New Jersey campaign and to lead a national fundraising drive for the all-important Super Tuesday primaries on March 8, 1988. I would be calling upon mayors in other urban areas across the country—New Orleans, Oakland, Philadelphia, and Washington, D.C.– to contribute to the effort.

In New Jersey we raised money to fly Jesse in to give us direction and motivation. He was a tough cookie to satisfy. He was about image and style. He wanted a Lear jet (he didn't want to travel on a commercial plane), so at great cost we provided him with one. We put him up in a hotel suite (no budget room, please) at great expense to carry his campaign statewide. He created excitement everywhere he went. People just wanted to be a part of the democratic process—people who loved Jesse Jackson, his eloquence, his star presence.

The most important thing about the Jesse Jackson campaign was not whether he could win—and we were certainly trying to win as many votes for him as possible—but that he would be a vehicle for expressing, our needs, and our hopes. We kept thinking; what would it be like if there were no Jesse Jackson in the presidential debates, in the party conferences, in the smoke-filled deal making rooms? If there were no Jesse Jackson, Blacks would have been shut out of the party process completely. Jackson was a minority candidate, and he was able to air our concerns on prime-time media. Who had more charisma? Who excited people more on the convention floor? No one republican or democrat was a showman like Jesse! Run Jesse Run, he was running and actually believed that he could win.

I was aware of the report that Jackson had embellished his role at the scene of Dr. King's death. Dr. King did not die in Jackson's bosom, as he had claimed. I knew that he had referred to New York as "Hymietown" in a private conversation with a reporter when he ran for President in 1984, and the accusation of anti-Semitism. None of those things discredited him with the African American community. Blacks believed that he was victimized by the media and the Jewish community. He was still considered our hero, our motivator.

However, that's not to say that Jackson did not have his detractors among African Americans. Mayor Wilson Goode of Philadelphia didn't like Jackson; he thought he was an egomaniac. Goode wanted to resist Jackson's candidacy in Philadelphia, but then he would have had to start by fighting his wife and daughter, who were campaigning for Jackson, he told me angrily, "Jesse has a spell over women voters!"

My mentor, Mayor Coleman Young of Detroit, thought Jackson was a "born liar" and used a forum at the University of Pennsylvania's Wharton School, in which I also participated, to bash Jesse. Young had made me agree not to say anything in my remarks in praise of Jackson. He followed me to the podium at the Black Student's Forum at Wharton and immediately called Jesse a pathological liar, and said that "Mayor James, if he would tell the truth, would agree with me." From my seat I shouted him down for his bias remarks. In the end, Jackson won Detroit.

Jesse Jackson had a way about him that could win people over despite the criticism. He would walk into a room and get down on one knee in front of someone seated or standing in the audience and shake that person's hand. And not only would he speak to invited VIP personalities at a gathering, he would make sure to seek out the janitors and the cleaning ladies and shake their hands, as well.

Nothing Jesse ever did or said dimmed the love and support that he received in New Jersey. Although I disagreed with him at times, I also knew he was very sincere about the "rainbow coalition." Wherever he went, whatever he did, he always demanded an integrated team. "Sharpe, I can't go out there, it's an all Black crowd, find some diversity he would challenge me."

In hindsight, maybe it was wrong of him to make the "Hymietown" remark, but he apologized. The Bible says if one offers an apology, we must accept. We must forgive, forget and move on. Any man who walked with Dr. Martin Luther King, with the multi-hued crowds surrounding him in Birmingham, Selma, and Chicago, could never be anti-Semitic.

If I could help both Jesse and Donald Payne win both would become the first African American officeholders; the first African American President and the first African American Congressman from New Jersey. We wanted to dispel the opinion put forth by Robert Kennedy that it would take about fifty years to elect a Black man President. We perceived Jesse Jackson as a "rainbow candidate," a man for all of the people.

Wherever Jesse Jackson, Sr. traveled he brought magnetic charisma, history, excitement, and promises of hope and controversy. He wrestled with the legacy of his mentor, Dr. Martin Luther King, Jr., in concert with his personal civil rights, social justice and political beliefs. He was an in demand undisputed civil rights leader helping to elect hundreds of African American local elected officials encompassing his worldwide crusade as an eloquent speaker. He was a voice for the voiceless, a leader's leader and a clergyman. Jesse was not shy in giving help and most certainly not shy in asking for help.

Excitement ran up and down the state from Wildwood in South Jersey to congested Westfield in the North. It was show and tell time for the neglected urban communities. It was the time to participate and demonstrate our voting strength.

As a newly-elected Mayor in 1986 and having been appointed one of the state coordinators for Jesse, I felt obligated to hit the trenches and support an all out GOTV effort for Jesse. I knew that a big voter turnout for Jesse, especially in heavily democratic Essex County, would also guarantee a victory for Donald Payne in the 10th Congressional District, where his base votes were located.

I preached from every street corner for an obligatory vote for Jesse. I simply told the truth that without Jesse there would have been no Ken Gibson in 1970, no Sharpe James in 1986, and no hundreds of local elected officials throughout the state and nation. "We stand on his shoulders and now it's payback time." I told the people. "Who answered our call in 1970?" I asked "Who came to our rescue here in Newark?" I challenged voters. "You know who. Remember May 1970 when electing Ken Gibson the first African American mayor of a major northeast city, who came to our rescue?" I asked. "Let me tell you."

I told the story of how a tall, flamboyant, articulate, courageous, yet controversial young man wearing an afro and a dashiki, came to our rescue. Jesse Jackson walked along Bergen Street in the heart of the South Ward drawing thousands of people from their homes. Soon it became a parade with a festival atmosphere in support of Ken Gibson for Mayor and his Community's Choice Team of which I was a member. There was excitement in the air. It's time for a change was the hue and cry from every street corner. "Our time has come," cried impeccably dressed senior citizen, Bessie McDonald, wearing her trademark large brim church hat.

Everyone wanted to join in the fun. Sound trucks were blasting and children were dancing on open flat bed trucks. People were throwing confetti from their windows! Seizing the moment, Jesse ended the rally with one of his fiery rebel rousing speeches on the importance of voting or registering and then voting.

Jesse cried, "Too many people have died for your right to vote. You can't stay home. If you do, Ken will lose. Let's remember! You can't hope him in. You can't pray him in. You can't buy him in. We must vote him in." The crowd would now be dancing in the street. The crowds were ecstatic. Ken Gibson had won and become the first African American mayor elected in a major northeast city.

Even when Jesse left town, Jesse was still in town. He would wear out your telephone and patience seeking donations for his Chicago based operation People United to Save Humanity (PUSH); and the National Rainbow Coalition, an organization fighting for social justice, civil rights and political activism. Jesse was always involved in some breaking news activity. He was always raising money.

Jesse knew no limit when calling on friends for favors. His favorite words to end all of his speaking engagements were "Please, now I want all the doors closed and nobody should leave. We are going to have a fundraiser." This last act would always follow his speech, despite the fact that in most cases he had already received an honorarium for his mere appearance.

Watching Jesse go after donations was like watching a Barnum and Bailey Ringling Brothers Circus. Jesse was the quintessential Master of Ceremony. He would say, "Ladies and gentlemen, boys and girls of all ages;" he went after everyone, no one was spared.

Jesse could have been called Jesse James on these occasions. He would start out saying, "Please no jingle, jingle, no silver contributions. Now listen to my instructions carefully. I want the following persons to stand and make a pledge. All of you wearing Rolex watches, Bally shoes, Armani suits, Versace shirts; women with the Louis Vuitton and Gucci handbags, please stand. Can you now start coming forward with cash or checks in hand or fill out a pledge card? Do I have a $1,000 donation, how about $500, anyone with a hundred dollars? Please hurry and come forward." You would think that Jesse was collecting church tithes. No such luck.

We needed Jesse. We loved him. Now in 1988 he was running for President. You never turn your back on a friend. We left no stone unturned getting out the vote for Jesse Jackson, statewide from Ocean County to Bergen County. Where we lacked money, we had heart and stamina. It wasn't easy going against the State Democratic Party and its sizeable war chest.

We put together a grassroots organization, and although we didn't get those big, fat checks, we got the $50, the $75, and the $100 contributions, creating hoopla up and down the state. We identified Black and White supporters all over. It was the same kind of organizing

I had done helping local politicians running for office. We were able to garner about 33 percent of the New Jersey primary votes for Jesse Jackson, a cause for celebration.

One drawback, though, was New Jersey's primary rules which allowed frontrunner, Massachusetts Gov. Michael Dukakis, to walk away with more than 80 percent of New Jersey's delegates to the convention, even though he received only 63 percent of the popular vote. Jackson would receive only 10 percent of the delegates. The Jackson camp thought the rule was unfair, and we challenged it in court.

In a state with a policy of the winner take all of the convention delegates, the Democratic Party had to call an emergency meeting and take notice to avoid a court fight. We were demanding proportionate representation based on percentage of votes won. We were putting to test the American doctrine of the one man one vote philosophy.

After weeks of wrangling, however, the state Democratic Party offered a compromise. Jesse Jackson would be allowed a third of the New Jersey Democratic delegates to the National Democratic Convention and a prominent speaking role at the convention. It was a clear message that every vote does count. Jesse Jackson was a happy man in New Jersey.

In addition to the nine delegates that Jackson had won in the June 7 primary, Jackson supporters would get to choose eight of New Jersey's 38 at-large delegates, plus two at-large alternate delegates and three members of the national convention's standing committees on rules, credentials and the party platform. So, we ended up with 17 of the state's 109 pledged delegates, and we accepted that.

The Democratic Party felt that it was better to compromise than to foster two attitudes among Jackson delegates, neither of which the Democrats could afford: One was hostility and combativeness at the convention. The other was lack of enthusiasm for the Democratic ticket. I was glad the party leaders chose to bring us into the fold. They gave us concessions, because they wanted to bring the same energy, the same drive that we brought to the Jackson campaign to the Democratic ticket in November.

In the end we all won. Jesse won because he had gotten more exposure than any other Black candidate running for President. He had a voice that even White America had to stop and listen to. In 1972 Shirley Chisholm didn't have a chance; she didn't have the national and international recognition that Jesse did. He was in the race all the way, and stirred the convention in Atlanta, Ga. with his "Keep Hope Alive" speech. Jackson's supporters won, because our message and platform was included in the national Democratic platform. The Democratic Party won, because it was able to hold on to its core of support—Black voters.

After Michael Dukakis and Texas Senator Lloyd Bensen won the Democratic Party's nomination for President and Vice President to go up against George Bush and Dan Quayle, they received the complete cooperation of Jackson's New Jersey supporters.

Shortly after the convention, Dukakis flew into Newark to kick off his New Jersey campaign. He asked me to come out to the airport to meet him and ride with him to a couple of rallies in New Jersey. His car pulled up, and the Secret Service agent—not I—opened the wrong door, the rear door on the side that Dukakis was sitting. I walked up to the car, attempting to get into the car, and Dukakis said, very coldly, "I don't slide!"

I was startled. I went around to the other side of the car and got in. Ever since that campaign, when anyone on my staff would try to get into my car on my side, I would say "I don't slide." That's become known as the Dukakis rule in my circle.

It was hard for the Jesse Jackson army to rally behind Dukakis as the standard bearer because of his lack of warmth and communication. We went through the motions, because he was a Democrat, but he was never able to galvanize the enthusiasm and support that he should have had. That's why he lost to Bush. He was the wrong candidate at the wrong time.

Now the focus turned to South Ward Councilman Donald Payne in his effort to become the first Black U.S. Congressman from New Jersey. How was he doing in the 10th Congressional District? For twenty years (1968-1988) I had partnered with Donald Payne to build a strong South Ward Democratic organization for producing votes. In order to get elected to a city, county or statewide office, one had to come through the South Ward Democratic stronghold. Peter W. Rodino, who had represented the 10th Congressional District for 40 years and who was then 78 years old, had announced that he was retiring at the end of his term.

The 10th Congressional District, mostly in Essex County, was 58 percent Black and the only district in New Jersey that could elect an African American. It was a district that the federal court had carved out in 1972 so that an African American could be elected to the Congress from New Jersey. Before that, Black voting strength was diluted by placing parts of Newark in neighboring suburban districts.

Payne ran against Rodino, unsuccessfully, in the 1980 and 1986 primaries. In 1988 Payne felt that Rodino should give up his seat in order to get an African American in Congress before the 1990 Census was released. The census, he feared, would undoubtedly show a loss of population in the 10th District which would lead to the creation of a new 10th District with more suburbs. The chances of a Black person getting elected to Congress from New Jersey would then surely be diminished.

I supported Payne both in 1986 and 1988, because in 1971 he knocked on my door and asked me to be a district leader in the South Ward Democratic organization. From 1971 to 1988 we were close associates from the same ward, living in the same neighborhood. Payne was the party chairman of the ward, and I was his district leader. We worked together.

Payne and I were political allies. Every candidate running for office simply had to visit our Bergen Street Headquarters during their campaign to ask for an endorsement or ask us for help. During these meetings Payne would sit at a front desk, like a member of the Supreme Court deciding on a significant case. I used to think; He should also wear a robe. He loved it. A real Shakespearean King Lear.

Payne would teasingly and cunningly proffer obligatory support for democratic candidates to evaluate their reaction. He was secretly waiting for the candidate to offer money to pay his district leaders, office staff and office utility costs. Donald Payne never had a benevolent heart. He was a businessman.

Donald Payne was obsessed with his singular ambition, to replace the "Godfather," legendary Watergate Commission Chairman and Congressman of the 10th Congressional District, a household name throughout his voting district, having served forty years in office, the Honorable Peter W. Rodino.

"Pete," as he was affectionately called was a native of Newark. He was more than eighty years of age, showed no evidence of slowing down or quitting, answered every letter and telephone call, and was running for re-election. I used to see him at every New York Giants home football game at the New Jersey Meadowlands. He was always in good spirit and full of energy. "Hi Sharpe," he would say, and then flash that Hollywood Clark Gable smile, his winning trademark.

Donald having lost to Rodino in 1986 was ready for the rematch in 1988, he had asked me to use my influence to get Jesse Jackson to support the campaign. He wanted Jesse to come to Newark during the final week of the campaign to drive his GOTV effort.

Jesse's reaction was, "Sharpe, that cheapskate won't even send a plane or pay for your hotel room, let alone buy you a beer. How am I supposed to abort my Presidential campaign and get there, walk?" he had argued. "I don't like riding camels," he said, laughing.

I, too, knew that Donald still had his first dollar, and always came to fundraisers after the ticket collector had left the door. I told Jesse, "This campaign is bigger than cheapskate Payne, and I will send you a Lear Jet and you will have the President's suite at the downtown Hilton Hotel. We need you to energize his campaign." Jesse was happy. Jesse was on his way. When I met him at Newark's corporate jet landing strip, at the old North Terminal, I noticed that the Lear Jet looked more like a fighter plane than a corporate jet.

As Jesse stooped and twisted to get off the plane, I could not help but think that he would have been more comfortable sitting first class on a regularly scheduled Continental flight from Chicago to Newark. The flight hostess had to equally twist and stoop to exit while carrying Jesse's luggage. Jesse approached me, bent down on one knee, shook my hand, and gave me his famous wide grin; then standing he patted me on the back and said, "Great flight Sharpe. Let's get started."

I thought to myself, *At $2,200 for the Lear jet versus $495 on Continental Airlines, it should have been a super flight. In fact, I thought, We could have put a down payment on the plane itself.*

Once in the Presidential suite at the downtown Hilton, we mapped out a weekend strategy for Jesse to speak at churches, senior citizen buildings and a repeat crowd teasing walk down Bergen Street.

Everywhere that Jesse went he drew large crowds and his message was the same. Above the hue and cry, Jesse would say, "Keep Hope Alive, Vote For Donald Payne, No Payne No Gain. Remember, you can't wish him in; you can't buy him in; you can't pray him in; you got to vote him in. You must vote on Nov 8, 1988 for Donald Payne for Congress." Watching Jesse in action, I saw our 1970 campaign all over again. I thought of the old Rule, "If it's not broke, don't fix it."

However, the real excitement and, I believe, a campaign home run, was not planned. We were returning Jesse to his hotel suite at the Hilton about 5 p.m. for some much needed rest. Studying the landscape, I realized that the Hilton Hotel, adjacent to Newark Penn Station, at this hour was an "active beehive." There was a sea of people leaving from work in mass, rushing to get on busses to take them home. *Hey, I thought, most of them live in the 10th Congressional District. Why not stop each bus and have Jesse say, "Hello?"* I thought. The drivers will think we want to board the bus. Just a "Hello, vote for Donald Payne" and off to the next bus. Of course Jesse was all smiles, willing and ready to show his face to a dog catcher, if he felt that it would help Payne.

I was beginning to recover from the price of the Lear Jet. *He's worthy,* I thought! What excitement we created, what a traffic jam gridlock we created, it was bedlam in front of Newark Penn Station at rush-hour time. *Maybe the New Jersey Transit police officers will arrest us,* I thought. We were proudly wrong.

Women were screaming and fighting to shake Jesse's hand, some wanted to just touch him, others wanted to rip his shirt off, kiss and hug him; others wanted to take a picture together, an autograph; and the police officers wanted our photographer to take pictures of them with Jesse Jackson. Then there were bus drivers leaving their seat and posing with Jesse. "This is unbelievable,"

When the excitement and gridlock had ended Jesse had boarded fifteen plus buses and had shook over a thousand hands. Many were chasing Jesse between buses to shake his hand. "We love you, Jesse; we're going to vote for you and Payne," they shouted out while blowing kisses as they departed.

Although Payne had lost in 1986, he won in 1988, and became the first African American Congressman from New Jersey. We celebrated all night. He had big shoes to fill in the person of the Honorable Peter W. Rodino.

We sent a happy and smiling Jesse Jackson back to Chicago on a Lear jet. I stood and watched as it climbed through the low-hanging clouds into the sun and headed west. As I thought about the expense of paying for the Lear Jet, I came to only one conclusion, "He was worthy."

We had made history in electing the first African American Congressman from New Jersey and Jesse was assured of a prominent voice in the National Democratic Organization having received 33% of the votes from New Jersey. Even more importantly I felt, it would not take another fifty years to elect an African American President.

"Yes," I said, "Jesse was worthy." Now, let me go pay his Lear jet invoice.

James Florio For Governor – 1989

I received a telephone call from Congressman Jim Florio asking to meet with me. "No problem," I said. "Please have our secretaries schedule a mutually convenient time and place. I look forward to seeing you," I told him.

Jim had lost the 1980 governor's race against Brendan Byrne in what was the closest governor's race in New Jersey's history. It had sent a clear message that every vote does count. Planning for his second race for governor, Jim had an added asset, an attractive second wife, Lucinda. She was a very lovely, warm, charming and friendly person. With Lucinda by his side, Jim now became a more attractive candidate.

Jim never had a warm personality and often talked like James Cagney in the movies. A hairline scar across his chin made him even more tough looking. He was a strong, predictable no humor career politician. Our meeting went well and I was impressed by the lack of frill or promises in his conversation. I truthfully felt that his no nonsense approach to government, and his history of delivering as a Congressman, would be good for Newark and the State of New Jersey. I was hooked!

As I had done for Senator Tom Bradley, Ted Kennedy for President, Jesse Jackson for President and Donald Payne for Congressman, I walked the state for Jim Florio and raised more than $500,000 for his campaign. With his attractive wife Lucinda in tow, holding his new grandson, Matthew, Jim had a new image, a new smiling personality, and he won. Happy days are here again. At least I thought so. I would soon learn differently. I would soon meet the real Jim Florio.

Soon after his election to governor, Florio arrived in Newark to speak at the Mutual Benefit Life Insurance Building. When he arrived, Governor Florio pulled Pam Goldstein, my communication director, to the side and told her, "Pam, don't you ever schedule me to speak after Mayor James. I must always be scheduled to speak first on the program. I hope that you will remember that," he said. "Please don't make that mistake again." Pam told me he had spoken to her in an irritating manner.

After the meeting Pam was still in shock and trembling when she told me of her conversation with the Governor. "Mayor," she said, "I was scared the way he was talking to me!"

I placed my hand on her shoulder comfortingly and said, "Pam, just do what the Governor asked. I don't care where or if I appear on a joint program with him. What angered him?" I asked.

Tearfully, she replied, "He thinks you're a better speaker."

"Pam that's nonsense," I said. "We need the Governor's help for Newark, give him what he wants. Pam was still shaking when I left her; the Governor had scared her out of her wits.

Later during his tenure in office Governor Florio called again and asked if I could have dinner with him and his Chief of Staff, Joe Salema, at the Manor Restaurant in West Orange. I said "Sure Governor, I would love to." The Manor has plates the size of a Direct TV disk. I was anticipating a large sumptuous meal. Unfortunately, the portions of food served could have fit on a six-inch plate.

Before the meeting I had called my Chief of Staff, Jackie Mattison, into my office and advised him of the planned dinner date with the Governor. Jackie would accompany me. I asked him, "Why do you think the Governor wants to have dinner with me?"

Jackie smiled, and said, "I'm sure he wants to personally thank you for your generous campaign contribution. He wants to give you a face-to-face thank you, and ask how he can be helpful to the City of Newark."

I felt very good after receiving Jackie's insight into the upcoming meeting. I then anticipated a much earned thank you from the Governor. I remembered the photos taken when we gave him the checks.

Well, after we had finished the appetizers, dinner, and dessert the waiters were cleaning our table and I was still waiting for the thank you. Joe Salema was blowing his cigar smoke in my face, and yet there was no mention of any thanks for your campaign help. Then suddenly Governor Florio turned to me and said, "Sharpe, we are waiting for you. I replied, "Waiting for what Governor?" He turned to Joe and said "Tell him."

Salema explained, "Most of the cities, at the request of the Florio Administration, are changing their municipal calendar year to coincide with that of the state. Cities are switching from a June to June calendar year to January through December. We have been waiting on Newark," Salema stated.

I asked Governor Florio, "If we were to switch, where would the monies come from to make up for the six months loss of revenue to pay bills?" Joe explained that we would float a $110 million bond from a company they had selected. Governor Florio, said, "It's easy, Sharpe. We have made all of the arrangements."

I thought privately of borrowing the money and placing the debt on the backs of Newark citizens for years to come. Was it a good idea? With the Governor staring at me with steel eyes; Joe still blowing smoke in my face saying, "Come on Sharpe, come on Sharpe, it's good for Newark. You are the last one." I politely told them, "Let me think about it. I will get back to you." They did not look too happy.

Once outside I turned to Jackie and said, "Some congratulations you promised me. I can't even breathe now. Was that a Cuban cigar he was smoking?" We never did change our municipal budget calendar year. We never borrowed any money, while Jersey City, East Orange and other cities had mortgaged their municipality's future.

Newark did not help the governor's selected bond company make its 10% profit or $11 million; a company owned by one of the governor's top aide's brother. The company eventually made more than $300 million switching municipal budgets to the state's calendar year. Thereafter, the governor, for some strange reason, appeared to become paranoid that Sharpe James was going to run for governor and had to be stopped. The familiar rumors surfaced that James was too powerful, had too much, and that you can't trust Sharpe James. He must be stopped. Two methods of attack developed.

First, the governor decided to create another highly visible African American supporter and rival for me. In my mind I was thinking, The Governor is saying the hell with Sharpe James, I will create my own Nigger!

Later, Governor Florio aligned himself with Mayor Cardell Cooper of East Orange, New Jersey, a fellow African American. Cooper, a native of Newark, was someone I had helped as a teacher and coach. I knew his family. I was proud of his election as Mayor of neighboring East Orange, population 60,000. He was matinee handsome, tall, curly haired with pearly white even teeth and a flair for dress and flashy red ties.

Cooper was highly successful and had a bright future. He was a young African American man on the rise. There was only one problem. Cardell Cooper wanted to be Sharpe James. He ordered the same town car I had, added the same security arrangements I had, and all of this for a city of only 60,000 people.

Without a doubt, Mayor Cooper failed to realize that these benefits were saluting my title and office (Newark being the largest city in New Jersey), not necessarily the man himself. East Orange, being one-fifth the size of Newark or the size of a ward in Newark, could never offer the economics, political clout, or voting tally that Newark could muster for any candidate. Just like Rochester or Buffalo could never be New York City or Scranton could never be Philadelphia, East Orange could never be Newark; therefore, Cardell Cooper could never be Sharpe James. However, this did not stop Florio and Cooper from trying. Cardell needed more visibility.

Bypassing Newark, the largest city in the state, Governor Florio immediately appointed Cardell Cooper a Commissioner for the New Jersey Sports & Exposition Authority. He walked with, talked with, and had public meetings with Cardell. I was ignored and put away with moth balls.

Interestingly enough, though, on a visit to Newark, Cardell came to City Hall and said, "Sharpe, you got too much: you're on the Board of Directors of the New Jersey League of Municipalities; Vice President of the New Jersey Conference of Mayors; President of the National League of Cities (NLC); Board of Trustees for the United States Conference of Mayors (USCM); give me something."

"What do you want?" I believe I asked him.

Finally, Cardell said what he had come for, "Hey, I got an idea, Sharpe, instead of rotating the leadership for New Jersey's Urban Conference of Mayors, let me take over the organization with your support?"

Little did Cardell know; I had no illusions about my titles or any of the offices or positions I held. I said, "Fine," and Cardell became the first permanent President of the organization. I even looked forward to our next meeting. At least, I did at that time.

The next meeting of New Jersey's Conference of Urban Mayors was in Atlantic City. I made the two-hour drive. My spirit for new young leadership, and especially for a native of Newark, was effervescent; a sharing of power; a passing of the baton. I just knew I had done the right thing.

As I approached the hotel meeting room, I was approached by Cardell Cooper and Mayor Wayne Smith of Irvington, another youthful, African American and recently elected NJ mayor. Cardell, grabbed my arm and said that he wanted to go over the meeting agenda with me. We went over the agenda, item by item. Finally, I said, "Fine, there is no problem."

As I turned to walk away, Cooper grabbed my arm a second time and said "There is only one thing I want you to understand."

"Sure, what's that?" I said.

"When we meet with the press at the end of the meeting, I will do all of the talking and you should refrain from making any comments. I am the President!" Cooper said.

I just looked at him, still feeling weary from the long drive to Atlantic City.

At the end of the meeting we stepped outside and the press ran up to me for an assessment of the meeting and the status of urban city issues. I thought of what Cardell had said. I saw the expression on his face standing nearby. *What should I do?* I gave one of my best interviews ever. I never looked at Cardell. I never attended another meeting. It was now his show. I had better and bigger things to do. Once again I knew that they were saluting the title and office not necessarily the man. Rather sadly, Cardell did not know this.

Losing a title was not a loss to me, but like a dentist, though, they wanted to extract more from Sharpe James. One day I had just jumped out of the car and was walking on Broad Street near Newark's four corners,

Broad and Market Streets, when a prominent businessman ran up to me and said, "Don't turn around or look at me. I have just been told that Florio's man, the New Jersey Attorney General, Robert DelTufo, has subpoenaed all of your fiscal records, personal and campaign, and is launching a full scale investigation of you. What did you do to tick off Governor Florio? Don't look at me. Remember, I did not tell you this." He turned and disappeared into the crowd of noon day shoppers.

When I reflected, losing a title was no problem, but the thought of losing my personal freedom took me to the office of Raymond A. Brown, Esquire. He would know how to handle this political attack.

After being subjected to five years of negative press, the review of more than 1,000 personal checks that I had written, interviews with donors, searches, and talking to government snitchers, the investigation of my office from the Florio Administration that had started with a roar, suddenly and quietly ended. At a press conference regarding an unrelated matter, a reporter asked U.S. Attorney Michael Chertoff–who the state's Democratic leadership had labeled a "monster" that we had to get rid of–"What about Sharpe James' investigation?" Chertoff turned to the crowd and said, "He didn't do anything! He had a birthday party! The case is closed."

When someone later reminded me of Chertoff's statement, I recalled the remarks of Labor Secretary Donovan who, under similar conditions, had remarked, "Where do I go and get my dignity back?" Chertoff was a highly respected and competent true professional law maker, a staunch religious man. He was not running for any public office.

I would soon learn that the next U.S. Attorney General appointed to New Jersey would have political ambitions and not be so pious. His goal was not to obtain justice, but to win at all cost, by hook or crook. Justice would not be blind under his tenure.

Bill Clinton For President – 1992

In 1992, the United States Conference of Mayors (USCM), on a non-partisan basis, offered its leadership, the opportunity to participate in the 1992 Presidential election. I chose to spend time in Little Rock, Arkansas, in support of Bill Clinton for President. It provided me an opportunity to meet the leaders of his campaign and an inside view of his campaign organization, strategy and planned GOTV effort.

After attending many campaign sessions and going on a tour of Little Rock, Arkansas, the highlight of my trip was getting to meet, greet and have a sit down breakfast with Bill Clinton in his favorite hometown restaurant. It was a small diner and the southern menu consisted of grits, eggs, sausage and biscuits.

It was clear from the beginning that Bill came to eat. Politics was put on the back burner and everyone became part of Bill's extended family. Little Rock and Bill reminded me of the days when it was cheaper to fly People Express than to drive. The pilot would take your ticket, luggage, fly the plane and hand you your luggage after landing, a real "no frills experience."

Little Rock, Arkansas was a "no frills city." It made Newark, New Jersey look like a major Metropolis. My visit to Little Rock would provide me a once in a lifetime beautiful experience to meet the next President of the United States, face-to-face, before he became President.

When President Bill Clinton asked the leadership of USCM to help him get his stalled Crime Bill through Congress, I joined Mayors Richard Daly of Chicago, Bob Lanier of Houston and Jerry Abramson of Louisville to lobby other elected officials to pressure their Congressmen and U.S. Senators to vote on the Crime Bill. Once the Bill passed, the President had promised to add 100,000 cops to the mean streets of America to curb inner city crime. "Let's render our streets safe" was the hue and cry.

To highlight its importance and to give the bill even more momentum. President Clinton invited more than two thousand guests, nationwide, to the White House Rose Garden, where we would give a passionate speech in support of the Crime Bill. Since we were all Democrats, the President wanted a prominent Republican Mayor to join us on stage for a bipartisan effort.

Mayor Rudy Giuliani of New York City, who did not participate in the United States Conference of Mayors or the National League of Cities Conferences, the two most prominent local government leadership organizations, had originally refused to attend. His huge ego would not allow him to partake with the duly elected mayors of America. As a former prosecutor he was "holier-than-thou." He never saw a camera he didn't fall in love with or a press conference he didn't attend.

However, he changed his mind after his demand to be flown from New York City to Washington, D.C. with the President on Air Force One was met. He wanted and received a media grand entrance, waving his hand as he stepped off Air Force One with the President.

Mayor Daly, a real tough guy and strong supporter of the Crime Bill, was livid over the quid pro quo arrangement. Seated next to me in the Rose Garden, he said, "That grandstanding egotistical S.O.B. should be kicked off the stage." He refused to look at Mayor Giuliani. He was really ticked off.

After the introductions only two of us were selected to speak for the group. I spoke, telling of the horror and devastating effects of crime, loss of lives, property and hope in our inner cities where people were afraid to leave their homes. "Citizens are prisoners in their own homes," I said. "If we can fight abroad we can bring the fight home to the mean streets of America." I hoped to impress upon the guests the urgent need to pass the Crime Bill, now.

The setting, pageantry, crowd and beauty of the Rose Garden was indescribable; an occasion like *Alice in Wonderland!* Congress got the message. The Crime Bill passed, overwhelmingly. Our group had delivered a strong and powerful message on the importance of public safety. President Clinton later thanked each one of us in a heartwarming letter.

Adopting this cooperative strategy gave me some perks that I hadn't expected. In the months ahead I was able to pick up the telephone and speak directly to President Clinton. "I'm sending federal dollars to Newark under the Crime Bill to hire 200 new police officers, Sharpe," he told me on one occasion. "Good luck to you!"

I was even given an opportunity to ride with him in his bullet proof presidential vehicle from a Newark rally at Louise A. Spencer School to his next stop in New Jersey. Once the thick steel plated door was sealed it was sort of scary, like riding inside a vault, I became oblivious to the elements outside. My phobia and claustrophobia were tested as I forced a smile for this wonderful, historical invite, all the time wondering how I would get out in case of an accident.

President Clinton, being just Bill, spoke openly to me about the attempt of the Democratic Party to get him to drop out of the Presidential race because of the Jennifer Flowers rumors. "No way would I retreat, Sharpe, no way," he calmly said. I was flattered to be sitting next to our President, a Rhodes Scholar, behaving like he was my next door neighbor talking over the fence. Bill was a smart and talented regular guy who also happened to be President of the United States of America.

After our police recruits were trained, graduated, and sworn in as police officers, they immediately hit the mean streets fighting crime, reducing it by 50%; auto theft went down 60%. Newark was no longer the carjack capital of America. The first question reporters asked, "What will Newark do when the federal dollars run out?" was something I never considered. This thought paralyzed many mayors and prevented them from accepting federal funds under the crime bill. My thinking was that if we could save just one life, I would address the fiscal question later.

Now that our city was viewed more favorably, long time community activist, Elizabeth DelTufo, decided to test the city's safety. Elizabeth, the widow of the late, US Attorney Honorable Raymond DelTufo, was now Director of the Newark Boys Chorus. Joined by renowned Metropolitan opera star, Jerome Hines, they spiritedly walked from Highway 280 exit, on First Street in the North Ward, to Newark Symphony Hall on Broad Street located in the Central Ward. They both proclaimed Newark a safe place to live, work and visit.

DelTufo and Hines were ecstatic and jubilant following their walk, reminiscent of Dorothy and the Tin Man in *The Wizard of Oz*; all roads led to Newark. Their unselfish act on behalf of Newark generated voluminous positive press and suddenly Newark was "on a roll." Councilwoman Gayle Chaneyfield Jenkins said, "Newark is a destination city." And we did not stop there.

Newark was always seeking public and private partnerships. The telephone kept ringing and we kept answering it. Newark's leading newspaper, and my public enemy number one, *The Star-Ledger*, now proclaimed that Newark "was hot." They reported that "Newark is one of the best places in New Jersey to invest your money. I could not believe the headlines put forth by my tormentors.

My initial response was our time has come, let's keep the telephone ringing with people interested in investing in Newark. Like Cleveland,

Ohio, once called the mistake by the lake, and now America's comeback city, Newark was moving from "urban blight to urban bright."

Nelson Mandela – 1992

One night, I answered my home telephone and a Maya Angelou sounding voice asked, "Is Mayor James Sharpe (a common error with my name) home to accept a call from Nelson Mandela?" Thinking this was possibly a crank telephone call, my instant response was, "This is Stevie Wonder!" The voice replied, regally once again, "I beg your pardon! Is this the home of Mayor James Sharpe?" The voice remained resonant, calm and dignified. I quickly switched to a passive but appropriate response, "This is Mayor Sharpe James speaking," I replied. "One minute please," she responded.

After a short pause, the dignified, humble and gracious, recognizable voice of Nelson Mandela, said: "Mr. Mayor, this is Nelson Mandela. Thank you for accepting my call. I am scheduled to visit New York City later this month. On this occasion, would it be possible to meet with you in Newark, to explore the wonderful renaissance occurring there? You certainly must be proud."

Hearing Nelson Mandela's voice made me feel like I was being hypnotized, or that I had been given a tranquilizer. He was casting a spell over me. Just thinking of a meeting with this most courageous, legendary, humble leader, President of the African National Congress (ANC), a Nobel Peace Prize winner, and a former political prisoner made me tremble.

He continued, "As President of the African National Congress, I, too, must create a renaissance for all of South Africa. Can our secretaries arrange a mutually convenient date, time and place to meet in Newark?" Nelson Mandela's telephone call to me was like dreaming the impossible dream. Nelson Mandela was my hero. He was bigger than life.

My mind raced to recall that two years earlier Nelson Mandela had been released after serving 27 years in prison, much of the time spent in solitary confinement. Apartheid was now banned in South Africa and his party was no longer outlawed. Mr. Mandela was traveling to New York to speak before the U.N. Security Council on the recent violence against Blacks in his nation under the White minority government of President Frederik W. de Klerk.

When I most enthusiastically met Nelson Mandela at Newark International Airport and presented him the key to our city, I felt small and humble in his presence. He was a towering, erect, strong, warm and worldly humanitarian. He maintained direct eye-to-eye contact with me. I don't think he even blinked an eye.

Again feeling inadequate, I used the phrase spoken by Randall Robinson of Trans Africa, in 1987 when we both addressed a crowd of more 10,000 at a union rally in Bermuda with Bishop Tutu's daughter. "Mr. President," I said, "Although we are separated by a great ocean, the blood that binds us is much thicker than the water that separates us. We are family."

Mr. Mandela smiled and we were ushered to seats in a private lounge. Once seated, he spoke about his desire for global communication, trade and economic development opportunities for his country. "I must improve the lot of my people," he most graciously stated."

I suggested that we form a joint committee to explore economic trade and business opportunities between South Africa and Newark. I told him that Newark had a great port. I mentioned a possible sister city relationship involving one of his cities. He listened intently and replied that he was agreeable to future talks. He stood, extended his hand and gave me that wonderful sincere cheerful cheek smile with those penetrating eyes.

Later, we would meet again at Gracie Mansion in New York City, where Mayor David Dinkins was hosting a United States Conference of Mayors meeting. The highlight of the event would be the unexpected arrival and speech of Nelson Mandela. He was the biggest celebrity among celebrities.

As Mandela spoke from the rear steps of Gracie Mansion facing the garden, he was wearing a sweater vest. It was baking hot and the sun was beating down on him. He calmly spoke showing no discomfort whatsoever. Standing next to me under a large blue tent, to shade the sun, was Mayor Coleman Young of Detroit. He leaned over and whispered, "Hell, Sharpe, he's been speaking for over thirty minutes and no beads of sweat, shit, now I know why he could last twenty-seven years in prison. That Brother got some mean genes," he said.

Mayor Young was a tough old rascal. He once said to me, "Sharpe, stick with me and I'll teach you the ropes," He hated Reverend

Jesse Jackson whom he called a "fake," regarding his role on the day Dr. King was shot. "Do you really believe he had Dr. King's blood on his sweater?" Young had asked me. Mayor Coleman Young was from the old school and took no prisoners.

His toughness could be confirmed by speaking with Congressman John Conyers of Detroit, who tried to unseat Mayor Young in his old age under the banner, "It's time for a change." The only change he got was the knock out Coleman gave him in winning his re-election.

Mean genes or not, Nelson Mandela was the undisputed heroic figure for the oppressed and suffering. A former boxer and lawyer by training, Mandela was able to articulate like a professor of sociology when denouncing apartheid. He was pure and simple. He spoke the truth without editorializing and without fear. He spoke from the heart. He made the impossible seem possible. He was my hero. I felt like I had met deity in my conversations with him.

As president of the ANC Mandela took a leadership role in South Africa even though he was not president of the country yet. That wouldn't happen until two years later when Blacks all over South Africa lined up five miles long and waited hours in the hot sun to cast their ballots for the first time in their lives. I recalled seeing the first historic voting ballot containing both names and pictures, so that even the most illiterate person could vote. Nelson Mandela was a mighty man of valor. He was worthy. In 1994 He became South Africa's first Black president.

James McGreevey - 2001

James "Jim" McGreevey was diminutive in size and extremely loquacious. What he lacked in size he made up for in his speaking ability. McGreevey would have made a good Baptist preacher. Instead, he chose to become a politician. He had been elected to the New Jersey State Assembly and later would become Mayor of Woodbridge, New Jersey, the fourth largest city in the state with a population of about 100,000. In 1997, when no one gave him a chance of winning the governorship of New Jersey, he had lost in a very close election to the incumbent governor, Christine Todd Whitman.

Now it was the year 2001 and another election was underway. McGreevey was now confident that he could put the Democrats in charge of the State House. The only problem was that a more popular and flamboyant candidate, Robert Torricelli, whom Democrats had all backed for United States Senator in 1996, when Jim was put out as the sacrificial offering against an unbeatable Christine Whitman, now wanted to switch from his just won U.S. Senate seat to the governor's seat, or from Washington to the State House.

"Bob," as Torricelli was affectionately called, was about the same height as McGreevey; but with a little more weight, polish and curls. He was rounding up Hollywood beauties to hold his arm in almost the same numbers as supporters. Bob was a "player," a paparazzi favorite. He loved the limelight. He loved beautiful women. He loved driving in the fast lane.

Jim McGreevey felt betrayed by Bob and the Democratic Party. "Nobody gave me a chance against Governor Whitman in 1998, and look how close I came to winning," he would tell anyone who would listen. "Now you want to deny me a second run," Jim belted out angrily. "What are we running a beauty contest?" he asked. "Torricelli is all frill and no substance," he decried.

"McGreevey lacks presence," Torricelli said. "He talks a lot, but I will deliver for the State of New Jersey. Next week I will announce the support of over two-thirds of the 22 county leaders for my run for governor." Then, he believed he should be given the party's nomination for governor.

New Jersey Democrats were divided. They truthfully liked both men, although for different reasons. While most people were sleeping on the issue, three political musketeers and known mavericks went to work. They had no permanent friends, only permanent and pressing political agendas. They had mastered the art of deal making.

In his book, "The Confession," McGreevey speaks about a dinner with me, arranged by Senator Ray Lesniak with my aide, Calvin West and democratic strategist, Regena Thomas. The dinner took place at Club Millennium, a nightclub on Clay Street in Newark. The owner of the club was my son, Elliot.

McGreevey highlights the dinner by mentioning how dark the club was, how loud the music was and that he was blinded by the pulsing laser lights. This made the chapter interesting to read, but McGreevey neglected to mention in his book the real meeting that took place when he asked me for my endorsement of him in his run for governor. Maybe he forgot. I didn't.

It was a clear Friday night. A full moon lit the sky above. One block long, tree-lined Wilbur Avenue was one of the smallest and picturesque streets in Newark's Weequahic section. There were nine beautiful homes on each side of the street separated by a well maintained grass island.

The tightly knit homeowners were preparing for bed, as one window light after another turned to darkness. I had gone upstairs and was reading a few chapters from the book *Endurance* about Shackleton's incredible North Pole voyage, by Alfred Lansing.

All of a sudden my normally sleeping security officer, in an unmarked vehicle in front of my home, was repeatedly ringing a special security bell, calling me to the front door. I could not recall the last time that he had activated this select security system at 10 p.m. I rose from my chair, and looked out the window before going to the front door.

The security officer entered the foyer and said, "Mayor, we have three strange White men walking up and down the block apparently lost. One of them says his name is McGreevey and that they are looking for you. Do you know them? Should I tell them to leave? They look kind of funny!"

I opened my outer glass framed door, stepped just outside and saw three colleagues in the persons of State Senators John Lynch, Raymond Lesniak and a waving Mayor/State Senator James McGreevey. "Sharpe, I hope we didn't wake you. We need to speak with you," McGreevey said. "It's very important, it couldn't wait until tomorrow." I dismissed my security officer.

Wearing my full-length, burgundy cotton bathrobe, I invited them in and led them into the living room. They were dressed casually. Jim and I sat facing each other in wing chairs and John and Ray sat between us on the sofa facing the fire place. I offered each a drink, but they were not thirsty. They looked desperate and worried.

"Hey, no problem," I said. "You are always welcome at any time, how can I help you this evening?" I asked.

"Sharpe, this is very serious and we need your help," Senator Lynch said, leaning in from the sofa.

"What happened?" I asked, growing somewhat uneasy and apprehensive. "What's wrong? Someone get hurt? What's going on?"

Again Lynch, now with his hands waving in the air said, "You know that Jim almost beat Whitman when he ran for governor?"

"I know that," I replied.

Lynch continued, "Well we believe that Jim is the best Democrat for us to take back the State House in 2000."

"Everything is in place for us to move out of the cellar and up to the second floor majority conference room, with windows," Senator Lesniak added, laughingly. "Just think some much needed fresh air. We lost everything and being in the minority is no fun and no windows, I want to see some grass again."

"Jim is a hard campaigner and we simply can't afford to blow this opportunity. We need to win," Lynch added, "All of my numbers point to a big victory."

I stood up and said, "Wait a minute, you are preaching to the choir, I agree with you. So why is it necessary for you to tell me this at 10 p.m. on a Friday night?"

"Unfortunately," Lynch stated, "Bob Torricelli plans to announce next week that he has the support of a majority of the county chairmen behind him. I don't believe that he is telling the truth, but he could mess things up. We've got to go on the offense. We've got to kill his momentum right now!"

All of a sudden, McGreevey jumped up and very emotionally blurted out, "I'll bet that S.O.B. will show up hugging some movie star or a Miss America candidate, hell, he should move to Hollywood and run for Governor of California. Sharpe, this is not fair after I busted my chops running against Whitman," McGreevey said. "I could have won with a little more support, and especially from Bob. Torricelli is nothing more than a hotdog," McGreevey concluded.

I sat in the wing chair, rubbing my chin. It was obvious to me that the three gentlemen sitting before me were serious. McGreevey, in fact, was quite distraught. I wondered what they wanted from me. As though reading my mind, McGreevey started to speak again.

"Sharpe, I need this favor," he said moving closer. Placing his hands on my shoulders he said, "You've got to do this for me."

"Do what" I asked?

"You can do it," Lesniak said.

"You are the only one who can pull it off." Lynch joined in.

"Do what?" I asked again.

They were all singing the same song over and over again, "You can do it." McGreevey was now in tears and wiped his eyes before returning to his chair.

My living room became quiet and McGreevey's tear drops wet the kelly green carpet. No one spoke. Everyone just stared into space. It was a weird, highly emotional setting. If I didn't know better we could have been at a séance waiting for Houdini to appear.

Finally, Lynch stood up and said, "Sharpe, here is our plan. We need you to call a press conference on Monday and endorse James McGreevey for Governor. You know how to do this."

"Wait a minute," I interrupted Lynch. "You want me to call a press conference, endorse McGreevey and that's a big thing?"

"Bigger," Lynch replied.

"Jim will win." Lesniak then spoke, "Torricelli will not run if you endorse McGreevey, trust me."

"He will drop out," Lynch said.

I couldn't take it anymore. "Hey, what are you guys drinking or smoking that makes you think Torricelli will drop out simply because I endorse McGreevey?" I asked.

"Trust me," Lynch said. "He will drop out."

McGreevey, with his voice cracking, was on his feet again, "Sharpe, Sharpe, you've got to save me, just listen to them, they have done their homework. Just listen. Please shut up and listen."

Lynch repeated himself, "If you endorse McGreevey, Torricelli will drop out."

"Okay, okay, enough sermons," I said. "I will call a press conference on Monday. But, I want some of your Central and South Jersey supporters to join with my supporters, is that a deal?"

I angrily gave my misgivings learned from past experiences supporting other politicians. I reminded them that I had stood up for Tom D'Alessio when all of his so-called friends deserted him. They had refused to stand next to him at his press conference when declaring his innocence after his indictment.

"I got my brains knocked out with five years of investigation, under the banner: 'The man standing beside him, Sharpe James, will be next.' This time I will surface only when all of our supporters are in place, no more solo flights. No more respect for the candidate. We are all in the boat together, sink or swim, okay?" I looked at them waiting for a sign.

We all stood and gave each other a big hug. The clandestine meeting was over. "You guys can leave," I said. "I've got a lot of work to do between tonight and Monday, a lot of work. Thanks for visiting urban America."

All day Saturday my staff worked the telephones obtaining a ballroom at the Robert Treat Hotel in downtown Newark, inviting all of our supporters, Essex County political leadership and of course, the press. "A full Monty." I wrote my speech.

Monday at noon the Robert Treat Hotel was alive and buzzing with excitement and the second floor Atlantic conference room was packed like a sardine can. The hallway was also crowded and noisy. It was show and tell time.

As arranged, I stayed hidden in the first floor restaurant until I got the word that everything was in place. Even my political enemies were fighting to get near the podium. Senate President Richard Codey and Congressman Donald Payne, never camera shy, were standing at the podium. Politicians sure like to pose in front of a standing room only crowd with cameras rolling. It was time for my entrance. It was time to get serious.

Struggling through the crowd, giving a few handshakes, a few hugs, and receiving some lipstick smears I stared out at the men and women, who had no idea what I was about to say. It was time for my speech. The podium belonged to me. After all, I was paying the freight and taking all the risks:

"Ladies and gentlemen, today I rise to remind you that 'promises made should be promises kept.' Four years ago, when Congressman Donald Payne wanted to be the first African American United States Senator and when Robert Menendez wanted to be the first Hispanic

United States Senator from New Jersey, we denied them and chose Robert Torricelli as our candidate. We felt he was more qualified and the best candidate. He won and has become a great United States Senator. He has made New Jersey proud.

"When Jim McGreevey asked to run against Christine Todd Whitman for Governor, we all said yes. We all gave him no chance to win; yet, he surprised us and almost won. Since then he has never stopped campaigning for governor, and now he wants a second chance. 'Promises made should be promises kept.' In politics all we have is our word.

Therefore, we should continue to support Torricelli for United States Senator, and we should continue to support James McGreevey for governor. 'Promises made should be promises kept.'"

The overflowing crowd roared with approval. The next day *The Star-Ledger* headline statewide read, "James endorses McGreevey for Governor, 'promises made should be promises kept.'"

On Tuesday, the following day, Torricelli dropped out of the race for governor, confirming what old pros, Senator's John Lynch and Raymond Lesniak, knew was simple politics. They understood that if a democratic candidate for governor could not carry the democratic stronghold, Essex County, they could not win; and if a Republican could not carry republican stronghold, Bergen County, they could not win the governorship. You must start out with those political bases locked up. McGreevey now had Essex County and Bob Torricelli did not. McGreevey was the democratic candidate for governor, and went on to win the State House.

While I kept my word, "Promises made should be promises kept," I had lost a friend. Bob Torricelli never spoke to me again. To make matters worse, when his Chief of Staff Jamie Fox, became Deputy Director at the Port Authority, he would hold the same grudge and deny Newark services and contractual rental fees for airport land until my successful court suit.

Jim McGreevey would go on to become a good and popular governor. He also became a good personal friend of mine. Our friendship was put to the test, however, when he and Governor Pataki of New York decided to honor 9/11 heroes by changing the name of Newark Airport to "Liberty International" without any input from the local government. It was insulting to Newark to say the least. We were not opposed to honoring 9/11 heroes it was being left out of the decision making process that we opposed. I forcefully reminded McGreevey that it was our land, (Elizabeth, NJ owned a small portion) our airport and the Port Authority of NY/NJ had a lease to manage it, not take it away from us.

McGreevey suggested adding Newark to the end of "Liberty International," but it was not acceptable and we threatened to demonstrate if necessary. "No one will ever remember the name, Newark, if it is placed at the end, only 'Liberty International' will be quoted and remembered," I warned him. I could hear the airline stewardess saying *Please fasten your seat belt and pull your chair forward, we are preparing to land at Liberty International Airport*, with no mention of Newark. Just the thought was painful to me.

After several heated debates, McGreevey reluctantly compromised with the name "Newark Liberty International Airport," and our lease was extended until 2065 (the previous lease expired in 2031), a first year payment of $100 million annually thereafter with $12.5 million per year until 2036 set aside to capitalize projects in the City and $3 million per year in supplement rent. We also won an escalation of rent payments every five years in proportion to the growth in airport and seaport revenues. Happy days were here again.

I signed a proclamation formalizing the lease agreement on October 31, 2002 at Newark Liberty International Airport with the Port authority Deputy Executive Director Michael R. DeCotis. Governor McGreevey was in a bubbly mood as he stood before the cameras sermonizing, "This is a finalized lease that benefits all parties and we fulfill a promise to rename our historic international airport to honor all the heroes who have defended our country through the years, especially the heroes of September 11."

I echoed his meaningful patriotic thoughts and added, We are creating an economic engine for the region for public and private

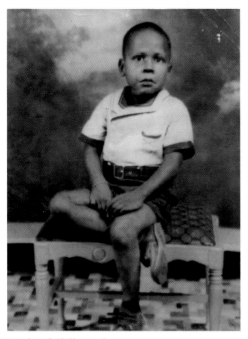

Early childhood, 1939

Early school picture, Newark, NJ
circa 1945

On Emmet Street in Newark
with neighbor Kevin McGuiness.

Graduation picture from South Side
High School ("Bulldogs") in 1954.

In the Army 1960, Schweinfurt Germany.

In 1964 I married Mary Lou Mattison from Walhalah, SC.

1970 Black & Puerto Rican Convention Community's Choice Team:
(L–R) Ramon Aneses, Ted Pinckney, Donald Tucker, Ken Gibson, Earl Harris, Dennis Westbrook & me.

Elected south ward councilman, 1970. (L–R) City Clerk Harry Reichenstein, me, Frank Megaro and Mayor Elect Kenneth A. Gibson

My family circa 1978.
(L–R) John, Mary,
Elliott and me
holding Kevin

Campaigning for mayor in 1986

Ashe/ Bollettieri
City National Tennis
Program started in
Newark, 1987.
(L–R) Arthur Ashe,
Sharpe James and
Nick Bollettieri.

Receiving honorable doctorate degree
from Montclair State College with
Senator Wynona Lipman, 1988. Also
recieved honorable doctorate degree
from Drew University in 1991.

Black history presentation to Mayor
Sharpe James (r) by US Senator Bill
Bradley, (c) 1989.

Campaigning
(state coordinator) for
Donald Payne for congressman
and Jesse Jackson for president,
1988.

State Coordinator &
Fundraiser for James Florio
for Governor, 1989.
The check is for $200,000.
me (c) and (r) James Florio.

Newark ABC Celebrity Tennis Match with
(R–L) Governor Tom Kean, Arthur Ashe,
Boris Becker and me.

Presenting medallion to my hero,
Nelson Mandela, at Newark
International Airport, 1992

Newark recipient of USCM City Livability Award 1992, for leadership and development of partnerships

Me and Newark's own, Whitney Houston, circa 1992

James' NHA Implosion Program (Columbus Homes) 1994

WYNONA LIPMAN GARDENS, FORMERLY CHRISTOPHER COLUMBUS HOMES
300 TOWNHOUSE UNITS

Replacement housing for demolished Columbus Homes.

With the greatest;
"Float like a butterfly, sting like a bee,"
Muhammad Ali.

Mayor Sharpe James welcomes
Dalai Lama to Newark in the 1990's.

Sharpe James (in red) with other members of the Rainbow Yacht Club (RYC).

Overnight guests at the White House with President Bill Clinton and First Lady Hillary, 1994.

State Senator Sharpe James introducing his bill #S-2030, the first bill to abolish dual office holding in the state of NJ, 1999.

State Coordinator for James McGreevey for Governor. (L–R) Sharpe James, Dina Matos McGreevey, James McGreevey and John Corzine

Congresswoman Shirley Chisholm visits Essex County College in Newark, NJ, 1999.

Celebrating with Rev. Al Sharpton after winning an unprecedented fifth term as mayor in 2002.

With then U.S. Senator Barack Obama at Essex County College, Newark, N.J., 2004

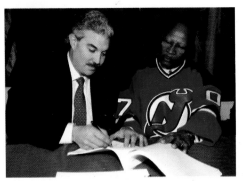
Signing agreement with NJ Devils' principal owner, Jeff Vanderbeek, to build Prudential Center, 2005

Receiving award at Petersburg FCC. Me in center with 2 fellow inmates.

Cheering, flag waving crowd greets former Mayor Sharpe James, home at Newark Penn Station, 2010.

redevelopment projects and providing jobs for our people." The airport and city would merge together in building a new oasis.

Congratulatory remarks were made by Port Authority Chairman, Jack G. Sinagra and Port Authority Executive Director, Joseph J. Seymour. I only wish that I had been a drinker for the amount of beer, wine and champagne that was served ending this historical, spirited occasion. Jim and I were friends again. As governor he always tried to do the right thing.

It was McGreevey's personal life, however, that the spotlight would focus on. Only two years into his term it was discovered that his traveling aide and the person he was recommending for State Security Director, Golan Cipel, was in fact his secret lover. Cipel was a disgruntled lover now blackmailing the Governor. Jim McGreevey, rather than stay and fight charges of infidelity and defend his sexual preference, chose to quit. To me he is still James McGreevey, former Governor. James McGreevey is a good person, was a good governor, and remains a good friend.

Jon Corzine – 2000 & 2004

There's an old saying "Follow the money and you will find your answer." With McGreevy's resignation, rumors began to swirl on who would take his place. Senate President, Richard Codey, had been sworn in as acting governor until the next election. He was the popular odds on favorite to take McGreevey's place.

Once again, the question was about campaign war chest. Everyone was wondering if Codey could get his wallet to match his personality and quick wit. While he was robbing his piggy bank to get an exact count of funds, the man we had just labored to make United States Senator, stepped forward for the job.

Once, a shy, withdrawn, uncertain and tongue tied candidate for public office, United States Senator, Jon Corzine, now wanted more. He had tasted the perks that came with holding public office and now was addicted. He had name recognition, a high profile national office, and most importantly, no one to match his political or personal war chest. He would spend like a drunk or whatever was necessary to win. To most he was viewed as a cash cow. To a few he was a sugar daddy.

Corzine, a former obscure and unknown Goldman Sachs executive, had walked into my office and asked for help a few years earlier. "Sharpe," he had said, "I have been told that you helped Bill Bradley, James Florio, Jesse Jackson, Donald Payne, Bill Clinton, James McGreevey, and Robert Menendez, do you think you can help me become a United States Senator?" More questions followed: "How can I win," was one of the first. Still later he asked, "Sharpe, should I wear contact lenses? Should I shave my beard?"

Corzine really wanted to remake himself. He was totally different from other political candidates that had sought my help. He was not overly loquacious like McGreevey, not indifferent like Florio, nor did he have a holier-than-thou attitude as Bill Bradley had. He was also not a consensus type individual like U.S. Senator Robert Menendez. *If elected, Corzine will begin a new breed of politician,* I thought.

In the beginning Corzine was very shy to the point of always looking down when speaking before a group. Rarely would he look you in the eye, and he appeared nervous. He often closed his eyes when speaking. When he first walked into my office with his gray speckled beard and horn rimmed glasses, he looked like one of the Smith Brothers on the cough drops box. I thought to myself, *He has a lot of money and we have a lot of work to do.*

I had never asked for money from any candidate that I helped and I never received a penny from Jon. I had to believe in the person and his program in order to crank our organization into gear. Our political labor was always viewed as a crusade for and a love affair with the candidate. We were committed from the beginning to the end, during good times and bad times. I told Jon, "We are going to make you the next United States Senator from New Jersey." For the first time that day Jon looked me straight in the eye and smiled.

I remember saying, "Jon you are worth more than $400 million, stop worrying about how you look and what other people are thinking and saying; if anything they want to be you. I'll trade places with you tomorrow." I told him that we should work on name recognition, "Get out and press the flesh," I had said. "Let's spend on advertising. We need to build an army of supporters, and you need to learn how to give a three minute speech looking people dead in the eye."

Jon was very receptive to my suggestions. He appeared to trust my instincts and even learned to smile more. I remember his smile when I said to him, "Please keep wearing that Mandela sweater vest look." We put a full court press on changing Jon from Wall Street to Main Street. He learned quickly and became a folk hero. He was the no frill political candidate for the United States Senate. He even learned how to talk in front of a group without looking down and without closing his eyes.

Corzine became simply the guy next door that you could go borrow an egg from. When the polls closed on election night, our new folk hero had been elected United States Senator from New Jersey. Jon bought himself a victory. He certainly could afford it. Money wasn't everything, but it sure beat whatever was in second place.

Now, all of a sudden, while still learning on the job, Jon wanted to be governor. He had been advised that acting governor, Richard Codey, was the perceived front runner and apparent heir to McGreevey's vacant seat. Jon, however, was now drunk with power and money and would not waiver in his desire to become governor. He viewed the governorship as being CEO and Chairman of the Board at the statehouse as a substitute for his days on Wall Street. When he read newspaper articles stating Codey was getting serious and mounting a campaign to become governor and building a war chest, Jon became angry. He called and said, "I want you take a message to Senator Codey."

I said "Jon, what message? What's your beef with Codey?"

"Well, I'm the United States Senator; I'm funding the State Democratic Organization; you tell Codey that if he is thinking about challenging me for governor in the primary, he can forget about being Senate President If I'm elected. Then he paused, and said, "Tell Codey that he might not even qualify for dog catcher." I could tell that he had a frown on his face from his tone of voice.

Jon continued to rant, "Tell Codey not to think about entering the primary, tell him to play it smart and he will keep his Senate presidency."

I thought Dick was our strongest candidate and that he would respond with an angry retort. I was dead wrong and terribly disappointed when I delivered the message and he simply smiled, laughed it off, offered no response and later folded his tent on his quest to become governor. Jon Corzine had scared Senate President Dick Codey out of his wits. Corzine's money was talking for him. Jon Corzine was now a consummate politician seeking more power and fame.

Rumor had it that being senate president was laden with hidden perks that Codey didn't want to risk giving up if he lost in a primary race. In fact, it was alleged that he had helped a friend turn a $2 million investment into a $100 million plus revenue stream. More interesting, was that State Senator Wayne Bryant with less clout, less perks and less on his plate had been indicted, convicted and sent to a federal prison in West Virginia for abusing his office. The targeting of minority officials was again the topic of discussion.

Nonetheless, after Codey decided not to run in the gubernatorial democratic primary, the door opened even wider for Jon Corzine. My telephone rang, it was Jon. He wanted me to meet him at his South Jersey, Toms River headquarters as soon as possible. He was all excited and explained that he had learned that Doug Forester, his Republican opponent, was going to run a negative campaign for governor and would oppose all urban initiatives; especially the proposed Newark arena and that he would target the Newark Housing Authority.

Harold Lucas, the Housing Authority's embattled director was under fire for having a lavish executive office. Jon also stated that Forester was going to raise questions regarding the city of Newark's decision to purchase new municipal garbage trucks, each the size of a Sherman tank, using federal grant dollars. "Can you meet with me tomorrow?" Jon asked.

I replied, "No problem."

I was pacing up and down Corzine's South Jersey headquarters thinking what a great opportunity he had to expose Forester's bias campaign plan to divide our state. When Jon entered the room, an hour late, we took seats at his conference table and he began to rehash the negative campaign Forester was planning to run using TV ads and personal appearances. I looked at Jon and said, "Great, you need to expose him, you need to remind voters of the words of Dr. Martin Luther King, Jr., 'An injustice anywhere is a threat to justice everywhere.' You should portray diversity as strength, not a weakness. Let's get started!" I was so enthusiastic. "When do we call a press conference?"

Jon remained strangely silent for a moment then looked me squarely in my face with cold steel eyes and said, "I can't!"

I immediately asked, "Why not?"

Jon slowly said, "Because I want to win." He repeated "I can't do it. I want to win. Sharpe, whatever urban initiatives Forester opposes, I will also oppose. I can win this thing! I can be governor. I can be governor," he kept repeating to himself. His mind was made up. There was nothing else to talk about.

I was stunned beyond belief. The man, who didn't think that he could be elected United States Senator, was now addicted to the idea of being elected governor. He would do anything within his power to become Governor. Silently, I drove back to my office in Newark and violated every rule of "Politics 101," never put anything in writing which can come back to haunt you.

I wrote a personal letter to Jon Corzine, soon to be the next Governor of New Jersey, telling him he was wrong to abandon the urban community in order to solicit suburban votes. I challenged him to take the high road and not the low road. I asked him to denounce Forester for dividing our state along racial lines. With all the facts on the table, I felt that maybe he would change his mind.

I was absolutely wrong. Two weeks later Jon Corzine was denouncing the proposed Newark arena (Prudential Center) as a waste of the taxpayers' money, while supporting the proposed Soccer Stadium for mostly White Harrison, New Jersey. As I watched him perform at his press conference, ranting and raving against urban America, against the arena, against the Newark Housing Authority, I wondered if we had created a monster with no morals.

Yet, the height of Jon's hypocrisy didn't come until after his election to governor, when he attended opening night at the arena that he and Mayor elect, Cory Booker, had condemned, called a waste of tax payer's money, and a criminal act by the James Administration. On opening night, Devils' fans found Corzine and Booker smiling broadly, while cutting the ribbon at the arena they had predicted would never be built. They were praising the arena and proudly wearing Devils jerseys. They showed every tooth in their mouths as they mugged for the cameras. And, just to add salt to the wound, Mayor-elect Booker referred to it as "My arena."

I had recently retired as mayor and was seated visibly in the fourth row. I was not introduced, nor asked to speak or even acknowledged. The

Devils organization that I had fought so hard for, raising $185 million to build the arena, putting together a dream team of municipal administrators to bring the plan into fruition, on time, and under budget, discarded me like garbage from their kitchen.

Although I had not been indicted or accused of any wrongdoing, the Devils organization had used the excuse of my investigation by the U.S. Attorney's office for treating me like I had leprosy. They were also trying to avoid negative headlines. In my estimation the Devils' real motivation was they wanted to get in bed with the new mayor-elect, hoping for any freebies they could wrangle out of the city. Being naïve, the newly elected mayor fell for it and this romance would soon cost the city millions of dollars. They were all true political hypocrites. They spoke out of both sides of their mouths. Governor Jon Corzine, Mayor Cory Booker and the Devils were perfect together.

I had labored to make Jon Corzine a U.S. Senator and Governor of New Jersey. I had advised him of the importance of diversity, equal opportunity and the need for justice being blind. Once he succeeded in becoming United States Senator and Governor, he resented any advice from me. We were never on speaking terms thereafter.

In fact, when I led a Newark delegation to Trenton for a private meeting with the Governor to discuss municipal aid, he secretly invited the press and tried to embarrass the delegation. The statehouse reporters said no other governor in history, that they could remember, had invited the press to come and hide out for a privately scheduled meeting in his office.

The reporters asked, "Why is Corzine doing this?" I had no answer for them other than Jon was now flexing his newly acquired political muscles. To underscore his vengeful behavior, Jon even invited disgruntled council members and community activists from Newark who were opposed to our municipal aid agenda. He really wanted to embarrass and silence me. He wanted the man who had helped to create him, yours truly, out of the way. I represented the past that he was running away from.

Jon Corzine wanted me to become a political prisoner. In 2008, at my trial he ordered his State Attorney General to assign one of her lawyers, Perry Primavera, to join the Christopher Christie prosecution team against me. Interestingly, Primavera would be the assistant prosecutor who jumped up in the air and uttered the illegal summation to the jury saying, "We have no smoking gun, no real evidence and no one will take the stand and testify that James did anything wrong, however, I exhort you to, use your imagination and send a message." The jury did use their imagination and sent a message as instructed, a message that the justice system is bias.

As governor, Jon Corzine developed a set of expectations for the citizens of New Jersey and a different set of expectations for himself. For instance he saw nothing wrong with him doling out cash to campaign workers once he was elected to office, which is illegal. He saw nothing wrong with him living in New York City three to four days a week while serving as governor of New Jersey, a position later made legal by his Attorney General Zulima V. Farber. Zulima was later rewarded by being fired for appearing at the scene where her close personal friend was receiving a traffic summons.

Corzine saw nothing wrong in using his clout to get friends out of jail, or to negotiate the largest union contract in the state with a close personal friend, a union executive officer. This was clearly a conflict of interest, but Jon went to court to keep from revealing their exchange of e-mails which he feared would expose him.

From Goldman Sachs to the senate to governor to CEO of MF Global, where 1.6 billion dollars in clients' funds went missing, Jon Corzine has been on a roller coaster of changing identities. His legacy reminds one to "be careful of what you ask for, you just might get it." Jon was a rich boy who saw no evil.

CHAPTER THIRTEEN

Philanthropy

"It is easier for a camel to go through the eye of a needle,
than for a rich man to enter into the Kingdom of God."
-Matthew 19:24

A biblical reference in Timothy 6:10 states, "The love of money is the root of all evil." This statement does not rule out the importance of money to purchase goods, pay for services and other normal living expenses, but it distinguishes those who use money to live from those who simply love to accumulate money. Some people's lust for money far exceeds their basic needs; they accumulate money that they will never spend.

A prime example of a person who lusts for money could be Bernard Madoff, who was convicted of using a Ponzi scheme which swindled his investors, many of whom were close friends, out of millions of dollars. Once convicted, Madoff showed no remorse for his actions. U.S. District Court Judge Denny Chin called Madoff's ruse, "an extraordinary evil."

People like this are possessed with a zealous insatiable goal of making money. Because of this there is a tendency to label the rich as an elitist group, not caring about mainstream America, especially the poor and the disadvantaged. They are accused of being indifferent and selfish. They are the exact opposite of the poor man who will buy everyone a drink after work on Friday: "Hey bartender run the bar on me." Seldom will you hear this statement coming from a rich man. One values money and the other spends money foolishly.

Fortunately, during my tenure as Mayor, I had an opportunity to meet some wealthy men and women who were rich by birth, or acquired wealth in their lifetime, and were dedicated to the well-being of others. They humbly practiced the art and tradition of philanthropy. They were willing to give freely of their property, money or time to advance the welfare of others; they possessed a desire to make a positive difference in the world at large.

Locally, I promoted the philosophy "never look down on a person unless you are going to pick him up." A sincere belief in brotherhood and the milk of human kindness is a worthy principle. Interestingly enough, the belief in philanthropy is not new. It existed during ancient Egypt and Greece, where Royal families gave gifts to establish libraries and universities; and the medieval church supported hospitals and orphanages.

During my tenure as Mayor I had the pleasure of meeting, face to face, two outstanding philanthropists in the persons of Ray Chambers and Doris Duke. They were like angels sent from Heaven, and Newark greatly benefited from their vision, leadership, dedication, courage and of course their generous benevolence. They were role models among role models.

Without Ray Chambers and Doris Duke's love for Newark there would be no New Jersey Performing Arts Center (NJPAC), Newark Ready Scholar's Program, Urban Screens Multiplex, Newark Boys and Girls Club; or, the giant among giants, the state-of-the-art 18,000 seat Prudential Center hosting the NHL New Jersey Devils, Seton Hall University Big East basketball and formerly the home court for the NBA New Jersey Nets before their move to Brooklyn. Chambers and Duke's visionary support and contributions to Newark went even further than their brick and mortar contributions.

How do you put a price tag on an idea to uplift the people? How do you add up so many acts of kindness? What can you offer multi-millionaires for the countless hours they spend in Newark at meetings, visitations and activities in support of your city? Chambers and Duke were joined by the Prudential Insurance Company of America which was founded in Newark and has never abandoned its birthplace.

Every Prudential CEO and President has treated Newark as a member of its extended family. Prudential has led in social, infrastructure, housing and educational contributions for a better city and quality of life.

Some noteworthy, Prudential leaders, during my tenure in office included: retiring CEO and President Robert Beck, Robert Winters and especially Art Ryan. They all deserve medals of honor for their philanthropic attention to the city of Newark. In fact, there would be no Giants, Jets or MetLife Stadium in the Meadowlands if Prudential had not stepped in when New York banks frowned upon the idea of financing a stadium in New Jersey.

Art Ryan and his lovely wife Patricia were community activists as well as philanthropists. Patricia was quite comfortable in the boardroom raising money for neighborhood groups or Military Park or hosting holiday concerts for the young and the old. Together, Art and Patricia greatly assisted the Newark school system, NJPAC and the "fee-based" buses that circle downtown Newark shuttling patrons between NJPAC and the Ironbound restaurant section of the city for only a dollar. Whenever a major project, that would revitalize the city, required financing, Prudential would always step up to the plate and greatly assist.

Prudential's outstanding work in Newark was buoyed by the Victoria Foundation and its former impresario Executive Director Catherine McFarland. The Victoria Foundation President was a member of the Chubb family that founded the Victoria Foundation, the debonair Percy Chubb III, who enjoyed wearing colorful golf attire. At those NJPAC board meetings that I attended, I kept thinking that at any moment he would take out a golf club and tee off. Each year The Foundation would publish a lengthy and distinguished list of grants provided to community based organizations and non-profits in Newark.

Under neighborhood revitalization the Victoria Foundation supported New Community Corporation and La Casa de Don Pedro. Other recipients included the Boys and Girls Clubs of Newark, Apostles' House, Above the Rim, Aspira, CREST Community Development Corporation, FOCUS Hispanic Center for Community Development, Habitat for Humanity, Newark, Ironbound Community Center, Leadership Newark, New Jersey Historical Society, NJPAC, Project GRAD, QUEST INK, Newark Symphony Hall, Newark Public Schools, Queen of Angels School, United Vailsburg Service Organization and the list goes on and on. Their heartfelt benevolence is surely felt in the City of Newark.

If any businessman were to receive a prize for assisting the city, the late great Robert Van Fossan, chairman and chief executive officer of Mutual Benefit Life would win in a landslide. He was one of the few, or the only one, who made it to the top himself, having started at the bottom of the ladder. Van Fossan was comfortable jumping over debris strewn rat infested stagnant water filled basements to explore the need for a South Ward Industrial Park. He never complained about insane daily 5 a.m. meetings to explore ways to better the city of Newark.

Van Fossan earned the right to be the spokesman for New Jersey businesses. He lent his personal strength to keep the New Jersey Symphony Orchestra and Opera in the city of Newark. When some weak leaders of the Symphony threatened to move out of the city, Van, as he was affectionately called, said, "Go, go ahead and move, but remember that we, the Newark business community, provide 75% of your operating budget and you won't receive another dime; go ahead and move." The Symphony Orchestra remained in Newark. Van was tough. He was fair. He was dedicated. I loved that guy. He was for real.

Likewise, it was my many after hours' meetings with philanthropists Ray Chambers and Doris Duke which have made everlasting impressions upon my cerebral hemisphere. They have contributed so much to the city of Newark and have provided so many wonderful and treasured memories with their many acts of kindness. Each of them possessed a deep, spiritual and visionary viewpoint of life. Both felt that their life on earth had a meaningful purpose and a goal to achieve. Perhaps it was best expressed by writer, George Bernard Shaw, who wrote this favorite quote of President John Fitzgerald Kennedy:

> *There are those who look at the way things are,*
> *asking why?*
> *I dream of things that never were,*
> *and ask why not?*

Ray Chambers

Both Ray and Doris were looking for a better world and people; they wanted to challenge the status quo. They felt a personal obligation to challenge and redirect the id and ego energy in man's existence. Meeting them often challenged one to raise their own level of consciousness, thinking and action in bettering their community. In their presence I felt compelled to dream the impossible dream.

I give heartfelt recognition and praise to Ray Chambers, a graduate of Newark's West Side High School. Ray became highly successful when he and William Simon founded Wesray Company which introduced "leveraged-buyout," where investors could make vast profits by acquiring companies and enhancing their efficiency. In one of their most celebrated acquisitions, in January 1982, Wesray purchased Gibson Greetings Inc. for $80.5 million and one year later took it public at a valuation of $290 million. There were many other profitable (Champion Sports Wear and a home run in purchasing Avis Rental Cars) investments.

Ray became fabulously wealthy and since then has dedicated his life to improving the quality of life for others. As the founder of the Amelia Foundation, he is one of the leading philanthropists in the state of New Jersey. He has spent a lifetime assisting at-risk youth and helping to rebuild the City of Newark. He courageously led the fight to build NJPAC in Newark; Urban Screens Multiplex; the revitalization of West Side Park and indirectly he is responsible for bringing the state-of-the-art, 18,000 seat Prudential Center to Newark. He also saved the Boys and Girls Clubs in Newark. Ray Chambers' earlier successes and commitment to Newark energized others to invest in Newark.

Interestingly enough, Ray is embarrassed and painfully shy in accepting any awards for his exemplary achievement. He did it not for praise, but for personal fulfillment and a sense of responsibility. Case in point one need not be praised for helping a senior citizen across the street; it was the right thing to do.

I further recognize another gift in Ray that has greatly benefited the city of Newark, the state of New Jersey and America. It is his investment in the human spirit and righteousness of man as opposed to mere mortar, bricks and steel projects.

One day Ray spoke about evangelical pastor, Rick Warren, who wrote and sold 20 million copies of his book, "The Purpose Driven Life;" and the next day Reverend Reginald T. Jackson, Barbara Bell, myself and others were on Ray's private jet flying to Orlando, Florida, to personally meet Pastor Warren who was scheduled to preach before an arena crowd of 10,000. After the prayer session, Ray invited the pastor to host a religious revival in Newark, in concert with local clergymen. Of course it immediately became a hot potato among local clergyman who asked, "Why should we allow a White clergyman from outside to host a revival in Newark; it sends the wrong message?" If they couldn't get the credit for the revival, they would prefer not to have it. The city of Newark would be the loser.

My first meeting with Ray Chambers took place in my office shortly after I was first elected Mayor of Newark. Ray had come to ask if I was aware of a program where one of its graduates had returned to his high school and offered scholarships to everyone in the senior class.

I replied, "Are you referring to Eugene Lang who was invited to speak to a group of sixth graders in Harlem and told them, "If you will study and finish school, I will personally pay for your college education?"

Ray, sitting ramrod straight and unemotional said, "I'm not sure if it's the same program, however, my idea is to expand the program."

"If it's the same program I believe that he paid college tuition for everyone in the class who graduated," I said. "What would you do differently?" I humbly asked Ray.

Unfolding his arms and with piercing eyes, Ray said he would like to offer a program giving every 7th grader a chance to attend the college or university of their choice, if they could maintain a C average through high school and thereafter. "We could also offer them tutoring and mentoring programs as well as employment opportunities after graduation," he had said.

I was speechless. I thought I was dreaming. I wondered if I had heard him right. Without a doubt Ray Chambers embraced the philosophy of the United Negro College Fund, "A mind is a terrible thing to waste."

Ray was still sitting erect, calm, and unflappable, yet there was excitement in his eyes as he explained his educational proposal. "We need to help these young students," he proclaimed as though he were speaking about his own children; "they represent our future," he had said.

I sat before this wonderful man flabbergasted, recognizing the magnitude of his proposal. I simply could not believe that he understood what a program like this would cost. I decided to bring some hard reality into our discussion. I politely interrupted and said, "Ray, wait a minute, funding one class or several classes like Mr. Eugene Lang did was an expensive undertaking. Your plan to include every 7th grader would cost a lot of money, like millions of dollars," I said. "Are you aware of the potential cost before going to the drawing board?"

Ray, still showing controlled excitement, was unfazed by any mention of cost. Then he abruptly said, "Maybe $15 million?"

I was scared to repeat the amount and remained silent. Everything happening was unreal to me as a newly elected mayor. Ray shattered the silence by asking, "When do you think that you can convene a meeting with the superintendent of schools? We need to get started as quickly as possible."

Now I was alive. Now I was animated. This is real. Now I could speak. "Tomorrow if possible," I said, excitedly. "I will be in the Superintendent's office tomorrow morning. There should be no problem getting all of us together to achieve this commendable goal."

I asked Ray if he had a name for his program and he softly responded, "The Ready Scholars Program." I thought to myself, *there are going to be some "ready" and very happy students and parents who have never dreamed of higher education opportunities like this for a member of their family.*

What a gift from Ray Chambers making it possible for low-income families to dream great dreams with his heartfelt assistance, a blueprint for achieving them. The Newark Ready Scholars Program for all 7th graders became an instant success story and a role model for the nation. If only you could clone Ray Chambers.

Ray did not stop there. Without his efforts to build an art center in Newark it may never have happened. At every obstacle, and there were many, I would see Ray standing by his window, arms folded, looking at the city below. He remained stoic and obviously in deep thought. He had already raised a record $60 million for this public project, and he and Robert Van Fossan, of Mutual Benefit Life, had put up a $26 million letter of credit. Still we were having all kinds of problems.

I remember once when I walked over to him and said, "Ray, you can quit and I would understand. With so many ups and downs and the state reneging on so many promises, why suffer?"

Ray turned and looked at me with his steel eyes, and calmly and with steel determination said, "Sharpe, if it was easy, it would have been done already. Let's continue."

Ray was a man on a mission to improve the quality of life for all in our city. In moving the city forward he added to his agenda the Boys and Girls Club of Newark, the Urban Screens, local entrepreneurships and a West Side Park restoration program. Ray's determination reminded me of the time I asked Bob Massey, who sold Jefferson boats out of Point Pleasant, if the vessel I had purchased could take eight-foot seas? Bob looked at me and smiled, "Sharpe the boat can take it; the question is 'Can you take it?'" Here was Ray during a storm not fretting, not quitting, so the question was could we the City of Newark as the recipient of his benevolence take the day-to-day tribulations encountered fighting for an arts center. Ray was ready. Were we ready was the $64,000 question?

Ray Chambers demonstrated leadership ability during the building of the arena. He was the first person to reach into his pocket to purchase parcels of land needed for the arena footprint. He did so for the good of the city and the state. Someone had to step up and take a leadership role. He filled that vacuum unselfishly.

I will always cherish and remember the courage and grit that Ray demonstrated chastising former New Jersey Governor, James McGreevey in the Democratic conference room in Trenton. McGreevey had reneged on his promise to lobby the New Jersey Senate and Assembly to fund an arena in Newark. McGreevey who loved to talk tough, like a Baptist preacher, suddenly became speechless and embarrassed. All he could do was stare at the walls. Then he looked to me for help. I offered none. He deserved none and was about to tear. Judgment day had arrived.

Ray, showing emotion on this rare occasion, accused McGreevey of not being a man of his word. "You demonstrated callous weakness," he had said. If I had been asked to comment, I would have simply said, "Amen." The conference room, where so many political deals had been hatched, was now silent and without answers. Politics suffered a terrible blow that night.

Eventually Newark would showcase a world-class performing arts center. Newark would also (after a James McGreevey plan to sue the

Port Authority of New York and New Jersey for increased rents) receive a $1.2 billion settlement with $450 million in cash. The state-of-the-art Prudential Center was funded in part with this money.

It should be recognized that much of the development in Newark would never have happened without the vision, participation, courage and philanthropy of Ray Chambers. He loved people. He loved the city of Newark and he wanted a better America. As the Bible teaches us, "He was worthy to be praised."

Doris Duke

As a young man I read about the opulent wealth, glamour and intriguing lifestyle of one of America's richest daughters, Doris Duke. When she was born she was called "The Million Dollar Baby." Upon the unfortunate death of her father in 1925, Doris, at the age of twelve, became one of the richest girls in the world. Her father was James B. Duke, a tobacco millionaire who founded the American Tobacco Company. He, himself, was a philanthropist who in 1924 donated more than $100 million to Trinity College, which later changed its name to Duke University.

At Age 30 Doris was handed a check for $30 million. As an heiress she had it all. Some say she had as many husbands as imposing and magnificent mansions around the world, especially her estate in Hawaii called "Shangri-La," located on Diamond Head. Like the Pyramids along the Nile, Doris' estate in Hawaii was exotic and exciting, something to remember.

I could not think of J.B. Morgan, the Rockefellers or Vanderbilts without thinking of Doris Duke. Yet, she was quite different from the others, notwithstanding gender. For one thing Doris enjoyed being a member of the First Baptist Church of Nutley, New Jersey, a Black congregation. She enjoyed singing in its choir. When she died she left the founder and esteemed pastor, the late Reverend Dr. Lawrence Roberts, one million dollars. Yes indeed she was different from the other "old money" making families.

When she was not in Europe or Hawaii Doris was tending to her plush acres of Garden of Eden-like property and secretive 2,700-acre estate in Hillsborough, New Jersey. "Duke Farms" is located in Somerset County. It was here that she had fought and won every attempt by the local government to reduce her acreage for public use or to run utility lines across her property. She was willing to spend millions of dollars to protect her privacy. "Just leave me alone," she advised the authorities. "Just go away," she fired back through her lawyers.

Doris' lead attorney was the highly respected, unflappable Donald Robinson. He loved to dance, and was a carbon copy of Hollywood's legendary film star Edward G. Robinson; so much so that I often wondered if they were relatives. Donald represented the prestigious Robinson and Robinson Law firm in Newark.

One day as I was reading *The Wall Street Journal* in my office, the telephone rang; it was Donald Robinson who had always supported my annual fundraiser, which was creatively disguised as a fun-oriented birthday party with more than 1,500 guests in attendance. "Please," I would implore my guests, "no politics tonight. Let's have some fun." Don would arrive early and spend more time on the dance floor than any Chamber of Commerce business member. He was a highly knowledgeable, skilled and talented lawyer, and unlike some other corporate leaders and lawyers who were cold and stiff, Don was a people person as well.

Don could enjoy a good laugh and often joked with me. "Sharpe, this is Don, my client Doris Duke, would like to invite you for lunch at her home," he calmly said.

"Doris Duke?" I eagerly, excitedly and surprisingly responded. "Is this a joke?"

"Sharpe, I'm her attorney why would I be joking?" he replied. "Yes, Doris Duke, wants very much to have lunch with you at her home," he repeated.

Since I was silent, Don continued talking. "She likes what you are doing in Newark, She said you are creating an exciting renaissance and would like to talk to you about the proposed art center for Newark," he said. "She thinks it's a great idea and would like to explore the project with you. With your permission, I will call your secretary and schedule a convenient meeting at her home for lunch. Okay?"

"Don, for Doris Duke, I am ready to meet, greet and eat twenty four hours a day, so I will wait for your call. "Let's do it."

A few weeks later I walked out of City Hall onto Broad Street, and a chauffeur opened the door for me to step inside of one of the longest limousines I had ever seen. It almost blocked the whole front of City Hall. Stepping inside, Don was seated comfortably on a soft blue leather couch across the front of the vehicle. He was more than two body lengths away. Décor lights and well-stocked bars with a sink and television set lined the interior. As I moved the length of the luxury limo and sat next to him, Don greeted me, "Hi Sharpe, thanks for joining me, we are on our way to Morris County."

In that brief moment I thought of my humble beginnings in Jacksonville, Florida, and I knew that this was "a day that the Lord has made." The double stretch limo eased out of the city and raced up Route 280 then Route 80 heading to Morris County like a Concord jet; beauty, speed, no sound, it was like being on cloud nine. We were totally insulated from the driver and the outside world. The President's limo, which I had ridden in, could not offer any better accommodations. Ms. Duke's limo was top shelf all the way.

Don offered me a choice of soft drinks and snacks like a flight hostess. *We must be flying*, I thought. No one will ever be able to tell me that mayors don't travel in style after this trip. Although not normally a drinker, I just had to pick up the rich looking Tiffany glassware and sample some of the world's finest chilled champagne. It was cold, frosty and bubbly. I said to myself, *not too much, don't get carried away*. I vividly recalled a certain Rainbow Yacht Club member who after drinking four glasses of champagne started talking gibberish and calling every female in sight "cutie." So, I stopped after emptying one tall frosted stained Tiffany glass.

During the drive to Morris County, Don proudly spoke of the friendship between Doris Duke and Imelda Marcos, the former first lady of the Philippines who had been charged with fraud in a New York Court. He explained that he had been given five million dollars by Doris to go and bail her out. "The lady with the four hundred pair of shoes," he had laughed.

Don was aware of, and spoke fondly of, Doris's involvement with the First Baptist Church of Nutley and Pastor Lawrence Roberts. He said she sang in the church choir and immensely enjoyed the church congregation. Don mentioned the enormous gift Doris had given Pastor Roberts. He paused for a moment and then became very serious;

"She really wants to get involved helping the City of Newark. She has been following your work. Doris learned philanthropy at an early age from her father," he added.

With all of the wonderful promises made by Ray Chambers and now Doris Duke, and because Don was my friend, I asked the forbidden question. "Don," I said, "tell me the truth, who has more money, Ray Chambers or Doris Duke?"

Don propped up and laughed, "Sharpe, please don't ever compare old money with new money, remember that. When Doris Duke writes a check for five million that's her petty cash fund," he said. "Just remember that tobacco has been here a longtime and her father and grandfather were in the tobacco industry, also Duke Power Company has been here for some time, Doris will never have to worry about money," he said.

The driver then spoke over an intercom system announcing that we were approaching the Doris Duke estate. I thought he said we were preparing to land. Soon the Limo stopped at a stately guardhouse. I could not see another house in sight. I asked Don, "Where is the house?" He quietly responded, "About a half mile up the road."

The security person at the gatehouse was on the telephone speaking to someone. He hung up, turned to the limo driver and said, "You may go forward." We drove on a road surrounded by tall trees and every imaginable plant life shading the area like the Appalachian trial. A tall concrete wall was the outer boundary. A few minutes later we were surrounded by more beautiful trees, flowers and a sculptured landscape as far as the eye could see, with an open courtyard of manicured grass. It looked like Augusta, Georgia ready for the U.S. Open Golf Tournament.

Man, it must take an army to maintain these grounds, I thought. To the right of a large decorated brick patio with outdoor furniture for entertainment was a towering and flowing Charleston style Mansion. At any minute, I thought Scarlett O'Hara from *Gone with the Wind* would appear in her splendor.

We exited the limo, and led by Don I approached the huge, natural wood front door. Almost immediately a tall, smiling, swashbuckling gentleman said, "Please come in and have a seat. Ms. Duke is upstairs she will join you momentarily."

When I stared closely, the gentleman was wearing knickers and his silk shirt was adorned with medals. *He must have just stepped from a pirate ship,* I thought to myself. I took my eyes off the "butler," and following Don's eyes, I stood in amazement at the richness, elegance, opulence, exquisite artwork and beauty of the interior of the mansion, which was breathtaking. It was definitely "Gone with the Wind" all over again. I couldn't believe that people lived like this. *She must have a staff of fifty persons to maintain this place,* I thought.

The center mahogany staircase reminded me of the center staircase pictured on the Titanic. The plush beet red carpeting we were standing on had to be at least four inches thick. The huge center chandelier was spectacular with the finest crystal reflecting on a gilded ceiling and moldings of gold. I could not help but think, *this is not a home, it's a museum.* Then I thought, *it might be larger and most certainly better looking than our award winning Newark Museum.* Before we could get comfortable in huge Victorian chairs, with a glass of juice in our hands, the butler announced the arrival of Ms. Duke.

We stood and turned to the center hall staircase as a tall, willowy, fragile looking yet stoic and regal looking Doris Duke appeared at the center on the balcony. In a clear, concise, measured and unemotional voice she said, "Hi Don, Hi Sharpe," and began what seemed a difficult yet graceful descent down the winding staircase. Later I would learn that she had a bad knee.

This was my first sighting of the legendary Doris Duke. Don and I both stood, almost at attention, as if we were going to be inspected by a drill sergeant. Personally speaking, I could have felt no different than if I were meeting the renowned Queen of England. In my mind Doris Duke was no ordinary person. She pointed toward two glass double doors and said, "Let's have lunch on the terrace."

We followed the butler out to the terrace and were graciously seated. Soon we were served red wine. Doris, said, "I'm glad we could get together and talk, Sharpe. I have been reading about you and Newark. I am fascinated by your plan for an arts center. Please don't give up this idea. I, too, want to see Newark prosper. I want the people of Newark and the state of New Jersey to have a better life."

I sat there in amazement. Unable to say anything, I smiled at the lovely lady sitting before me.

Doris smiled back and said, "I truly believe that an arts center can energize people and prove that there is strength in diversity. Tell me, why are you pushing for it? How do you see it benefiting Newark?" she asked.

Don, who had been silent throughout this exchange, turned and looked at me waiting for my answer to his rich client. His job was to get me there. Now I was on my own. Just as I was about to answer the question, the butler, wearing his medals, began serving our lunch. Her important question was put off until after lunch.

Lunch was dominated by small talk about travel, her pets and world affairs; how the local township was constantly harassing her over the size of her estate. She said the township inquired about building some condominiums, a public park, and why not allow us to cross your property with utility wires? "This would save the township some money," she mimicked their offer. "When I reminded them that I was willing to spend a million dollars in court to fight their encroachment, or a blight declaration, they backed down," Doris said. "I pay my taxes and I want my privacy," she said. "I do not bother anyone."

We finished a delicious lunch of a tossed salad and baked salmon. We had tasted the finest wines from around the world. Doris' five dogs had now accepted me as a member of the family and were jumping in and out of my lap, wanting to be petted.

Doris said, "They like you Sharpe," while shooing them away. Truthfully speaking, I did not like the dogs licking on me, even though they were rich dogs and probably had someone assigned to brush their teeth. They behaved as though we had come to see them. They were overly friendly and craved attention. They responded instantly to any command from Doris, like children to their parents. Her dogs were treated like people. I figured *their dog house is probably bigger than my house, unless, of course, they each have a private bedroom in the mansion.*

After lunch we moved to a sitting area on the terrace as the butler cleared the table. Don, always the lawyer protecting his client, then said, "Now, why an art center for Newark, Sharpe? I believe that was the question Doris put to you before lunch."

For at least thirty minutes I told Doris of our struggles and progress in Newark. I explained to her that Newark was the dumping ground for every social program in the state (jails, prisons, methadone clinics, halfway houses, welfare hotels, x-rated movie houses and HIV-Aids housing) which I did not oppose, however, they were creating an imbalance and negative image for Newark. "I'm tired of hearing people say I wouldn't want to be found dead in Newark," I said to her. I paused to see if I was boring them and surprisingly both were still attentive and listening to my rambling.

I continued, "In order for Newark to survive and grow, the city needs an economic and racial balance. We need to attract middle-income people by building middle-income housing; and we need to become competitive in the arts, entertainment and sports. We need to become a destination city. We cannot survive as a mere reservation for the poor, with failed high-rises as our postcard. For the naysayers who do not believe in my dream that Newark can host an arts center; to those blue blood suburbanites who say that they will never attend the center if it's built in Newark," With great passion I said to Ms. Duke, "if we build the best mousetrap the people will surely come." I thought I had talked too long and then shut my mouth. I needed their feedback.

Doris and Don had sat silently and just listened. They had not interrupted me. When I had ended, Doris stood up clapped her hands and said, "Sharpe, you are sharp; that's just what I wanted to hear, and I want to help. How soon can you bring me a model of the arts center? I want to see it. I want to contribute and make your impossible dream a reality. I truthfully believe it will have a positive impact not only in Newark, but the whole state of New Jersey as well," she said. "How long do we have to be dependent upon New York City for the arts?" she asked. "I have already discussed this with Don and he believes in the project too."

Once again it was Don the diplomat to the rescue, "Let's toast," he said. "Here's to a new arts center in Newark." Now I was really enjoying the bubbling champagne. I didn't care about any side effects. I was in love with Doris Duke. I wanted to marry her. She could have a prenuptial agreement on her assets. *Doris with all of her money is a down to earth person,* I thought.

A horseman appeared in the great distance riding toward the open terrace. Soon the horseman was very close; he stopped, dismounted and walked toward the terrace. Removing the cap and shaking the head, a long roll of hair unfurled, and now approaching us was a beautiful and physically fit young lady.

Doris stood, greeted her, and then turned and said, "Sharpe, I want you to meet my daughter, Chandi." Chandi extended her hand and said, "Pleased to meet you, Sharpe, Hi Don." She joined us at the table and immediately asked the butler for a cold drink. "Whew, I'm tired she said." While she quenched her thirst, Doris repeated her enthusiasm and the value of an arts center in Newark.

"It sounds like an interesting project," Chandi said. Looking at her mother and me she offered her support.

With our youthful new arrival our conversation turned to national and world events and people around the world. I casually told them of my recent trip to Japan with the United States Conference of Mayors. The biggest hit in Japan at the time was Madonna. I told them that her performance was equal to a Michael Jackson production. "They went crazy in Japan over her singing and dancing." I told them. "I thought I was on Broadway."

Doris said, "I believe that Madonna is appearing here, in New Jersey, at the Meadowlands."

"I think I have seen some advertising of the event," Chandi said. "It looks like Madonna will be in New Jersey."

"Well, Sharpe said that she was well received in Japan, why don't we go see her in New Jersey," Doris said. "Sharpe, can you see if there are any tickets available? Can you arrange for security personnel to get me in and out of the Meadowlands without a hassle?" Doris asked.

Don responding first, said, "My office has heard that the meadowlands is completely sold out, no tickets whatsoever. All requests are being turned down. This might be Madonna's first appearance here in New Jersey."

Chandi stood and said, "Let me make some calls to New York or Los Angeles, I know some people connected to the show." When she returned, she asked "How many tickets do we need?"

Excitedly, Doris responded, "How about thirty tickets, we could go in three limousines. Now Sharpe, can you get us in and out, Doris asked again?"

I responded that I knew the security manager at the Meadow-lands. "I don't believe it will be a problem," I said.

Chandi left the terrace again to go and order the thirty tickets from her friends. (later I would learn that Chandi Heffner was Doris' adopted daughter).

It was agreed upon that we were going to see Madonna's concert at the Meadowlands. We had thirty reserved tickets and everyone was really excited. This called for another standing round of cold bubbly champagne toasting. These folks really know how to celebrate—*one more round and Don will have to carry me to the limo*, I thought to myself.

I was feeling a little light-headed when Doris asked if she could give me a tour of her property. Without any hesitation, I said, "I'd love to go on a tour." A sturdy golf cart was brought to the terrace; and with Doris behind the wheel, Don and I were off on a tour of this beautiful Garden of Eden. Driving along the path, Doris proved to be a connois-seur of birds, animals and plant life, as she pointed out various species and rattled off their history as they came into view. From her travels around the world Doris had stocked her Garden of Eden, as I called it, with every imaginable type of flora and animal life.

Walking freely about were beautiful white swans, pink flamin-gos, peacocks, black and white ducks, and a multitude of flowers in various colors; there were gardenias, gorgeous rows and rows of red roses and exotic cherry blossoms all thrilling to the eye. All of the wildlife completely ignored us as though we were trespassers and they were at home.

As we crossed miniature bridges, I asked Doris about the possibility of the lakes running dry; Doris laughed, and said "No, no, my father always had pumps built in his man-made lakes to maintain a certain level of water. He was a great engineer," she said lovingly and solemnly.

"If you haven't noticed, I make a hobby of giving animals, from around the world, a home," Doris said. Suddenly, she stopped the golf cart in front of a rustic barn like structure. "Come on in," Doris said. "I want to show you something very unique for Morris County."

Don and I followed her inside and there stood two very large and tall humpback camels staring at us like we were expected. "How do you like them?" a beaming Doris asked, as she moved closer to rub the face of one. I thought to myself, *no one ever accused us of having camels in Newark. Maybe some crack cocaine, but no camels.*

"Sharpe," Doris called while removing a box of graham crackers from a nearby shelf, "Why don't you feed him?" I thought *I must be hearing things. Here I am a city mayor, meeting a camel face-to-face, and being asked to stick his hand in the stall and feed him.* Just then the camel got excited and roared showing his massive, monster sized teeth. Doris, smiling, said "Go ahead and feed him, Sharpe, he loves graham crackers."

I love my fingers, too, I thought. He could just bite off my fingers, or as I had read in the encyclopedia they can spit in your face. What a terrible situation to be in. I did not want to insult my hostess by saying no, nor did I want to show my fear of losing my fingers. What do I do? *Oh well,* I thought, *if I should lose my fingers, with Doris money, I'll be the richest fingerless mayor in America.* Doris handed me a stack of graham crackers, I placed them in my right hand and trembling with fear, turned away, closed my eyes and stuck my hand towards the camel's mouth.

I nervously made a silent prayer and waited for the excruciating pain and flow of blood. After a brief moment, feeling nothing, I opened my eyes, and to my surprise the crackers were gone. I asked Don what had happened. He was silent; the camel used his lips and tongue to re-move the crackers two or three at a time.

"He loves you," Don said.

"So the dogs and camels love me," I said. Everyone laughed. Little did they know that I loved that camel too, he didn't bite off my fingers. Now jubilantly I patted the camel's face, as Doris smiled. We returned along another scenic road to the main house.

Don and I thanked Doris for her kindness and extended warm farewell greetings. I told her that I would secure a model of the proposed arts center for her; and that I would work on the security arrangements for the Madonna concert at the Meadowlands. We stepped inside the luxury limo, and waved goodbye as it began to ease down the tree-lined road. Doris was standing and waving from the terrace like Scarlett O'Hara in *Gone with the Wind*. The massive mansion became smaller and smaller. We exited past the guardhouse and headed to Route 80, eastbound. Soon the Garden of Eden was replaced with miles and miles of highway concrete, concrete barriers and metal road signs giving directions to motorists. No birds or beautiful plant life adorned our route home.

It was now that I could truly appreciate the estate of Doris Duke all the more. I had just left a real Garden of Eden, a private paradise in Morris County. Doris' estate was a place you wanted to return to. You simply could not see all the beauty and wonder in one visit.

Trip To The Meadowlands

On at least three occasions I met with the Meadowlands security manager to plan for the entrance, seating arrangement, security and exiting of Doris Duke and her guests when attending the Madonna concert. As advertised, the concert was sold out. I had advised Doris that my wife and I, along with my personal security, would arrive first and confirm the special arrangements. I would meet her at the club entrance about one half hour prior to the start of the concert, and escort her to her seat. Doris was still excited about seeing Madonna.

On the night of the show I stood just outside the club entrance and watched as three gleaming, powder blue stretch limousines eased up to the curb. With club administrators, security personnel, security workers, ticket takers, and ticketholders all cramming and jumping up to see who the VIP persons were; you would have thought that the President of the United States was arriving.

Everyone was pushing and shoving trying to look into the tinted windows of the limousines. Security personnel were struggling to keep the on-lookers under control. When all was quiet and everything was under control, I approached the lead limo and signaled to the driver. The driver exited the car and raced around the vehicle, now joined by private security personnel, reaching to open the door. A long slender leg was extended followed by a remarkably tall, calm, casually but impeccably dressed, Doris Duke.

Standing to her full height, wearing dark glasses, Doris turned to study her surroundings, looking like a million dollars she said, "Hey Sharpe, we made it, this looks like a nice place. Please introduce me to your wife."

Shaking hands with my wife, Doris said, "Well Mary, we can both suffer together tonight. I hope we are not sitting too close to the stage." Don Robinson then introduced Mary and me to the members of Doris' entourage. Doris then turned and said, "I'm ready, let's go." She was really excited!

With the Meadowlands security manager leading the way, we followed with a party of thirty guests, three Newark detectives and arena security personnel. As we entered the club entrance, a peaceful group of onlookers kept staring and asking, "Who is that?" Some whispered aloud "Is that Doris Duke?" Some asked out loud "Is that Doris Duke?" We had advised everyone not to confirm or deny any questions about our mysterious guest with the large entourage. Still, you would have had to be blind and dumb not to recognize an important person with her carriage, mannerisms, designer clothes, Hollywood like dark glasses and surrounded by a posse.

I had arranged for Doris and her guests to sit in two empty rows of press box seats, each row ending with a sitting security officer. We led the group to their seats just before the start of the concert, and the group would not depart until after adjacent concert goers had left. My mission was to isolate Doris from those who might wish to speak to her, request an autograph or take a picture of her. This was to be her fun night out without any paparazzi headaches.

As concert goers, still curious, flocked to our area to stare, point and whisper about our mysterious guest, Doris never looked their way, acknowledged or showed any concern as she shared conversations on what to expect from Madonna with my wife and others. It was obvious that she had experienced this public reaction on many occasions and knew exactly how to focus her attention away from the gawkers.

As the lights dimmed, indicating the start of the concert, Mary, Don and I were smiling and amused when Doris took out cotton balls and placed them in her ears. When we asked her, "why?" Doris replied, "You told me about some of her songs and language in Japan, I don't wish to hear everything and some of her music is really too loud, I'll be okay. We are here to enjoy ourselves," she said.

Madonna did not disappoint a standing room only crowd as she sang, danced and crawled to the beat of her Pop music. Her dancing, with her group, would rival Michael Jackson and his entourage of dancers. Doris watched intensely and commented on various songs she liked, and deplored some activities of Madonna on the stage. At times Madonna went from to being pure burlesque to a brusque woman.

Throughout the concert we observed Doris as a fabulously rich, down to earth person. She was friendly, warm and clearly fiercely independent in thought and action. At the end of the concert we all huddled together and gave reviews on the exciting concert, there were no naysayers.

After concert goers sitting near us had departed, the Meadowlands security manager appeared and joined with the security personnel to escort the party to the waiting limousines. As we exited the arena and reached Doris' vehicles she turned and gave Mary, Don and me a hug; others from her entourage were shaking hands and still talking about the excitement of Madonna's performance.

Doris said, "Sharpe I'll give you a call about the arts center when I return from Hawaii." She stepped inside her limousine, a security person closed the door and it pulled away very slowly with everyone waving. Suddenly the vehicle stopped, we moved forward to see if anything was wrong. Doris' window lowered, she leaned outside and with a broad smile said, "I forgot, the next time we will host Madonna's show in Newark. Please do not forget to send me plans for the art center, Sharpe, and thank all of you for a wonderful evening."

This time we waved good-bye and the limousine did not stop. It was headed for the New Jersey Turnpike; onto 280 West, exiting onto 80 West and the Duke Farms in Somerville, New Jersey. If it were not for Doris Duke, Madonna would have been a star all by herself on and off the stage that night. Unfortunately, with Doris Duke in attendance, Madonna had to share the spotlight, since no one could overshadow the fully-grown Million Dollar Baby.

Doris wrote me several letters from Hawaii. She wrote of wanting to help Newark with the building of the arts center. "Let's meet again when I return," she wrote. Then suddenly and unexpectedly the world was mourning her death, and questions were being raised. Questions that deserve answers, but will never be answered. Everyone started fighting for her money.

Based on Doris Duke's letters to me and her sincere interest in the arts, the Duke Foundation made a donation to NJPAC. Doris believed in diversity. Doris wanted to help Newark. She was lovely to be with. She, too, was worthy to be praised.

CHAPTER FOURTEEN

James Defeats Cory Booker

"Let Sleeping Dogs Lie!"

U nder my administration Newark went from what Harper's magazine had called "The worst city in America" in 1975, to being awarded the "Most Livable City" title. From 1995 to 2000, under recently appointed police director, Joseph Santiago, the crime rate decreased 52% and auto theft declined by 60% percent. Newark was experiencing an economic boom and received three fiscal bond-rating upgrades based on our financial stability. The largest newspaper in the state, *The Star-Ledger,* wrote an editorial saying that Newark was on a roll.

With our world-class performing arts center, award winning Society Hill Townhouses at University Heights, the new Bears/Eagles waterfront minor league ball stadium, the Newark Legal Center, Seton Hall Law School and the Newark Center, a new Rutgers University Law School, Gateway Office Buildings 2 and 3, the Dr. Martin Luther King Federal office Building and courthouse, Home Depot, the James/Gibson new aquatic center, Malcolm X Shabazz Athletic Complex, a $35 million Hope VI Neighborhood Grant and the refurbishing of our museum, library and Newark Symphony Hall, the city was on a roll.

Yes, the city was on a roll, and the achievements we could boast of were many. I had demolished all of Newark's failed family public high-rises and replaced them with state-of-the-art townhouses. The James administration brought Blue Cross/Blue Shield back to Newark, and added IDT, MBNA and an IHOP. With our new train to the plane airport station, along with ten new hotels we had become a destination city.

Everyone wanted a piece of Newark, now. Everyone wanted to be Mayor of the up and coming new Newark, especially a young man, who in 1996 rented one room in a carriage house for that specific purpose. This young man had, in 1998, narrowly defeated four-term incumbent, Councilman George Branch, of the Central Ward, in a run-off election. George simply ran out of money.

Still, the young man was not satisfied. He wanted more. Shortly after his Central Ward victory, rumors began circulating that the newly crowned Central Ward Councilman and Rhodes Scholar, Cory Booker, was running for mayor of Newark in 2002. He wanted to defeat four-term incumbent Mayor Sharpe James. "It's time for a change, James is too old," he had said.

Booker didn't know it at the time, but I was thinking about retiring. *Why not pass on the baton? Why not groom some young person to become the next mayor? Why not just retire and go fishing or play tennis?* These were my thoughts at the time. My family and I had discussed my retirement many times when we sat down at the dining-room table for a meal. The fact that I had earned a pension from the City of Newark that could sustain us quite comfortably was all the more reason to retire.

Booker's ambitions, qualifications, and goal offered me an opportunity to retire. *No more beatings from The Star-Ledger. No more personal harassment because city employees did not do their job and had to be disciplined, no more bearing the weight of being the Mayor of the largest city in New Jersey, a Mayor on call 24 hours a day.* With someone younger and qualified to succeed me I thought more and more of retiring.

Yet, after Cory Booker's publicity stunts, one after another, and his blistering personal attacks on my record in office, I knew that I had to protect my legacy. If I decided not to run again, *The Star-Ledger* would say that I was scared to run. They would write that Cory Booker, who had been saying that everyone in my administration was too old, and too much a part of the past; that it was time for new ideas and a new direction, had forced me out. I knew *The Star-Ledger* would write that I was afraid to face him in an election. All the good work that I had done, work that even Booker himself had acknowledged, would now be in question, and I couldn't live with that.

Having coached championship teams in the Army, in Newark public schools and at Essex County College, I became more determined than ever to win the election and silence Booker's attacks on me. The more he pushed, the more aggressively I responded. It became a matter of victory or defeat with me; and I planned to "take no prisoners."

I decided to run on my record of progress against Booker's inexperience, but he proved to be a formidable foe. Not only did his talk of "saving" Newark capture the attention of the national media, CBS News, *Time magazine* and *Newsweek*, but money came pouring to him from wealthy supporters outside of Newark. His formidable war chest forced me to spend more than I ever had in a campaign, making this the most expensive mayoral race in Newark's history. Booker publicly boasted that he would raise $5 million to run. No one in Newark had ever spent more than $500,000 in a municipal election. He spent the money, though, and should have learned a valuable lesson, "Let sleeping dogs lie!"

The sound system was blasting out my theme song, "Sharpe James, He's Our Mayor and Ain't Nobody Gonna Beat Him." Everyone was singing. It was around 11 p.m. on May 14, 2002, election night, when I took the stage in the Grand Ballroom at Newark's Robert Treat Hotel, the place was packed with my staff and supporters dancing and drinking. There was jubilation all around me, and it wouldn't stop. Only moments before, they had learned that I was on my way to an unprecedented fifth term as Newark's mayor. The scene reminded me of the 1970 election victory celebration for Newark's first Black Mayor, Kenneth Allen Gibson.

Now, as I looked out over the celebration of my victory at the Robert Treat Hotel, I thought about how my opponents would have loved to have seen on the front page of the morning's newspapers: "Newark's Mayor Fails to Win Fifth Term—a reprisal of the Mayor Gibson headlines 16 years ago.

If the press could have its way, I was washed up, I had stayed too long, and I had nothing more to offer. Their odds-on favorite was Cory Booker, a charmer, who at 33-years-old was half my age; he was the new kid in town, raised in an affluent, predominantly White Bergen County suburb, a Stanford University graduate, a Yale-educated lawyer and a Rhodes Scholar. Booker, one could say, was heir to the civil rights struggle and the kind of politics that brought me into office. He attracted national media attention with his youthful looks, his powerful connections, his fund-raising ability and his message of fighting corruption and "It's time for a change."

I had never before faced a challenger like Booker. He was a charming and imposing sight. He never stopped smiling, showing his pearly white teeth. He reminded me of the New York Giants running back Tiki Barber, just so photogenic, with the prematurely balding shaved-head look, owlish eyes and fair-skin. Booker hugged and kissed everyone. He gave bus rides to Atlantic City and bought gifts for senior citizens. He had the money to buy votes. He had no shame in wanting to win.

In 1998, after getting elected to a first term as councilman from the Central Ward, Booker had become a media darling. He was bright and articulate, for that I congratulated him. But he kept bragging about upsetting the 16-year incumbent George Branch. It was not enough to get elected at a very young age, 29, but he made it too personal; "I, Cory Booker, defeated a 16-year incumbent. I denied him a fifth term." Later on I would realize that he was thinking of defeating a 16-year incumbent mayor, Sharpe James.

Booker soon made it clear after elected to the Council that he was anti-council members, anti-administration, and anti- City of Newark. He perceived himself to be a Mother Teresa, a saint. He set himself above the other members of the council. In his mind they were corrupt, in his terms, old-fashioned, not skilled, not knowledgeable, too entrenched in power; he was the maverick. Booker behaved as though he was Newark's savior, and that he was the crown prince. Perhaps he felt that with his academic credentials he deserved more. Going after the perceived weak Central Ward seat was only a stepping-stone for him. Cory wanted more back then, he wanted to be Mayor.

As the legendary, longtime, charismatic and popular Newark Mayor, I was the only obstacle standing in Booker's path. It was now "D-Day," time for Booker to implement his "six year take over plan." I am sure that he felt confident that he had done his homework.

From his first days in Newark in 1996, Cory Booker was in awe of my success. At every opportunity, he studied my storytelling, relaxed speaking pattern (even taking notes), ease with senior citizens, and like me he began hopping up on the stage when called to the podium and dancing at every social event. He watched my hand shaking, hugging and kissing everyone. Booker confided in one of his supporters that I was cool and well liked by the people. Privately he would articulate that I was a good mayor.

The leading newspaper called me "Mayor for life." For all of these exemplary reasons, Booker hated me. Booker wanted my job. Booker wanted to be Mayor and had the blessings and support of *The Star-Ledger*. "They promised to help me," he told Essex County Freeholder, Linda Cavanaugh, during the annual legislative train ride to Washington, D.C. "I'm going to take James' place. I'm going to defeat James," he had bragged. Freeholder Cavanaugh told me, "I was surprised and felt uneasy with his swagger as a newly elected official. That boy is on an ego trip," she had said.

For his entrance into Newark politics, Booker decided, in 1998, to put his Stanford University and Rhodes Scholar credentials against four-term Central Ward incumbent and popular George Branch, who was a high school dropout and former boxer. Booker knew that the Central Ward had just added 1,500 new voters who lived in Society Hill, at University Heights, an award winning tree lined upscale middle income K. Hovnanian townhome neighborhood. Residents at Society Hill likened it to living in Boca Raton, Florida or Forest Hills in New York City. Booker, although a stranger and an outsider, felt that he could easily sell his Stanford University and Rhodes Scholar academic credentials to the new homeowners in Society Hill. George Branch had not catered to these new homeowners.

It was a backroom political move, choosing the weakest candidate on the Newark Municipal Council, to oppose in launching Booker's political career. A game of chess was being played with human beings as pawns. George, or "Buddy Gee," as he was affectionately called, was a street smart, jive talking, joke telling down-to-earth guy. He was a person everyone loved. He was a person Booker had underrated when he decided to challenge him for the Central Ward seat.

In a spirited campaign of the pro versus the ego maniacal novice, George received more votes than Booker on May 12, 1998, only to fall just short of the required 50% plus one vote needed for an election victory. Now, out of money, Branch would lose to highly financed Booker by about 300 votes in the June run-off election.

Booker's political career could have ended on the night of May 12, 1998. It was a simple case of Branch running out of money rather than Booker winning on merit. Being an outsider over-shadowed his exemplary academic credentials against a popular local hero.

Still Booker got his prize. He had a ringside seat on the City Council which enabled him to launch his ambitious goal. He was never really interested in being Central Ward Councilman. He spent very little time in the Central Ward. He was more comfortable sitting on Oprah Winfrey's couch begging for her money, debating national TV host, Conan O'Brien, or on a panel show being loquacious with Tavis Smiley. Booker also liked to be seen with an attractive woman on his arm in an attempt to prove his masculinity.

In his adopted city, Newark, it was never about serving his constituents, he had bigger ideas. He was producing a film entitled "Street Fight," showing how he had defeated both opponents (Branch and James) in his first run for the city council and mayor. Of course, taking a hint from Clint Eastwood, Booker was the writer, producer, director, editor, and received star billing for his self promoting film. I, Sharpe James, was portrayed as the villain, the buffoon, the bad guy.

Cory Booker told everyone who would listen that *The Star-Ledger* had promised to support him. They had been building him up. Historically, Newark was a city with many African American heroes; many trail blazers had emerged, and much blood had been spilled during the civil rights movement. Stories like the recall of South Ward Councilman, Lee Bernstein; the school board fights; and the Newark riots could fill a newspaper.

There were other stories of courageous people that went untold, like Louise Epperson, a woman, who single-handedly fought all powerful, Mayor, Hugh Addonizio, for promising to relinquish 250 acres of land in the heart of Newark for the current UMDNJ, now sitting on fifty acres of land, displacing thousands of citizens. There was the story of former Newark Teacher's Union (NTU) President, Carole Graves, who went to jail fighting for a quality education for Newark school children.

Other noteworthy Newarkers include the late Essex County Freeholder and Councilman-at-large, Earl Harris, "The Silver Fox," who fought the state and county to locate Essex County College in Newark. Timothy Still who led the federally funded United Community Corporation (UCC) antipoverty movement in Newark was also a trailblazer. United Community Corporation, a neighborhood program, produced Jesse Allen, Earl Harris, Donald Tucker and me. We all became elected officials thanks in part to our UCC experience.

Former Newark school teacher, Harry Wheeler, the brainchild of Newark's political growth, who was blessed with a golden tongue and an expansive vocabulary, cannot be forgotten. It was often said that Harry could sell snowballs to the Eskimos. The charismatic State Assemblyman, George Richardson, who formed a third party when kicked off the Democratic line, also deserves recognition. Essex County Freeholder, Charles Matthews, and of course our first Black Congressman, the Honorable Donald Payne are not forgotten.

Nor can we forget renowned poet, playwright and community activist, Amiri Baraka. Yet, none of these heroes, our native sons and daughters, ever received two paragraphs of recognition in *The Star-Ledger*. Their good work and sacrifice was taken for granted. They were totally ignored. They were not *The Star-Ledger*'s pick. Cory Booker was *The Star-Ledger*'s choice for the next Mayor of the city of Newark.

Cory Booker, who owned no property in Newark, thus paying no taxes to the city, who used a fake residency, an empty apartment in Brick Towers with a futon and two chairs won *The Star-Ledger*'s endorsement for Mayor. Why did Booker choose Brick Towers to claim as his residency, a public low-income housing complex? Because, he could exploit the people living there for his own personal gain.

Booker sermonized to White audiences, "Every time I walk out of my apartment I see filth lining the hallways, drug dealers, criminals, barefoot children, seniors with no teeth and a man called "T-Bone" who is trying to kill me." He would travel the nation preaching this story to White folks. He always painted Newark in a negative light. He wanted his stock to rise by knocking or stepping on Newark. He was not a native son of Newark and he did not love Newark.

My only question at the time was, why live there if it's so bad? Move out. Noted Newark historian and Rutgers University's distinguished professor Dr. Clement Price, accused Booker of creating a "T-Bone" character in order to raise money from White suburbanites. "He's being threatened and he needs money—a subliminal message to pour campaign funds on him to increase his political war chest." Dr Price was quoted as saying, "I personally view "T-Bone" as a fictitious character, a sympathy ploy from Booker's creative imagination." On the street Booker's T-Bone experience was called a bold-faced lie.

Booker, the outsider, predictably was given five full pages of coverage in *The Star-Ledger*, including one where he is standing at a wash basin when he was only two years old. All of the real heroes of Newark received limited or no coverage at all in the *Ledger*. It was now clear to all that *The Star-Ledger* was promoting Cory Booker for Mayor. *The Star-Ledger* wanted Sharpe James out of office. One reporter, a Newark resident, speaking anonymously, said *The Star-Ledger*'s position was clear. "Sharpe James kicked us out of City Hall, and we will kick him out of City Hall," a quid pro quo arrangement.

The Star-Ledger was boiling mad at me for kicking them out of City Hall and for getting re-elected in 1998. For years the *Ledger* had enjoyed a private office suite on the same floor as my office at City Hall. From this advantage point they had full access to my administration and oftentimes interviewed guests in my waiting room, employees walking the hall, those having lunch in the municipal cafeteria or participants attending city hall ceremonial presentations. They would sometimes interrupt and interview on-duty department heads for one breaking news story after another. They had it all. We were transparent in every aspect of government. *The Star-Ledger* had the best of two worlds.

When I noticed that most of their inside coverage consisted of one negative story after another, I concluded that the city was being exploited. To add salt to the wound the *Ledger* assigned one of its editors, Joan Whitlow, to write an exclusive weekly column on the Mayor's Office. It, too, quickly became a weekly smear column. Joan cranked out more than sixty negative articles in a row without catching her breath. My supporters dubbed her column the "Witchlow column." She earned the title of the "smiling dragon lady" and bearer of bad news.

I called for a meeting with the *Ledger*'s popular editor, Mort Pye. Mort, a thin, petite, tight lipped, scholarly looking quiet gentleman, welcomed me to his crowded office. "Mort," I said "what about some balance in *The Star-Ledger*'s coverage of Newark? There are a lot of good things happening in Newark, so when are we going to read some success stories? We just built over 1000 units of state-of-the-art townhouses, an award winning new elementary school, and new shopping malls. Where are the stories?" I asked.

Mort gave me his tight-lipped smile and nervously, waving a pencil thin finger at me, said in a quiet measured voice, "Sharpe, you just don't get it, you don't understand our business. We cover plane crashes not plane landings. Our job is to sell newspapers, you just don't get it."

I did get the fact that the *Ledger* had no intention of presenting any balanced coverage of Newark while I was the mayor. I did get the fact that I was wasting my time talking to him. I humbly thanked him for the meeting and politely left.

Later, when my administration advised me that the mayor's office needed more space in order to better serve the public, I did not hesitate to consider the space that *The Star-Ledger* was using. My staff had recommended that we relocate *The Star-Ledger* from the second floor. The only space the city could find to accommodate them was at 215 Central Avenue, about a mile from City Hall, which they promptly refused to accept. Instead their anger led them to rent space across the street from city hall, where they could easily reach and spy on my administration. Now I had my own personal worst enemy, the largest and most powerful newspaper in the state, *The Star-Ledger*. To retaliate they wanted to kick me out of City Hall. They wanted me to crash land for full coverage.

The Star-Ledger could not wait until 2002. They were salivating in anticipation of witnessing my defeat. James' days are numbered was the hue and cry in *The Star-Ledger* office. The 2002 campaign for Mayor was on.

Leaving a municipal breakfast meeting at a private dining room at the Gateway Hilton Hotel one morning I passed through the public portion of Bentley's Restaurant, when a voice yelled out to me, "Hey Sharpe, your days are numbered." The remark was followed by laughter. I turned around and saw Elnardo Webster, Jr. a former law firm colleague and confidante of Cory Booker, seated at a corner table with a group of friends. "Sharpe, how about taking $300,000 and retiring?" he had asked.

I approached Elnardo's table and asked if there was something wrong. Becoming highly animated and excited, he stood up and said, "Sharpe, Booker has raised $5 million dollars to run for Mayor and you don't stand a chance. Why don't you just quit old man? You haven't done one thing for Newark." Again, his friends roared with laughter.

Charles Jones, my aide, who was with me, was stunned by their open rudeness and disrespect. He looked at me with disbelief. I kept my composure; staring Webster in the face, I asked him if he really wanted me to name one thing I had done as Mayor? Before I could start, he yelled in a sarcastic tone, "Yes, yes, go ahead; think of one good thing you did as Mayor." All of his friends, gleaming with delight, were now staring at me.

I bit my lip, took a deep breath and, while waving my right hand in slow cadence, said, "Here is one thing I did." Elnardo and his group quieted down. "Here's one record of service that might interest you," I said.

"In 1989, when your father was having some difficulty I helped him." Everyone at the table was now very attentive; they waited to hear more.

I told them about a time when his father got into some trouble and needed assistance. "When your father could not find a job in his native city of Jersey City, he came to my house seeking help," I had said. "I recommended him for a job with a youth program that I had created in partnership with the Newark Board of Education. That job saved his household and put you through college. He held that job for twenty years or more. He's still on that job today, as we speak. That's one thing I did, that might interest you."

Elnardo and his supporters remained silent with bowed heads and no further words were spoken. I turned and left the restaurant. He continued to support Booker for Mayor; however, he made a change in his attitude toward me. Whenever he met me in public he would greet, meet and respect Sharpe James. I never told that story again, even when his father was up for Superintendent of the Roselle School System. In fact, I personally congratulated him. I believe the lyrics in one of my favorite songs, "We fall down, but we get up."

During the 2002 mayoral race a Star-*Ledger* editorial reported of the progress in Newark under Mayor Sharpe James' Administration. Newark was a city that had been written off, and was now prospering, a city on a roll. As Mayor, Sharpe James had courageously moved the city from urban blight to urban bright, and had been named 2001 Mayor of the year. Newark was a city steeped in its renaissance and becoming a destination city.

As I read the article, I could not believe that at last *The Star-Ledger* was going to endorse me. *Hey, I might just hit a homerun,* I thought. Then, the curve ball came, and I struck out. *The Star-Ledger* wrote of a need for change and they portrayed Cory Booker as a "Mother Teresa", "Florence Nightingale" or "Pope Paul." Booker would ride in on his white horse and save the dumb, poor and drugged people of Newark. He would be Newark's savior, Newark's Lord. He was perfect without sin. "Booker for Mayor," was their mantra. "It's time for a change!" The 2002 campaign for Mayor was heating up.

Booker was out telling the world how bad the city of Newark was, how corrupt it was, and how unsafe it was: "Sharpe James hasn't done anything. Sharpe James cares only about downtown and neglects the neighborhoods. We need new ideas, we need a new strategy, we need a new mayor, and I'm the agent for change," he said. It was a smear-and-fear campaign, and it was working. Booker was the darling of celebrities and the media. He never saw a camera or reporter that he did not like. He loved to spin falsehoods. He loved lecturing to the poor or the rich asking them for money.

In the national political arena, Newark's mayoral race became a fight between the younger generation of Black politicians and the older, civil-rights-era generation, between the whiz kids and the bridge builders. Booker's 2002 campaign army was the best financed and best dressed in the history of any Newark election. Booker outfitted his "Team Booker" with Timberland boots, designer jackets and colorful Team Booker T-Shirts and caps. He even provided a cell phone and rental vans for all of his key campaign workers.

Team Booker looked so good that they could have marched in the opening ceremony of the 2002 Olympics in Athens drawing applause; or, by adding military weapons they could have replaced our troops in Iraq. Booker desperately wanted to deny me an unprecedented fifth term. Meanwhile he continued working on the campaign movie documenting his anticipated victory.

Halfway through our heated campaign I received an emergency police call of possible trouble at the Dayton Street public housing project. "You better get over here quickly," my police director said. When I arrived at the housing development, I found my army of supporters on one side of the street staring down Team Booker on the opposite side. They were engulfed in a tense shouting match with tension mounting.

I called my Dayton Street area coordinator, Tawanna, to come over and explain the problem. She smiled and said, "There's no problem Sharpe, they want to cross the street and canvas the projects. We want permission to cross the street and beat them out of their fancy uniforms; just give us the word," she had said.

The traveling reporter, who was standing next to me, was visibly shaken, scared to death, she wanted to leave. She turned to me and said, "Are we safe here, can you control that tough looking mob?"

I looked at her and said, "What mob? You mean my supporters?"

"Supporters?" she questioned me.

I told her that they were my campaign workers and she had absolutely nothing to fear. She was shocked and turned a bright shade of red.

Compared to Booker's well-dressed army my workers looked like they were preparing to dance with Michael Jackson in "Thriller." Tawanna again asked, "What do you want us to do?" I advised her not to interfere with them canvassing the projects, which they had every right to do. I was trying to diffuse a potentially explosive situation with no blood spilled. Even with Tawanna ready to make war, allowing them to canvas the area was the legal and moral thing to do. Their presence would not change anything; the Dayton area was considered my home turf.

There was no surprise on Election Day when, with a tremendous GOTV effort, we trounced Team Booker in the Dayton Street district. We had won by might not fight.

This election sent a nationwide message that the youth movement could not simply walk in and take over calling for "A Change." Congressman Jesse Jackson Jr., who came to Newark to help, had explained the situation to Cory Booker. He told him to "Stop saying that

I have endorsed you because of our youth. While I respect you and recognize your many talents, and we are both young, in this election, I am endorsing Mayor Sharpe James," he had said.

Jesse Jr. further said, "My father, Jesse Jackson Sr., and Sharpe James built the bridges we cross; they fought in the civil rights movement to open doors for us and our time will come." I was humbled and shocked that he came to Newark, uninvited, to straighten out the misuse of his name and alleged support for Booker. His father, whom I had assisted in many campaigns, was a no show.

In summary, I believe the 2002 mayoral race was not about age. It was about past performance on the job. Jesse Jackson Jr. was a man of principle, a man of courage. He echoed what I have believed since my humble beginnings in politics, some thirty-eight years earlier. A belief that our youth should join forces with the current leadership to learn, contribute, challenge and eventually take over (accept the baton) rather than attempt a hostile takeover while they are ill-prepared to govern.

Our youth should be a part of the solution, not the problem. Unfortunately Booker was too cocky! When he started his campaign for mayor, he created flyers showing two boxers in a ring, Muhammad Ali and Sonny Liston. Booker's head was superimposed on Ali's body, and he was standing victorious over Liston's prostrate body, with my head tacked on it. But, this veteran heavyweight champ was nowhere ready for a knockdown or knockout by the novice Booker. If necessary, I would have given him "a rope-a-dope" punch to the belly. He still had a lot to learn.

When I formally kicked off my re-election campaign in March, I campaigned at Wynona Lipman Gardens, where more than 500 people showed up. I looked around and said, "Where are we, In Boca Raton, In Georgetown, or in SoHo, New York? Maybe we're in Miami Beach? No, no we're at the once notorious Columbus Homes site, now an oasis of urban revitalization!" The media and Gov. McGreevey's representatives could not believe that we had transformed this public housing site from being one of the worst in America to one of the best.

Governor McGreevey was there and he had the crowd singing, "Ain't Nobody Going to Beat Sharpe James." Even when the music stopped, they continued acappella. Visibly emotional I told them, "Kenneth Gibson mixed the mortar. I've been laying the bricks. By working together we put a roof over our heads, created jobs, improved our schools and we're not going to let any carpetbagger come in and take over. We are going to defeat Booker, the carpetbagger."

The Rev. Al Sharpton who had come to Newark two days earlier, to address my Mother's Day breakfast, came back on Election Day. He arrived around 3 p.m. We took him around to senior citizens' buildings and he spoke to residents in their lobbies. We went to bus stops where people were coming home from work. We went to the Weequahic High School polling station. Eventually we ended up in the Pathmark supermarket on Lyons Avenue just before the polls closed. Everywhere we went people wanted to come up and touch Al Sharpton, get his autograph or have their picture taken with him. He knew what to do and say, like a pro.

"Come and meet Mayor James in the produce department," Sharpton shouted through a bullhorn. "He has always been producing in Newark, producing housing, producing more jobs, producing an arts center and baseball stadium. Come on down and meet Mayor James in the produce department, now," he had said. It was my last chance to get my message across that the choice voters had was between a candidate with competence versus one without competence, experience versus inexperience.

I have never believed in pre-election polls. The late Councilman-at-Large, Earl, "Silver Fox", Harris, used to get real loud when saying, that "The only poll that counts is on election day." Earl and I used to joke that "You can fool some of the people all of the time, all of the people some of the time, but never all of the people all of the time" (Abraham Lincoln).

Cory Booker lost to me during our one locally televised debate. He became nervous and tongue-tied. He lost the senior citizens vote, the public housing vote and he lost badly in the South and Central wards. It was still a close race, though, because of his support in the predominantly White and Hispanic North and East wards of our city.

Booker believed that he could fool all of the people all of the time in Newark. He was badly mistaken. He spent more than $5 million, donated to him by the rich and famous. With support from television star, Oprah Winfrey and far right groups, Booker would still lose the 2002 race for Mayor. In 1996 he had underestimated Councilman George Branch, but was lucky enough to win in a run-off. Now in 2002 he had underestimated me. He had disrespected me and there would be no run-off.

Cory Booker never congratulated me on winning in 2002. No telephone call, no letter and no concession speech. His ego had been badly bruised. He thought he could buy an election. He failed to realize that he could not defeat the people's choice for Mayor. I had been selected and elected as a delegate from the 1970 Black and Puerto Rican Convention. I was the people's choice.

Just prior to Election Day, Booker had personally called the U.S. Attorney, Christopher Christie, and asked him to have federal marshals supervise the election. Christie had invited both of us to meet with him. It was later reported to me by a reliable source that Christie subsequently told a class he was addressing that Cory Booker had brought a team of ten or more lawyers with him and tried to tell his office what they should do. He had said, on the other hand, James came alone and was led to his office by his then assistant, Paula Dow (who later became Essex County Prosecutor and thereafter State Attorney for New Jersey). During the meeting Christie said James only asked for fairness for both sides on Election Day. "I found him to be a real gentleman," he had said.

Despite the rumor put out by Booker's camp that I had hired gang members to be campaign workers, there were no reports of irregularities on either side. By mid-afternoon U.S. Attorney, Christopher Christie, confirmed that it had been a "very fair election." No formal charges have ever been filed.

The Star-Ledger reported that Booker made another call to U.S. Attorney Christie in 2006, after defeating State Senator Ronald Rice and taking office as Mayor of Newark. He allegedly asked Christie to investigate his political nemesis, Sharpe James. "I want you to look into his spending habits. I have these bills that I will not pay. My administration will assist you," Booker allegedly had said. "James might be planning to run for mayor again or even governor." I wasn't there, I didn't hear this conversation, but I believe it happened; the beginning of the conspiracy against me.

Only one name surfaced to oppose Jon Corzine in the 2010 gubernatorial race, that name was Christopher Christie. Booker, the political climber, saw an opportunity to crush prominent Democrats seeking upward mobility. He didn't care whether a Democrat or Republican occupied the Statehouse for now. He was young and ambitious. He would be a future candidate for higher office. He wanted Corzine to lose his re-election bid, and me to rot in a federal prison. He saw himself as becoming the Democratic standard bearer to rescue the party.

I was not particularly concerned about any rumored investigation because I had been investigated over a four year period, which ended in 1995, by then U.S. Attorney Michael Chertoff. Unfortunately that was the past. This time the U.S. Attorney appointed by President George W. Bush was Christopher Christie, who had his own political agenda and wanted to be governor.

Because Cory Booker had refused to communicate with me after his 2002 defeat, and continued to hold a grudge in 2006, even after winning the Mayor's seat, he could not adequately transition over to his newly elected position. He did not allow me to explain to him normal and routine overlapping transition bills from one administration to the next. He especially needed to understand, as the newly elected mayor, and a novice, the policy for paying for police security that the city council had granted me during the transition. He needed to understand the policy for the storage of twenty years of memorabilia and government papers. Instead, being political, he called U.S. Attorney Christopher Christie again.

Both Christie and Booker had a mutual agenda. They both had aspirations for higher political office. Christie would become governor of New Jersey in 2009. He was re-elected in 2013 but his eye is on the presidential race for 2016. Following Senator Lautenberg's death early in 2013, Booker would win the senator's seat in a special election. Booker's eye is probably on the governor of New Jersey's seat for 2017, and then maybe the White House.

Booker and Christie wanted to politically silence a leading Democrat. He and Christie wanted me in a federal prison for life. Moreover, I learned that justice was not blind. I learned the hard way what can happen when you have an unscrupulous egotistical mayor and an overzealous prosecutor using their office to advance their own political agenda.

I learned that I was a target.

CHAPTER FIFTEEN

A Target

Remember the parable of the "Monkey?" The higher he climbs up the tree, the more his ass is exposed. Politically speaking, and otherwise, the higher you climb in life, the more you are exposed. By 2002 I had climbed higher than any other Black man in the political arena in New Jersey; this, plus the insatiable political ambition of a United States Attorney, made me a TARGET.

Chris Christie was a top fundraiser for the 2000 George W. Bush presidential campaign. He was rewarded by being appointed U.S Attorney for the District of New Jersey in 2001, succeeding Robert J. Cleary. Now at age 47, Chris Christie, formerly a highly controversial Morris County Freeholder, was in a position to fulfill his lifelong political dream of being elected governor of the State of New Jersey.

Numerous newspaper articles alleged that U.S Attorney Christie was using his office to campaign for governor. He made it a practice of selectively targeting high profile elected officials to accuse of criminal wrongdoings, preferably Democrats, African Americans and Hispanics, with one or two Republicans (Essex County Executive James Treffinger was one) sandwiched in for perceived balance. For the most part many of Christie's GOP supporters would not be investigated. For example, GOP State Senate President, James Bennett, with mounting allegations of wrongdoing, suddenly, at the pinnacle of his power, quietly quit ending all investigations.

Similarly, GOP supporter and State Senator Martha W. Bark of the 8th District, under state investigation in 2006 for alleged no show part-time jobs paid by the Burlington County Bridge Commission and the Burlington County Institute of Technology ($330,000), retired from the senate at the end of 2007 and had her investigation dropped.

The internet had gone wild inquiring about the status of her investigation. Senator Bark said she did work, but "did not keep detailed records" of what she did. Despite evidence to the contrary, calls to the State and U.S. Attorney's offices fell upon deaf ears. She was no longer a target.

Rumor had it that Christie was still salivating over a plan to bring me down. GOP Senators Bennett and Bark simply did not warrant the prize that I would bring him. As mayor of the state's largest city, state senator, college professor and a Democrat, who had never lost an election, I was on his radar screen. I was viewed as a trophy to adorn his wall and boost his resume. I would further his political ambitions. Like the monkey parable, "My ass was exposed."

Christie became obsessed with the idea of bringing the longest tenured mayor in the history of Newark to trial, thus winning a political conviction. He had mastered the art of political showmanship convictions. Then Governor Jon Corzine had said he was "concerned about Christie's recently disclosed conversations with President Bush's political advisor, Karl Rove, in 2004." It was alleged that Christie had discussed running for governor with Rove. As a sitting U.S. Attorney that conversation may possibly have been in violation of the Hatch Act, a law preventing federal employees from using their offices for partisan purposes.

During that same year Christie obtained permission from my former director of housing production, in the Department of Economic Development and Housing (DEHD), Basil Franklin, to wire him in order to get information regarding me. Franklin had quit my administration in anger after I had named a more qualified, White director, Al Faiella, to replace, Harold Lucas, who was appointed Assistant Secretary of HUD by President Bill Clinton. Franklin wanted that job.

The prosecution had learned that housing developer Basil Franklin was flirting with Tamika Riley, a Newark housing developer. I personally believed that Basil would have left his wife for Tamika Riley. The government had evidence that Basil and Riley had been kissing, hugging and rubbing one another in her car in front of his home.

This evidence was enough to coerce Basil to become a cooperative witness for the government. They didn't want Basil, whom they considered a small fish, they wanted me. They offered to remove Basil from the investigation and make him their star witness, if he cooperated and helped them entrap me.

On May 18, 2004, Basil Franklin signed an agreement, allowing FBI Special Agents, Durrant III and Graves, Jr., to place a body wire on him to record conversations that might be conducive to the plan. As a disgruntled former employee he would be perfect to assist in targeting me.

Christie also had the enthusiastic help of Mayor Cory Booker. *The Star-Ledger* had reported that Booker had called Christie after my retirement in 2006 and asked him to investigate routine overlapping city council approved travel expenses, storage of my city hall memorabilia and security costs while ignoring the fact that all of my expenditures were reviewed and approved annually by the city council. Thus Booker and Christie formed a personal relationship behind the strategy to disgrace, render fiscal hardships and to imprison me. Both wanted me out of sight and out of competition for mayor or governor.

With this setup in place, Christie could turn his attention to raising campaign funds. If you are planning to run for governor on the GOP ticket, you need GOP supporters with money. Christie faced strong criticism for awarding lucrative federal monitoring positions, in no-bid contracts, to GOP friends, supporters and allies.

Professor Alexandra Natapoff of Loyola University stated in her 2009 book Snitching that "Christie's use of the Deferred Prosecution Agreement (DPA), an attractive mechanism for companies under criminal investigation to avoid a conviction, to funnel a no-bid $52 million contract to his friend and former boss, John Ashcroft, a Republican, led to congressional hearings on a possible conflict of interest and the establishment of new DPA guidelines." Christie himself refused to fully cooperate in the hearings.

At issue was the awarding of a no-bid contract to Ashcroft to serve as the monitor for a DPA involving the medical supply company, Zimmer Holdings. Zimmer hired Ashcroft at the suggestion of Chris Christie, the U.S Attorney in New Jersey investigating the company. Other ethical and fairness questions followed Christie as well.

David Kocieniewski, writing in the *New York Times* (June 26, 2009), pointed out that questions were raised when Christie awarded a multimillion dollar, no-bid contract to David Kelley, another former

U.S Attorney, who had investigated Christie's brother, Todd Christie, in a 2005 fraud case involving traders at the Wall Street firm, Spear, Leeds & Kellogg.

Kelley had declined to prosecute Todd Christie, who had been ranked fourth in the investigation; an investigation by the U.S Securities and Exchange Commission (SEC) involving twenty traders who earned the largest profits for their company at the expense of their customers. The top three were indicted, as were eleven other traders.

Christie also faced censure over the terms of a $311 million fraud settlement with Bristol Myers Squibb, where he deferred criminal prosecution of the pharmaceutical company in a deal that required it to dedicate $5 million for a business ethics chair at Seton Hall University School of Law, his alma mater.

Other criticism included Christie's acceptance of campaign funds and the resulting public finance matching funds from a law firm (Stern and Killcullen) that received a lucrative no-bid federal monitor contract (DPA) worth more than $10 million in legal fees while Christie served as the state's U.S Attorney.

On August 18, 2009, Christie acknowledged that he had loaned $46,000 to first assistant U.S Attorney for New Jersey, Michele Brown, two years prior, while serving as her superior as the state's U.S Attorney, and that he had failed to report either the loan or its monthly interest payments on both his income tax returns and his mandatory financial disclosure report to the New Jersey Election Law Enforcement Commission.

Rep. Bill Pascrell Jr. (D-8th Dist.) urged federal authorities to investigate Christie's failure to report income from the loan on his taxes.

Democratic State Chairman Joe Cryan who filed a complaint with the State Election Law Enforcement commission against Christie said, "Christie continues to fail to live up to the ethical standards he sets for others."

Similarly Christie acknowledged that he bought and sold stock in a travel and real estate company while it was under investigation by the U.S Attorney's Office that he led at the time.

Even when receiving a simple parking violation Christie set himself above the law. New Jersey Progressive Politics and News reported that Christie was not issued a traffic ticket after an accident that injured a motorcyclist in 2002. Christie was in the wrong, driving the wrong way down a one-way street. To exert his position and power Christie identified himself as U.S. Attorney and then faulted the victim. He lectured the motorcyclist as he was being placed in an ambulance. He showed no remorse whatsoever.

Clearly, Christie perceived himself to be above the law when there was conflict of interest or ethical issues. He would prosecute others for the very same alleged violations. Now he was abusing the powers of his office to target me, in order to enhance his resume in his campaign for governor. This practice had been a proven successful GOP strategy.

Just as former GOP Governor Christine Todd Whitman had taken and released copious pictures of her leaping from her SUV and frisking an African American male during a raid in Camden, New Jersey helping her to win re-election, now GOP U.S Attorney Christie, seeking to become governor, wanted a picture of me going to jail. It was never about fair play or justice. It was about winning at all cost.

After I received numerous subpoenas from the U.S. Attorney's office, my staff attorneys, Raymond M. Brown and his father, the legendary Raymond A. Brown, visited the U.S Attorney's office to make inquiries regarding the subpoenas. They asked if there were any questions that needed to be answered. "How can we save the government money?" they asked.

The U.S. Attorney's office responded that they had no questions. "There is nothing we want to tell you," they said. The government was not interested in any answers. They wanted publicity, they wanted me. The buzz was that Christie was seriously thinking of a run for governor in 2009.

Not satisfied with bragging about the indictment and convictions of State Senator John Lynch, Mayor Barnes of Patterson, Essex County Executive James Treffinger, State Senator Wayne Bryant, Assemblymen Alfred E. Steele, Passaic Mayor Samuel Rivera, Passaic Councilman Marcellus Jackson, Patterson Housing Authority deputy director Benny Ramos, Guttenberg Mayor David Dellie Donna, Passaic Councilman Jonathan Soto, Patterson School Board President Chauncey Brown 111, or State Senator Joseph Coniglio, Christie wanted a bigger fish, a bigger trophy; he wanted to add the name of Sharpe James to his resume, "by any means necessary."

If the highly dignified former U.S Attorney, Michael Chertoff, could not find any criminal wrongdoing or corruption by me during the 1990's investigation, Christie's office would look for "circumstantial factors;" disgruntled employees or align me with an obviously guilty co-defendant that might sway a mostly White suburban jury. "We want Sharpe James" was the hue and cry from Christie.

Because of my success with the renaissance occurring in Newark, because of my independence and because I was fighting for the citizens of Newark, I became a political target for attacks from within and outside the political arena. I had a big mouth, I pointed out what had been accomplished in Newark under my administration. Thus, my conviction would be a prize worthy of being hung on the U.S. Attorney's wall, with the caption, "I brought him down."

Even with this knowledge, I was not totally prepared for eight years (1991-1995 and 2004-2008) of witch-hunts that were orchestrated against me by state and federal authorities, and by politicians and foes who supported this course of action because of personal jealousy; or the fact that they could not defeat me at the polls, or felt threatened that I might seek higher office.

In hindsight, I realized that I would have been better prepared both mentally and physically had I taken the pattern of harassment demonstrated in prior cases that had targeted Black elected Officials more seriously. Unfortunately, I guess that like so many other successful Black officials, I, too, fell victim to the notion that because of my prior success and impeccable honesty that the issue of color was behind me. Perhaps I was naïve for thinking that I was finally living in a post-racial society.

In addition to Basil Franklin being wired, Christie recruited and wired Tamika Riley as well. Now, she was on their side. Ms. Riley had a public relations contract with the City of Newark and had received permission from the Newark Board of Education to produce a Weequahic High School student magazine, *Beyond the Cover*. Riley had been the public relations agent for NBA Boston Celtics player Eric Williams, a native Newarker, who wanted to give back to the city by building affordable housing.

When Eric's pro basketball schedule interfered with development meetings, Riley and her mentor, Diane Fuller Coleman, formed a nonprofit organization, "Building an Empire." They submitted an application to obtain an abandoned building in Newark to serve wayward women. Their application was turned down and a personal dispute ended their relationship.

With the assistance and guidance of Basil Franklin, Director of Housing Production, Riley formed her own TRI company, submitted an application and with the approval of the city council (then councilmen Cory Booker, Luis Quintana and Augusto Amador voted in her favor, et al) purchased nine abandoned properties from the city of Newark. She paid the same price as everyone else had. She did not receive any steeply discounted prices, nor did she receive any assistance from me or my office, as charged in court by U.S. Attorney Christie and unequivocally refuted in court by the law, evidence and both government and defense witnesses.

The contract called for Ms. Riley to rehabilitate the properties before selling them. She rehabilitated the first two and sold three others without rehabilitating them. She had violated the terms of her contract. This was enough for U.S. Attorney, Chris Christie to put his plan to become governor in motion.

One morning, at 6:00, in 2006, FBI and IRS agents raided the Jersey City home of a half sleeping, half naked Tamika Riley. Armed with search warrants for her home and office in Newark, she was advised that she would be indicted, arrested and convicted for "flipping" properties in violation of Newark's municipal contract; a failure to file personal taxes for the last five years and for welfare fraud. It was alleged that she was receiving rental assistance while earning money.

Timidly, she asked, "What is flipping?"

An agent explained that she was accused of not rehabilitating the properties prior to selling them, and secondly receiving rental assistance while earning sizeable profits from the sale of properties purchased from the City of Newark. She was advised that she could spend the next 10-15 years in prison.

Of course, she was advised that she could escape all of these charges by cooperating with the government in targeting Sharpe James.

"We will let you walk," the agent had said. Under these intimidating conditions before sunrise, a frightened Riley with no legal counsel in attendance agreed to allow special agents to wire her office, her telephone and to wear a body wire for conversations. She was told by the agents, "You are now on our side, welcome to the team."

As a government cooperating witness Riley was given a private cell phone number to reach FBI agents. She visited their office frequently and was told to stay in constant contact. Later when the electronic eavesdropping equipment produced no recordings involving me, the government panicked. They needed some damaging evidence of corruption or some criminal activity and had found none. Basil Franklin's body wire had produced no criminal wrongdoing either.

To advance their case, the government called Riley in and asked her to testify that after selling her properties she gave some of the money to me. The government wanted to show the court that I had received an economic benefit from Riley's violations. This was the quid pro quo arrangement they wanted to present to the jury. They wanted an easy conviction. They wanted Riley to lie. They had no evidence against me. Riley went ballistic and said to them, "At your request I have exaggerated a close personal relationship, I have allowed you to wire my telephone, office and body, but, on this false money matter, I can't lie." She was adamant.

"I never once told Mayor James that I was developing properties," she had said. "We only talked about the Weequahic High School student magazine project; I asked him to meet with celebrities visiting Newark, like Little Bow Wow, JaRule, JaHeim, Isaac Hayes, Hip Hop King Russell Simmons and others," she had said, adding, "I can't lie and say that I gave money to the Mayor when I did not. What more do you want from me?" It should have been apparent that she was visibly shaken.

"I will not lie. He was not involved in any of my real estate transactions. I can't lie against the Mayor," she had said. She told them that I had never asked for any money. She told them that she had called my secretary, Deborah Moore, and asked how she could thank the city council and mayor for supporting her concerts and hip hop festivals in Newark.

Ms. Riley was told by Ms. Moore that "The Mayor never wants anything from anyone. He believes that his job is to help people." Deborah had suggested to Ms. Riley, "Just buy a ticket and show up at his annual fund raising birthday party, just show your face and have fun. His reward is happy constituents and supporters." Deborah let Ms. Riley know that, "The Mayor will be there, and he will be the first person on the dance floor doing the electric slide. Please come and join the fun."

The FBI agent was not happy and advised Ms. Riley that she would be indicted along with James as a co-defendant if she did not continue to cooperate. "Do you want me to change my testimony," she had asked? "You have my previous FBI testimony exonerating the Mayor," she had said.

The next day Ms. Riley observed that her car was being followed. She pulled to the side of the road and stopped. She called the FBI headquarters using the private number that they had given her. A senior agent on the telephone told her the FBI agent would pull along side of her car and perhaps she should talk to him. Immediately, the FBI car pulled up to her parked car, the window went down, and the agent asked Ms. Riley if she had changed her mind; would she cooperate? She replied, "No I will not lie."

"We gave you a chance, you will be sorry," the agent had said to Ms. Riley.

The very next week, on Madison Avenue in Jersey City, with a helicopter overhead, more than a dozen federal Marshalls in riot gear had barricaded the street. Fully armed with machine guns and a battering ram, they broke into a private home during breakfast and dragged out a half naked female, with one breast exposed. It was Tamika Riley.

For publicity purposes Christie had alerted the press. He wanted Riley to look like a "strange woman, a harlot." His goal was to poison the minds of any potential jurors. Justice was not blind. He was abusing his authority as an officer of the law.

Now, the former fully cooperating witness, a former member of the government's team, became my co-defendant. What was her real crime? She would not lie for the government. They had wanted to create a fictitious paper trail of me receiving money. It was Christie's belief that the government needed Riley, (as the government later stated in their response to my appeal) an alleged tax and welfare cheat, seated next to me to win a conviction. They wanted a jury verdict based on my guilt by association. This government strategy portraying James on trial in the company of an alleged unsavory person would help to convince the jury that he had to be guilty of something. He would appear to be a bad guy in the eyes of the jurors.

Tragically the government had abandoned their cooperating witness. Riley had been used and abused by the government. I was their target and now she was the weapon to be used against me. U.S. Attorney Christopher Christie had no shame. He was not about justice. He was about winning at all cost to pad his resume by hook or crook. There was no justice. He was running for governor.

CHAPTER SIXTEEN

Retirement, 2006

Thirty-eight years is a long time to serve the public (1970-2008). My body was feeling as though I needed a comprehensive physical and psychological examination. I felt like I had gone fifteen rounds with Mike Tyson, without him biting my ear, just his punches alone. This brings to mind a time when Mike and former New Jersey Commissioner of Athletics, Larry Hazzard, visited me in my home. Mike was in the kitchen talking. Because of Mike's soft voice another guest asked me, "Who is that 'faggot' in the kitchen." Although offended by this remark, I always believed that I saved my guest's life that night. It was a reminder, please, "Don't judge a book by its cover."

While I was feeling the fatigue of having served my constituents for the past thirty-eight years, my ecstatic supporters were screaming at the top of their lungs, "Four more years, four more years." Some were even chanting, "James for Governor in 2009. He will do for New Jersey what he has done for Newark, make it better," they cried. "Happy days are here again" businessman Ruben Johnson had shouted. It struck me that running for public office can become an addiction for the candidate and even for his followers.

For example, in New Jersey's 10th Congressional District, my beloved late Congressman, Peter W. Rodino, of Watergate fame at age 89, after having served for more than forty years, had rescinded several announced retirements. Pete simply would not quit and had to be beaten out of office by Donald Payne.

I was accused by several of Rodino's colleagues in Congress of helping to force him out of office in order to elect an African American congressman. My heated response was that he was not kicked out, he was voted out. Sometimes we stay too long. If it had been a vote for respect, love and serving your country well, Rodino would have won in a landslide. Unfortunately, this was a vote saying enough is enough; times are changing; and pass the baton.

United States Senator from New Jersey, Frank Lautenberg is another example. Facing re-election in 2008 at age 84, Lautenberg refused his party's request to step down for a younger candidate; instead Frank jumped down on the floor and started doing pushups to demonstrate his physical fitness. Later he produced a campaign film entitled; "I'm running" starring himself as a jogger.

In the film Frank was out front leading the pack. Rumor had it that Frank had hired a group of golden senior citizens to be part of his jogging entourage. Frank knew how to win; this was his undisputed message to party officials. They left him alone. On November 4, 2008, he won a fifth term as the U.S Senator from New Jersey. Now his same detractors are lining up against him for his 2014 run at age 90.

Across the Passaic River from Newark, Frank Rodgers had served as mayor of Harrison, New Jersey, a small town working class community, for fifty nine years. Many persons do not live that long; and certainly many marriages do not last that long. No candidate would utter the popular words, often used against an aging incumbent, "It's time for a change." They loved Frank Rodgers in Harrison. He was their hero. He was their mayor for life. Still, there is the question of how important is age?

Since Hollywood actor, Ronald Reagan, ran for the Presidency in 1984 at age 76, and won in a landslide, age has become less of a factor when running for public office. Reagan's remarkable retort, "I will not exploit your youth and inexperience," to his youthful challenger, Walter Mondale, might have contributed to this perception.

At age 69, I wrestled with thoughts of living, working, possible retirement, life after retirement and even death. I asked myself, *Is it really noble to stay on the job and die; or should one serve well and then retire?* If we wait too long, until we die, we obviously and without a doubt lose the option of retirement and enjoying hard earned pensions. To aid with my decision on the question of service, life and retirement, I thought about some noble people hoping to learn from their example.

Dr. Martin Luther King, Jr. sermonized that like any other man "I would like to live a long and productive life," however, it didn't matter to him anymore because he had been to the mountain top. He did not want to be eulogized as a man who had earned a doctorate degree from Boston University; authored more than sixty books; received a Nobel Peace Prize or as a man whose face had graced the cover of *Time magazine* as "Man of the Year." Dr. King was a very humble person. He wanted people to remember him simply as a man who loved humanity.

Dr. King said that he wanted to be remembered as a man who cared for the sick and poor, clothed the naked and visited those in hospitals and prisons; that he was a drum major for justice. Of course, I personally can never forget his profound, captivating, motivating and memorable, "I Have a Dream" speech at the 1963 March on Washington, it was simply hypnotic.

Moreover, like President John F. Kennedy, Dr. King did not live a long life; they lived a good life. So the real challenge is not how long one lives but how well one lives. Both men of valor never had the opportunity to weigh the question of retirement. Retirement is not always an option.

From my viewpoint, and God willing, there are four major events in our lives and two that we do not control. There is a time to be born, a time to live and if you are one of the lucky ones, a time to retire and of course a time to die. Unfortunately and disrespectfully, man is constantly trying to manipulate and control all four events, a mistaken and bold attempt to play God.

My Army combat buddy in Hohenfels, Germany, Elvis Pressley, with his matinee good looks, extraordinary singing voice and sans curls did not wish to die. He took pills for everything thinking that it would bring him immortality.

My good friend and supporter Doris Duke with her immense fortune, many husbands, many mansions, a personal zoo and her wonderful belief in philanthropy, did not wish to die. She spent money to control her environment.

I remember reading that highly eccentric, reclusive, aeronautical genius and billionaire Howard Hughes tried to defy death. He wanted to live within a germ-free environment.

Our beloved United States Senator Edward Kennedy fought long and courageously against brain cancer. He, too, wanted to live.

And to challenge the finality of death, baseball Hall of Famer Ted Williams was cryogenically frozen, perhaps in the belief that he or a part of his body would return one day.

With the exception of Ted Williams, none of these legendary and highly successful personalities had an opportunity to experience retirement before death.

With a much lower profile, portfolio in life and record of achievement, my mind and body was ready for retirement. I was not ready for the senior choir to sing, "Let the work I've done speak for me." I wasn't ready for the junior choir to sing, "Remember me."

With my retirement from my mayoral and state senatorial positions, I would be officially ending thirty-eight years of uninterrupted public service. I was now 69 years of age. I wanted to spend more time with my family. I wanted to do the things I'd always enjoyed like boating, fishing, tennis and traveling. I wanted to visit old friends, like former Mayor Ken Gibson, and talk about our beloved city of Newark. Ken and I both still lived in and loved Newark. We sometimes got together at community gatherings discussing our scars from political combat over the years; just as our hero Muhammad Ali showed his scars from the ring. Yes, it was time to retire, I thought. Yes, it was time for the career Democrat to pass the baton.

My plan also included retiring from my position as a tenured professor and Director of the Urban Issues Institute at Essex County College (ECC) in 2007. I had already officially retired as athletic director for ECC after providing two decades (1968-1986 then 2006-2007) of exemplary service.

When retiring from the Senate in 2008, I was giving up my positions as vice chairman of the Senate Budget and Appropriations Committee, overseeing the state's $30 billion spending plan, and the vice chairman's seat on the Community Affairs Committee. I had served for nine years (1999-2008) as a dual officeholder.

I was considered one of the most powerful elected officials in the history of New Jersey, and with the retirement of Mayor Richard

Arrington of Birmingham, Alabama in 1999, I was the last of the civil rights leaders elected to office during the 70's. Understandably my body was tired. I had to accept the fact that I was not getting any younger, not superman, nor was I indispensable. It was time for retirement.

Surprisingly, I discovered after retirement that it wasn't so bad sleeping late, nor did I miss the hectic pace and daily challenges of the office. *I should have retired earlier,* I thought to myself. The questions I asked myself everyday now, were, "Will it be golf, tennis or boating in the morning? Should I take my wife out to dinner this evening, attend a Broadway play, or a movie?" I had too many new choices.

I remembered when I had asked my American Tennis Association (ATA) doubles partner William Mallory, who had retired three years earlier as supervisor of athletics for the Newark Board of Education, "What do you do every day now that you are retired?"

He couldn't wait to answer, "I get up and go to work every morning."

I replied that I didn't know he had taken on a new job? Now with his chest sticking out, he said, "I thought you knew"

"Knew what?" I asked.

Bill smiled, and said: "I get up every morning and go to work to play golf in the morning and tennis in the afternoon or tennis in the morning and golf in the afternoon."

I had been ambushed. Trying to get even, I asked, "Well, what about in the winter?"

Now with his chest still sticking out and becoming animated with his arms flailing, Bill said, "I thought you knew; we fly to Myrtle Beach."

I had no further questions for Bill. I accepted the fact that "LOVE" (6-0, 6-0) is a game called tennis. I had lost the match.

Nevertheless and thanks to Bill's insight, I adopted a simple life-style of taking in movies with an extra large bag of buttered popcorn, my favorite candy, Raisonettes, and a large diet soda; or standing in line on Broadway in New York City, at the discount ticket window, hoping to get to see a Broadway play.

When the weather was good there was always the opportunity to go boating with members of the Rainbow yacht club. I could also learn golf in the morning and play tennis in the afternoon or tennis in the morning and learn golf in the afternoon.

In the winter when Bill and his gang flew to Myrtle Beach, I used my membership card for the local downtown YMWCA to go swimming and partake in physical fitness classes. I even challenged Mary, a former league bowler to show off her "back-up" curve.

Like the tune from the Broadway play Gypsy, "Everything is coming up roses for me and my gal," everything was coming up roses for me and my family. Mary is a retired educator and able to travel with me anywhere we want to go. Our three sons are all grown up and doing well on their own. Our oldest son, John, a graduate of Rutgers Law School works as a supervisor analyst for a local hospital. He is the only of our three sons who has expressed interest in a career in politics. In 2010 John was the next highest vote-getter for Councilman-At-Large.

My middle son, Elliott Sharpe James is a graduate of Hampton University. He is a licensed real estate agent and owner/manager of the Key Club, in Newark. Elliott is athletic, like me. He enjoys tennis and keeping in good physical condition.

Kevin Sharpe James, my youngest son, briefly attended Essex County College. He is a former Newark fireman. He is currently a New Jersey longshoreman. Kevin is a sports enthusiast as well, only from a spectator perspective, though. He's the ladies' man in the family and enjoys wearing designer clothing.

Indeed, life was good, and then, just as I was beginning to really enjoy the excitement of being retired, a rumor surfaced again that I was being targeted by United States Attorney Christopher Christie. It was the same political rumor that he was running for governor in 2009, and needed to convict a prominent African American Democrat to launch his gubernatorial campaign. It was the same political rumor, which had surfaced before, that he wanted publicity to appeal to his base GOP conservative voters.

Again, the talk was that he had violated his oath of office, and possibly the Hatch Act, by turning the supposedly nonpolitical U.S Attorney's office into his campaign office. He was building a case against me before a grand jury, where it was well known that a U.S Attorney could indict a ham sandwich.

U.S. Attorney Christopher Christie wanted to enhance his campaign for governor by "bragging" that he put Sharpe James in prison by hook or crook. Justice was not blind. It was now obvious that I would not get to enjoy my retirement.

CHAPTER SEVENTEEN

Indictment/Arrest/Arraignment, 2007

*"As a former federal prosecutor, I'm aware of
the fact that you can indict a ham sandwich"*
By Hon. William. J. Martini

O h what a beautiful morning," or at least I thought so. I was
enjoying my retirement and the military training I received
in Germany, had me up and out of bed at 5:30 a.m., in the
bathroom brushing my teeth. Another blessed morning to start good
grooming, I thought.

Our beautiful stained glass bathroom windows, which diffuse
the rays of the sun, had been left open. A cool breeze flowed through
the window screen. By chance I looked out across my front lawn and
saw two suspicious unmarked vehicles parked near my driveway. *This is
unusual,* I thought. Suddenly I heard the roar of two helicopters circling
above my house. This was very strange. I hadn't called for any emergency.
What could it be?

I decided not to call my friend, Bill Mallory, for golf or tennis that
morning. Instead I called my lawyer, Raymond A. Brown. I explained the
situation to him.

Ray said, "Well, there's been a rumor going around about a possible
sealed indictment against you. I suggest that you drive straight to my office,
I'll meet you there."

I dressed, got into my car and headed to my lawyer's office.
The two unmarked vehicles followed me to Ray's downtown Gateway

Office. After I parked the car and got out, an occupant from one of the two cars that had followed me got out of his car and continued following me on foot to the entrance of the office. He never spoke a word, but stared me down.

Inside in his office Ray explored the ongoing investigation with me, the hearsay accusations, and my being a target. "They have been trying to pin something on you for twenty years," Ray said. "People are making plans to run for governor in 2009; anything can happen in a political season. From my experience, I believe that they are planning to make a big splashy TV breaking news arrest of you. I think that they want to hold you over-night in jail for publicity purposes."

Ray reminded me that former Essex County Executive, James Treffinger, was arrested in the morning while eating breakfast. He had been handcuffed and shackled in front of his wife and children. It had been alleged that while investigating Treffinger, the U.S. attorney had obtained a wire tape with him saying that the U.S. Attorney didn't know the difference between a cook book and a law book. This had made the U.S. Attorney, Chris Christie, furious. "They might have worse plans for you," Ray had said. We both sat in silence for awhile. We had run out of options.

Suddenly Brown jumped up and said, "Let's go."

"Where are we going? What are we doing?" I asked.

Brown serenely said, "You are going to turn yourself into the FBI. They are following you around. Let's end this nonsense.

"I'm going to the federal courthouse to prepare for your imme-diate release after the arraignment; I do not want you held overnight. I intend to spoil their plan," Ray said.

With all of this orchestrated hoopla going on I could only think of my favorite songstress, Diana Washington, singing, "What a difference a day makes." We were now driving to the brand new state-of-the-art waterfront FBI headquarters. As Mayor, I had been widely criticized by the Board of Trustees of the New Jersey Performing Arts Center for granting the land and rights for the FBI to build such a project adjacent to the NJPAC. This was part of my Newark impossible dream project.

When plans for the FBI headquarters were made public, I received a visitor. NJPAC's CEO and President, Larry Goldman, came to my office and said, "Sharpe, please reconsider your terrible decision.

That ugly fortress like structure doesn't fit in with our plans. Please kill the project," he had said. "It's the wrong facility to occupy space in the performing arts district. You are making a serious mistake," Larry had warned me.

While he was berating me, I only wished he knew the beating I had taken for supporting the construction of the art center. Local residents had screamed at me, saying, "You are building another extravagant edifice for White folks. We don't need it," cried poet, play writer, Amiri Baraka. "It will be the kiss of death for Newark Symphony Hall; you are selling out to the White folks," he had screamed.

The antagonism and protest grew even worse after we learned that the site contained an old African American cemetery. We had to honor and respect the ancestors. Now the Black community was accusing me of selling out to the White carpetbaggers, who only wanted to make a buck in Newark.

How quickly I learned that there were no easy decisions for mayors. Do I give in to the naysayers or the "NIMBYs," the not in my backyard protestors? I had decided to keep Newark on a roll. I decided to err on the side of progress. I kept my word to support the construction of the waterfront FBI headquarters.

My thinking was "a bird in the hand is worth two in the bush." For too long we had witnessed a vacant waterfront with one plan after the other eventually failing. That was then.

During construction a portion of the building caught fire and the Newark Fire Department promptly responded. As fire fighters were climbing in the building and putting out the fire, the FBI Director raced by me, hands waving, and screaming "Everyone leave this site, get off this property, now, get out. 'Who is in charge?'" he had asked.

The Fire Chief met him, and pointing his finger at me, said "The Mayor that you just passed." The FBI Director turned quietly and walked back towards me. Before he could speak I asked, "Do you want us to put out the fire?" He remained embarrassingly silent.

Unlike my previous visits to the still under construction FBI headquarters, I was not the mayor now. This time I was not overseeing a fire; or seeking a tour of this highly technological and bomb proof facility. A facility built by several contractors, each kept in secret of the others work for security reasons. This building had its own physical fitness center, private radio shop and medical facility. A structure Batman would be proud of. It was purposely designed to make it hard to get into and even harder to get out of. There were moving concrete barriers. Unknown to many, it has a unique system of cameras watching over the city. Unknowingly I became proof that they work.

One day I arrived one half hour early for a scheduled tour of the building and decided to park my car two blocks away and read the newspaper. I had just reached the editorial page when suddenly an FBI agent tapped on my car window and said, "Mr. Mayor you can arrive early, they are waiting for you." *This is unequivocal proof that the roof top cameras do work and are being monitored,* I thought to myself.

However, this was a different day. On this occasion they were not expecting me. They had no idea why I was reporting to them. They looked surprised. Attorney Brown turned to one of the FBI agents and said, "You are looking for Sharpe James, well, here he is." When both agents looked at each other they seemed stunned and genuinely surprised. My attorney said, "You must have a warrant out for his arrest, why else would you be following him around with helicopters circling over his house?" Neither agent responded. Ray walked directly up to an agent and pointing toward me with his hand said, "Well here he is, do your job."

The agent, still in shock, replied "Well all right, all right, we will look into this." He turned to make a telephone call. An unfazed Ray Brown never stopped talking. "Sharpe, you stay here. I want you guys to take care of the Mayor," Brown said to the agents. "I have some work to do at the federal courthouse." He left, and the agents immediately got on the telephone trying to figure out what to do next.

I am still thanking the late Ray Brown to this day for his legal knowledge, courage and insight. He was working hard to assure that the Pre Sentencing Office would receive, interview and set bail for me before its 4 pm closing. Attorney Brown wanted me before a federal judge as quickly as possible for the arraignment. It was Brown's plan to foil the government's publicity stunt.

After Brown's departure the FBI agents quickly went from knowing nothing to knowing everything. They took me to their basement laboratory and had me photographed and fingerprinted. The Black FBI agent, with a snarl on his face, told me not to move, despite the fact that we were in a bomb proof, escape proof room. He roughly cuffed my hands tightly behind my back. Then they took me upstairs and shoved me into an unmarked vehicle and transported me to the federal courthouse.

The agents drove directly into an underground parking facility where both agents, without speaking, turned the engine off and exited the car. I was left handcuffed, wrist bleeding, in the back seat of the car with no air conditioning; the temperature quickly rose from 60 degrees to about 90 degrees. After a length of time alone in the car, I began suffocating from heat exhaustion. I was hot and thirsty, and started choking. I was bleeding from the wrist. They were treating me like a caged animal and there was no help around.

When the agents finally returned and opened the door I simply fell out of the car, dripping wet. I thought I would die. They didn't care. "Move," the Black agent growled, pushing me roughly. It was obvious to me that he was showing off for the White FBI agents, letting them know that he could be mean to a Black person. I knew they were still mad because I had turned myself in. I had denied them the publicity they were expecting for my arrest.

I was taken to the courthouse laboratory, and although the equipment was the same as in the FBI headquarters, I was again photographed and fingerprinted. That was easy. Then they locked me in a steel cage and told me to strip naked, "Make sure you take everything off," roared the Black FBI agent. After I was naked, federal Marshalls made a meticulous and degrading search of all of my body parts and cavities, searching for weapons.

As they fondled my penis, I kept asking myself *are these guys perverts?* Finding no weapons they left me nude in the cold steel cage for over an hour. Finally, they told me to get dressed, leaving my jewelry, watch, belt and tie in a bag. I thought the worst was over, but I was wrong.

Now it was slavery time; a reenactment of the movie, "Roots." If I thought being handcuffed was uncomfortable, now I was handcuffed and manacled with chains and leg irons. I felt as though I had just gotten off a slave ship, heading to the auction block. I was overwhelmed with feelings of being disrespected, mistreated, persecuted and helpless to do anything about it, even before I reached a courtroom.

I wanted to ask the question, *Is all of this necessary for an alleged nonviolent crime when the person being charged has no prior arrests or history of ever committing a crime?* Once convicted, they will tell you to travel five hundred miles alone, to surrender yourself to a federal correction center. What's the difference? *Why a defendant is considered a threat for flight or capable of inflicting physical harm while standing in the courtroom with FBI agents, and not when told to report to a correction center to be locked up?* Are we just creating more and more jobs in the criminal justice system? *It doesn't make any sense,* I was thinking.

I was told to follow the agent down the hall. *How?* I thought. I had to hobble, skip, jump, trip and hop behind the fast walking agents. Once entering the elevator a female agent pushed my face against the wall screaming not to look around. I could sense another person being placed on the elevator with me.

The female and the Black FBI agents who escorted me were verbally and physically brutal. Each wanted to prove something; the female agent showing that she could be tough and the Black FBI agent definitely out to prove that he was not "my brother."

Finally, after this weary and difficult journey, in a disarrayed sight, I was standing before a Federal Judge in a blinding, overcrowded, wall-to-wall standing room only courtroom of reporters, photographers, agents, federal officials and some thrill seekers; all anxiously awaiting the burning at the stake; a desire for a modern day lynching. I questioned myself, had I killed someone? "Where is the guillotine?"

"Order in the court, order in the court," now echoed throughout the courtroom. Order was quickly restored. The Judge read the indictment against me: "Mail fraud, Fraud involving local government, receiving federal funds; and a conspiracy to defraud the public of honest services."

In laymen's terms, Sharpe James created a fraudulent South Ward Redevelopment Plan (SWRP) to benefit Tamika Riley directly, and himself indirectly; he sold land to her at steeply discounted prices; steered properties to her; participated in the fraudulent sale of properties with Riley; and deprived the public of his honest services.

This is all bull shit, I thought. Under the Faulkner Law, which Newark is governed by, I lacked the legal authority as mayor to commit the crimes they were charging me with. *I am an innocent man,* I thought while standing before this modern day lynching mob.

I had served as a councilman for sixteen years prior to becoming mayor. I knew that as mayor, under the Faulkner Act, I could not legally set the price to sell or convey land to developers. The city was selling abandoned properties "as is" under the South Ward Redevelopment Plan (SWRP) without using any HUD or federal funds. Riley was approved by the members of the city council and paid the same price as every other developer. Three members of the current city council, Augusto Amador, Luis Quintana and former central ward councilman, and now Mayor Cory Booker, had met with Riley, named her a developer, approved her project, set the price of the land and voted to sell municipal properties to her. She was never assisted by me or my office.

"The government is lying," I whispered to my attorney. "They are narrating a story to the press without any evidence or facts to support it." I touched his arm to get his attention and said, "I lack the legal authority to set prices or sell land. I've been both a councilman and mayor, I know the law," I said. "What's going on? This is a circus. This is a joke. Where is the justice?"

The Judge finished reading the five-count indictment. Cameras were flashing in every direction. The courtroom artist was vigorously drawing lines and shading colors. The FBI agents and the U.S. Attorney's office staff were standing proud and erect. They all wore smiles and were giving one another a thumbs up, a suggesting that "We got him."

It was like a celebration, a weird environment to be in. Thoughts of a lynching party came to my mind. I wondered *how many others have suffered such an injustice.*

The judge asked, "How do you plead?"

Is she crazy? I thought. "How do I plead?" *I shouldn't even be here to plead.* "Why is this happening?" I asked myself.

Again the Judge asked, "How do you plead?"

Quickly I snapped back to reality and looking at the Judge, I said, "I plead not guilty your honor."

Now the cameras lit up like the Fourth of July, blinding me. Reporters started racing for the nearest exit to feed their networks breaking news; some were trying to paw at my defense attorney and gain my attention. We had no intention of honoring this blood thirsty entourage. I had lost my image but not my personal dignity.

Again I was ordered to hobble, hop, skip and jump back to the federal court detention room. After the chains and shackles were removed, I put my shoe laces in my shoes and got dressed. As a new guard opened the door to allow me to leave, he turned and said, "Mr. Mayor, hang in there, what they did to you upstairs was all wrong, good luck." He closed the door and walked away. *At least I met one decent guy,* I said to myself.

I had been arraigned, now I got to meet with my attorney in the Probation's Pre-Sentencing Office. I felt like it was feeding time at the zoo as I struggled through media personnel to reach the office of Ms. Annette Gautier, Supervisor in the Pre-Sentencing Office. I was only there through the wisdom and noble effort of my attorney, the honorable Raymond A. Brown. The government had planned to hold up the arraignment until her office was closed for the day, thereby getting to hold me overnight in jail. Attorney Brown was trying to thwart the government's plan.

The government's plan was for a mid-day arrest. Brown had gone to the federal courthouse to arrange for a judge to handle the arraignment as quickly as possible; then he asked if the Pre-sentencing office would receive, interview and set bail for me before closing. Brown was relentless in his pursuit for fair play. He was a lawyer's lawyer.

Once we were in her office, Ms. Gautier handed me a form to fill out and started asking questions about my finances, properties and the possibility of bail. While reviewing my answers her telephone rang. I watched as her face became taut, her complexion changed, her eyes widened and her body jerked back. Removing the telephone from her ear as for relief, we could hear the loud voice of U.S Attorney Christopher Christie coming through the receiver, and it was not pleasant.

Attorney Brown and I looked at each other, sensing a confrontation between the two. Ms. Gautier continued her spirited conversation with Christie, showing emotional stress. She frequently removed the telephone from her ear, and we could overhear Christie's loud, demanding voice questioning Ms. Gautier. When she hung up she looked at both of us and said, "I'm sure you heard that call from the U.S Attorney Christopher Christie."

Without saying a word Attorney Brown and I shook our heads in agreement. Brown nudged me with his elbow and I knew what he was thinking. We both had to be thinking that we would no longer be able to complete this mandatory task in a timely manner. We thought Christie had won the day.

I thought about the possibility of remaining in jail overnight. Even more importantly, though, Brown and I were both embarrassed to have placed Ms. Gautier in this highly volatile situation. We were afraid that she was not trained to play politics. U.S Attorney Christie had really put some fear in her.

After gaining her composure Ms. Gautier turned to us, still visibly shaken. We were wide-eyed, nervous, tense and now puzzled as to what would happen next. We leaned our elbows on her desk to find out her next move. The office was quiet.

Ms. Gautier straightened up in her chair, tugged at her clothes to get comfortable, took a deep breath and said, "Where were we? Oh yes, your house at 59 Wilbur Avenue can be used as collateral. Attorney Brown and I were stunned at this courageous response, following her telephone confrontation with Mr. Christie.

Ms. Gautier proved to be a highly respected, exemplary and a very competent professional. She exhibited objective behavior for the government, court and the defendant. She was not a political pawn. She was a no nonsense person. No pushover. She knew her job. She was about justice.

When passing the huge statue in front of the Dr. Martin Luther King Federal Office Building and Courthouse, Ms. Gautier must have known that Lady Justice wore a blindfold. She knew that justice was blind. During my entire ordeal I never met a more honest, professional and courageous government official than Ms. Annette Gautier. Like the hit song by Larry Graham she was, "One in a million." She is my hero. She is justice's hero.

Interestingly enough, Ms. Gautier was less than five feet tall and handicapped. This never stopped her from doing anything; walking from her private office on full display to greet visitors in the foyer and then leading them back to her office; holding conferences or visiting you in your home even climbing stairs. She was undoubtedly the tallest person I met in the federal courthouse.

Because of her professionalism, fairness and courage, I was officially released on bail until my trial date. My home on Wilbur Avenue was held as collateral. My next challenge was to figure out how an innocent man should defend himself against the United States of America?

Will the others I come up against be more like U.S Attorney Christopher Christie, who embraces a personal philosophy of winning at all cost, or Ms. Gautier; a true objective professional and believer in justice for all?

"Will justice be blind for me?" I asked.

I will soon find out, I said to myself.

CHAPTER EIGHTEEN

No Fair Trial Possible, 2007

Jury Selection

"Can anything good come out of Nazareth?"
"Can anything good come out of Newark?"
"Can justice be blind?"

In life one must "stand for something or you will fall for anything." I stood for the revitalization of Newark against all odds. As an articulate, independent, flamboyant, un-bossed and highly profiled politician for thirty-eight years, I had ruffled many feathers and created many enemies.

Despite the feathers that I ruffled I have always believed that we, as Americans, are a fair and just people. I believed that justice is blind, as depicted by the Roman Goddess of Justice, "Justitia," who frequently adorns courthouses and courtrooms. Justitia is most often depicted with a set of weighing scales typically suspended from her left hand, carrying a double-edged sword in her right hand, symbolizing the power of reason and justice, and wearing a blindfold. To me the blindfold symbols that justice is or should be meted out objectively, without fear or favor, regardless of the identity, power, or weakness of the individual charged with an infraction.

To move Newark from urban blight to urban bright, a designation conferred by the New Jersey Conference of Mayors, when they named me "Mayor of the Year" in 2001, I had to say no to a lot of influential people, step on the toes of some and embarrass others. By choice and by the needs of my people, I could not play the role of being the "Good Ole Boy" or a "Stepin Fletchit," an ebony character, grinning and tap dancing. Nor could I be bought by a job or title. I did not suffer from any Negro amnesia, as many Black leaders do, as charged by the Reverend Al Sharpton.

Thus my love, courage and defense of Newark made me an easy target. I wore Newark on my shirt sleeve. I inherited a sick city requiring major surgery, not mere symbolism or tokenism. We needed real help not patronizing freaks. We needed real supporters and friends of Newark, not curiosity seekers, the lonely-hearts or urban enemies; we needed those who would put their hands in the fire for Newark.

My attacks on Phil Donahue, Johnny Carson, Jay Leno or George Zoffinger, who was Chairman of the New Jersey Sports Authority, and a host of other local and state officials for their unwarranted and relentless criticism of Newark, created even more enemies for me. Phil Donahue, at least, had the decency and courage to offer a public apology for denigrating Newark.

My political enemies could not defeat me at the polls, so they decided to make me a political prisoner instead. The sixty four thousand dollar question being asked on the street was could I receive a fair trial? Is justice really blind? After the arraignment I met with my staff lawyers, personal lawyer and my criminal defense lawyers Raymond A. Brown, Raymond M. Brown, Alan Bowman, Tom Ashley and Alan Zegas. Together you could not find more diverse, multi-talented, hardnosed and gifted practitioners of law. Individually they differed in dress, style, court manners, savvy and their approach to interpreting the law, but together they were dynamite.

Legendary attorney Raymond A. Brown was considered the dean of criminal lawyers in New Jersey. His legal career resume could earn him a Nobel Peace Prize. Without fanfare and with a minimum of debate, they all agreed that I could not receive a fair trial in Newark, which housed the closest Federal District Courthouse.

The Dr. Martin Luther King Federal Office Building and Court-house, is a beautiful structure in Newark, which required the city to declare it a blighted area in order to create the site. It is a state-of-the-art building, located in an area that was once residential, and where angry homeowners had heckled and threatened to tar and feather me for relocating them.

The courthouse, a magnificent facility, is only a short distance from equally impressive Newark City Hall, with its golden dome, and a mere two blocks from our new Prudential Center superstructure.

My lawyers believed that due to my fierce independence over the years and constant fights with *The Star-Ledger*, I could not receive a fair trial. I was a marked man. They believed that *The Star-Ledger* wanted my scalp and wanted me out of office because they could not dictate or control me. The attorneys unanimously agreed that I would be convicted if the trial was held in Newark.

The questions I asked were, "Wouldn't the people of Newark be aware of my good record in office for more than three decades? Wouldn't they be able to attest to the significant progress that we have made? What about the ongoing $10 billion renaissance occurring in Newark? I have never taken a dime or tried to hurt anyone. I have always tried to help people," I offered in my defense. "Wouldn't the people of Newark understand that legally I could not commit the crimes leveled against me? They know the difference between the duties and legal authority of the Mayor and the Council."

"Sharpe, Sharpe, slow down, you don't understand how a jury is selected," Brown, Sr. said. "Most of the jurors will not come from Newark; the Court will draw from neighboring counties a pool of registered voters which will guarantee you a mostly suburban, mostly White jury."

"That's what the government is counting on to win their case," Attorney Ashley vigorously stated. "Their plan is to stand a long-term urban politician before a mostly White suburban jury and call him a bad guy; that's how they win, even when they have no case. James is a bad boy; he's seated next to an alleged tax and welfare cheat; he must have done something wrong, so put him away," Ashley illustrated.

Their suggestion was to hire Dr. John Lamberth, who came highly recommended, to conduct a poll in the three New Jersey Federal District Courts (Camden, Trenton and Newark) to test potential jurors in order to determine what they knew about Sharpe James and what they knew about the charges being leveled against Sharpe James? A poll designed to test how far the negative images of me, portrayed by *The Star-Ledger*, had reached other parts of the state. The poll would determine if I could receive a fair trial.

Dr. Lamberth could craft a telephone questionnaire, which would enable him to answer those questions within a 5 per cent margin of error, my attorneys told me. Attorney Raymond A. Brown said that trials are often won by jury selection alone, notwithstanding the evidence and witnesses produced at trial. "Jury selection is the highest priority in crafting your defense," he had said.

There was some talk about petitioning Federal Judge William J. Martini to conduct the trial in lower Manhattan, entirely outside of New Jersey, to thwart the heavy influence of *The Star-Ledger*. "Sharpe, it's that important," they continued to remind me. "All we want is a fair chance to win this case on the merit of the evidence and witnesses presented at trial," Ashley said.

When my lawyers finally met with Dr. Lamberth, they advised him of my on-going feud with *The Star-Ledger*. My thirty-six years, as a councilman, mayor, and state senator who would not bow to the demands of *The Star-Ledger* or the media, made me a target. "Sharpe has been a maverick, bold, independent and a self made politician," Raymond M. Brown said. The attorneys explained to Dr. Lamberth that I was a long term urban mayor hated by the press and a "target" by the U.S. Attorney's Office. "Christopher Christie is running for governor," Brown, Sr. stated. "He will do anything to win."

My experience has been somewhat similar to that experienced in 2008 by Vice Presidential candidate, Sarah Palin. As an independent voice, she was simply never accepted by the press. She was considered an outsider. To *The Star-Ledger*, Sharpe James was an outsider. The Star-Ledger was running a campaign against me, personally, and against the James Administration simultaneously. It appeared that they were never going to get over being kicked out of Newark City Hall. They were playing a childish game of payback.

After Mort Pye's retirement from *The Star-Ledger*, his replacement, Willse, adopted Mort's philosophy and took it to a new level. At his first public speaking engagement, before the Newark Fund, a group of Newark businessmen who were active in the revitalization of Newark, Willse spoke proudly and candidly about his intentions for the newspaper.

I heard that Mr. Willse delivered a brilliant speech on the workings of the newspaper and its many challenges. When the floor opened for questions, Gustav Heningburg, a Newark businessman asked Willse why he could not purchase the Essex County edition of *The Star-Ledger* at the Newark Liberty Airport. He advised Mr. Willse that only the Union County edition, which does not cover Newark news, is available at the airport.

Heningburg, a longtime Newark businessman and activist, had pulled off one of the most successful open air concerts in the history of Newark, "Love Festival." The concert drew over 100,000 participants who crowded into Newark's Weequahic Park. Heningburg was also the individual who had served as chairman of the transition teams for Mayor Kenneth Gibson in 1970 and for me in 1986. Heningburg said that Willse became annoyed at his question.

"Willse looked surprised and appeared angry at the question," Gus had said. After he recovered from the question he proceeded to shock the entire group by saying, with a smirk on his face, "Who in their right mind would want to read anything about Newark?" Gus said that all the good things that Willse had said that day were now lost in this unwarranted and unsolicited attack on Newark. The business leaders in the room were supporters of Newark. They too were shocked at Willse's negative attitude toward the city. The die was cast.

Shortly thereafter Mr. Willse assigned Joan Whitlow, a divorcee from a racially mixed marriage, to write exclusive weekly articles about me and the James Administration. Interestingly enough, and although I am older than she, during our youth we were both members of the Weequahic Park Tennis Club. Oftentimes I carried her as my doubles partner, although she couldn't hit the side of a barn with a tennis ball. Because she was dating a member of our club we decided to tolerate her poor tennis game.

To prove her loyalty to *The Star-Ledger* (job security) and not our tennis club, Joan ran off about two dozen negative columns about the James Administration. It appeared that she could not find anything good to write about Newark. She brought to mind the Biblical quote, "Can anything good come out of Nazareth?" I kept wondering if her writings would find any good in Newark. Joan saw the glass always half empty and never half full.

The idea of assigning a Black reporter to Newark was designed to thwart any charges of racism. Joan even criticized my desire to build an arts center (NJPAC) in Newark. She was against our plan to build a minor league ball stadium in the city. She was against everything the James Administration put forth to improve the quality of life in Newark.

I just knew that Whitlow would write something positive about the city when we decided to bring the arrogant Port Authority of NY/NJ to their knees. The city initiated a lawsuit against the Port Authority for not paying Newark a fair rent for our most valuable airport land. Newark's contract with Port Authority was based on a share of their net income. We witnessed millions of dollars being squandered away in excessive salaries, perks, unnecessary office space and questionable purchases. They had even built a $2 million tunnel to nowhere and then closed it.

There was nothing left after Port Authority deducted expenses from their net income. The gravy was long gone. We demanded a new contract, one where rent was based on a percentage of their gross income, not their net income. We wanted some of the cream from the top, not the dregs from the bottom.

After about seven years in court, we settled for about $1.2 billion. It was the largest court victory for a municipality in the history of New Jersey. We took $450 million in cash for special projects and for property tax relief. With the money we received we could now move forward with building a world-class arena in Newark. Strangely enough, Joan and *The Star-Ledger* used much ink criticizing the amount of money that we received. "Sharpe didn't get enough money," they cried. He sold out. He should have waited". Again *The Star-Ledger* was attacking me.

Joan Whitlow and *The Star-Ledger* were of the opinion that building an 18,000 seat arena in Newark for the New Jersey Devils and a possible NBA team was a waste of money. She even criticized the expense we incurred for the city's preparation to receive the Pope, who was visiting Newark and other major cities. Everything negative about Newark appeared highlighted in the statewide edition of the "*Ledger*"(for jury poisoning) and anything approaching good news about Newark was not covered or limited and buried in the Essex County (local readers only) section of the paper.

In their desire to get me out of office, The Star- *Ledger* promoted candidates to run against me in 1994 and 1998, both candidates lost badly. What infuriated the *Ledger* the most was the unexpected defeat of their golden boy, Stanford University Rhodes Scholar, Cory Booker, in 2002. The *Ledger* was confident that all of the positive press they created for Booker, pages and pages of unwarranted praise, would win him the election with a landslide. It didn't happen. The voters saw through this smoke screen. Booker was all smoke and mirrors.

Now they were really mad at me. *The Star-Ledger* hated me more than ever. They increased their venom against me; calling me a bully, Darth Vader, and machine politics. They called me a racist during the campaign (even though Booker and I were both Black); they called me Boss Tweed, Boss Daley or "Hizzoner for life."

The film Booker produced, "Street Fight," portraying me as a ruthless and vindictive politician, a thug, while portraying him as the good guy, was made out of spite. He was trying to explain why he had lost to me. He felt embarrassed. His ego had been hurt. After all he was supposed to be the golden boy and savior of Newark. What was left for my enemies to do to me? Jury poisoning became the new goal against me.

My lawyers impressed upon Dr. Lamberth that The Star- *Ledger* would stop at nothing to get me out of office, to destroy my family, image and legacy. They were out to get me at any cost. There was a war against Sharpe James at city hall and those out to get me were hurling mortars.

My attorneys emphasized to Dr. Lamberth that "no way" could I get a fair trial in Newark. "We must explore the other two federal district court areas of Trenton and Camden," they said. "We must find out how far across the state The Star- *Ledger*'s negative campaign against Sharpe has reached." Ray Brown, Sr. asked Lamberth, "Can you craft a questionnaire that will bring this evidence out for our evaluation? Can you sample opinions about James statewide?" Tom Ashley reminded everyone, "We have to petition the court right away."

Questions were being fired left and right at Dr. Lambert. Then, there were no more questions, just silence in the room. Dr. Lamberth, who resembled Kurt Douglas, had been listening intensely and taking copious notes on a yellow pad. He paused, looked over the group, smiled and with measured words replied, "That's the business I'm in.

That's what I do best. Please feel free to review some of my other studies." He was all business. The size of his resume and studies could give you a hernia carrying them. We had the right man.

My lawyers excitedly received Lamberth's response, and immediately hired him to conduct his study. The question was simply, in which federal district court could I receive a fair trial? "We do not have much time," Ashley repeated.

The results of Lamberth's highly professional and definitive federal district court study would prove to be an eye-opener on the powerful influence of *The Star-Ledger*. His study would also point out the tactics of the U.S Attorney's office prior to going to trial.

Poisoning The Jury Well

Once I was indicted the government began with innuendoes on the charges and then made frequent leaks to *The Star-Ledger* of every negative inference they could dream of. They were determined to poison the mind of any potential juror. My co-defendant, Ms. Riley, was being portrayed as a strange woman, a welfare and tax cheat.

The Star-Ledger carried a false front page story that I believe was provided by the government, accusing me of watching an adult movie  while I was a guest of Shaquille O'Neal in a Miami Hotel. The story was instantly refuted by the hotel. "We have no equipment to determine what any guest was watching during their stay here," countered the Miami Hotel writing to the government. The government did not care. Their false leak had already served its purpose. They had knowingly lied. The people read it. The damage was done. It was an act of jury poisoning.

The government lied about me and Tamika Riley spending a week together at a luxury resort hotel in California, when they knew she was at home due to the death of her grandfather; another lie was that James was parking his car illegally on court street during the trial, the property owner told them that he had given me permission to do so; another lie was that I had traveled to Memphis, Tennessee with Ms. Riley, when they knew she was already there as a guest of Isaac Hayes. Witnesses testified that Ms. Riley did not fly to Memphis with us.

One false story after another would get into The Star- *Ledger*. A false leak that Riley and I flew to Atlanta, Georgia together. A false leak that $600,000 had been stolen by the defendants; when the evidence proved that without a doubt the government was deliberately lying and leaking stories to the ever cooperative, and in waiting, Star-*Ledger*, in order to paint both defendants as unsavory and unscrupulous individuals. They were jury poisoning statewide.

Finding jurors who had not read all of these daily pre-trial leaks, stories, incidents and false information was going to be difficult. Federal District Court Judge William J. Martini called both sides into his chambers and read the riot act on the wrongfulness of participating in leaks and misinformation. He asked both sides not to issue press releases. "Stop it, stop it," he had shouted. He was tired of all the false information circulating about the trial, "It is a disservice to the court," he said, warning both sides.

I found all of this quite interesting since only the U.S Attorney's Office was holding press conferences and issuing press releases. Judge Martini was preaching to the choir. He was too late. The government's plan to pollute and poison public perception of me, portraying me as a bad guy, immoral, and by implication a criminal person, had already occurred.

Results Of Study

Finally, Dr. Lamberth called a meeting and presented the results of his study. Rather sadly he pointed out that the prosecution strategy of poisoning the well (jury pool) was in evidence. Before sharing the study, he reported that:

> "Defendant must give the government its due: it has succeeded in shaping public opinion to the point where it will be exceptionally difficult, if not impossible, for defendant to obtain a fair trial. The government's drafting of the indictment in a way that appeals to the interests of the public in the salacious, raises serious concerns about the integrity of the investigative and charging process, and raises equally, if not more serious concern, about how to deal with the damage the government's conduct has caused. By charging through innuendo, and the media's pervasive reporting and re-reporting on the charges,

a devastating toll has been taken upon defendant, placing in jeopardy, perhaps irreparably, his due process and fair trial rights.

"The palpably destructive effect that the indictment has had upon public opinion is demonstrable," Dr. Lamberth said.

The renowned statistician with special expertise in jury surveys polled potential jurors in three federal vicinages (Newark, Trenton and Camden) then released the results of his study, which demonstrated how difficult it would be for me to receive a fair trial anywhere in the State of New Jersey:

In Newark, 80 percent of respondents had heard about this case, and of those polled, 50.2% thought Mr. James was guilty. In Trenton, 81.7% of those polled has heard about this case, and of all persons polled, 53.3% believed that Mr. James is guilty. In Camden, 40.5% of those polled have heard about this case, and 38.4% of all persons polled believed Mr. James to be guilty.

Dr, Lamberth noted in his report a representative sampling reflects the degree of prejudice existing against Mr. James. Respondents made comments such as these:

- He's a crook—he is a disgrace as a public servant— I'm very happy that he is no longer mayor.
- I don't believe that he wasn't charged with more offenses.
- I just remember that through the years he has misused his office.
- That he was a fraud—that he stole money from the government.
- It absolutely disgusts me to hear about anyone in his position or any high position doing those kinds of things.

Although Dr. Lamberth found a statistically significant variation in Camden with respect to prejudice than he did in Newark or Trenton, no doubt, if venue were changed to Camden, more people there would become familiar with the case, and it would likely result in the same levels of prejudice already existing in Newark and Trenton. Moreover, trying the case in Camden presented its own set of difficulties given the number of documents involved and the location of witnesses.

Under these circumstances, we did not seek to change venue, but it was palpably clear that extraordinary measures needed to be taken in order to filter out those jurors who already were prejudiced against me based on reading *The Star-Ledger* and comments made by the U.S Attorney's Office before trial.

One of the procedures recommended by Dr. Lamberth was to automatically exclude those jurors who had heard about the case. My defense attorney would request that the Court adopt such a procedure, and that the Court, also, permit defense counsel to question potential jurors.

As other courts have noted, there are times when the customary protections in voir dire (the questioning of prospective jurors or witnesses) are inadequate. For example, it has been recognized that "Adverse pretrial publicity can create such a presumption of prejudice in a community that the juror's claims that they can be impartial should not be believed." Patton v. Yount, 467 U.S.

The Star-Ledger and the prosecution had done their "poison the jury" homework. We were faced with no fair venue in the state of New Jersey. Therefore, it was our decision to address the possibility of not receiving a fair trial by exercising our constitutional right and strongest weapon of voir Dire' by joining with the Court and government in developing a jury questionnaire; and then to question and examine the attitudes of those being selected to sit as jurors.

The only weakness would be the failure of jurors to tell the truth during "Voir Dire." The perceived color of the jury and expected favorable conviction is the measuring rod for far too many indictments against African Americans. Most wins are because of jury selection and more often the color of the jury; not because U.S. Attorneys are so much smarter or their ability to present the evidence or their courtroom savvy.

With all of this information we found ourselves swimming uphill trying to plan for a fair trial. Also, in federal court proceedings where the prosecution goes first and last, was not in our favor.

For some strange, unexplainable reason the Pulitzer Prize winning book by Harper Lee, *To Kill a Mockingbird,* kept resurfacing in my mind. *Can it happen years later in real 1ife?* I asked myself. *Can I really receive a fair trial? Can justice really be blind?*

Jury Selection

The fundamental principal governing the jury system is that a jury must be unbiased, and without predisposition for or against a defendant. The Sixth Amendment provides that an individual accused of a crime, "has the right to a trial by an impartial jury." Thus jury selection is the most important action determining the result of a trial by jury. It can overshadow the trial evidence and at trial testimony of witnesses, which should be the basis for the jurors deciding its verdict.

During the course of a trial, if certain issues arise with one or more jury members, the Court has the authority to meet with a juror, and conduct further questioning on any relevant issue. "The bias of a juror rises to the level of structural defect in the proceedings, and thus requires significant review, and should not be subject to a harmless error review." See William v. Netherlan, 181 F. Supp. 604 (E.D. Va. 2002)

I learned firsthand that it is possible for a jury to find you guilty when the law, evidence and trial testimony is overwhelmingly in favor of the defendant; and innocent when eyewitnesses and evidence link one directly to the commission of a crime. Therefore nothing is more important than the makeup of the jury.

My personal experience convinced me that all too often jurors walk into the courtroom with a preconceived notion of the defendant's guilt. Many jurors possess an attitude of "Why else would the United States of America be bringing this person to trial?" In many cases you are guilty until proven innocent as opposed to being innocent until proven guilty. The opening remarks of the judge, "It is not the duty of the defense to prove anything; it is the responsibility of the government to prove its case beyond a reasonable doubt," helped to relax me. As the defendant, I knew I was not guilty.

Unfortunately in this scenario a defense lawyer might fall victim to the notion that all he or she has to do is refute the government's charges. With a strategy like this, the defendant will more than likely be found guilty. With overreaching prosecutors portraying you as unethical and corrupt, the defense attorneys need to prove your innocence as well as refute the government's case. They must labor before the jury and give evidence of your innocence as well as counter the government's character assassination of you.

Despite the fact that evidence and witnesses clearly refuted the charges in the indictment against me at my trial, the government, by using Rule 404b "Prior acts of bad conduction," put my character on trial. In cases like this, most jurors believe the government. However, armed with the results of Dr. Lambreth's study, we planned to address the various issues in our jury selection.

My defense team was of the opinion that bad publicity from *The Star-Ledger* and my being a veteran politician combined with an indictment purposefully written to portray me as salacious, a debaucher, a crook, all too-powerful and that I was a bad seed had been planted in every federal court district. With this realization our worst fears had come true. Dr. Lamberth had concluded in his study that I could not receive a fair trial anywhere in the state. We had to put our faith in his belief that our only chance for fairness was to select fair and impartial jurors.

The manner in which we decided to seek the truth from prospective jurors was by voir dire examination. The prospective jurors filled out a questionnaire, created by the court, with input from both the government and defense, with the right of each (government and defense) to question the juror on his or her answers to determine if they could be an impartial juror. My defense team convinced me that, "You only need one juror on your side."

The jury pool consisted of more than three hundred registered voters summoned to the federal courthouse. They did not look like a friendly group to me, and most certainly not like a group of my peers. We had to pick twelve jurors and two alternates. The judge allowed both sides five peremptory challenges.

We probed for hidden prejudices of potential jurors. We reviewed individual juror questionnaires and explored their lives; where they lived, where they worked, level of education, preferred reading material and their feelings about politicians. We also questioned previous personal court experience that would suggest bias. "Have you ever served as a juror? Do you or any member of your immediate family know the defendant or work at City Hall?" Whether the juror had any prior involvement in political campaigns for or against the defendant was also asked.

We were desperately seeking due process through a fair and impartial jury of my peers. The only weakness would be if jurors failed to tell the truth during the voir dire process. This important factor, we had no control over. The most we could do to alleviate this was to employ utmost due diligence in exercising all of our rights and peremptory challenges (the right to excuse a juror who might not be impartial).

Once we had selected twelve jurors and two alternates, Judge Martini gave them a formal "jury charge" as the sitting jury in a criminal case. We felt that it was mandatory that the sitting jury be attentive and most importantly, fair and impartial, for they would have the last word and answer the most important question: Do you find Sharpe James guilty or innocent? My trial would soon begin.

Is justice blind?

CHAPTER NINETEEN

At Trial

"At the last came two false witnesses."
-Matthew 26:60

My highly publicized trial commenced on February 27, 2008 before the Honorable Federal District Court Judge, William J. Martini. *The Star-Ledger* had published articles calling Judge Martini the best man for the trial. He had been appointed a federal judge by President George W. Bush. Prior to his appointment he had served as a councilman, Passaic County freeholder, congressman, federal prosecutor and he had practiced law in the city of Newark. Martini was considered a no-nonsense judge, and he was wealthy by inheritance.

Newark was the selected venue for the trial rather than federal district courts in Trenton or Camden. The opening of the sparkling new Dr. Martin Luther King Federal Office Building and Courthouse had given Newark a new skyline and image with its open courtyard, tot playground and large glass windows inviting the rays of the sun.

In front of the federal complex stands a statute. At the top of the building is a large American flag. On days when the flag is blowing westerly you can smell the delicious and exotic Portuguese cuisine emanating from restaurants located in the Ironbound section of the city. If I close my eyes I can envision a table of exotic seafood and a pitcher of Sangria.

Whenever I had to visit the courthouse I found it to be an inviting structure. I had never before feared going inside. I grew up believing in the justice of "America, the beautiful, the home of the brave, the land of the free, and a country based on the fundamental rights of the individual. After all, this is the land of Lincoln. "All men are created equal; justice for all; and of course, a man is innocent until proven guilty by a jury of his peers." I had been taught to respect our criminal justice system. That was my mindset going into court.

The government classes I had taught at Essex County College often stressed Patrick Henry's declaration "Give me liberty or give me death." Hadn't we established this fundamental belief with the Revolutionary War? American history had been so reassuring to me, convincing me that I could get a fair trial. My belief in the American justice system made me fearless. No racism here! What do I have to fear? Once the truth was brought out, my name would be cleared.

I thought of Newark's plan with former Secretary of Commerce, Ron Brown, to purchase adjacent land to the Peter W. Rodino Federal Building, U. S. Post Office and the new Dr. Martin Luther King Federal Office Building and Courthouse. The plan was to add a hotel and commercial shopping mall to create a connecting federal square. We had put together a strong local financial team to achieve this goal. Everyone was excited and waiting for groundbreaking.

Ron Brown was an exceptional man; he had the looks, knowledge, business experience, personality and articulation to have been elected President. Brown was given no chance to be elected the first African American Chairman of the Democratic Party, yet, he won in a landslide. His intelligence, pressing the flesh and winning smile was contagious. I always felt that matinee handsome Ron Brown with his coiffure moustache, could sell snow balls to the Eskimos.

When we last met in his office in Washington, D.C., to explore the Newark federal square project, Brown had said, "We will not fail because I'm sitting behind the desk that once belonged to the legendary FBI Director, J. Edgar Hoover. All of the information needed is here at my desk," he had laughed. Ron's savvy, style and dignity were one in a million. If Ron had lived, it is conceivable to me that Barack Obama would have been the second, not the first African American President. What a tragic loss of talent.

I was now scheduled to have my day in court in the very building that I had fought so hard to bring to Newark. I suppose many of the homeowners who were forced to relocate were laughing. I could almost hear their voices, "Hey Sharpe, do you still want a new federal courthouse in Newark?" Of course, jubilant boisterous group laughter would follow.

On the morning of the trial I woke up as usual at 5:00 a.m. I brushed my teeth, shaved and showered and went into the kitchen for a cup of hot tea with lemon, honey and two slices of whole wheat toast topped with more honey. This was an important day in my life. My face had appeared on every major television network. "Former Mayor Sharpe James due in federal court tomorrow morning to face charges," the anchors had blasted over the television airwaves.

I walked to my living room window to see if the reporters were still camped outside. Surprisingly, there were still occupied vehicles awaiting my appearance. I could see two cars with their interior lights on. One driver was raising a cup to his mouth and reading a newspaper. I thought to myself; *These guys are like buzzards. They circle the wounded waiting to attack. They never go away.*

I checked the clock again, the plan was to meet my lawyers, Thomas Ashley and Alan Zegas, in the parking lot behind the federal courthouse at 8:00 a.m. We were due in court at 9:00 a.m. Tom had reminded us not to be late. We had to go over a few things prior to court. *It is time to get moving,* I thought.

I wore my dark blue pinstriped business suit, a white shirt with a standard collar, no cuff links, and President Bush's look-alike toned down blue tie, nothing fancy today. I brushed my crew cut hair, anchored my attire with ribbed, black cotton socks fitting neatly into my spit shined black Johnston-Murphy dress shoes. Looking in the dining room mirror, I looked the same as the year I was voted "Best Dressed Political Official" by the Fashion Institute. I had no intention of appearing in court irresponsibly dressed. My life and legacy were on the line.

Driving myself to the courthouse, I noticed in my rearview mirror that the cars that had been parked in front of my house were in hot pursuit. They knew where I was going and would be waiting. Like clockwork, Tom, Allan and I arrived at the same time, parking in the lot behind the federal courthouse. We would have to walk about two hundred feet before reaching the front corner of the building leading to the main entrance. We would then have to walk another one hundred feet to the front door. Although still out of sight, we could hear the buzz, talk and excitement of reporters and TV camera men perched in front, waiting my arrival.

Each reporter wanted to be the first to interview me; the first photographer to sell a picture of me arriving in court to placard all over television again would be a hero. They wanted a scoop. They wanted something new. They wanted "Breaking News!"

The reporters and cameramen were huddled around a very large concrete sculpture of the head of Lady Liberty. I, again, chuckled to myself. I hope that Lady Liberty will not peep from behind her blindfold and see that Sharpe James is a Black man. *No cheating,* I thought. *Only time will tell.*

Just as we reached the corner of the courthouse and made the turn toward the main entrance, becoming visible, chaos broke loose. Reporters and cameramen came wildly rushing toward us, pens, pencils, mikes and cameras in hand; some were falling and others tripping over the concrete guardrail separating the walkway from the grass. Others, now walking backwards to keep my face in front of the camera, were bumping into concrete walls, railings and each other. It was a very hectic and chaotic scene.

The reporters fired the same old questions at me; "Mayor James, how do you feel?" "Mayor James, are you guilty?" "Is Tamika Riley your girlfriend?" "Did you sell her land at steeply discounted prices?" "Mayor James, do you think race is a factor in this case?" "Sharpe, what do you think of the government asking for a twenty year sentence?" "Mayor James, do you think that you can get a fair trial?" "Senator/Mayor, what do you want us to call you?" "Do you think Mayor Booker had anything to do with these charges?" "Mayor James, what is your defense?" "Please say something," they badgered me.

With the vigorous help of court security personnel, we kept moving, although I was being pushed, shoved, grabbed by the arm and intimidated. I gave the same two answers repeatedly as we approached the entrance; "It's a beautiful, God-given day!" and, "I have no other comment."

"Mayor James, don't you want to say something to your constituents?"

"Thank you, no comment," I said.

"Are you guilty?"

"Will your wife be in court?"

They continued to ask questions. I continued walking. Ignoring the reporters and using all of our muscle and energy we held hands in order not to get separated. Finally, we bravely pushed through the courthouse doors. Battle-weary, we stood facing the metal detectors. I was out of breath. Tom Ashley, my attorney, sweating with his "GQ" clothes now soiled said, "I hope this is not the way we have to enter every day." Once through the metal detectors we took the elevator to the fourth floor for the courtroom of Federal District Court Judge, The Honorable William J. Martini.

The last time I had been in a federal court, was many years earlier when I was a character witness for the legendary Junior Gardner. At the time he was the most powerful African American Longshoremen leader in America. The courthouse was located near Wall Street in the financial district of Manhattan. It is a mammoth facility. It was so huge that I thought I was in a church cathedral. The seating capacity was for over 500 persons. A sound system was used to communicate.

In the Newark courtroom, I sat in a relatively small, comfortable; semi-teak paneled studio-like setting. It was like sitting in a parlor on a cruise ship. The room looked to hold between 100-150 people; the jury box was to the left. We sat squarely facing the Judge off to the right of the center aisle and the government sat facing the Judge to the left of the center aisle. My co-defendant, Tamika Riley, and her lawyer sat to my right with their table at a perpendicular angle facing the jury.

Once everyone was seated; the court clerk appeared and asked everyone to please rise for the Honorable William J. Martini. Judge Martini entered the courtroom. He was small in stature, and had a youthful, smiling face, gorgeous crop of wavy brown hair, and bird-like piercing stern eyes. He immediately addressed the members of the jury, thanking them for their willingness to serve. "It is a duty and a noble cause," he had said. He advised them that he planned to maintain a strict schedule and stressed the importance of being on time. He asked each juror, individually, if they could be objective, fair and impartial. He cautioned the jurors to keep in mind:

"Being a long tenured politician is not the issue and one should harbor no good or bad feeling: just examine the testimony and evidence presented in court and from the witness stand; infidelity in itself is not a crime unless it furthers a crime; conspiracy charges had to be linked to acts of wrongdoing; an illegal agreement between partners and proven beyond a reasonable doubt; the defense has no duty to testify or to defend themselves; and if they choose to exercise this right, you should not hold that against them. Again it is the evidence and testimony presented in this court that you weigh. The burden of proof never shifts to the defense. Can you listen to all the testimony and evidence before rendering a decision? Can you be fair?"

Judge Martini was calling this trial the "Public interest" trial of the year. In my mind it was the paparazzi interest trial of the year. I thought all trials were of public interest. I felt that he was putting added pressure on the minds of the jurors; a demand that the jurors do something drastic. As I looked around, I saw that the blood thirsty media would not go away. The jury had been seated and was ready to hear the evidence.

The Star-Ledger, a newspaper that had enthusiastically endorsed all of my mayoral opponents; the paper that had for twenty years attacked, vilified, mocked and printed one negative article after another about me was in the house. Just prior to the start of the trial, and after reviewing the government's indictment on the internet, feature column writer and my political nemesis, Tom Moran, had written that "James will be acquitted; James will walk," he had said.

Moran had stressed the fact that there was "No political or financial benefit for James." Later Robert Braun of The Star-Ledger would write, "Where is the crime? He was merely doing his job as chief executive officer... What mayors do not recommend developers," he had asked?

Reading these comments, my lawyers warned me of over-confidence. Tom Ashley spoke of one flawed common thread at every federal trial is an assumption by the jury that the prosecution (The United States of America) and FBI agents are always telling the gospel truth. Another historical belief is that the defendant and his witnesses are always lying. "Good guys and bad guys, notwithstanding the amount of evidence and testimony in favor of the defendant."

A tragic failure of many juries is not to recognize that many prosecutors have personal and political agendas; an opportunity to build their resume when seeking higher office or entry into politics; a failure to believe that all politicians are not corrupt. Since the O.J. Simpson trial, prosecution has become a prime time major sporting event, a trophy event. To me this mirrors the words of former President Ronald Reagan; when he was asked what his cold war strategy was, he replied, "We win, they lose."

While this tough talk might be good philosophy in defense of our country, it should not be the acceptable philosophy of an over-reaching and politically motivated U.S. Attorney. My case was a prime example of a political prosecution by a U.S. Attorney running for public office. It became a grand opportunity to appeal to his conservative constituents by bringing down a highly successful, highly visible and prominent African American leader. It had become a proven and success-ful GOP strategy when running for public office.

From the very beginning of the trial the government recognized that they had no real evidence of any criminal wrongdoing. They were limited in their ability to present a case on the legal argument that I had broken some law, stolen some money or bribed someone. The wiring of Basil Franklin in 2004 and later Tamika Riley, had produced no evidence of wrongdoing.

As a first order of business, Judge Martini had asked the prosecution if they had any wire-tapping or surveillance evidence to submit in court. Lead prosecutor, Ms. Germano, had stood and replied, "None your honor." The case should have ended right there. They didn't even have a case, this was a publicity stunt.

The tapes that the prosecution obtained were favorable to me. They were hiding (in violation of the Brady Law dictate to turn over favorable evidence to the defense) my conversations when I had informed Basil of the proper and legal procedure for acquiring land. This occurred when he attempted to compromise my honesty by seeking municipal land after he had resigned. At the time, I did not know that he was working for the government; nor did I know that he was wired. I simply spoke the truth.

The government also lacked confidence in the witnesses they had recruited and rehearsed their testimony with. With these weaknesses, and the absence of any evidence of wrongdoing on my part, they had to come up with a scheme to win a conviction. The U.S. Attorney had assigned a female lead prosecutor to appeal to the members of the jury. He had selected a blond tough-talking, medium height Phyllis Dillard look alike, Assistant U.S. Attorney Ms. Judith Germano. She had less knowledge, qualifications or experience than Assistant U.S. Attorney Phillip Kwon, who would assist her at trial. Apparently the U.S. Attorney's office felt that the never smiling, unfriendly, and hostile Germano, could best wage a war of character assassination against me.

The prosecution team was aided by Perry Primavera, an attorney from the State Attorney's office. Then Governor Jon Corzine had a vested interest in my demise as well; he, too, thought that I might run for governor of New Jersey.

My defense team was led by a fashionable, pin-striped suited, Rutgers University graduate and former basketball star; a person mentored by the late renowned and legendary criminal lawyer, Raymond A. Brown, and now a leading criminal lawyer himself, Tom Ashley. He was being assisted by case law and computer whiz associate, Alan Zegas of Chatham, New Jersey. They were a knowledgeable and formidable team in the courtroom and could not be intimidated.

Alan arrived in court early everyday to set up his computer and printer. He took notes faster and more accurate than the court stenographer who would often correlate notes with him at the end of the day. I faced a five count "political" indictment:

"Mail Fraud; Fraud involving local government; Receiving Federal funds; and conspiracy to defraud the public of honest services."

In laymen's terms, the government was saying: Ms. Riley mailed her contract creating a charge of three counts of mail fraud; some time during my tenure as Mayor the City of Newark received HUD federal dollars, so that was interpreted as one count of fraud involving local government although no HUD dollars were involved in the South Ward Redevelopment Plan (SWRP); and lastly, because I was an elected official,

I had deprived my constituents of my honest services, thus the fifth count. Here we had the most bogus charges a politically motivated U.S. Attorney running for Governor could dream of. None of the charges would be sustained by the law, evidence, or testimony of witnesses in court. U.S. Attorney Christie was trying to pad his resume.

Judge Martini professorially explained each count to the jury. Unfortunately, he failed to explain the form of government under which the City of Newark is governed; The Faulkner Act, Mayor Council Plan C. How could the jury objectively evaluate my conduct as it related to my authority and duties in office without this vital information? Each juror would have a mindset of his/her own city of residence and its form of government. Under some forms of government the mayor is a "boss" figure, someone who controls everything, this is not so in Newark.

Interestingly enough, all of the sales were approved by then Central Ward Councilman, Cory Booker, Newark's current mayor. Incumbent council members Luis Quintana and Augusto Amador also approved those sales. Along with the rest of the city council members, they decided upon the price of the land. Every single sale of property to TRI was made pursuant to NJ.S.A. 40A: 12-13 (c). By law, the mayor does not have the authority to do what the government alleges I had authorized and promoted; an improper sale of land to an unqualified individual. The statutory framework expressly authorizes private sales of real property to a private developer, as set forth by resolution and ordinance, "When acting in accordance with the Local Redevelopment and Housing Law."

In legal action, Council of the City of Newark v. James, 232 N.J. Super. 449 (App. Div. 1989), the Appellate Division held that pursuant N.J.S.A 40A: 12-13(c), the City Council has the express authority to determine which parcels of land will be sold and the conditions for such sale, including price. Because the express language of N.J.S.A. 40A:12-13 authorized the sale of property by resolution or ordinance, it provided the City Council with the sole authority to determine the pieces of property to be sold and the conditions for their sale. Id. at 453. Inasmuch as only the Council can act by resolution and ordinance.

It follows that the statute (NJSA 40A: 12-13) assigns to the Council, not the Mayor, the function of selling municipally-owned real property." Id. at 454. The Court rejected the Mayor's claim that the Council's role is limited to approving sales. Id. at 454. The Court did not deem it necessary to determine whether the functions in dispute were legislative or administrative because the statute's language clearly assigned the functions at issue to the Council. Id. at 455.

I believe this information should have been explained to the jury by Judge Martini. All of this vital information was ignored by Judge Martini. It was vital because there would be no testimony that I had interfered, lobbied, corresponded or had any quid pro quo arrangements with the DEHD, city council, or Tamika Riley.

The jury heard only the government calling me "All too powerful," inferring that I controlled everything. This could create a false belief that Newark had only one elected official; only one ego to satisfy. I wondered if the Judge or any member of the jury had ever heard of Councilman-at-large Donald Tucker, Dr. Ralph T. Grant, Jr., Bessie Walker, or Earl Harris; they should have abandoned this false belief after seeing and hearing the testimony, demeanor, knowledge and savvy of councilpersons Gayle Chaneyfield Jenkins and Dr. Mamie Bridgeforth. Gayle personally shut-down FBI hecklers from the witness stand, twice. This act should have convinced anyone with common sense that there was more than one political ego to satisfy in Newark. Now the trial started.

As predicted, the government opened its case by telling the jury that Mayor James was all too powerful. "He's too powerful and we want him removed from office." Isn't it sinister to believe that a Black man should not dream the American dream? I sat in court wondering; *When did it become a crime in America to stay in school, get an education, serve your country then return home to get a job, marry, raise a family, serve your community and invest wisely?* 'Be all that you can be.' Isn't this the American dream?

During the trial Judge Martini had to remove one juror for misconduct. First, the juror was seen on the elevator greeting and embracing a government witness, which drew a warning from the judge. Later, it was reported that the same juror was going around the city saying, "What goes around comes around." A native of Newark, he was referring to the fact that the city of Newark had issued a blight declaration to seize his father's property for a public good, and he was still angry. He blamed me as the mayor, although mayors could not legally blight an area or create a redevelopment project. The city council had the only statutory authority to ask the central planning board to study a blight declaration request.

After a conference with the juror and confirming that he had in fact made the comment, Judge Martini excused him from the jury and an alternate was selected. No other member of the jury was questioned to see if the comments had polluted other jurors. The defense took the position that Judge Martini should have polled other members of the jury, especially those members who had lunched with the dismissed member every day, to see if he had contaminated them with his biased personal opinions. The judge's failure to do so raised the question of whether the jury could be fair and impartial in its decision-making.

In court, I received a rude awakening to the real world in which we live. The whole trial was a rush to conviction and making one false assumption after another. I sat in the courtroom under the microscope, on pins and needles waiting for the government to put forth its legal argument of my alleged criminal acts. *If I unknowingly broke the law, I should be sent to prison,* I thought to myself. *Where did I possibly go wrong?* I kept asking myself. *Did I make a mistake?*

When lead prosecutor, Germano, began ranting and raving, calling me a bad person; "He's no good, vindictive, too powerful, controls people and was stealing money from the poor people of Newark," I touched Tom Ashley's elbow and whispered into his ear, "Who is she talking about? Who is she describing?"

Without even looking at me, staring straight ahead and becoming a ventriloquist Tom said, "You, they are talking about you. Calm down and get used to it. This is only the foreplay. Welcome to federal court," he had said.

The prosecution was leading a personal attack against me. It was an attempted character assassination at its best. It was an act of jealousy and racism at its best. *This isn't a trial, this is a public lynching,* I thought. I sat there in total disbelief watching one government witness after another testify, and not one of them accused me of any wrongdoing. They had been told to create a relationship between Ms. Riley and myself, and that's what they tried to do. *Why am I in court,* I thought to myself.

Later, Tom whispered to me again, "In federal court, unlike the state courts, federal prosecutors get two bites of the apple," he explained. "They get to go first and last; brace yourself," he warned.

The trial was a painful, uncomfortable and humiliating experience for me. Sitting in the courtroom for hours and hours, listening to untruths about me being spewed by the government was very difficult. The real hurt was that these men and women who had taken an oath of office to serve honestly and honorably were behaving like striking rattlesnakes, and there was nothing that I could do about it. In reality they were out to win at all cost, even if they had to lie.

The United States of America versus Sharpe James had been reduced to: May the best team win. *May the best liar win,* I had thought. The trial was never about fair play and justice. Hey, it was not a level playing field. *It's not fair.* The government was using 150 attorneys against my two; they citied 200 different law cases as legal references (knowing and praying that the defense team would not have the time to research them); worse of all, they still felt a need to make personal attacks against me and to outright lie ("James spent a week with Riley at a luxury hotel in California"). The government ignored the evidence that she did not attend the fundraiser in California for the United Negro College Fund. They knew that she was home grieving the loss of her grandfather who had died.

"James flew to Memphis with Ms. Riley" the prosecutor had stated in court, knowing that she was already in Memphis as a guest of Isaac Hayes. The government knowingly lied and would continue to do so throughout the trial. The Truth had no place in the minds of the Christie prosecuting team. *This is not a trial. This is nothing but character assassination. This is Jury poisoning at its best.*

At one point the lead prosecutor, Ms. Germano, launched a vile and biased personal attack against my success, personal income and lifestyle. She was obviously jealous and wanted members of the jury to be jealous as well. "This man has too much on his plate," she had said before screaming to the jury:

> *He's been elected for five terms; he makes more money than the governor; he's a dual office holder (mayor and*

*state senator); he controls the department of economic and
housing development (DEHD); he owns a summer home,
he has a swimming pool, a yacht and a Rolls Royce, he
travels to exotic places; he's all too powerful.*

She was denigrating a Black man's success and lifestyle. For the
first time in my life, I had a different view of America and our criminal
justice system. I wondered if this was the country I had risked my life
serving in the United States Army in Germany. Could this be America,
the beautiful that preaches opportunity for all? I was not on trial for
stealing any money. After holding two jobs for over thirty years I did
not feel a need to apologize for owning my home, car or a boat of my
choice. I had a right to purchase whatever I wanted and could afford I
was personally offended by her racially biased attack.

Judge Martini had to interrupt the lead prosecutor at least four
times during her tirade to remind the jury that what she was accusing
me of was not illegal. "I want you to know that it is not illegal in New
Jersey to be a dual office holder," he had said. "It should be noted that
the mere fact of being mayor, you control and supervise various departments, nothing illegal about it," he had said. "No, no the officer cannot
describe his car in the garage," he said. "The officer has testified that he
didn't open the garage door, Ms. Germano, please, please move on,"
Judge Martini had said.

Ms. Germano wanted the officer to confirm to the members
of the jury that I owned a Rolls Royce. My antique model was being
exploited as though I had committed a crime. All of this had nothing
to do with the charges against me. What I believed she wanted to plant
in the minds of the jurors was that, "This Nigger has too much!"

In my opinion no matter how many times Judge Martini corrected
her, the damage from her unwarranted character assassination had already
occurred. As stated in the "Bruton Ruling," *you can't un-ring the bell.* I had
been portrayed before the jury as an all-powerful monster who should be
imprisoned for life for achieving the American dream.

As Ms. Germano's monotonous voice reverberated through-
out the courtroom walls, I thought to myself, *apparently, she has never
seen an America where individuals from humble beginnings or who were*

born into poverty, pulled themselves up by their boot straps and turned their lives around. She doesn't know of any courageous individuals who achieved the American dream against the odds.

I figured that Ms. Germano never knew that Walter Cronkite, the most celebrated CBS news anchor, was a high school dropout or that Howard Hughes, our eccentric inventor, motion picture producer, aviator and billionaire was orphaned at age 17 and quit school. No she couldn't have known. She wanted to win at all cost. I was nothing more than a guinea pig to her. She put forth no legal arguments. *Who is she to determine that I have too much on my plate,* I thought. *I'm just an Old Black Joe experiment to see if she can convince the jury to convict an innocent man.*

Witnesses

From our knowledge of the Bible we know that witnesses lied against Lord Jesus; "At the last came two false witnesses." At my trial there were eight false witnesses who took the stand, placed their left hand on the Bible, raised their right hand, swore to tell the whole truth and nothing but the truth so help me God, and then obnoxiously proceeded not to tell the truth under oath (Rosemarie Posella, Christine Malanga, Robert Moore, Adelino Benevente, Derrick Foster, Prentiss Thompson, Augusto Amador and Vivian Casiano). They had no shame knowing that they had each cut a deal with the prosecution to save themselves or family members.

I sat at the mahogany defense table gripping the legs of my chair to keep from bolting from my seat as untruths spewed from their vicious forked tongues. While each witness could not speak of any criminal behavior or wrongdoing on my part, they tried to portray me in an unfavorable light to support the government's case. They made every attempt to shame me before the jurors. They were lapdogs for the government.

Each of the eight witnesses had a personal guilt to hide. Each was involved in a quid pro quo arrangement. It was Barnum and Bailey Ringling Brothers circus time. The worst was my former secretary, Rosemarie Posella, wearing a Diana Ross style wig and platform shoes to grow her five foot frame. She had rehearsed her testimony so much that she sat sideways and looked directly at members of the jury, swaying her head like a King Cobra Snake, peeping over her reading glasses, hanging from a string around her neck for dramatization.

Rosemarie repeated the story she had rehearsed the night before in a meeting with the government on the third floor of the federal post office, across from the federal courthouse. Accidentally and unexpectedly, my wife, Mary, had met a visibly nervous and shaking Rosemarie and her husband as they were entering the post office for a rehearsal. The next day in court she gave a 100% flip flop from her previous FBI and grand jury testimonies. Sitting on the edge of her seat and shaking her head like a rattlesnake she testified:

"Now I have a new opinion. Now I think they were boyfriend and girlfriend, although I have no proof. My memory has improved with age. I am changing my testimony."

Ms. Posella offered no proof to support her changing opinion that my relationship with Tamika Riley had gone from being a business and friendly relationship, to a romantic one. Having previously testified, strongly, that she had no knowledge of a romantic relationship, "How should I know what relationship they might have had?" She now thought that something could have been going on. Obviously feeling guilty, she left the witness stand and immediately held a press conference in the courthouse hallway with Robert Braun, of *The Star-Ledger*. Now she offered her third story of the day saying, "Sharpe James was good to me; I like him a lot." I wanted to ring her neck for deceitfully lying.

After I read the newspaper article the next day I told my wife that Rosemarie's conscious had to be bothering her. No one begged or received more from my administration than Rosemarie. I had given her troubled son three jobs; and I gave her unemployed daughter a job as well. I gave her husband, a Newark police officer, a car to commute to their home in Point Pleasant, New Jersey.

Still, Rosemarie was not satisfied. She wanted more. We increased her secretary's salary to more than $75,000 and she was chauffeured to Penn Station in order to catch the early train home, when her husband was on duty, thereby beating the rush hour traffic. She still was not satisfied. She demanded that I give her another raise before I retired in order to boost her pension. She wanted a going away present and a party. I said, "No!" I was tired of Rosemarie playing everyone for a fool.

She was angry that I refused her request. She complained to my executive secretary, Deborah Moore. The only truth she spoke on the witness stand was that: "He wouldn't raise my salary to help my pension; and he did not give us a party or a gift when he retired," she had testified. Rosemarie suffers from acute greed. Rosemarie had no shame, she perjured herself and the court did nothing.

Unknown to Rosemarie, the government had to share the written statement of her planned testimony with the defense where she had stated that "James and Riley had a business and friendly relationship." This was the testimony that she accidentally left with the prosecution. She had also previously testified that: "How should I know if he has a girlfriend? I leave work every day at 4 p.m. in order to catch the early train home."

Another false witness, Christine Malanga, of Gateway Travel Agency, could not remember that she had personally arranged, invited, paid for and assigned rooms to everyone on a Gateway Travel sponsored Sharpe James Civic Association inspection trip to the Dominican Republic. She had made an effort to get us to book a civic association trip using her travel agency. As a witness, she could not remember the details even with her e-mails, air and hotel reservations in front of her.

Malanga's ruse, probably at the government's request, was to establish a relationship between Tamika Riley and me. She was trying to falsely convey to the jury that I had invited Ms. Riley on the trip, and possibly shared a room with her. The travel records indicated that she had invited everyone, made the reservations, paid for and assigned rooms to everyone. Malanga had personally invited Ms. Riley and her close personal friend, Fredrica Bey, on the trip as a peace offering because Riley had accused Malanga's agency of getting all of City Hall's business.

On cross examination by my defense attorney, Christine had to admit that she had arranged and traveled with me on more than a dozen civic association trips. Ashley then asked Malanga if Riley had ever gone on any of those trips.

"Again, I ask you, was Ms. Riley on any of those trips?" Ashley barked. "Was Riley there?"

"No, no, none," She reluctantly answered.

She could not lie this time. Chris was cooperating with the government because it was alleged that she had overbilled the city on numerous trips. She was protecting her travel agency and her pocketbook.

Following Malanga to the witness stand was a nervous, sweating like a bull police officer, Robert Moore. I was informed that Moore had run from the Newark police headquarters on Franklin Street to the courthouse to avoid reporters. I was not surprised when I learned of this. He had run much faster the day a Newark Housing Authority employee caught his fiancée' with Moore in a police vehicle on Van Velsor Place. Hundred- meter Olympic Champion, Usain Bolt, could not have caught Moore on that day. Brother Moore was scared out of his wits and running for his life.

Once on the witness stand, Moore, who had been the security officer on a trip to the Dominican Republic, tried to outperform Malanga in loss of memory. As a security officer, charged with protecting the Mayor and the lives of others, he could not remember anything. When my attorney, Ashley, asked him who his roommate had been in Santo Domingo, he replied, "I forgot." When asked where he had slept? Moore replied, "I can't remember."

Moore was incredulous; a fifteen year veteran of the Newark police force not remembering where he was and where he had slept while on security duty. I felt like jumping out of my chair and punching him in his mouth. I restrained myself, though. At a minimum Moore should have lost pay for impersonating a police officer.

The government had, of course, rehearsed Moore's testimony, too. Like Christine Malanga, Moore's job was not to tell the truth regarding the whereabouts of James and Riley on a trip sponsored by Malanga's agency. The government did not want the jury to know that Riley and I had arrived and left the Dominican Republic at different times and had separate quarters during the short span of only two days. Their vagueness would leave it to the imagination of the jury. The government believed that the jury would take the hint that we shared a room together, after all who will believe a politician?

After lying on the witness stand, a sweaty, twitching and nervous Officer Moore raced back to the shelter of the Franklin Street police headquarters. He was also hiding from having been investigated for hosting illegal fundraisers in my name, and never turning in the monies he had collected. Moore was scared to face reporters, the FBI and especially the groom to be of the young lady he had in his police vehicle.

Since the government could not find any evidence of fraud, conspiracy or corruption to use in my trial and since Judge Martini had told them, "Do not use those words in my courtroom; you did not prove any," he had said, the government fell back on creating the illusion of a romance or the suggestion of infidelity in itself to present before the jury as a federal crime. With this philosophy in mind our prisons could have been filled with the likes of President Lyndon Johnson, Bill Clinton, Newt Gingrich, Jesse Jackson, former mayor Anthony Guiliani, Governors James McGreevey, Jon Corzine, Eliot Spitzer, David Patterson, and the list goes on.

With nothing else to hang their hat on, the prosecution continued the alleged "close personal relationship" and a "breach of honest services" angle. The government recruited two more police officers, Adelino Benevente and Derrick Foster, to testify for them. I believe that Benevente had been told by the Booker administration that his son, who had recently dropped out of Essex County College, would be kicked out of the Newark Police Academy if he did not cooperate.

Officer Derrick Foster had been without a gun for over two years for assaulting a female witness who had implicated him in the theft of funds from our municipal courts. I believe that Foster was promised the return of his gun and a favorable assignment if he would cooperate with the government.

Both officers were salivating and eager to testify. Both were prostituting themselves. Foster apparently forgot that he had been fired from my security detail. Without thinking, Foster created a fictitious trip to a boxing match in Atlantic City that involved stopping for half an hour at my summer home, on the way back to Newark.

Foster alleged that I gave him, Riley and another police officer (he could not remember who) a tour of my summer home. Again, the purpose of this testimony was to show a possible relationship between me and Riley. Foster testified that Riley and I left the group alone and was somewhere in the house for about half an hour. Yet, he testified, unlike Rosemarie, that "I did not think that they were boyfriend and girlfriend."

So which liar do you believe, Rosemarie or Derrick? On cross examination from my attorney, Foster, wearing a silly grin on his face, with his head bobbing and weaving, looked and sounded foolish. He knew that he was lying and was not a member of my security detail during the time span the government wanted him to show a relationship. When my attorney asked him, again, what year, date and time was this boxing match? Foster replied, "I don't recall."

"What hotel hosted the fight in Atlantic City?" Ashley asked.

"I don't remember," Foster testified.

"Who was fighting?" Ashley asked.

"I forgot," Foster testified.

"What was the name of the other police officer with you?" Ashley asked.

"I don't remember," Foster testified.

The government wanted Foster to create a relationship between Riley and myself for the years 2001-2002 during the time she was receiving properties. The problem for Foster was that he had been fired from my security detail in 1999. His only choice was to lie, play dumb or tell the truth. He chose to lie and play dumb.

I sat in court in total disbelief, thinking, *How desperate is the government to recruit witnesses who lie and have no idea of what they are talking about?* I wondered if this is what justice is all about. Derrick Foster couldn't even keep a straight face on the witness stand; it was like a joke to him. He would do and say anything to get his police gun back.

The next witness up was cry baby police officer, Adelino Benevente. I guess he was remembering how he had begged me to take him off patrol duty (he had been demoted) at Broad and Raymond Boulevard. Perhaps, he was thinking of the $2,500 check I wrote, after his check had bounced like a basketball, to pay the balance for his mother and children to take a cruise. He was embarrassed at the thought of cancelling their reservation and asked if I could lend him the money.

Adelino Benevente could have been crying for the damage his children had done to my summer home when his family was invited to a Fourth of July celebration, and they knew no better than to pelt my house with the white rocks covering my waterfront lot. I thought of throwing them in the water at the time for causing $1,000 in damage.

Then, I thought better and decided to send them home early. Observing Benevente on the witness stand, I thought that at least for the moment he was sober. That was a victory in itself.

Adelino tearfully testified that on one or two occasions he had dropped me off at Riley's home and waited in the car. What he failed to say is that Riley was hosting a reception for one of her public relations clients, who at times included Eric Williams of the Boston Celtics, a native of Newark; Little Bow Wow, JaRule, JaHeim or the late Isaac Hayes who had headed a Christmas holiday event at Newark Symphony Hall.

Tamika Riley had surprised me by introducing Little Bow Wow to Newark at the four corners (Broad and Market Streets) before a record crowd of more than 5000 fans. We had predicted a crowd of only 500-1,000. Following the event Little Bow Wow and I appeared on television together promoting the City of Newark. Tamika even persuaded Eric Williams to distribute 2,000 turkeys to the poor and JaRule paid for more than 200 senior citizens to attend our annual picnic at Ms. Riley's request.

Adelino also testified that he had purchased an air conditioner on sale for Riley on his off duty day at the request of Deborah Moore, my executive secretary. He claimed to have installed it in Ms. Riley's bedroom window. Ms. Moore allegedly, told him to use my personal credit card as Ms. Riley had left the money in our office. Adelino had spent no more than ten minutes in Riley's apartment and probably under the influence of booze he became an instant interior decorator.

I believed that it was totally out of character and disingenuous for Benevente to testify that Riley's apartment did not impress him. He did not like the covering on the floor or the furniture in the kitchen and living room. He was disappointed by the way her apartment looked. *What right does he have to evaluate the apartment of Ms. Riley which is in better condition than his home and looks ten times better?* Is what I thought.

I believe Adelino Benevente was following the government's orders to denigrate Riley, to make her appear to be a strange woman, a shady character, a lady of possible ill repute, even a harlot. They wanted to portray Riley as a person in need of money or unable to provide for herself; a person in need of Sharpe James was Adelino's orchestrated brain washing to the jurors. Adelino wanted the jury to believe that I was Riley's Sugar Daddy, so he gave them what they wanted. His whole testimony was despicable.

Again, I wanted to jump up and punch this alcohol breath, foul mouthed police officer in the nose. It's one thing to want to help your son graduate from the police academy. It's another thing to believe that you have the right to judge, falsely criticize and put down others, behaving like a deity. I wanted to cross examine Adelino and ask him only one question: "When did you clean up your act of booze, tobacco and womanizing to become a judge of others?"

In summary, Rosemarie Posella, Christine Malanga, Officers Robert Moore, Derrick Foster and Adelino Benevente all suffered from not telling the truth. They suffered from acute amnesia trying to aid the prosecution by creating a false relationship between Tamika Riley and me. Each had something to personally gain from their dishonest and flawed testimony.

The government, recognizing the fact that there was still no testimony of any criminal wrongdoing against me, recruited one of their favorite informers, a member of my Rainbow Yacht Club boating group, Prentiss Thompson, to testify. Thomas was a former director of security for the Newark Board of Education and a former assistant Essex County prosecutor.

When I first hired Prentiss, many years earlier while I was director of a summer youth program at Montclair University, his name was Prentiss Newton. When I had asked him about this discrepancy, he got up and left my house without speaking. It's still a mystery to me; is he Prentiss Thompson or Prentiss Newton? He has accepted checks in both names.

Prentiss bragged to me about once climbing a tree and video-taping former Essex County Prosecutor, Patricia Hurt. He was angry at her because she would not promote him. He wanted her to get fired or to resign her position which became a reality due to a controversial driving incident and her questionable conduct in office. When Prentiss was not promoted under former Essex County Prosecutor, then State Attorney General, now Superior Court Judge, Paula Dow, he quit and lobbied for his son to be promoted.

Prentiss was fired as Director of Security for the Newark Board of Education by Newark School Superintendent, Eugene Campbell. He was accused of spying on his supervisors. Eugene had said, "Prentiss spent more time spying on them than stopping the theft of Board of Education equipment and supplies." As a member of our yacht club, I had assisted him in getting an interview for a similar security position at the University of Medicine and Dentistry of New Jersey, and at Newark Rutgers University; both institutions turned him down.

Prentiss has always been highly controversial. He has a serious ego problem. He is also very stingy. Whenever we had meals together at the marina, just before the check would arrive, he would get up and go to the bathroom; leave and then board his vessel, never to return to share in the cost of the meal. He has mastered this routine. Now, Prentiss "Whatever" was a government informant. Tom Ashley advised me that Prentiss had served in this role before. At my trial he was taking the stand while holding two full time jobs as Director of Security for the Newark based New Community Corporation (NCC) and a full time administrator for the city of Irvington, New Jersey, under Mayor Wayne Smith.

Interestingly enough, while the prosecution was attacking me for owning a summer home, a boat and being a dual officeholder (mayor and state senator) they saw nothing wrong with their informant and witness, Prentiss Thompson, owning a home in Montclair, New Jersey, two or more summer homes and a brand new luxury 41 foot Carver motor yacht. He was on their side. I was the bad guy.

Similarly, the government saw no wrong having Wendee Bailey testify against Tamika Riley for not filing taxes for five years; only to learn on the witness stand that Bailey herself was remiss in filing her own taxes over a period of five years. We learned that government witnesses can do no wrong if helping the government convict people, especially innocent people.

Unbeknown to me, Prentiss, an alleged "close friend," had been spying on me and had called the FBI over a dozen times advising them of my whereabouts. He had also contacted members of the Rainbow Yacht Club (RYC) looking for pictures of me participating in various club activities.

Prentiss couldn't wait to be called to testify. He was a professional on the witness stand. He lived for this moment. My attorney, Tom Ashley, said "I hope I don't have to go toe-to-toe with this nut; he has too many skeletons in his closet. I hope he will be a gentleman and just cooperate."

Prentiss, with erect posture and beaming, took the witness stand. Behaving like a movie star, he wanted "ready, action and roll the cameras;" his testosterone was active. With tight lips and clenched fists, he testified that he had arrived, unannounced, at my home inquiring as to the procedure for acquiring Newark property under the South Ward Redevelopment Plan (SWRP). He further testified that I had recommended him to the Rosa Agency where my son was employed. He tried to portray me as "All Powerful" using the prosecution's words. He stressed the point that I had said, "Your application will have to go through me to get to the City Council."

Prentiss Thompson and the government failed to understand that all land applications go through the administration to get to the city council. He had raised his voice when testifying as though it would make his testimony more credible. His intention was to make me appear the all too powerful boss, controlling everything and everyone thereby; I had to be the one who gave land to Ms. Riley. The legal and statutory role of the city council became non-existent. Prentiss portrayed me as the Mayor and the nine-member City Council, all by myself. What did he know? He was an informant, not a student of government. He was on a mission of destruction. He was a hit man.

I had explicitly said to him during his unexpected visit to my home, "Prentiss, you first have to file an application with the administration. They will evaluate your proposal and assist you."

"I don't know how to prepare a proposal or anything about real estate," Prentiss had said. "Is there a shortcut," he had asked?

"If you need help visit the Rosa Real Estate Agency on Bloomfield Avenue. My son works there, they will be more than happy to assist you. They are one of the best in the business, a one stop shop real estate agency. Then you can submit your application to the city," I had said.

"Well, well, all right," he had sheepishly responded. He walked out of my home, put on his helmet, jumped on his motorcycle, fired the engine and raced off. Of course he never filed an application. The next time I saw Prentiss was when he was on the witness stand testifying against me. He obviously enjoyed being praised by the FBI; it did something for his inferiority complex.

In hindsight, I believe that Prentiss, too, wore a body wire. I know that he was sent by the prosecution and that he was trying to trick me into making an unlawful statement. While he could not salivate at his attempt to trick me; he could add my name to the list of those he had tried to destroy, including former Essex County Prosecutors Patricia Hurt and Paula Dow; and former Newark Superintendent of Schools, Eugene Campbell. I am sure that there are many others whom we do not know about. Prentiss Thompson loves spying on people and destroying the lives of others. That's the job of an exemplary government informant. Prentiss cannot be trusted.

Still not satisfied, the government recruited the worst witness of all, Tamika Riley's former secretary, Vivian Casiano. She had been fired by Ms. Riley and the government wanted her to suggest that I had purchased gifts for Riley and took her out to lunch. They wanted this testimony despite the fact that Ms. Casiano had never met me and had no proof, other than a vivid imagination. "I think the flowers came from Mayor James," she had testified. "I think her jewelry came from Mayor James. I think he bought her a fur coat. I think she went to lunch with him," she said. She was a liar's liar on a mission to destroy.

When the defense asked Ms. Casiano the name on the florist card she replied, "I do not recall." When asked "When and what coat did Mayor James purchase for Ms. Riley?" she replied, "I don't know, but she was wearing one in the office."

"When did she have lunch with James?"

"I don't remember."

"When did James visit her in her office?" Ashley asked.

"I don't know," she testified. Her job for the government, like that of the other government witnesses, was to try to create a false relationship, invent false gifts and false meetings.

The government was now looking beyond a conviction on the charges of fraud or corruption (no broken law, no evidence, and no witnesses) and hoping for a conviction on "deprivation of honest services," which was vague and non descriptive. Their theory was that James signed a contract for a close personal friend, viewed as an alleged conflict of interest, and notwithstanding the law that my signature was not needed on a resolution passed by the municipal council, which was binding in itself.

Ms. Casiano was so untruthful, so hostile, and belligerent; she refused to answer specific questions on cross examination by Riley's attorney, causing Judge Martini to issue a warning to the jury after her testimony, to weigh the credibility of each witness. She had greeted and hugged a juror on the elevator raising the question of jury misconduct. Clearly, Vivian Casiano was not a credible witness. The government should have apologized for placing her on the witness stand. They were blowing in the wind and desperate to find some evidence of wrongdoing.

It was quite evident to me that the government wanted their next witness, Newark Corporation Counsel, Joanne Watson, on their side, lock, stock and barrel. They put out the red carpet for her and tried to bamboozle her using every method possible. I sensed that she was under tremendous pressure. I knew that she was fearful that Mayor Booker might remove her as a municipal judge if she did not cooperate. She had a home mortgage, a troubled marriage and kids to feed. She was between a rock and a hard place.

Joanne had worked for the City of Newark for over twenty-seven years as assistant corporation counsel, corporation counsel, business administrator and back to corporation counsel. She knew municipal government inside out. My last appointment as mayor was to nominate her to fill a municipal court judge vacancy. She had come to me with a hardship story of raising two children and having a significant suburban home mortgage. "Mayor, I am asking that you please appoint me a municipal judge before you retire," she had said in her humble way.

In retrospect, I could not have retired and allowed the new administration to sweep Joanne out with their new broom. She would have been jobless and panic stricken. Now she was being intimidated by the government to help them put me in a federal prison for twenty years. She had made two tough decisions. Fearfully, she met with the government to shape her testimony while trying to protect her job. She refused to meet with my defense attorneys. She forgot the fundamental rule of law that a witness does not belong to the prosecution or defense. She wanted to please the government. She wanted desperately to remain a municipal judge. She wanted to stay in favor with Mayor Booker and his administration.

The government wanted Joanne to testify that it was a conflict of interest when I signed the contract page selling land to Tamika Riley; yet, she knew that we had not signed the contract page for the sale of land in another unrelated matter on McClellan Street. The courts had then ruled that the sale was valid by mere passage of the city council resolution. At best any signature was merely ceremonious. Thus, Ms. Watson knew that my signature was not needed on the contract once a resolution had been successfully passed by the city council.

Ms. Watson was under enormous pressure and fearful of doing the wrong thing. Feeling the heat from the government, she testified truthfully, yet ambiguously on the question of "honest services." I could tell that she was scared out of her wits. The full truth would have set both of us free. She was concerned about job security and her home mortgage.

Joanne held up well under tremendous pressure when the prosecution asked her to respond to a barrage of questions including: "What does it mean to say that no one should have an interest in the contract or a financial standing? Does an alleged undisclosed close personal relationship have to be made public? Is disclosure required? Is it a conflict of interest?" *Should one recuse his or her self under such circumstances?*

Ms. Watson testified that she was not aware of any conflict; "If the Mayor had a conflict he could disclose it to me as the corporation counsel," she had said; it was not clear if a conflict of interest meant in the contract itself, or to have received a financial benefit; upon receiving a complaint her office would investigate to determine when a social relationship material warranted one to recuse themselves, or if it is immaterial; "Is going to lunch or dinner with a developer a crime?" she had asked.

On the question of who set the price to sell land, Joanne testified: "Riley did not receive any steeply discounted price; she paid the same price as everyone else." On the question of steering property to Riley, she testified, "James did not steer any property to Riley or attempt to assist her."

On the question of Senate Bill 967, Watson testified: "Senate Bill 967 had absolutely nothing to do with Riley and did not grant any new powers to the Mayor. The Bill was simply to clarify existing powers and duties of the mayor and council under the Faulkner Act." On the question of the South Ward Redevelopment Plan (SWRP), she testified: "The SWRP" was a huge success in eliminating blight and raising property values." On the question of signing the contract for developers to purchase municipal land, she testified: "The contract was valid by passage of the city council resolution. The mayor's signature was not needed. At best it was ceremonious."

Newark Corporation Counsel Joanne Watson was truthful in her testimony, and refuted the government's case against me. Even though her highest priority was saving her job, family and home, Joanne did not compromise her integrity. I personally felt that Judge Martini should have ended the trial after her testimony.

Two courtrooms were being used to accommodate the overflow crowd at my trial. The second courtroom that opened contained a television monitor with audio. FBI agents and the United States Attorney's staff had been ordered to occupy seats in Judge Martini's courtroom for support. "Fill all the seats," they were told. "Keep James' supporters out." This strategy worked well until Judge Martini, apparently tired of listening to the heckling of witnesses by the FBI agents, threatened to remove them from his courtroom. At a sidebar conference he warned a defiant Ms. Germano to control her government supporters or they would be removed from the courtroom.

Federal Agents heckled government witness who took the stand and refused to follow the rehearsed testimony leads of the prosecution during questioning. In plain and simple language they were heckling witnesses who refused to lie under oath. The government's star witness, Basil Franklin, was heckled and badgered on the witness stand and labeled a "turncoat" because he truthfully testified that I did not assist Riley in any way or interfere in the handling of her DEHD application. He also testified that Riley was a qualified developer, even more qualified than some others in the program. Ms. Germano was shaking her head and waving her hand like a mad woman. She looked as though she was about to explode. She wanted him to lie on the witness stand.

Basil, who had allowed the government to wire him in 2004 to entrap me, now refused to lie under oath. He knew the defense could call other witnesses and trip him up if he lied. He did not want to perjure himself. Still Germano kept pressing him to change his testimony; she even asked for a recess to question his testimony. He was their star witness. He was the only person Ms. Riley dealt with in the Department of Economic Development and Housing (DEHD). He was the only person who could charge me with wrongdoing.

Basil Franklin refuted the government's charges against me. Again, I felt that the case should have been dismissed. The New Jersey Redevelopment and Housing Laws did not grant me the legal authority to create the South Ward Redevelopment Plan (SWRP); mayors are not allowed to create redevelopment projects by law. Only the city council can request a blight hearing study by the central planning board, and then vote nay or yea to blight land after conducting a public hearing.

The testimony of Basil Franklin, Joanne Watson, Regina Bayley, London Farley, Robert Marasco, Gayle Chaneyfield Jenkins and Dr. Mamie Bridgeforth, had refuted all of the government's charges. I sat there in total disbelief watching and listening to one witness after another refuting the government. *Why am I even in court?* I thought to myself. *This is all wrong. The government never had a case. This is a waste of the taxpayer's money.* The government still would not quit, though. Judge Martini would not dispense justice.

Germano was back at the lectern making faces, kicking the leg of the lectern, crossing and uncrossing her arms and legs while screaming to the jury that Riley was not qualified, she told the jury that Riley was receiving rental assistance; she previously owned a clothing store that had failed. This brought a strong objection from Riley's defense attorney, which was sustained. Germano continued to rant that Riley had no development experience and was not deserving of any property. Being even more dramatic, she rushed toward the jury, stopped abruptly, threw up her hands and said, "She had Mayor James that's how she got those properties." Still standing before the jury, Germano sarcastically said to the jury, "She had a hook, that's how. James was her hook." I thought she had said, crook.

Ms. Germano had totally ignored all of the testimony by her own government witnesses (Basil Franklin, Joanne Watson, Regina Bayley, Robert Marasco and London Farley). Clearly she was not about fairness or justice. This was a modern day lynching by the prosecution. A desire to win at all cost; a desire to build resumes on the backs of an innocent man. *Just kill another "Old Black Joe."*

While my defense team, throughout the trial, had been overly respectful citing the law and presenting evidence, Ms. Germano had aggressively attempted to paint a false picture for the jury. I was being portrayed as King Kong, standing on top of the Empire State Building holding a defenseless and helpless screaming blonde, and like the ensuing planes in the movie, the jury was supposed to shoot (convict) me down. I was a bad guy. Tamika Riley was a bad girl. By the time the prosecution rested its case against me I had a splitting headache.

For the first time I realized why so many defendants cop a plea or plea bargain rather than go to trial. It's not just because of the legal cost; it's not because government resources are unlimited, which we all know to be true; the truth is that the government can and will abuse its position and the defendant in court. The government is not about justice. The government is about winning at all cost.

The government will wake up the dead to testify against you. They will threaten members of your family and friends to testify against you. They will search back under "Rule 404," prior acts of bad conduct, in order to tell the jury that you stole bubble gum at age three. To them it's a sporting event and they want the trophy.

When a weary and tired Judge Martini called for the defense to present their case, it didn't take long for my defense attorney, Tom Ashley, to point out the legal deficiencies in the prosecution's case. He pointed out that under the Faulkner Act only the city council had the legal authority to set the price and convey land to developers, not the mayor. He showed that under the New Jersey Redevelopment and Housing Laws only the city council could propose and vote to create a South Ward Redevelopment Plan "SWRP," not the mayor.

Ashley presented to the Jury city council resolutions, passed by members of the city council, asserting their legal authority; even evidence where members of the council changed what land they wanted to give to Ms. Riley; with the resolutions, Ashley pointed out that Riley paid the same price as everyone else, she did not receive properties at any steeply discounted price as the government had falsely portrayed. He thoroughly went over the testimony of each witness where they had refuted the government's charges in counts 1-5:

- Government's star witness, Basil Franklin; "Riley was a qualfied developer, more qualified than some others; James did not assist her in any manner." "He never instructed me to give anybody property or to work with anybody directly, he did not interfere in the process." "She was treated no diferently than any other developer."
- City Clerk Robert Marasco; "Riley paid the same price as everyone else." There was one price for everyone, no steeply discounted prices."
- Joanne Watson; "The SWRP was a huge success; Senate Bill 967 had absolutely nothing to do with Riley or granting the mayor more power; James did not assist her; the contract is valid without the signature of the mayor."
- Councilwoman Gayle Chaneyfield Jenkins; "We, the city council, set the price and convey land to developers, it takes five votes; Senate Bill 967 involved a dispute between the mayor and council over commercial land on McClellan Street; the Mayor did not lobby me on behalf of Riley. The 'SWRP' created over 8000 new units of housing and property value went up."
- Councilwoman Dr. Mamie Bridgeforth; "We wanted women and minorities in the 'SWRP'; Riley was a qualified developer, one did not need any prior experience as long as they could put a strong development team together; it is the duty and responsibility of the city council to set the price and convey land to developers." "It's the job of the city council." "The mayor did not lobby me on behalf of Riley."
- London Farley; "The 'SWRP' was a huge success." "I was part of a project review team and Mayor James did not interfere in any manner."

- New Jersey State Senate Analyst George Leblanc; "There was nothing improper about James' State Senate Chief of Staff inquiring whether or not TRI/Riley was qualified for a state grant; they never applied, nothing ever happened, again there was nothing improper."
- DEHD secretary Regina Bayley; Question: "Did Sharpe James ever write a letter to the department on behalf of Riley?" Answer: "No, no, I don't believe the Mayor would ever write a letter like that."

Ashley reminded the members of the jury that there was no effort by defendant James to influence members of the City Council on behalf of Tamika Riley. "There are ten elected officials in Newark not just the Mayor," he had passionately argued. His deep and strong voice resonated throughout the courtroom grasping the attention of the jurors and courtroom attendees.

Tom Ashley stressed to the Jury that the prosecution's opening charge, that defendant James had provided a steeply discounted price for Riley, was false and the government knew it to be false. Ashley stated that even Judge Martini had refuted this charge when responding to an earlier question from the defense; "I'm aware of the fact that there is no evidence that the defendant [James] provided a lower price for her [Riley]," Judge Martini had stated.

Before the jury Ashley emphasized that there was no corruption, no fraud, no chicanery, no deceitful behavior, no benefit to the defendant and the city did not lose any money. "There was no crime; therefore, there was no deprivation of honest services. Any disclosure of an immaterial alleged close personal relationship in itself would not have rendered Riley ineligible to purchase land in the SWRP." He summed up.

Pausing before resting his case, Ashley was about to take his seat, however, before he could sit down a visibly angry Ms. Germano, who had been sitting on the edge of her chair and bobbing throughout his presentation, leaped to her feet, twisting and waving her arms with clinched fists and started firing back, accusing me of stealing city monies from the poor.

Judge Martini interrupted her, and asked "What monies did defendant James steal?" All the court testimony had supported the fact that I had not received any economic benefit; my defense attorney had stated that, "I did not receive one dime." Judge Martini waited for a response.

Somewhat shaken by his question, Ms. Germano paused for a moment, and then said, "Stealing properties."

Judge Martini said, "Oh, that's your interpretation."

After another pause Germano continued; "He also traveled to exotic places; he was a do nothing politician, he was all too powerful and headed a corrupt administration." Obviously, she was enjoying herself.

Again, her remarks warranted a caution from Judge Martini. He angrily admonished her, telling her to "Stop it! I don't want to hear these generalizations about corrupt administration, all powerful, didn't do anything good. I don't want to hear it. Don't talk in terms of the history of corruption unless you've proven that. You didn't prove that in this courtroom as far as I am concerned."

The courtroom fell silent. Germano, standing limply at the lectern, flabbergasted, silent, near tears looked toward her assistant prosecutors for help. Both Kwon and Primvera had their heads bowed at the prosecution's table. They had no legal rebuttal. They could not rescue her. She had crossed the line of fairness once too often. In the absence of any real crime, she was pressing the jury too hard.

Watching Germano standing in a hypnotic trance, I could imagine what she was thinking. I was sure that the prosecution wanted to lynch their star witness Basil Franklin for not lying on the witness stand. They had wanted him to point the finger at me when the government knew all along that it was Basil himself who was enamored with Riley. It was Basil who was flirting and exchanging gifts with Riley. It was Basil who had been intimate with Riley. It was her own star witness, Basil Franklin, who was Riley's "Hook," a title Germano tried to give to me.

The government had egg on their faces when they had to advise my defense team, under the Jencks Act (prosecution must turn over evidence favorable to the defense) of the following evidence:

"Be advised that in or about December 2001, defendant Riley purchased a plane ticket for Basil Franklin to Guyana. He did not repay her. Tamika Riley flirted with him, and on two occasions, after Riley drove him home, they kissed and 'rubbed' at Franklin's home."

Also, according to Dwayne Robinson a housing production employee, during one meeting at City Hall, Mr. Franklin purportedly stated in substance and in part: "I'd like to spank your (Riley) little hiney on this table."

On many occasions Basil had gone to lunch with Tamika Riley. The government was always aware of who had assisted Riley obtain property. They knew that Basil was only doing his job. There was no crime. The investigation should have ended there, right? Not if the U.S Attorney is running for governor. Not if you are out to win at all cost. Not if you have a "target." Not if you have a Black politician that you can stand before a mostly suburban, mostly White jury."

In presenting the closing argument before the Jury, Special Assistant, U.S. Attorney, Perry Primavera, uttered the frustration of the prosecution when citing the lack of evidence and at trial testimony to sustain their indictment. "We have no one who is going to take the stand and accuse the defendant of any wrongdoing; we do not have any smoking gun evidence, we just want you to connect the dots. We want you to use your imagination." He then jumped up, clicked his heels and shouted at the top of his voice, "Are you going to make a statement, say it loud and clear, SEND A MESSAGE!" He implored the jurors.

My defense attorney, Alan Zegas, leaped out of his seat screaming, "Objection, objection; followed by attorney Tom Ashley who was in the air behind Zegas screaming, Objection, objection, your honor; both attorneys challenged Judge Martini to declare a mistrial. "The prosecution has used a highly inflammatory and illegal summation to the members of the jury," Tom Ashley said.

Judge Martini sustained the objection. He called for a sidebar; again he asked both sides how to best clean up the illegal utterance before the jury; once again he was faced with cleaning up after the damage had been done; once again, according to the Bruton ruling, "You can't un-ring the bell."

Prosecutor Primavera had illegally said it, the jury had heard it. "Send a message," that all politicians are guilty before they walk into a court of law; send a message that an African American cannot dream the American dream; send a message that racism in America is still as fundamental as motherhood and apple pie; find this innocent Black man guilty. That was his send a message after presenting no evidence or witnesses to charge me with a crime.

Germano, Kwon and Primavera never spoke of justice, fairness, objectivity or given a true interpretation of the law. They never referenced the evidence as presented in court. I was never considered innocent until proven guilty. I was never viewed as a human being. I was never viewed as a man with a wife, children and career, to them. I was much like the character in Ralph Ellison's book, *The Invisible Man.*

My trial had lasted six long tortuous weeks. The jury was about to receive instructions before being sent to deliberate on a verdict. The silence in the courtroom mirrored the seriousness of the occasion. Spectators and supporters were attentive, yet nervous.

My thirty-eight years of public service had been demonized by the prosecution and New Jersey's leading newspaper, *The Star-Ledger.* Looking down at the defense table in front of me I wondered; *How many people have sat here while their lives were on pause?* They left behind stains from cups and ink. They left scratches from pens and briefcases that had slid along the mahogany surface. They left behind telltale signs of an emotional chapter in their lives. Once all was said and done, evidence of my story would also be embedded in the fine wood grain.

My heart beat faster as I sat waiting for the verdict. It had been six weeks of nightmares, six weeks of tossing and turning, six weeks of not sleeping. It had been a very frightening and painful experience to endure, especially when you know in your heart that you did not commit a crime. When you know that the government is using you to advance personal careers. Six weeks of the government, with its unlimited resources, firing challenges in all directions to keep you off-balance; to keep you on the defense and spending money. Their aim was to break me physically, mentally, financially and spiritually. *Still I shouldn't be nervous,* I told myself.

One thing in my favor, Tom Moran (no friend of mine), a writer for *The Star-Ledger*, had predicted "Sharpe James will walk." There was no benefit to him. "The government has not proven their case," he had written. Even Robert Braun, a columnist for *The Star-Ledger*, covering the trial, had written, "What is James' Crime? It seems every mayor can pick and choose developers to recommend to the city council, the government has no case." Of course I agreed with Braun. *That was my job,* I reflected.

I could not help thinking how the supposed "jury of my peers" was no more representative of me, than the all-White jury in Tom Robinson's trial in the book, *To Kill a Mockingbird*. In my case, ten of my jurors were White suburbanites; a lone Black female suburbanite, who would never look at me, and a weird young Black male from Newark who brought issues to the court. The fact that his issues were being supported by the government who had removed all other potential Black jurors made his presence even more disturbing.

The jurors' display of fatigue mixed with boredom presented an odd spectacle in the courtroom. Though, no louder than a hum, one juror could be heard snoring at intervals; having fallen into a deep state of sleep. Another juror's head dropped onto the shoulder of the juror to the right of him. This would have created an awkward situation for the man on his right, except that he, too, was sound asleep.

In all honesty, there were moments that sparked the jury's interest. They paid attention when they heard words like "conspiracy," "corruption," "too powerful," "make too much money," "theft" and a few other negative words and phrases that the prosecution emphasized. During those moments I noticed a few glares at me from some jurors that said, "Just another corrupt politician," or "Just another corrupt Black politician."

As a group, the jurors seemed let down by the anti-climactic evidence regarding the torrid relationship I was said to have had with my co-defendant. No witness ever testified that we had shared a room, held hands, kissed or was intimate. They had to live with an alleged "close personal relationship." They had to live with Rosemarie saying "I think they were boyfriend and girlfriend."

Most of the jurors looked relieved after the closing arguments were done. They quickly learned that they had to listen and pay close attention to the judge giving the jury instructions before deliberation, the weighing of the evidence. I was dumbfounded, when I realized that Judge Martini wasn't going to explain to the jurors the different job descriptions of mayors. This information wasn't in the instructions to the jury. How could they decide my fate without considering my job description? How could they decide my fate without knowing the role of the City Council, since the Mayor and Council jointly govern the city? I felt that Judge Martini was remiss with his instructions, leaving the jury with the impression that I could just wave my hand or a magic wand and do as I pleased. They needed to know that the independent City Council could not just go all willy-nilly and approve anything, either. The jury wasn't reminded of this.

The judge did instruct the jury on what was needed to place the first three charges under the umbrella of a conspiracy and fraud. He explained that for the government to establish conspiracy, four things must be present. Two or more parties must have a mutual understanding to carry out an unlawful scheme, as charged in the indictment. The members must be willing participants and during the conspiracy, at least one of the members must knowingly carry out one of the overt acts described in the indictment. Lastly, the wrongful or overt act must be carried out during the time of the allegation with the intention to advance the conspiracy.

While the judge continued instructing, I looked over at the jury; most of them had ambiguous expressions. I wondered how much of the information they had absorbed. A few seemed distracted by all of the spectators in the courtroom and weren't focused on the judge at all. I wondered if the judge could have done more to clarify the law and define the role and duties of jurors.

I pulled my eyes away and looked down at the old mahogany table again. Something about the whole trial was nagging at the back of my mind. When I looked back at the judge, he was stating that there were no victims. The City of Newark did not lose any money. "There was no evidence that Riley received any steeply discounted prices." He told the jury, that "The prosecution's summation was not evidence or facts and you must weigh your judgment solely on the trial testimony and the evidence as presented in court." He reminded the jury that the law required them to find the defendants "guilty beyond a reasonable doubt." Finally, the jury was dismissed for deliberation; to try and reach a consensus.

The evidence was in my favor, but something didn't feel right. I weighed the evidence again. The accusations of the government were so unrealistic, they were surreal. I wondered if I should have been flattered or insulted by the abilities they claimed I had. I was this sinister entity according to them. The government's attorneys did all but draw a picture to drive their point across. They did it so much that it formed an image in my mind; none of which resembled me in the least.

It would take someone with special abilities to make so many people bend to his will. The prosecution drilled the premise of how I had maliciously misused my authority to the jurors over and over, again. Yet, the testimony by many witnesses made it hard for the government to pull together the chain of events they had suggested.

The government showed no interest that two White women, Maria Inglasia and her partner had made more than $3 million participating in the same South Ward Redevelopment Plan (SWRP). They paid the same price as Riley had, and even less than Riley on their Osborne Terrace property. The government ignored this fact. Sometimes you just want to make sense of things and this was the best I could do with the prosecution's theory. The five-count indictment was fraudulent at best. I counted thirty-three witnesses that had all testified overwhelmingly in my favor. Not one had given evidence to substantiate corruption, conspiracy or fraud. No testimony was given to suggest a torrid affair with my co-defendant

Meanwhile, Christie and his lead prosecutor, Ms. Judith Germano, held their third or fourth press conference and announced, "With a guilty verdict and a twenty year sentence, and at age 69, Sharpe James will most likely die in prison." Following this announcement they gave themselves high-fives to the cheering of members of the U.S. Attorney's office, followed by free flowing bottles of champagne. Ms. Germano, still not satisfied, had screamed, "We want him in the prison kitchen scrubbing pots and pans," which had led to another outburst of applause and laughter. The celebration was not about justice, it was an opportunity to make fun and sport of the public humiliation of an innocent man.

As I was leaving the courtroom on the first day of deliberation, almost everyone seemed to be talking about the strong aroma in the air. People talked about it to each other, some were talking about it on cell phones. It was talked about on the news and in the newspapers. Everyone appeared to agree on the scent, "acquittal." From spectators to reporters the interpretation of the trial was the same; the prosecution had not proved its case. Considering the charges and the lack of evidence and witnesses to sustain the charges, no one expected the jury's deliberation to take much time.

An open-and-shut case for acquittal was the hue and cry? The jury had been out for five days; five agonizing days waiting for the results and my fate. The tension began to mount. The jurors kept requesting more food, more dessert. One member of the jury weighed more than five hundred pounds and ate ice cream for lunch I was told. At one point a juror became ill and had to be driven home by a United States Marshall. Rumors began to circulate of possible jury tampering. There were rumors that individual jurors were being pressured for a guilty verdict before they could go home.

Finally, on the fifth day the jurors made a request to review the testimony. They wanted the transcript of the complete testimony of Joanne Watson, Newark's Corporation Counsel. This was interesting, since her testimony refuted the first three counts of the indictment and part of Count Five. Her testimony had no bearing on Count Four. They had asked for further clarification on honest services. Judge Martini advised them to read the testimony of council members Augusto Amador, who had twice taken a group to Portugal without reporting it to ELEC, Gayle Chaneyfield Jenkins and Dr. Mamie Bridgeforth.

Shortly after receiving the transcripts, to everyone's surprise, the jury sent word to Judge Martini that they had reached a verdict. The jurors were tired and wanted to go home. They asked to be dismissed for the day; they wanted to deliver their verdict the next day. There was mixed reactions to this news, but like it or not we all went home to wait another day. As we exited the building, words of acquittal were still floating throughout the courthouse.

I stepped outside of the Dr. Martin Luther King Jr. Federal Office Building and Courthouse and paused for a moment. I looked at the statue of Lady Justice wearing a blindfold and judging the sins of mortals. In one hand she holds up the scales of justice. She uses this to weigh the strength or weakness of a case. "Is justice blind?" I whispered, as I passed Lady Justice. "I'm counting on you tomorrow; please no pressure from the government." *I will know tomorrow,* I thought.

How do you show up in court to hear your verdict? You show up composed and confident. It was time for this nightmare to come to an end. The halls of the courthouse were overflowing with friends, family members, supporters, spectators, and reporters. People were chomping down on cold turkey and ham and cheese sandwiches. Business was booming in the courthouse coffee shop. A few ego-driven opportunists were competing for attention from the press and cameramen.

I opted not to make any statements to the press. Most of their questions were about an acquittal. They were there for sensationalism; I was there for justice. I walked with dignity; head high, revealing no emotion. My co-defendant, Tamika Riley, avoided the press, as well. She appeared to be composed. Our attorneys, though, showed the strain, tension and anxiety of the moment, as we all took our places in the courtroom.

"Court's in session! Court's in session!" The words rang-out throughout the courtroom. A swarm of people in the hallway raced into the courtroom to secure a seat. They were the lucky ones. The ones that didn't land a seat were sent to the second courtroom with the monitor. "Please rise for The Honorable William J. Martini," the clerk said, announcing the judge, as he entered the courtroom. "Please be seated," Judge Martini instructed, after taking his seat. He was solemn, all businesslike.

"Has the jury reached a verdict?" the judge asked the bailiff.

"Yes, Your Honor," he replied.

"Please bring the jury in," Judge Martini requested.

In single file the jurors entered the courtroom. With blank expressions they walked with their eyes looking straight ahead. Each juror took his/her seat, making sure not to look out into the courtroom.

"Has the jury reached a verdict?" Judge Martini directed his question to the jury foreman.

"Yes, Your Honor."

"May I see it?" In a sea of silence a sheet of paper was passed from the foreman to the bailiff to the judge. Judge Martini read the paper and passed the paper back to the bailiff. The bailiff returned the paper to the jury foreman.

Judge Martini read aloud each count of the indictment, then, he looked over at the jury foreman.

"Will the defendants please rise," the judge said.

This was the moment. I rose from my seat. Once both of us were standing, the judge turned to the jury foreman.

"On Count One, how do you find the defendant, Sharpe James, guilty or not guilty?"

"Guilty, Your Honor," the foreman's words sent a shock wave through the courtroom. It was an unexpected jury conclusion in view of the evidence and testimony in my favor.

As the words clanged in my head, I lost focus for a moment. *How? What about the city council resolutions and evidence? What about the at trial testimony refuting the government's charges? The government failed to prove their case!*

Judge Martini continued. "On Count Two, how do you find the defendant, Sharpe James, guilty or not guilty?"

"Guilty, Your Honor."

This can't be happening, my mind cried out. *What's going on? This isn't justice. This is a lynching party.*

"On Count Three, how do you find the defendant, Sharpe James, guilty or not guilty?"

"Guilty, Your Honor."

To Kill a Mockingbird jumped into my thoughts. It sent a chill from the base of my neck down my spine. Now I knew what was lingering in the back of my mind all along. Tom's all White jury convicted him for what they believed was a higher cause. Had mine done the same?

"On Count Four, how do you find the defendant, Sharpe James, guilty or not guilty?"

"Guilty, Your Honor."

How is this possible, when there were no HUD funds received or used in the program? Are these people crazy? I asked myself.

"Send a Message!" the words of the prosecutor cut into my

thoughts. Earlier, the jury was told I was all too powerful, a dual office holder, owned a Rolls Royce, a yacht a summer home and earned more money than the Governor. The message was to bring me down. My jury consisted of ten Whites and two wanna (Negro amnesia) be Whites.

"On Count Five, how do you find the defendant, Sharpe James, guilty or not guilty?"

"Guilty, Your Honor."

The courtroom was completely silent. The alleged jury of my peers was behaving like a lynch mob. "Use your imagination and send a message." The illegal jury summation was repeating itself again and again in my mind. Now I understood firsthand why a hue and cry to reform the criminal justice system should be a high priority. I was to be the prosecution's poster child; an example of what could happen to any politician they decided to target. They were also sending a subliminal message that any alleged act of infidelity could become a federal crime.

By using the "Send a Message charge," the prosecutor had encouraged the jury to serve the prosecution and themselves, not justice. He was giving them a politician to destroy, even better, a Black politician. I was the sacrificial lamb. The temptation was too great for the jury to resist. *Where's the justice,* I thought, as I sank into my chair.

It took a moment, before I noticed that my attorneys, Tom Ashley and Alan Zegas, had bowed their heads in disbelief. They knew that the government had failed to prove their case; they had predicted and expected an acquittal. Even the judge appeared as though he didn't know what to make of the verdict. The prosecutors, who were sure they had lost the case, were now looking at each other in amazement. They too could not believe the verdict, even though it was in their favor.

Earlier, the prosecution had offered to throw out Count One in order to shift my sentencing from the 2002 guide book to the more severe 2004 one. In response Judge Martini had said, "Don't be so quick to say don't consider Count One. If that's the case, maybe I won't consider counts Two, Three, and Four." They wanted to bargain. It was evident that the prosecution wanted to inflict pain, by hook or crook, not justice. Judge Martini had suggested that there had been no mail fraud case in Counts 1-4; still he had denied the defense motion for an acquittal.

After the verdict, U.S. Attorney Christie again suggested a twenty year sentence. I knew that he had everything riding on this case. It was high profile and would be a great win on his political score card. Christopher Christie would soon announce himself a candidate for Governor of New Jersey. "I brought Sharpe James down," was his bragging 2009 campaign theme song! I believe that it was the prevailing attitude that he brought a bad Nigger down that helped win him the statehouse from Governor Corzine, who was seeking reelection.

My attorneys, family and friends helped clear the way for me to exit the courtroom. The prosecutor's words continued to reverberate in my head like an echo; it would start low and grow louder, "SEND A MESSAGE." Walking in a group, we pressed on as reporters and spectators tried to get my attention. They were pushing and pulling at me. It was like a riot scene.

As we struggled toward the exit doors I noticed more than a hundred cameras and the prosecution team waiting in front of the courthouse. I looked to see if they had a noose around a tree. A tall, dignified high level courthouse official grabbed me by the arm and said, "Wait, I will let you and your family out the rear door to avoid the mass of reporters and curiosity seekers." Somewhat surprised and confused by his act of kindness, I asked, "Why?"

The middle aged, handsome official said, "Because I feel you got a raw deal upstairs."

I stood spellbound, allowing him to quietly lead me and my family to the rear door of the courthouse. Unlike so many before me I was able to escape the noose and fire. I later learned that the courthouse official would come under heavy attack from Christie himself. Christie had wanted my life and blood spilled on the front steps of the federal courthouse. He wanted to give his staff more high-fives, and with free pouring champagne, dance over my ashes.

Days later I would hear more about the lone Black female member of the jury. She had allegedly told her beautician, two weeks prior to the verdict, "Sharpe James will be found guilty. The government has promised to escort each juror home once the verdict is rendered." *Was this promise to the members of the jury before reaching a verdict legal?* I asked myself. *Is this jury tampering? Did Judge Martini know about this arrangement? Why was it necessary before knowing the outcome of the verdict?* There had been no incidents or suggestions of violence forthcoming from my supporters. No courtrooms flare ups. No outburst! No threats to anyone! My supporters had, at best, been a model group of citizens.

The only heckling had come from the FBI agents and the members of the U.S. Attorney's staff. The only people who were admonished by Judge Martini were FBI agents and members of the U.S Prosecution staff. *Was this a quid pro quo jury tampering move by offering each member of the jury a ride home before a verdict is reached? By offering jury members protection, could the prosecution have been lobbying and urging for a conviction?* My speculations persisted. *Could the government have engaged in jury tampering? Did the government try to win at all cost?*

There is an old song now sung by Justin Timberlake, *What Goes Around Comes Around.* Assistant U.S. Attorney Phillip Kwon found utter delight and even salivated at my trial when questioning whether an African American mayor, such as I, had the right to own a 1989 antique car, a summer home and a fishing boat. It was quite obvious to me and others that he felt I had too much and that it was wrong for a public servant to be that comfortable. I wonder how he felt when the tables were turned.

During the 2012 New Jersey Supreme Court nomination hearing, the Senate Judiciary Committee raised questions about Kwon's personal wealth. They questioned his ownership of expensive and exotic properties and the matter of his mother who, as reported in *The Star-Ledger* (1/31/12), reached a $159,629 civil settlement with federal authorities for making over 222 cash deposits of slightly less than $10,000 each which were illegally placed in the bank account of KCP Wines & Liquor Corp., which she owned and where Kwon's wife worked. An alleged question of money laundering was raised.

While knowing everything at my trial, Kwon feigned knowing nothing about the questions raised at his hearing. He was consequently rejected by the Senate Judiciary Committee. The governor referred to Kwon's hearing as an act of "lynching" (what about Sharpe James). "What Goes Around Comes Around."

In time I learned other disturbing information that exposed the ugly bias in the jury decision making; information that convinced me that bigotry and racism are still very much alive and healthy in America. The jury had found me guilty when there was no evidence or witnesses to sustain any of the charges by the government. I received no justice. America was not so beautiful. Lady Liberty was not blind.

CHAPTER TWENTY

Petersburg Federal Correction Center
Petersburg, Virginia

One night I dreamed I was walking along the beach with the Lord.
Many scenes from my life flashed across the sky.
In each scene I noticed footprints in the sand.
Sometimes there were two sets of footprints,
other times there was one set of footprints.
This bothered me because I noticed that during the low periods of my life,
when I was suffering from anguish, sorrow or defeat,
I could see only one set of footprints.
So I said to the Lord.
"You promised me Lord, that if I followed you,
you would walk with me always.
But I have noticed that during the most trying periods of my life
there have only been one set of footprints in the sand.
Why, when I needed you most, you have not been there for me?"
The Lord replied, "The times when you have seen only one set of footprints,
is when I carried you.

Footprints in the Sand Mary Stevenson-1936

The over-incarceration of federal prisoners or slavery by another name takes a huge societal toll. Hundreds of millions of taxpayers' dollars are wasted; the human costs are even more. Individual freedoms are lost, family support structures are broken; and the acceptance of an overreaching prosecutorial philosophy, "to win at all cost" takes precedence. This factor, unknown to me at the time, I would soon learn by experience.

While Americans struggle with education, employment, health care and environmental issues, our country leads the world in the number of prisons built and the rate of incarceration. We incarcerate people at five times the world's average, and about 80 percent are for nonviolent crimes. Of the more than 2.4 million inmates in America, about 300,000 are incarcerated under the jurisdiction of the Federal Bureau of Prisons (BOP). The federal prison population increased at least three times the rate of state prisons since 1995, and costs taxpayers more than $5 billion per year. As of year end 2006, the Bureau of Prisons was 37 percent over capacity.

A vastly disproportionate number of those incarcerated for low-level drug offenses, under the crack cocaine guidelines, are African Americans. The number of Black federal crack defendants is ten times the number of White defendants. The strong racial correlation of federal crack defendants exists despite the fact that "Whites comprise a majority of crack users." The so-called war on drugs found one in ten Black men ages 25-29 arrested and convicted, partly because possession of crack cocaine (disproportionately used in Black communities) draws draconian sentences equivalent to having 100 times as much powder (White community) cocaine. America is in the arresting business.

A *New York Times* article written by Nicholas Kristof, reported that "Curtis Wilkerson, age 19, of California is serving a life sentence under the 'three strikes' rule, for stealing a $2.50 pair of socks. He already had two robbery offenses on his record. Similarly the state of Florida sentenced 17-year-old Terrance Graham to life in prison without parole for committing robberies. He, too, was convicted under the "three strikes" rule. U. S. Senator Jim Webb from Virginia has been leading the fight for reform in our criminal justice system. He stated, "Either we are home to the most evil population on earth, or we are locking up a lot of people who don't need to be in jail."

On July 29, 2008 at my sentencing hearing, Federal District Court Judge William J. Martini recommended that I be placed in a federal correction center (FCC) as close to my home as possible. After hearing this, inmates at Fort Dix, New Jersey FCC sent word to my supporters that they were anxiously looking forward to greeting the mayor of Newark. Many of those inmates had lived in Newark, and others had relatives living in the city. They had followed the trial in the newspaper and could not believe that I had been found guilty. "Sharpe, now you know how we feel." "Welcome to the club," they had said.

I quickly learned that where I was to be incarcerated was not a decision for Judge Martini to make. Once you are sentenced by the judge and become a convicted felon, you become the property of the BOP, the Bureau of Prisons. They get to decide how to carry out your incarceration. BOP, I was told, could assign you to a cottage in Alaska as long as they provided your basic entitlements of a cot to sleep on, three meals a day, a toilet, one hour of exercise daily, medical services and a chance to shower at least once a week. Mail privilege was also considered an entitlement. Prisoners had taken BOP to court in order to get a ruling classifying mail an entitlement and not a perk as television, telephone and commissary privileges are.

Shortly after being sentenced by Judge Martini, I received a letter from the BOP advising me, under the volunteer surrender program, that I was to report on September 15, 2008 not to Fort Dix, New Jersey, but to Petersburg FCC in Petersburg, Virginia, by 11 a.m.

Instead of traveling forty five minutes from my home, my family and other visitors would now have to travel six to seven hours to see me. If I failed to appear, I would become a fugitive of justice and a warrant would be issued for my arrest; they so warned me. BOP had spoken. Trial Judge William J. Martini was now history. My life was about to take a "Sharpe" turn.

From the t̶ ̶ ̶ ̶ ̶ ̶ ̶ ̶ 'ictment and throughout my trial the prosecuti̶ ̶ ̶ ̶ ̶ ̶ ̶ ̶s conferences where they would brag ̶ ̶ ̶ ̶ ̶ ̶ ̶ ̶ ̶ ̶ ̶ ̶ ̶nty year sentence, Sharpe James might ̶ ̶ ̶ ̶ ̶ ̶ ̶ ̶ ̶on. This prediction would elicit cheers from the ̶ ̶ ̶ ̶ ̶ng team.

Love in its essence is spiritual fire.

"We want James behind bars, in a cell for life, scrubbing pots and pans," they had cheered, sounding like a mixed chorus. The cheers were most often led by lead prosecutor Ms. Germano, I was told. They gave themselves high-fives like they had just won a championship trophy in a major spectator's sport. "Do they make coffins in prison," one member of the U.S. Attorney's staff had asked. My trial was never about serving justice, it was always about serving bloated egos in the office of the politically ambitious U.S. Attorney.

When I arrived at Petersburg FCC camp on September 15, 2008, the ceiling in the "beach area," (crowded beds in an open floor space) of the dorm was leaking profusely; buckets were scattered all over the floor to catch the rain. As if I had to be told, someone informed me that the roof needed fixing.

Over the next few months the number of leaks increased, as did the number of buckets to catch the rain. On September 8, 2009, almost one year to the day of my incarceration, at approximately 11 p.m., a large portion of the dorm ceiling collapsed, narrowly missing sleeping inmates. The debris consisted of concrete and steel rods. Any number of inmates could have been killed instantly in their sleep. BOP simply had inmates remove more of the loose ceiling and provided more and more buckets.

I thought this was ironic considering inmates received a shot (a reprimand) for having a dirty bunk or an unsanitary area. I thought to myself, which is more important, a falling ceiling or a dirty bunk? To add insult to injury inmates were called upon to lift and carry heavy new exotic cherry wood furniture to each of the dorm's administrative offices. This at a time when BOP was crying broke and the quality of inmate's meals were in question. When I left camp on April 6, 2010, the roof was still leaking with no repairs having been made and the ceiling was still falling. This was the life of being a prisoner even in a camp setting.

"The more things change, the more they remain the same." Some things never change. *The Star-Ledger* continued to vilify me even after I was locked up and out of the public eye. Six weeks after I arrived at Petersburg Camp, the headline, on October 26, 2008, read, "Bars Can't Keep James Out of City Politics."

The article further stated that, "Even from a jail cell hundreds of miles away, the 72 year old Democrat is still seeking to put his mark on the politics of the city he dominated for two decades." I had sent a campaign donation to a city council candidate, Charles Bell, involved in a Newark special election to fill a vacancy by the ouster of Councilwoman, Dana Rone. Rone had been accused of abusing her office of trust by interfering in a traffic stop by Rutgers University Newark campus police officers. It involved a family member. My act of generosity was misconstrued by the *Ledger*, of course, and made out to be a political maneuver on my part.

The Star-Ledger was ecstatic to report that I was behind bars in a cell whenever I wasn't washing pots and pans in the kitchen. Likewise the U.S. Attorney's office was elated. This is what they wanted to hear. This is what they had predicted. Fortunately, none of it was true. The Ledger has a history of writing articles without facts. Their reporters were known for not putting in an effort to print the truth. Even worse the Ledger never printed corrections like the New York Times. After this last attack on my character, Newark citizens started writing me letters about how wrong it had been for an innocent man; especially after all I had done for Newark, to be placed in a federal prison cell. "Mayor James we are praying for you," they most graciously wrote.

After reading The Star-Ledger headline, a fellow Petersburg camp inmate asked, "What bars are they talking about? What prison cells are they referring to?" I had never been behind a razor wire topped fence. I had never been behind bars. I had never been in a cell. "Petersburg Camp," said inmate Dwight Silver, "used to be called 'Sweetsburg.' Everyone loves Petersburg camp including former Mayor, Marion Barry, of Washington, D.C.; the lawyer for Imelda Marcos and other celebrities," he had proudly boasted. "We used to have benches outside and a picnic area for visitors until an inmate was caught having sex with his guest in the bathroom. Now the security guards sit and watch over us in one open room," he said solemnly.

"Sharpe, you can walk away from this place any day of the week and drive home. You can walk down to the James River and take a boat home." Silver had said. Listening nearby, inmate, John Doe, who had the body, build and muscles of Hercules, said he had been at Petersburg for six years and couldn't complain. He jokingly added, "Maybe we should pay to be here. It's my Bally's fitness center," he had said and then laughed.

Doe looked as though he belonged on the cover of Muscle magazine; and just to tease the women he sported four foot long, legitimate dreadlocks. I felt like writing The Star-Ledger and advising them that no one in camp spent any days behind bars or in a cell. But I knew that it would be a waste of time and energy. They didn't care about the truth. They just wanted to sell newspapers.

The team that had prosecuted me had wanted me in the kitchen; and on my first day in the chow line my case Manager, Mr. Tucker, said, "Hey James you look like a good kitchen man, come and see me later." During lunch I almost choked on the "chilidogs" thinking about being assigned to the kitchen. I had heard rumors that an inmate working in the education department was leaving, so half way through lunch I raced to building twenty-one, where the education department was located, to submit my resume to Ms. Tammy Monk, supervisor of the camp education program. "I'm interested in the possible opening for an education aide," I said to her.

Seated behind a cluttered desk in a cluttered office, Ms. Monk studied my resume, smiled and then with a puzzled and distorted face, said, "Well, I see you have a strong academic background and career ladder as a former teacher, coach, athletic director, professor, mayor and state senator. I do have one important question, though; with such a strong academic background, are you willing to take and follow my instructions? Would that pose a problem for you?" she had asked.

I recognized that I was being asked the question that would define my tenure at Petersburg FCC camp; would I be a problem or could I learn to take orders? I moved closer to her desk, thinking of my past meeting with Dr. Martin Luther King Jr., and the words he had uttered in many of his speeches; my hero gave me the answer I needed. "Ms. Monk," I said in a humble tone, "in order to be a good leader one must first be a good follower; whether I am asked to clean the toilets or teach math, I will do my very best. I can assure you that I will follow your instructions without hesitation. I'm a team player."

Later in the day when I met with my case manager, Mr. Tucker, I explained to him that I had been offered a position in the education department. He did not believe me. It took a telephone call from Ms. Monk to our unit manager, Mr. Larry Moody, who then turned to Mr. Tucker and said, "Hey, James belongs in education with his background." Tucker remained stone silent and appeared somewhat angry. I was now an education aide and had not been assigned to the kitchen to wash pots and pans.

At my trial Judge Martini, a former federal prosecutor himself, had told the prosecution team that he was aware of the fact that they could indict a ham sandwich. Once at Petersburg FCC camp that message became crystal clear to me. I was able to see firsthand the results of over prosecuting and unjust convictions leading to the warehousing (overcrowded) of poorly fed and poorly treated inmates costing the government billions of tax payers' dollars.

In my opinion this was a blatant attempt to dehumanize a youthful population under the guise of a so-called war on drugs. It was all because of the unfortunate drug overdose of Len Bias in 1987. Bias had just signed a million dollar contract with the Boston Celtics. His death triggered law enforcement officers to go after street level drug dealers. In reality it was a law enforcement sport where young men between the ages of 25-29 were targeted on street corners for selling crack cocaine (Black community) while violators dealing in powder cocaine (White community) or even those who had committed murder were sentenced to far less time. There was no real effort to catch the drug lords who had supplied the drugs.

My position is not to suggest that drug dealers should not be punished for their crimes, but raises the question of selective enforcement and parity in sentencing laws. I believe that the first step should be for congress to pass Senate Bill 1789, restoring fairness in federal sentencing guidelines for cocaine violators. Jayson Williams, NBA $80 million basketball star, after an eight-year court battle, received an eighteen-month to five-year sentence for aggravated assault in the shooting death of his limo driver and for his alleged cover-up attempt. At the same time a twenty-year-old street corner drug dealer will be put away for 15-20 years, with no remorse, for selling five grams of crack cocaine.

We need to revisit the cases of Terrance Graham, and Curtis Wilkerson, teenagers who were both sentenced under the "three strikes law." There must be a better way to punish youthful, nonviolent offenders other than having them spend a significant part of their lives behind bars. No one can tell you that prison life is fun. It stinks and degrades the individual. There was nothing funny about seeing men behaving like women; men jumping into showers with other men having sex, or seeing muscle bound freaks posing in the mirror; it is a sick environment. My advice to the young and old is to stay out of prison and out of harm's way. If you don't, you will be sorry, for prison is a compartment of hell.

In prison only the strong survive; others are turned into punks to be abused financially, physically or sexually. I was fortunate to be physically fit, and carried a title; "Hey Mayor." My big mouth made other inmates treat me with respect or indifference, but no hostility. Many inmates were not as fortunate as I was. I felt sorry for them. I prayed for them.

To minimize (cover-up or sugar coat) the government injustice of over incarcerating, FCC camps were created to house political prisoners, white-collar criminals and the non-violent street level drug dealers who could not survive the normal physical, violent and psychotic prison population. Still these camps are an environment where one could get killed for changing the television channel, or beaten for staring at someone.

Camp is also a trap for the weak and simple-minded inmates who are harshly disciplined and receive even more prison time for violating simple rules within the invisible walls of confinement. Inmates are not in cells and there are no armed security guards. Yet, they can't leave, they can't have a cell phone, there is no smoking or drinking, and no sex or acts of violence are tolerated. Even using bleach to wash clothes is a violation; bleach is contraband.

The camp is reminiscent of Skinner's box rat experiment, where rewards were given for right and wrong responses. Even though the camp has no walls, razor wire fences, cells or gun-toting officers, inmates are still restricted in individual freedoms. Various locations, social activities, movement and choice of reading and television material are off limits. You are constantly reminded that you are a BOP prisoner. There is still a bed-check. You are still counted at 10 a.m., 4 p.m., 10 p.m., and throughout the night.

I was scared of the prison medical facility where two dentists had to serve a 5000 (camp, low and medium) prison population. There were two doctors who gave the same pill for every ailment and a visit to the doctor's office never lasted more than 3-5 minutes before he would shout, "next." It was clear that the prison medical staff never took the Hippocratic Oath. There was no sympathy or tears for the sick. If you were not standing outside the health clinic at 6 a.m. try another day, week, or month or just die.

Your mouth can get you killed in prison. After witnessing a bloody fight between fellow inmate "Smiley" and another inmate, where the other inmate had been beat into a bloody pulp, I learned to keep my own mouth shut.

On another occasion I witnessed one muscle man going to the weight pile and bringing back the forty-five pound weight bar to pummel another muscle man over the head. Again blood was flowing like Niagara Falls. The startled inmate had knots all over his head. It was reported that he had told the other inmate, while arguing that you can't beat me anyway, I'm too strong for you.

The forty-five pound weight bar was more than the equalizer. All of these incidents were constant reminders that your mouth can get you in trouble, and that one can get killed in prison simply by saying the wrong thing at the wrong time. Sometime we have to give others their space for whatever reason. Prison life can make you an accident-in-waiting for someone with pent up emotions. One must remember to let sleeping dogs lie.

Having incurred the notoriety of *The Scarlet Letter* for being a convicted felon, inmates from the hood crave their own unique identity. They can't wait to discard their khaki work uniform and boots. On the streets they were known for their fancy clothes, cars, jewelry, stereo and video equipment or drug money. Prison life takes all of that glitter away and adds further embarrassment if you dyed your hair or wore a hair-piece. No hair tint or wigs are allowed in prison. I can still visualize TV sports announcer, Mark Albert, in prison without his hairpiece.

Thus inmates with low self-esteem struggle to distinguish them-selves at camp. To gain attention they wear weird hairstyles, beards and tattoos. They customize their prison grey sweat suits by adding white stripes, cuffs, patches, pockets and vary the leg lengths of their pants. They wear designer sneakers or immaculate white (status) sneakers, boots and even fancy bedroom slippers.

Inmates are always looking for an edge over each other, trying to defeat uniformity. Some inmates adorn themselves with two to four feet of straight hair, no hair, buns, pony tails, dreadlocks, braids or uncombed and wild looking hair like Ben Wallace of the NBA. One inmate kept his hair standing two feet straight up in the air with rods; others had patches of hair as though they had been scalped. Variations in prison dress and hairstyle meant show time for the insecure inmates. They had something to prove. It was show and tell time.

The only camp hair incident that I witnessed, occurred when a male prisoner arrived sporting "39 triple D breasts," with hair below his waist; drawing stares from everyone. Because many inmates thought he was a woman, the unit manager ordered him to cut his hair. He refused to do so, citing his rights. The unit manager had a couple of inmates forcefully hold the inmate in a barber chair and gave him a crew cut. He was kicking and screaming throughout the encounter. When I asked a fellow inmate if this action was legal, he smiled and said, "Sharpe, Mr. T was wearing extensions; his hair was not real but his tits are. Mr. T was seeking attention; he, too, fell victim to BOP rules and regulations."

Like in the movie *The Elephant Man,* inmates are crying out, "I am a human being, not just a number." After the haircut incident, I felt sorry for Mr. T (Tits) and asked him how he felt. He snapped his fingers, rolled his eyes and said, "Sharpe, you would be surprised how many freaks come out at midnight. I'm having a ball," he had said with a full smile. I had no more questions. I left Mr. "T" to enjoy himself.

Upon his release in January 2009, Mr. "T" underwent a complete gender transformation, from male to female. Apparently, to tease his former inmates, he sent pictures of the real Ms. T back to us. She was now a striking beauty and had the whole package of sex appeal.

Basically, unless inmates know you as "home boy" (from the same city or state); or from having previously entered and/or served time together, they are slow to embrace you. Most inmates, from street habits, shy away from eye-to-eye contact. When passing they will suddenly drop their head or look away, pretending not to see you. A polite greeting can be totally ignored; I don't know you, is the body language, and I don't want to know you is the clear message.

I, too, found myself passing inmates blindly and silently. This is not to say that other inmates have not gone to inmate.com (gossip) to learn everything about you. It would be a mistake to believe, which I learned the hard way, that you can be invisible in prison. Walking to the chow hall one day, an inmate who had never looked my way, never even spoken to me, suddenly placed his body squarely in my path; creating a roadblock. We made eye contact, and he smiled, gave me a fist greeting and amazingly called my name, "Hi Sharpe, or is it Mayor?" he said. "How are you brother?" I quickly learned the reason for the changing attitude and this sudden honeymoon behavior. He wanted something.

"Sharpe, my money is a little tight this month. I can't get to the commissary (inmate's store) could you help me out with some soup, tuna and ice cream?" he asked. Other times it was batteries, bagels, peanut butter, stamps, envelopes, popcorn, coffee and the list goes on. Of course, once you satisfy a fellow inmate's immediate fiscal need, they will go back to passing you without making eye contact and without speaking to you. One out of ten inmates will make good on their promise to repay you (by exchanging goods). When I raised a concern about this behavior, I was told to "Wake up, Sharpe." Being a con-artist is an inherent skill possessed by most inmates. "Get wise or they will break the bank," I was told.

I spent most of my time in the camp library reading or researching the law, preparing for my appeal. While there, I used an old battered typewriter to write this memoir. I joined an inmate's book club engaging in some spirited discussion on the writings of various authors. To stay focused and keep my spirit high, I found rapturous enjoyment in participating in the many religious services offered. I believed in the lyrics by Sam Cooke that "a change is gonna come" therefore, I had to keep Lord Jesus in my life. My faith, however, did not give me immunity from camp gossip.

From the so-called elite group of prisoners (white collar criminals) I heard over and over again, that many inmates are living better in prison than they were at home, if they had a home. These elitists would back up their belief by strongly suggesting that many inmates, while living in the hood, could not boast of having had a roof over their head, a single bed, three meals a day and full health coverage.

One inmate, who worked in the kitchen, called me over and pointed out another inmate. "When he arrived in camp he was near death," I was told. "Yea Sharpe," he said. "Prison saved his life, and there are many others who should be thankful that they are in prison. It's a free rehabilitation clinic for many," he had said, matter-of-factly. "Don't believe all that crap about how great inmates had it at home; you are now part of a population where lying is an art. Some of these brothers didn't even have food stamps," he said passionately.

This came from an inmate who, as part of the kitchen staff, served indescribable cakes and grits for breakfast. A rare change might see them stuffing us with the worst possible bad tasting dry cereal, grits in many forms and colors, or beef and flour gravy to pour over biscuits, which in the army we called "shit on shingles." We did not complain when breakfast consisted of oatmeal, eggs, pancakes, or French toast.

I learned that every BOP prisoner in America was served the same meal daily. Prisoners receive a heavy starch oriented meal for lunch and dinner consisting of potatoes in every form imaginable, macaroni and cheese, noodles, a variety of beans, burritos, chicken fajitas, rice and vegetables from the inmate tended garden; and of course more cake. Add to this the sweet water drinks that are served daily, it is no wonder that obesity in camp is a growing problem.

One inmate weighed more than 500 pounds and several others tipped the scale at 300-400 pounds. The oddity, though, was seeing these same inmates supplement their heavy FCC starch and sugar diet with high calorie microwave cooked meals; and then rush to the commissary for candy, cookies, soda and, of course, a pint of ice cream. It was a ritual for inmates to walk around once a week with a pint of ice cream in their hand as a badge of honor; a once-a-week treat, only because we did not have personal refrigerators. A few inmates had the ingenuity to make and sell ice cream; the first challenge was to steal a lot of salt to keep the ice cubes frozen.

I labeled this enterprise, along with the FCC menu, a way of killing yourself slowly. It was no secret that the BOP was striking it rich selling food to inmates through the commissary; charging for copying materials; and selling telephone minutes to call home, all at outrageous prices. Whatever items were in great demand at the commissary, the price would slowly increase day by day. BOP is making money off the inmates.

Even while complaining about the bad food, inmates will race to the mess hall everyday trying to be the first in line. On days when chicken is being served, you need to wear shoulder pads and a helmet to fight the mad rush.

While inmates smuggle in cell phones, cigarettes, drugs, alcohol and bleach, the correction officers (CO) are busy tearing apart nooks, wall vents, insulation wraps, tile ceilings, sinks and cabinets in camp searching for these contrabands. Theft from the camp kitchen had reached astronomical proportions. One inmate had enough stolen chicken in his locker to feed the entire camp. Some days the camp menu had to be changed due to inmate's theft of food products. Inmates working in the kitchen became entrepreneurs pilfering uncooked food from the kitchen pantry or cooked food to sell to inmates who were too lazy to walk to the mess hall or commissary.

A fellow inmate, Dr. Unknown, felt that stealing from the kitchen was an entitlement due to the low pay and poor food services that we received. He considered it an act of survival. I vehemently disagreed with him. After observing him stuff his pockets and sweat suit once a week with eggs and other food items, I felt the doctor was too involved himself to be objective. Everyone could complain about the low pay and low morale in prison, but it didn't give you a license to become a thief. He was defending himself.

Interestingly enough, stealing is not limited to inmates. A blind man cannot help but notice government managers and supervisors taking federal equipment and supplies for their personal or business use. For example, at camp the administration was still trying to figure out how two rolls of copper wiring, each weighing about 1500 pounds went missing. Unbelievably, they were questioning inmates. Even if Houdini was in prison he couldn't lift or make 1500 lbs of copper wiring disappear. Not all of BOP staff members were honest and most certainly they were not role models.

We were told that we were going to be locked up in a "safe haven" (prison) to be rehabilitated, to be purged of our criminal lifestyles. Well, someone made a mistake. The first thing we learned at Petersburg FCC was that there was a thin line between the vice world and being in prison. We learned that prison was not a safe and sane environment to rehabilitate prisoners. Everyday there was shocking news of BOP staff not living up to their oath of office.

Picking up the local newspaper we read about a Petersburg FCC female, senior correction officer, who was indicted and arrested for taking inmates to a local motel for sexual encounters. Shortly thereafter a second Petersburg correction officer was indicted and arrested for smuggling in and selling cell phones, marijuana and barber shears to inmates; and for planning to have inmates maimed or killed for cooperating with the ongoing investigation. Just think, for telling the truth in prison a correction officer would put out a hit on you. Inmates were not even safe in a federal prison.

After recovering from these horrible events, we inmates learned that our Petersburg FCC food management specialist was found guilty of stealing more than $100,000 in bogus overtime. Here we were complaining daily about the poor quality of the food and the food manager was pocketing money earmarked for prison meals. Our environment for rehabilitation was beginning to resemble the hood. Most times we simply ignored correction officers stealing government supplies and equipment.

Correction officers, managers and supervisors had a great advantage, who would believe a convicted felon testifying against a law enforcement officer or BOP personnel? Prisons have become another failed big business; a giant extraordinary waste of taxpayers' money (government waste) and a waste of human life as well. How many unnecessary single-family households are there? How many children are without a father?

Americans need to rethink our criminal justice system where inmates struggle to survive in a chaotic environment. The biggest perk at camp is watching television which is a means of connecting prisoners to the outside world. Take that privilege away and prison life would be unbearable. Inmates grab their chairs and race to one of the dorm television rooms to flop down in their chair claiming territorial rights in front of the television set. Late comers sit or stand outside the room, gazing in.

The daily fight in the television room becomes, "Don't change that channel." Deciding what to watch is a daily ritual. World News and ESPN Sports receive the most interest. Popular TV Series 24, Meet the Browns, American Idol, BET and Atlanta Housewives are some of the favorites for regular television. Watching anything else is subject to a fight generally settled by a majority vote. One inmate was killed in a confrontation over changing the TV channel. Rightfully, there is a selected Spanish speaking television channel.

I found it depressing being in an environment where inmates preferred watching two basketball games in a row rather than watch the 2010 Winter Olympics. "Sharpe, we don't want to watch that mess," one inmate scolded me. Another inmate screamed, "There ain't no Blacks (he obviously had never heard of USA Speed Skating Champion, in the short and long track, Shani Davis) competing," he had grumbled. I wondered what would be his explanation for Whites watching and supporting NBA basketball, dominated by minority players. Without Whites in the audience, NBA basketball would be in a recession.

Inmates preferred watching the first game of the basketball season rather than watch championship events in the Winter or Summer Olympics which occur only once every four years; even watching the World Series in baseball created a disturbance. Far too many inmates had no interest in learning anything new. While not fighting over the issue, I could clearly hear the words of Socrates, "Those who repeat the same thing over and over again and expect different results are insane."

How will inmates prepare for the outside world, if they continue doing the same thing behind prison walls for 10-20 years? I asked myself. One man entered prison with a strong liking for Walt Disney children shows, now at age 35, he was still daring anyone to turn off his Walt Disney show. The inmates TV room was not for the faint of heart; only the strong survived.

Besides watching television inmates are addicted to physical fitness and weight training. An inordinate amount of time is spent lifting weights and doing pushups, sit ups, abdominal exercises, leg lifts and jogging around the prison dirt track daily. It appears that everyone is seeking an "Adonis physique;" a self made sculptured body of beauty; a biblical mighty man of valor. "Just wait until the ladies see me when I'm out of here," appears to be the attitude.

Every day that I was incarcerated, I observed inmates stripped to the waist or in tank tops competing in the weight pile mirror, flexing their biceps, pectoral, deltoids, abdominals, triceps, trapezius and scapulae muscles, challenging others. "Man, I got you beat," they would argue. Since inmates are removed from the general population, some of them miss the admiration of a spouse, family member, girlfriend or significant other, so they develop a Narcissus complex.

Like in Greek mythology, Narcissus, who saw his own reflection in a pool of clear water and fell in love with himself, some inmates become just like Narcissus. "See how beautiful I look."

These bodybuilding inmates love to stare at themselves in the mirror at the weight pile or in the bathroom. They strip to the waist when shaving to allow for a full exhibition of their upper body muscles. Shaving is actually a secondary concern. Some never even wore a beard. I take my hat off to these brothers for taking care of their bodies, however, I question the mentality of those who believe they have to rise at 5 a.m. to run steps, jump rope, and shadow box or lift weights everyday for 5-15 years in order to stay fit. Even Muhammad Ali, Mike Tyson, Joe Frasier and Sugar Ray Leonard didn't train every day for 5-15 years to stay fit.

I believe that these inmates are advertising the fact that they have not found real enjoyment in reading, using the library, attending chapel services, critical thinking or the beauty of just plain rest and relaxation. Their addiction is weight training.

One inmate admitted to me that he could not concentrate long enough to read a book. He said, "I have become highly institutionalized. Most times I fall asleep when holding a book in my hand." He went through the same BOP ritual (exercise, breakfast, work, exercise, dinner and exercise, bed) each day like a robot. After seven years of incarceration never once had he set foot inside the library or the chapel. He never read a novel. He was not alone.

An inmate named Rick followed the same daily routine. Rick was matinee handsome with curly hair, pearly straight teeth, sported a six pack of well defined abdominal muscles when wearing a spandex bathing suit and to top it off, he had a winning smile. When he was released from prison and returned home to Myrtle Beach he could not find a job. When it came to seeking employment, he had no qualifications. His sculptured look was not a resume. His time in prison would have been better spent if he had studied for a GED, or taken a skills course.

As a GED teacher for the BOP, I tried to instill in inmates the importance of an education, learning to use the library and participation in job fairs. Investing time in studying was as important, if not more important than time spent at the weight pile. My message was that good looks and muscles, or just muscles alone will not guarantee you a job. In 2008 Congress passed, and President Bush signed into law, the "Federal Second Chance Act," which provided $165 million a year for substance abuse programs for inmates which included education and employment services (Job Fairs).

I encouraged inmates to take advantage of the "Second Chance Act" in order to add knowledge and skill development to their daily repertoires. Needless to say, my message was not received with any overt enthusiasm. In some circles I was viewed as a government sympathizer. BOP policy stated that inmates, who did not have a high school diploma or a GED, must participate in a literacy program requiring a minimum of 240 hours of instruction, or until the attainment of a GED certificate.

I will never forget the reaction of my class when I told them that they had to take tests without looking up the answers in the back of the book. One inmate jumped up and shouted, "Sharpe, we always look the answers up in the back of the book when taking tests, where do you come from?" Another inmate asked, "Sharpe, what are you, a BOP spy?" Another yelled out, "Hey Brother, you're just another inmate with eight numbers like us, and don't forget it. Don't come in here trying to rock the boat," he had said. He was right. I had choices to make.

Would I surrender to inmates' nonsense or take the heat for trying to bring about a change in attitude? I could not abandon the old philosophy, "If I give you a fish you will eat for a day, but if I teach you how to fish you will eat for a lifetime." Like my good friend, Joe Clark, the subject of the movie, *Lean on Me* or Sidney Poitier in the 1967 British film, *To Sir, with Love* where an idealistic teacher is confronted with a rebellious group of students, I found myself with quite a dilemma.

Situations where teachers struggle between winning the love and admiration of their rebellious students versus providing them with the academic tools they will need to survive in life require tough choices. This dilemma was even tougher in a federal prison where inmates viewed me as one of them, yet saw me in an authoritative position as well. At Petersburg FCC camp, I viewed teaching as challenging and a strained love affair. I decided to provide tough love, demanding that my students achieve, accept discipline and respect the rights and properties of others, whether they liked it or not.

Many inmates had dropped out of school to sell drugs and had lost the desire for study and learning. They had exchanged short-time pleasure for the long-time pain of being incarcerated. Every day I would face a student in the classroom who emotionally and honestly would say, "I don't want to learn." Or, "I can't read." They failed to understand that drug money couldn't buy knowledge. Knowledge is something that you have to acquire yourself.

Some of my students reminded me of Dexter Manley, the All-Pro defensive end for the Washington Redskins, who at the peak of his career embarrassingly confessed, after being voted the most valuable player, that he could not read. For thirty years he had been hiding this fact; guessing words, and pretending to know how to read. Unexplainably, he had graduated from high school a functional illiterate and was accepted into Oklahoma State University, where he became a star football player.

While Manley's public statement was embarrassing to him, it was also brave of him. It took a lot of courage for him to admit his handicap. One can't cure a disease without first recognizing the fact that the disease exists. As stated by the United Negro College Fund, "A mind is a terrible thing to waste," and Dexter was going to do something about it. He opened Dexter Manley reading clinics to help others.

In November 2009, I received a "call out" (inmate must report) that I should report to the main desk in the lobby of the dormitory, "spit shine from head to toe." No sooner had I received the message, three inmates approached me to let me know that I had been selected by the unit manager, Mr. Larry Moody, to be interviewed by a group of 35 newly appointed federal judges. They were touring federal prisons to learn about inmates and camp life.

My fellow inmates who were members of the Inmates Camp Board of Directors (I later learned they were self-appointed) informed me that I should refuse the invitation. Their reasoning was that I had just arrived and didn't know "shit" about camp life. I didn't know "shit" about how bad the camp administration was; and one of them should have been selected so they could talk tough to the judges. One inmate said to me, "Tell them to go screw themselves for giving out draconian prison sentences and tell them that the camp unit manager and warden should be fired." An inmate convicted of money laundering said, "Tell them that I did not deserve a 24 year sentence." Again, they stressed that they needed my help. Yet, they were saying, "Don't go. "Piss on them!" I was told, "We will handle this, Sharpe."

After listening intently to their highly emotional concerns, I politely advised them that they should speak to the unit manager themselves. I told them I was not mad at anyone. I was not about to start any warfare with the unit manager, warden or inmates. My goal was to get the hell out of camp as soon as possible. Also, I could only speak about the feelings of Sharpe James regarding camp life. "I don't have to be in prison for ten years to know the horror of being incarcerated," I told them.

At exactly 3:00 p.m. I was standing at the main desk in the lobby. My boots were spit shined like a polished mirror, my khaki uniform pressed to impress. A fresh, fade out prison haircut did not hurt either. Mr. Moody met me and escorted me to the camp chapel where the interview would take place. We were seated inside when someone yelled, "Out, out, move out," the strong voice demanded. Hurriedly we raced to the hallway and walked to a rear corner remaining out of sight.

Later we learned that a team of state police officers, federal marshals and sniffing German shepherd dogs were making an inspection of the facility while the federal judges remained on a charter bus parked directly in front of the camp chapel. We were told that the federal judges would enter first and be seated, while we waited in another room. Shortly thereafter, I was called into the chapel with my Petersburg FCC case manager, Mr. Tucker. We sat in two chairs at a front table, while the judges sat in chairs arranged in a horseshoe, facing us. Mr. Tucker opened by introducing me and reading the charges I was convicted of, fraud, mail fraud and fraud involving receipt of federal funds.

At times I did not know who Mr. Tucker was referring to since the charges were bogus and unfounded. Nevertheless, his remarks went well with the judges who now had a convict in front of them wearing a "Scarlet Letter" number #28791-050; and from the excited looks on their faces, they were ready to put me under a microscope. I felt as though I was their experimental guinea pig for the day. The group was evenly divided with both men and women. They couldn't wait to pepper me with questions. They were shooting them at me left and right.

"Mr. James, in your own words, please tell us why you were you convicted?" "What do you think of your sentence?" "What was your trial experience?" "What is your background?" "How is the administration at this camp?" "What programs are being offered in camp?" "Are the inmates taking advantage of the programs?" "Do you think that you are being rehabilitated?" "Are you happy here?" "What do you plan to do in life after leaving Petersburg?" they asked.

I felt like I was back in college taking my final oral examination. *Hey, slow down, blow the whistle, time out,* I thought to myself. I slowly and carefully answered each question, some were personal and others based on my experiences at Petersburg. The questions and rapport between us changed after one of the judges specifically asked me about my background. When I stated that I had been Mayor of Newark for twenty years; State Senator for nine years; vice chairman of New Jersey's Budget and Appropriations Committee overseeing a $30 billion state spending plan; and a college professor for twenty years, their eyes opened wide. Instantly, I could tell that I became less of a guinea pig to them.

Some of the judges shuffled in their seats, sat up, turned to one another, then looked me in the eye for the first time and with strange smiles began to pepper me with more academic questions. Now, the questions were about solutions to poverty, unemployment, crime, violence and recidivism. Now, we were partners in the war against crime. Now, we were fighting for reform in the criminal justice system. Once they knew my former status, I was elevated in their opinion; I was more human, more on their level.

"You were a Mayor for twenty years?" A woman judge asked. "As Mayor, what programs did you offer to thwart young men from going to jail?" another judge asked. "You speak about recidivism? Did your programs work?" "As a Camp teacher, what have you learned?" "Are there any recommendations you would make?"

Thinking back to my meetings with the inmates' ad hoc board of directors (and with the unit manager and warden in attendance), I kept my responses away from personal, hostile and negative remarks as they had suggested. I felt a need to tell these important Judges the truth about prison life. I felt obligated to take serious advantage of this opportunity, and not be confrontational, but cooperative instead.

I told them that they did not know camp life. I mentioned that people had told me to bring my tennis racquet and golf clubs. They told me that the camp is loaded with white-collar criminals, doctors, lawyers, accountants, politicians and financial people, all non-violent. I was told that these inmates are no threat to the community. "It's a country club," former inmates had told me.

"Well," I told the federal judges, "You should take some time and visit the Petersburg FCC camp dormitory." I told them that the camp I knew was overcrowded, approaching "warehouse" status and predominantly occupied by street level crack cocaine users and dealers. Many were high school dropouts requiring education, apprenticeship and skill development programs to address an alarming rate of recidivism.

I let them know that it was my opinion that every inmate leaving Petersburg would benefit from a high school diploma, or GED, or learn a marketable skill to compete in our local and global economy. I suggested that BOP develop a strong reentry program for inmates returning to society. One inmate had robbed a bank the day he was released so that he would be sent back to Petersburg; he had stated he had no family, no money and no place to stay. He wanted to spend the rest of his life in prison.

I questioned the long minimum and maximum sentencing guidelines for drug charges when many persons who had committed murder faced less time in jail. I mentioned the political disparity between sentencing for crack cocaine versus powder cocaine; and the evils of selective enforcement, destroying families and the failure of Congress to address this wrong.

I reminded the judges that the 20-to-life drug sentences all started due to the sad and tragic death of Len Bias on June 19, 1986. I emphasized the need for shorter sentences, 65% mandatory time as opposed to the current 87%, and consideration for non-violent inmates to be assigned to work sites in their local community. The government could reduce the expense of room and board and other related costs of housing non-violent criminals. I suggested that probation officers refer violators back to minimum or maximum prison facilities if the inmate did not adhere to program rules and regulations.

"There is also a need for incentive programs leading to more prison furloughs and the granting of maximum, not minimum, halfway house or home confinement," I said. My prosecutor and the probation office had angrily refused to grant me permission to visit my family at Christmas. I let the judges know that I strongly believed that inmates should be rewarded for good work ethics.

"Perhaps a report card can be kept to grade inmate's performance in apprenticeship programs, and maintenance of sanitary areas. While no guarantees can be given, at least consideration for good behavior might be an inducement. Presently there are no rewards or incentives to be a model prisoner. Only 'snitchers' are rewarded," I told them.

At the end of our informal exchange, I was most happy when the federal judges decided to visit our dorm and witness for themselves the severe case of overcrowding. Our unit manager tripped and fell over himself rushing to stop a judge from approaching my bed. The unfazed judge, standing erect, asked him if something was wrong. The manager was too embarrassed to reply; he just straightened up and rearranged his clothes. The judge then shocked me by saying with a pleasant smile, "I, also, attended the 1972 Democratic convention in Florida; good luck to you, Sharpe." I wondered what her title and status might have been way back then, now here she was standing before me as a federal judge.

Another highlight of my camp experience at Petersburg was to be granted community custody and being assigned to the "Back to Reality program." Our select group was allowed to visit local churches, courthouses and the Fort Lee Army base to speak to troubled youth, hoping to help them turn their lives around and avoid possible detention later in life. Not only was it exciting to leave the prison facility, it was even more exciting being well received by the students who accepted our message of avoiding mistakes that could lead to incarceration. "Prisons are miserable places; stay in school; respect your parents; hang with the right peer group and take advantage of a world that is full of opportunities just waiting for you to seize the moment," we advised.

I stressed to these young people, mostly Black and Latino, how fortunate they were to be living during a time when we had an African American President and Attorney General and a Hispanic who had recently been appointed to the Supreme Court. Within their reach, grants and scholarships for higher education were available. "Just think of the opportunities that lie ahead for you," I told them.

We all mentioned the fact that prison is not a good place to be. "Let no one tell you that prison life is fun; it's a horrible experience and degrading to individuals. It's a place where only the strong survive and where you can become a punk for other inmates to abuse financially, physically or sexually." We told them about the racial and class systems that exist in prison. These systems are quite visible at mealtime where Blacks, Whites, Hispanics, Asians, Muslims and the elite white collar criminals tend to sit together. Prison is not a hospitable environment. You simply can't trust inmates to be honest with you. I told the students that even old men like me are sentenced to prison where there is room for the young as well. "Age is not a determining factor," I told them.

One inmate, affectionately called "Daddy," who had been in jail for ten years of a 15 year sentence for selling drugs, shocked the young people by removing and waving his artificial limb in the air shouting, "Even the handicap go to prison. It's all about the choices you make in life," Daddy said. The Fort Lee Army Base conference room, filled with students, parents and army officers, fell silent. Daddy had made his point, having lost his leg in a train accident as a youth. Being handicapped did not excuse "Daddy" from serving a federal prison term. He was certainly physically able. He played every sport in camp and was a role model for younger offenders.

We were driven to the youth meetings by our unit manager or counselor who participated as well. Soon our names were in the press, and we were likened to the "Scared Straight" programs of the late 1970's. We emphasized that parents should set an example and stay involved in the lives of their children. "Our youth can't raise themselves," I sermonized to the parents. The local newspaper praised our efforts, convincing our unit manager to expand the program. Petersburg FCC was giving back to the community and had every reason to be proud.

I became a better listener while I was incarcerated; having learned that keeping your mouth closed could save your life sometimes. Oftentimes I listened to highly emotional debates on an inmate's perceived innocence or guilt. "I didn't commit any crime." "My lawyer was a joke and sold me out." "Man, the feds forced people to testify against me."

From my lower bunk at camp 407 I could observe, from the window, the visitors coming to our Petersburg FCC low and camp facilities. Unbeknown to the visitors, especially the women, hundreds of starving and lustful male eyes were watching them, sometimes making obscene remarks about female visitors. I listened to these remarks saying nothing, but observing that male chauvinism locked behind real and unreal bars was on display.

Some of the visitors were elderly, some obviously ill, and some handicapped using canes and walkers or wheelchairs. I found it rather painful to watch people bent over with muscle spasm taking half steps at a time, or being assisted to make the arduous journey from the prison visitor's parking lot to the main building or to the camp visitor's room. It was even more painful to me to have to listen to the endless chatter of inmates who never seemed to consider what our incarceration was doing to our loved ones.

While we debated our status in prison, many inmates neglected to think of the hardship our incarceration, notwithstanding our innocence or guilt had placed on our spouses, family members, loved ones, friends and supporters; especially those that were elderly, ill or handicapped. Those loved ones who, despite our guilt or innocence, were willing and determined to visit and demonstrate their uncompromising love and support for us, despite the hardships and pitfalls, were heroes as far as I was concerned.

Some who made the trip were turned away for being five minutes late; some were turned away because of improper dress (no hats allowed inside, no shades/or sexy dress attire); others because they were not on the visitor's list or too many (unless pre-approved we were limited to four) in number. The overflow would have to wait in the car. Still they kept coming. Perhaps their reasoning is found in the song, *Love is a Many Splendored Thing.*

These visitors were our true heroes. They were like the words in the song by Bette Midler, *You Are the Wind Beneath My Wings.* They are special and precious because so many of the people that we had helped, or our so-called friends, never took the time to pen a postcard or letter; those who disappeared and showed no interest during our hour of need; those who developed amnesia or adopted the philosophy, "out of sight, out of mind."

Of course, once we are free again, have money again, these same people will resurface and be in our faces asking, "Hey where have you been?" With our mugs posted all over the BOP website giving every possible piece of information about us, how can anyone not know where we were? In that instance we would be wise to adopt the words from a great musical score by Duke Ellington, "I sent for you yesterday, now here you come today." Hopefully they will get the message. Unfortunately, it's when you are experiencing bad times, or in prison, that you learn who your true friends are.

Notwithstanding my innocence, I did not blow up, act disrespectfully in court or hold press conferences attacking the racially biased prosecution. I followed the letter of the law and filed my appeal within the required ten days. I did not request to remain free until the ruling of the Appellate Court. I decided to go directly to prison and continue to communicate with my appeals lawyer while trying to help troubled young men in prison. From this prison experience I had some learning to do. I know that God has a master plan for all of us.

Petersburg Camp reminds me of a poem written by Robert Frost, *The Road Not Taken*. The poem starts out like this: "Two roads diverged in a forest; we took the one less traveled, and that has made all the difference in our lives." I'm sure that if given the opportunity again, most inmates will travel the regular highways and byways of life as opposed to the least (life of crime) traveled. Their experiment is over.

At camp the inmates respectfully called me "Mayor" and I called myself an inmate. We all wore the same number of letters on our shirt and pants. I reminded them that we were the same in status, and yet I thought how far apart we are. At their youthful age, forty-eight years earlier, in the same green khaki pants and shirt I had been sent to camp at Fort Benning, Georgia. I had a college degree under my belt. I was a member of the United States Army preparing to leave for Germany and the Berlin East-West border crisis. I wore the same khaki uniform yet for a different purpose. Then, I wore a nametag as opposed to a number. If the military draft had not ended perhaps many of these inmates would have worn a nametag and not a number.

We need to end the practice of allowing egotistical, career building and politically active prosecutors to abuse their authority by selectively and vindictively prosecuting innocent men and women. We need to stop them from embracing and practicing the "You can indict and convict a ham sandwich" philosophy. This constitutes an inhumane and savage practice that has made our prisons overcrowded, costing billions of dollars, a loss in human productivity and a breakdown in the family structure. Until we develop a means of ending prosecutorial abuses we should immediately reform our sentencing guidelines.

There is no reason that non-violent Petersburg inmates presently working in carpentry, the kitchen, garden, paint shop, and garage, electrical and plumbing shops could not perform the same services in their local community, thereby saving the federal and local governments millions of dollars. During my tenure as Mayor of Newark we used local non-violent state prisoners to clean up debris, vacant lots and our waterfront to reduce our municipal budget. Interestingly, the inmates enjoyed working outside and we appreciated their work. There were no incidents; it was a win-win situation for all.

By keeping these non-violent offenders at home, caring for their families, especially those with young children who need parental guidance, the government would not have to bear the cost of room and board, medical, recreation and other BOP services. Any inmate who abuses this privilege can always be sent back to a waiting cell behind a razor wire topped fence. Clearly it's time to put families back together, men back to work and to stimulate the economy. It's time to rethink our draconian selective sentencing laws. It's time to reform our criminal justice system.

From my personal experience, I wish to warn young men to stay out of trouble, stay out of harm's way and be careful who you hang out with. Many young men are sent to prison because of what their "so-called friends" did or for being in the wrong place at the wrong time as opposed to actually committing a crime themselves. Some say "We are what we eat;" and I say "You are who you hang out with." Please no self-serving, macho rhetoric about prison life not scaring you. It might just kill you.

I know that I am not the first to tell our youth that there is nothing glamorous or macho about being locked up in prison with or without bars. It's still prison, it's still restricted living under strict rules and regulations;

it's still personal freedom denied. Prison is still a compartment of hell. For those who dream great dreams about your future, it might be wise to learn the words in Langston Hughes' poem, "What happens to a dream deferred?"

"Does it dry up like a raisin in the sun?
Or fester like a sore — And then run?
Does it stink like rotten meat?
Or crust and sugar over—like a syrupy sweet?
Maybe it just sags like a heavy load
Or does it explode?"

Beware young folks; if you commit a crime your dreams will be deferred. You will place an unnecessary hardship on your family and loved ones. Stay out of jail "by any means necessary." Place a value on your freedom.

CHAPTER TWENTY ONE

The Appeal 2008

"The Unjust Verdict"

Eloquently stated by Dr. Martin Luther King, Jr., "An injustice anywhere is a threat to justice everywhere," is a clear message that we should seek to correct obvious wrongdoings. Justice was not "blind impartiality" at my trial. A wrongful conviction can be addressed in a court of law. "Federal rules of appellate procedures require a defendant to file a notice of appeal within ten days after the district court has imposed a sentence," so states the Georgetown Law Journal, 2008, page 820.

I had been found guilty on five counts of an honest services statute, which I had lacked the legal authority to commit; a grave injustice was enacted by a jury not of my peers. A jury made up of ten suburban whites and two "wanna-be-Whites," some of whom had made up their minds about my guilt the first day they entered the courtroom; thereby opting to sleep through the trial.

The verdict was reminiscent of Harper Lee's Pulitzer Prize winning novel, *To Kill a Mockingbird*. On July 29, 2008 Federal District Court Judge, William J. Martini, sentenced me to 27 months in prison. The overreaching prosecution had demanded a twenty-year sentence with the hope that at age 69, "Sharpe just might die in prison," so stated by a gleeful U.S. Attorney, Christopher Christie.

After my sentencing I asked for further clarification. I was told to speak to my pretrial sentencing officer if I had any questions. I learned that the probation office had already forwarded my records to the Federal Bureau of Prisons (BOP).

I was mad, angry and confused over the biased conduct of the prosecution, the premature judging, and the inattentiveness of the jury and the failure of the judge to grant a directed verdict of acquittal. The prosecution had admitted in its brief that there was no evidence that I had personally impacted the South Ward Redevelopment Plan's decision-making process. My co-defendant, Tamika Riley had paid the same price as everyone else. I did not assist her or receive any economic benefit, the city of Newark did not lose any money and there was no evidence of any deception, fraud or chicanery on my part.

The only witness whose testimony suggested a relationship between me and Ms. Riley came from my disgruntled secretary, Rosemarie Posella, who had perjured herself and gotten away with it when she changed her testimony to suggest that Ms. Riley was my girlfriend. Police officer Derrick Foster, had refuted Rosemarie's flip flop statement by testifying, "I did not think that they were boyfriend and girlfriend." *So which government witness do we believe?* I asked myself. Rosemarie, the snake, lying through her teeth with head bobbing for affect, apparently carried the day.

Judge Martini had called it, "A victimless crime," and had said, "James did not receive any economic benefit and the city did not lose any money. I think most of his conduct was conduct that was inherent in the very nature of his position as Mayor. There wasn't much in this case that suggested that he asked anyone to do something, you know, to not even have her apply; not to do anything." P 136 L 8-12.

Then why am I being sent to a federal prison, I asked myself, receiving no answer. *This is crazy. The criminal justice system is pure charades. Who can put on the best show?* I had to seek justice. I had to appeal.

My pretrial sentencing supervisor, Ms. Annette Gautier, was out of the office, so I was referred to Ms. Heather Maloney, a counselor in the same office. When I entered her office, she was smiling from ear to ear, as though she had just won the lottery. She asked if I was pleased with Judge Martini's sentence. Before she could finish, I twisted my face, sat down and turned my head to directly face her. Seeing my expression, she immediately changed her expression. With eyes wide open she said, "Well the government was asking for twenty years and Judge

Martini only gave you 27 months; didn't he show some real courage?" She started to smile again. "Don't you agree," she asked?

Regaining my composure, and doing my best to be respectful and polite to a person who had treated me with utmost professionalism, I took a deep breath and let it out slowly.

"But, I'm innocent of all the bogus charges. This is America, I should not have to spend one day in a federal prison. He should have thrown the case out. He should have rejected the decision of a biased, sleeping jury who never knew what a conspiracy was and never knew what form of government Newark operated under."

While Ms. Maloney listened intently, I spilled out all of the inconsistencies from my trial. "The government lied in court," I concluded, exhausted from my tirade. All of my statements had fallen upon deaf ears. There were no more questions or talk about my sentence. We just stared at each other. I could hear the wind outside her window. She offered no more smiles. She had retreated from my verbal defense salvo.

I broke the silence by telling her that I was going to appeal the verdict. Again, there was no response. I then asked Ms. Maloney if she could tell me, from her experience and knowledge, how many defendants appealed their guilty verdicts?

She thought for a while with her head down, looking at her desk. Then, she looked up, gave a friendly smile and said, "Very few."

I asked, "With so many convictions why so few?"

She leaned back in her chair, and with a very serious look said, "By the time defendants pay their legal fees, court fines, possible restitution and other expenses, most do not have any funds left to hire an appeal lawyer. No money would be my answer," she said.

I knew that she was right. I had just spent more than $800,000 only to be found guilty, and my lawyers wanted another $200,000 for the appeal. Lawyers want their money more than they want your freedom. I had ten days in which to file the appeal and having sent no check, I had not heard from my trial lawyers. They were demanding a third down and a signed contract for the balance immediately. Both Tom Ashley and Alan Zegas went in hiding and became unavailable until I could come up with the money. My repeated telephone calls to them fell upon deaf ears. I had to do something, time was running out.

The next day after my visit to Ms. Maloney's office I felt the need for some exercise to relax my mind and body. I grabbed my workout bag and drove to the local YMWCA where I had a gold club membership. Bally's Fitness Center on Highway 22, where I had another membership, was an hour's drive away and there was too much traffic.

As I entered the towering downtown YMWCA, I experienced an exhilarating feeling. I attributed it to being in a friendly and relaxed environment and seeing familiar faces. The people here looked physically fit, robust, energized and they exhibited wholesome attitudes. They were real people who appeared not to have a care in the world; reminding me of the Broadway musical "Gypsy," where "Everything is coming up roses."

"Hey Sharpe, glad to see you," was the chorus line from one patron after another as I walked the length of the entrance hallway to the locker-room. I changed quickly into my Wilson cotton sweat suit, Nike shorts and sneakers and entered the crowded weight room. Again, I was greeted by friendly faces and friendly hellos, "Hi Sharpe, where have you been man? You got to work those muscles;" followed by the obligatory handshake and hug. I was feeling better already. What a difference a new environment can make, especially after leaving the federal courthouse.

After some stationary bicycling, light weight lifting exercises, abdominal crunches, pushups, and some isotonic stretching exercises, I took a warm shower. Then I did ten laps in the pool and went into the steam room to relax.

The fitness gang was going through the daily sports news and gossip. "Hey Sharpe, we're so sorry about that crazy verdict!" "Those suburban jurors must be nuts." "After all you have done for Newark!" We still do not know what you were found guilty of, politicians recommend people all the time; where's the crime?" "I read she paid the same price as everyone else." "Hey, and 'getting laid' can't be a crime or all of us would be in jail, they would have to turn schools into prisons for the number of offenders." Each comment was followed by a chorus of laughter. "Judge Martini should know that; he was a politician himself," said police detective, Tyrone Singletary. "He talked tough during the trial but in the end Judge Martini was scared of Christie too," a stranger added.

I interrupted their heartfelt cries of sympathy and blurted out my concern about my appeal deadline and having not heard from my lawyers. "They want more money." I said. "I can't miss this deadline," I cried. I am in a box.

A brother, from Jersey City, whom I have always admired for his carved out muscles, six pack abs, and "Mr. T" look, was enjoying the steam with a towel covering his head. With sweat dripping from his Joe Louis granite like head, he removed his towel, sat up and said, "Sharpe, you don't need no lawyer to file an appeal notice. You can write down your case number on toilet paper, pay the fee and file yourself. They will accept it. Trust me. It's no big deal. Lawyers just want to make some money that's the bottom line. They are looking at you as a cash cow, old man," he laughed. "They are holding you hostage, forget those money bags," he said.

Just to make sure I heard him right, I sarcastically asked "How would you know? Who told you?"

The brother, now standing erect in the steam room like a mighty man of valor, like an Adonis, said, "Because I spent fifteen years in a federal prison. I been there and done that," he said. "If there's anything I know it's how to file an appeal."

Later, while in prison, I would think of this brother while working on my own appeal. I could flashback and picture him at the inmate's weight pile, with his abdominal and pectoral muscles on display, lifting weights for fifteen years while incarcerated. I could visualize him bench pressing four hundred pounds; warming up with 100 pushups, sit ups and pull ups. He was the real deal. I thanked him for giving me that piece of advice before I began serving my sentence.

It was another lesson for me to learn that you never know who you are talking to. You never know who can help you in life. I had pegged the brother as a former All American football player or an athlete, not a former jailbird. I certainly never thought he would know anything about the federal court system.

The next day I walked back into the same federal courthouse with more confidence, took the elevator to the same fourth floor, walked toward the same courtroom and this time I entered the federal court clerk's office on the opposite side of the hall. I did not use toilet paper as the brother had suggested; I simply turned in an 8" x 10" sheet of white paper stating that I wished to file an appeal, gave my case number and paid a filing fee of $450.00. The clerk, without looking up and unemotionally took my money, stamped my application and gave me a receipt.

I had made the ten-day deadline. I did not need to pay a lawyer to file. I remembered the old saying "He who represents himself, has a fool for a lawyer." I was no lawyer and no fool; I needed an appeals lawyer to argue my case. Feeling good about myself, I sought the law partner of the legendary, but now ill, Raymond A. Brown, Alan Dexter Bowman, Esq. Bowman, who shared office space with Brown, was a renowned litigant with his own practice. I wanted him to handle the appeal.

My first question to Alan was, "Why should I hire you rather than keep my trial lawyers who now know every detail of my six weeks trial, they have all of the trial laws, evidence and testimony in their heads?" I thought the question would embarrass him. I would soon learn that it did not; in fact, he perhaps had anticipated that question.

Showing no emotion, Alan looked me straight in the eye and said, "Because a good appeals lawyer will first evaluate the conduct of your trial lawyers to determine errors they made in representing you as well. Sharpe, many appeals are won based on errors by the trial lawyer in representing their client, as well as issues of insufficient evidence, the law, at trial testimony or mere prosecutorial errors," he had said. "Do you think trial lawyers are going to admit that they made mistakes?"

I had no answer. I only knew that there were many appeal issues which my lawyers had put forth; issues which could warrant a new trial or a directed verdict of acquittal. Unlike so many other defendants who had been railroaded by the prosecution and didn't have the money to challenge them with an appeal, I would take on the United States of America even if it put me on welfare. They had ruined my retirement and my life goals. U.S Attorney Christopher Christie had framed an innocent African American man in his desire to run for governor to bolster his GOP resume.

I would seek justice. My appeals attorney and I would raise the questions that would not go away. We went over the facts again and again outlining them sequentially. I could not let it go; I could not let the verdict stand. I wanted justice.

After the jury returned a verdict of guilty on April 16, 2008, the defense offered a motion that the United States adduced insufficient proof that the appellant participated in any form of a scheme to defraud, or in any fashion failed to provide honest services to the public, and asked for a judgment of acquittal on counts 1-5, which Federal District Court Judge William J. Martini promptly denied. However, throughout the trial he had ruled as follows:

Judge Martini: "No, no, I'm fully aware that there was no evidence that suggested that defendant James provided a lower price for Tamika Riley for obtaining these properties." 7/28/08 p. 53 L 2-4.

Judge Martini: "I think most of his conduct was conduct that was inherent in the very nature of his position as Mayor. There wasn't much in this case that suggested that he asked anyone to do something, you know, to not even have her apply; not to do anything." P 136 L 8-12

Judge Martini: To the government: "But don't talk in terms of the history of corruption unless you've proven that, you didn't prove that in this courtroom as far as I am concerned." 7/29/08, P-99-100, L-22-25; P-26 L-1.

Judge Martini: "I don't want to hear these generalizations about corrupt administration, all powerful, didn't do anything good, I don't want to hear it; you did not prove that in this courtroom." 7/29/08 P 100 L-1-5.

Judge Martini: "I had the benefit of hearing this trial. "This is not a bribery offense; this is not an offense where a public official was taking money directly to be influenced to approve some land deal or to award some contracts. And in this Court's opinion, that's a more serious offense than what happened here." 7/29/08 P 139, L1-11.

Judge Martini: Speaking to assistant prosecutor Phillip Kwon; "Kwon the SWRP was not indicted. I don't see how you could indict the program; and whether we like it or not, the SWRP helped develop the South Ward."

Judge Martini: "The City of Newark did not lose any money in this. In fact, these properties were put back on the tax roll within the same amount of time-nobody alleged there was a delay in developing them-and they got back on the tax roll and the City did receive taxable funds from these properties." (SA 1248)

Judge Martini: "There was no direct monetary benefit to defendant James." 7/29/08 P 135, L 19-20.

Judge Martini:"I know why we're here, because I found last week, we're here because there was a breach of honest services, and the failure of the Mayor to disclose his relationship while awarding contracts is a "deprivation of honest services".....I know a little bit about public service and I know that that's wrong." 7/29/08 P 30, L8-14.

Summing up Judge Martini's rulings during the trial and based on the lack of evidence provided by the prosecutor as well as the favorable testimony presented, I should never have been convicted. Now I would have to go through the appeals process in order to continue my pursuit of justice.

Judge Martini had been correct when he stated that the United States argued all counts 1-5 as honest service crimes which were before the Supreme Court. Also the United States did not adduce sufficient evidence to underpin any conviction of the various forms of fraud alleged in counts one through five. Their charges were refuted by the law, evidence and testimony of both government and defense witnesses and the trial judge.

These trial and post trial issues would now become the challenge facing Alan Bowman in his appeal. Sporting a light beard and with hawkish eyes he sat ramrod straight in his leather chair. Finally, he smiled and said, "It's an impressive list. Let's go back to your first question of why should you hire me? I believe that I'm one of the best appeal lawyers in the state," he said without a trace of emotion, a matter of fact statement. Bowman was steely eyed, knowledgeable and tough. He knew case law. He was all business and unflappable. He was a no nonsense guy.

"Will you represent me," I asked?

"Sharpe, let's go to work," he said. "I plan to stab directly and mortally at the legal and at-trial deficiencies clear and concise; from what I'm reading we can win against this injustice, we must tell the true story of what happened. There was no conspiracy, corruption or fraud; the government did not prove its case. I don't see how your trial lawyers lost this case."

I still believed that there was a Chief Justice "God Almighty" himself and a Supreme Court below him. If the law, evidence and at court testimony had proven me guilty, I would have had no recourse but to accept an honest verdict and serve my time. However, this was a bias and political decision divorced of any fair play or justice. I had been used and abused to advance a political career. I made a governor. I had been lynched modern day style. My appeal was on.

I had to report to Petersburg on September 15, 2008 so my appeal was left in the capable hands of Alan Bowman. We communicated by mail as he reviewed the trial transcript, testimony of witnesses, spoke with my trial lawyers and researched the law under which I was convicted. He requested several extensions before filing to make sure that he had all of the facts for a strong rebuttal based on the law.

On June 19, 2009 Alan Bowman filed an appeal of the guilty verdict to the U.S. Court of Appeals for the Third Circuit. At the beginning of 2010, after exchanging briefs (defense & government) and an oral hearing, we were asked to wait for the decision of the Supreme Court in the Jeffrey Skilling v. United States case on honest services fraud, 18 U.S.C. & 1346.

On June 24, 2010 the United States Supreme Court issued its ruling (a vote of 9-0) that limited the honest service fraud statue to cover only bribery and kickback schemes, which was not present in my case. They unanimously stated that the law against "honest services" fraud was too vague to constitute a crime unless a bribe or kickback was involved.

I should have been a free man. Every other defendant in America had their honest services charges dropped. Here in New Jersey Mayor Vas of Perth Amboy and former chairman of the Democratic Party in Bergen County, Joseph A. Ferriero, both had their honest services charges dropped.

Instead of my freedom, On June 28, 2010 the United States Court of Appeals for The Third Circuit, asked both the defense and government to file contemporaneous memorandums not to exceed ten pages on the effect of the Supreme Court's decision in Skilling v. United States, on my case before them. I thought it very strange for the U.S. Appeals Court to ask that my defense team and the government interpret the law; I thought that was the purpose of the Appeals Court, especially with a Supreme Court ruling staring them in the face.

On September 16, 2010 the Third Circuit Court of Appeals, being political itself, reluctantly dropped only count 5 of my conviction whereas it was specifically named "honest services" and confirmed my guilt on the other four counts. I perceived this as a grave miscarriage of justice, whereas the District Court had ruled that all of the counts were argued as a "deprivation of honest services." Then in a strange turn around, one month later, on October 21, 2010 the Third Circuit issued an order amending its opinion issued on September 16, 2010. The order stated in part:

Page 15, first sentence of the first full paragraph which reads:

"We cannot be certain of how the jury utilized the broad definition of an honest services violation given in connection with the entire conspiracy charge."

Shall read:

"Defendants have met their burden of showing a responsible probability that the jury utilized the broad definition of an honest services violation given in connection with the entire conspiracy charge."

Here they reversed their ruling. Again, I should have been a free man, but Christie's influence had even reached the Third Circuit Court of Appeals and continued to allow him to punish an innocent man. They, too, did not want to embarrass a former U.S. Attorney, now a sitting governor. This injustice continued to grow and multiply.

While serving my time at Petersburg FCC, I received a letter from a Newark municipal employee informing me that a member of the jury that had convicted me, had two parents working for Mayor Cory Booker, who had requested that I be investigated and who wanted me convicted. "Mayor Booker wanted you out of the way," he wrote. He apologized for the late notification because of name changes due to marriage.

I immediately notified my attorney. His post-trial investigation confirmed that at the time of my trial the juror in question, during "voir dire" examination (court questionnaire), was untruthful and concealed that both of his parents were employed by the City of Newark. He had also stated affirmatively that none of his immediate family had businesses or other dealings with the City of Newark or were in any way familiar with the Mayor, and had never participated in a campaign for or against the Mayor.

A review of records showed that both of the juror's parents were hired by me and both had supported me politically. Both parents were now working for the current Mayor, who was firing, laying-off, demoting and harassing my former supporters and contributors as an act of retaliation.

One of my supporters, Lucy-Garcia Brown, who had been a Senior Administrative Analyst in the Office of the Mayor under my administration, had been immediately transferred to the sanitation department and required to sit at a filthy, empty desk, devoid of a computer or any office supplies. The current Mayor hired several of his campaign workers to replace her, giving them her title. Lucy, I heard, went ballistic.

This quiet dignified lady now became an army of one against this injustice. She filed an "Act of retaliation" complaint against Mayor Booker in Superior Court and before the NJ Department of Personnel Merit Board Most Notable Cases dated March 28, 2007, page 65. The result was a ruling demanding that the City of Newark return her to her rightful title or face fines immediately (DOP Docket No. 2007-935).

The juror's parents could have faced a similar fate had he had answered voir dire questions correctly. Their jobs with the city would, without a doubt, have been in jeopardy from the newly-elected administration if they were known supporters or contributors to my campaign. It is a lugubrious possibility that the juror in question agreed to convict me on the mistaken belief that his action would somehow enhance his parents' job security or be viewed by the new administration as a demonstration of loyalty.

Had the defense known of these lengthy employment and political relationships, a request to excuse the juror for cause would have been made. At a minimum, a peremptory challenge would have been exercised to strike the juror.

From prison I badgered Alan Bowman to immediately file an appeal for jury misconduct. His response was that we had to wait until our first appeal was ruled on. By this time I had served eighteen months in prison and was scheduled to be released to Toler Halfway House in Newark on April 6, 2010.

When I stepped off the Greyhound Bus from Richmond, Virginia more than 500 supporters carrying signs and noisemakers greeted me at historic Newark Penn Station for a resounding welcome home party. I was in tears meeting my family and supporters. Reverend Ron Christian, of Christian Love Baptist Church, rushed me to Toler House where the staff was already complaining that I was late.

I would spend only about a month at Toler House before being released for home confinement until the end of my sentence, which would not occur until August 30, 2010. I was only allowed to leave home for work release at Christian Love Baptist Church and to attend church services on Sunday. I was also allowed to spend a few hours with my Attorney, Alan Bowman, who was preparing my second appeal by filing a motion for a new trial under Federal Rule of Criminal Procedure 33 (b) (1), grounded on "newly discovered evidence, jury misconduct."

I was released from home confinement on August 30, 2010. Alan and I worked diligently to file the appeal to the District Court on "Jury Misconduct" by April 18, 2011. After responding that our appeal was for good cause on April 20, 2011 and receiving briefs from both sides, Federal District Court Judge William J. Martini on October 25, 2011, denied us a new trial and even an evidentiary hearing. He stated "Maybe the juror was confused with the questions during voir dire," defending the incorrect and misleading answers of the juror.

Bowman was shocked by this decision and filed a third brief on April 22, 2012 before the Third Circuit Court of Appeals. Following another review of both briefs we were notified that the court had ordered a hearing before them scheduled for February 11, 2013. That hearing was cancelled; the overwhelming evidence in my favor (numerous irrefutable copies of campaign checks written out to me by the juror's parents, who even participated in my 2002 defeat of Cory Booker; the juror had lied under oath) was ignored. The system sided with Judge Martini. We then appealed to the U.S. Supreme court which refused to hear our case, again protecting the flawed "old boys" judicial system. Justice was never blind, never impartial and the deck was stacked. Apparently they were all members of the same country club; they knew my name and the hue of my skin.

CHAPTER TWENTY TWO

My Legacy

"Whatever you do for the least of
my people, you do for me."
Matthews 25:45

I recall the 1957 hit song by Johnny Mathis and its lyric, "It's not for me to say you'll love me. It's not for me to say you will always care." Well, it's not for me to write my legacy. I am simply following the advice of former Newark West Ward Councilwoman, Reverend Dr. Mamie Bridgeforth, who demanded that I write my own biography so that the bias press will at least have the truth before them. "Sharpe, don't you leave here without telling your story of achievement from the outhouse to the White House," she would whisper in my ear while playfully pinching my arm. So enclosed herein this memoir is my road map, or once again, in the words of Robert Frost, *The Road not Taken*.

Historically speaking, through the grace of God as an educator and public servant I traveled the world and crossed many great oceans seeking answers to the problems facing our local and global economy. I served as a Newark school teacher, college administrator and professor at Essex County College for twenty years (1967-1986, 2006-2007); Mayor of Newark for twenty years (1986-2006); Member of the Newark Municipal Council for sixteen years (1970-1986); New Jersey State Senator for nine years (1999-2008; United States Army Veteran (1958-60); community activist (Past President of the United Community Corporation Area Board 9 and President of the Weequahic Community Council); Athlete (tennis, baseball, skiing, soccer and swimming); family man and dreamer while serving thirty eight uninterrupted years in public office (1970-2008).

James the Educator

My educational training includes receiving a B.S degree from Montclair State University; M.S. degree from Springfield College; 6th year at Washington State University (WSU); and additional graduate studies at Columbia and Rutgers Universities. I was awarded honorary doctorate degrees from Montclair State University and Drew University in New Jersey.

Prior to becoming Mayor of the City of Newark in the state of New Jersey, I served as the first African American athletic director in the State of New Jersey at Essex County College (1967-86), where we won numerous conferences, regional and national championships. In 1972, at the Penn Relays (we had to sue to run in the event that accepted only four year colleges) our sprint medley team set a national record in besting the nation's most prestigious four year colleges. We were called "Champions without facilities." During my tenure at ECC I was honored as professor and administrator of the year. I took a leave of absence in 1986 to serve as Mayor and returned July 1, 2006 serving as Director of its Urban Institute until July 1, 2007.

In 1970 I served as the first African American Vice President and President of the Garden State Athletic Conference (GSAC), NCAA Region 19, presiding over all junior college athletics in the states of New Jersey, Maryland and Delaware.

Prior to my employment at Essex County College, I was an elementary school teacher, a physical education teacher and coach in the Newark Public Schools where I met my wife, Mary. In 1960 I was accepted as a graduate teaching assistant in the Department of Physiology at Springfield College, under the tutelage of the renowned Dr. Peter V. Karpovich.

I also served as a teaching and research assistant in physiology at Springfield College and Washington State University (1960-1963), where I provided technical assistance in publishing "Electrogoniometric Study of Locomotion" and "Some Athletic Movement," as well as "Energy Cost and Comfort of Walking in The Direct Molded Sole Boot with Anti-Personnel Mine Shank," with research physiologists Dr. Peter V. Karpovich and Dr. Phillip D. Gollnick (1960-63).

Service in the United States Army in Germany (USAEUR)

Prior to becoming a teaching assistant and graduate student at Springfield College and Washington State University, I served in the United States Army in Germany (USAREUR), where I was one of only ten soldiers out of 10,000 who won the "Expert Infantry Badge" (EIB) and was honorably discharged in 1960.

James the last elected official from Newark's historical 1970 Black and Puerto Rican Convention, and the last of the civil rights era elected officials from the 1970s.

My political career began when I was first "selected and elected" to be the candidate for South Ward Councilman as part of Newark's historical, November 14-16th 1970 Black and Puerto Rican Convention. I was part of the "Community's Choice Team," headed by civil engineer, Kenneth A. Gibson. I never dreamed of becoming or wanted to be a politician. I merely answered the call of the people who knocked on my door and asked me to participate in the convention.

On that historical day, July 1, 1970, out of the seven candidates (Ken Gibson, Donald Tucker, Earl Harris, C. Theodore Pinckney, Ramon Aneses, AI Oliver, Dennis Westbrook and myself) on the Community's Choice slate, four won. Ken Gibson was sworn in as the first Black mayor of a major northeast city, Newark; Earl Harris was elected Councilman-at-Large; Dennis A. Westbrooks would be Central Ward Councilman, and I was elected Councilman of the South Ward.

In 1999 with the retirement of Mayor Richard Arrington, Jr., the first Black mayor from Birmingham, Alabama, (serving from 1979 to 1999), I was the last of the civil rights era elected officials from the 70's still in office.

As Councilman Sharpe James

- I defeated a field of 15 candidates in 1970, winning in a runoff election against incumbent Councilman-at-Large Leon Ewing, who decided to run for the South Ward seat.
- I easily won re-election in 1974 with 80% of the votes.

- I was the first ward councilman to run unopposed for re-election in 1978.
- I was the first ward councilman to be elected Councilman-at-Large and the top vote getter in 1982.
- In 1986 I was the first Councilman to be elected Mayor.
- I was the first Mayor to run unopposed in 1990.

Councilman James Accepted A Jail Sentence Rather Than Vote For Newark Revaluation In 1976

I will always cherish the memory, and honor the courage of five Newark Council Members (Sharpe James, Donald Tucker, Hank Martinez, Anthony Carrino and Marie Villani) who defied a 1976 court order and accepted a jail term, rather than vote for revaluation which would have had a devastating effect on the already overburdened Newark taxpayers. We stood in solidarity for the citizens of Newark, putting their interests ahead of our personal welfare thus delaying revaluation for more than two decades.

No other elected Newark Council had demonstrated such a love of community and citizens, sacrificing themselves for the good of the people they represented. Our stand-up courage and fight eventually led to a "tax increase moratorium" granted by the New Jersey State Legislature resulting in property tax relief for the citizens of Newark.

Newark Had A Sharpe Change in 1986
Under James' Exemplary Leadership

On January 25, 1986, a *New York Times* editorial asked the question, "Who Can Lead Newark?" If elected, I had promised "A Sharpe Change." Well, after twenty years as Mayor and nine years as State Senator, I was willing to accept the opinion of the New Jersey Conference of Mayors, who named me "Mayor of the Year" in 2001. This gesture stated unequivocally that I had moved Newark from "urban blight to urban bright." The citation read, "Mayor James saved New Jersey's largest City, Newark." I, now, constantly remind people that although we didn't do everything, we did a lot to make Newark a better place. We loved our city and wore Newark on our shirt sleeves.

Newark Was A Struggling City

When I became mayor in 1986 Newark faced a $40 million budget deficit, was crime ridden, led the nation in auto thefts and was rated one of the worst cities in America according to *Harper's* magazine. We were the butt of every joke with Johnny Carson saying, "First prize contest winners will spend one week in Newark and second prize is two weeks in Newark;" and Jay Leno saying that "Newark stinks;" Phil Donahue stated "Who in their right mind would want to visit Newark?" I challenged each of these popular television hosts and made them apologize. I invited each of them to "Please come and visit Newark and see the progress being made."

In 1986 the police were on strike when I took office. They were handing out flyers at Broad and Market Streets saying that Newark was not a safe place. They were protesting Mayor Gibson's lay-off of police officers and his refusal to hire more. Newark was the crime, murder and auto theft capital of America.

Mayor James, keynote speaker promoting 100,000 Cops Bill on behalf of Bill Clinton before a nationwide group of Law Enforcement Officers in the White House Rose Garden:

In 1994 I joined President Bill Clinton to support his national program to hire a record number of police officers in urban cities, and traveled across the country promoting it. I was chosen to speak in the White House Rose Garden to lobby Congress to pass the 100,000 New Cops Bill. With its passage, Newark would receive monies to hire a record number of police officers which I believed would decrease criminal activity.

Passage of the 100,000 New Cops Bill catapulted Newark into a renaissance city with pride, prosperity and progress to follow. Newark is now a "Destination City" with planned programs and economic projects that will develop and surface over the next decade. Everyone now wanted to invest in Newark and some wanted to become elected officials in Newark. Following our renaissance we had carpetbaggers moving to Newark to run for office, using Newark as a stepping stone in their dream for higher office.

$1 Billion court victory over Port Authority of New York/New Jersey "Airport lease" with $450 Million upfront cash payment in 2006

It pleases me to report that in 2006, before retiring and with the help of some Honorable members of the city council (Council President & South Ward councilman Donald Bradley, councilwoman-at-large Gayle Chaneyfield Jenkins, West Ward councilwoman Rev. Dr. Mamie Bridgeforth and councilwoman-at-large Bessie Walker), we took the Port Authority to court and finally negotiated an unprecedented $1 Billion lease settlement with the Port Authority of New York/New Jersey for property tax relief.

It was not easy. We went, unannounced, to the office of Senate President and acting governor, Richard Codey, in West Orange and asked for his help. When he started rationalizing and playing politics as usual, the unexpected happened; our most dignified member of the group, West Ward Councilwoman Rev. Dr. Mamie Bridgeforth, stood and pointed her finger at Codey shouting, "My grandmother taught me that you can't piss in my face and call it rain water; we want our money now," Codey was shaken by her remarks turning beet red. He got the message and our money was on its way.

We demanded and received $450 million upfront monies to balance our budget; earmarked funds for property tax relief for the next four years; and made the building of the Prudential Center possible with a partnership payment of $185 million.

Our new lease would have our rental income based on the gross income of the Port Authority rather than their net income, which they could manipulate with excessive and unnecessary expenditures.

I am also proud of the implementation of the following programs and achievements during my tenure in office:

Newark's Society Hill at University Heights wins Harvard University "Dively Award" for best urban housing

In every ward and in the neighborhoods we witnessed new homes being built. Some of these homes were selling for more than a million dollars. We built the best mouse trap where citizens from all over the state and outside of New Jersey stood in line in the rain for one week, in 1987 to be the first to purchase state-of-the-art condos at University Heights, K. Hovanian's Society Hill. We proved that Newark could attract a middle class population.

We added the downtown rail link "From the train to the plane," connecting Newark's Penn Station to Newark Liberty International Airport. We lured IDT, MBNA and other giant corporations to Newark. Historically speaking, we became the first city in America to bring a corporate 500 company back to the city it had left for ten years, (leaving Florham Park and moving back to Newark) Blue Cross, Blue Shield.

Corporate America learned that the boondocks was no place to sustain a mostly clerical staff, who depended upon public transportation to and from work, and who preferred to chit chat in local restaurants during lunch time, rather than sit in a company cafeteria.

Added to these mortar and brick improvements, the James administration balanced twenty consecutive municipal budgets, and improved Newark's bond ratings by spending five billion dollars on economic development and infrastructure projects in Newark. The James Administration gave land and money to the Newark Board of Education to build state-of-the art new schools ($3 million for Central High School including a new pool) for our children to learn and increased recreational facilities for the worthy use of leisure time; thus reducing violence, crime and drug abuse (also reducing the rate of recidivism). We believed that providing adequate recreation was a deterrent to youth violence and a criminal lifestyle.

Newark Ready Scholars Program

I am most proud of the fact that thousands of students have been given an opportunity to attend colleges and universities of their choice because of the privately funded highly successful "Ready Scholars Program," that the city introduced in 1987. This program was made possible with the visionary and fiscal support of philanthropist, Ray Chambers. Every seventh grade student who maintained a C or better average could attend the college or university of their choice; as well as receive a mentor and promise of employment upon graduation. We owe a lot in Newark to the kindness, love and generosity of Ray Chambers (a proud graduate of Newark West Side High School).

Award winning "ABC (Ashe Bolletierri Cities) and Althea Gibson Tennis Programs"

As a longtime tennis player, I am proud that my Ashe/Boliet-tieri/City (ABC) Tennis Program, founded with the late Arthur Ashe, assisted students to achieve physically, academically and socially and became a national model for other cities. When Arthur called and asked me to meet with him and Nick Boliettieri about starting a national tennis program in Newark, I thought they were kidding at first. They proved me wrong.

They were sincere, committed and courageous. When reporters asked Arthur if I could play tennis, he said, "Sharpe cheats on line calls; he has never seen a ball in on his side of the net." I had no comment. I have never met two more honorable and dedicated persons in my life than Arthur Ashe and Nick Boliettieri. Because of the success of the ABC tennis program, we later added the Althea Gibson tennis program.

Past President of the National League of Cities (NLC) and Trustee for the United State Conference of Mayors (USCM)

The two most prestigious organizations representing local govern-ment are the National League of Cities (NLC), founded in December 1924, representing over 18,000 cities, villages and towns, and the United States Conference of Mayors (USCM), founded in 1923, representing 1,139 cities in the United States with populations of 30,000 or more.

I had been a member of the NLC since 1970. When I became president in 1993-94, it propelled me to the position of being spokes-man for urban America. As President of the NLC and a trustee for the United States Conference of Mayors, I traveled the USA, giving speeches before state municipal leagues on how to improve the quality of life in our cities.

As I traveled the length and breadth of the nation, I was learn-ing what the best practices in America were for addressing municipal problems. Of course, I brought back the best practices to explore here at home in Newark. I truthfully believe that the renaissance that took place in Newark, beginning in the 1990's was the result of my having looked at so many other cities and seeing what they were doing to solve their problems. I became much wiser, more knowledgeable and aware of what works and what doesn't work.

I had sixteen years of legislative (city council) and administrative (college) experience when I became mayor in 1986. I inherited a $40 million budget deficit, a crime ridden city with the police on strike, 10,000 abandoned buildings; a struggling city at the butt of every joke. We hit the ground running, though. With team work we were still able to create a renaissance. We spent over $5 billion in economic development. We improved our infrastructure, created jobs and made Newark a destination city. We improved Newark's bond ratings twice and Newark won the National Triple Crown for recycling, tree planting and improving the environment.

We were also recognized for our citywide housing construction and our private public partnerships. As *The Star-Ledger* begrudgingly reported, "Newark was on a roll," and we placarded our city with colorful banners to acknowledge it.

Some Most Notable Newark Improvements/Action by the James Administration:

- Never laid off a municipal employee
- Never raised the municipal portion of the tax rate
- Implemented an implosion program for Newark's failed Newark
  Housing Authority high-rises and replaced them with state-of-the-art townhouses
- Brought five or more new schools (Luis Munoz Marin Middle School, Science Park and Central High Schools, Belmont Runyon Campus and First Avenue Elementary in the North Ward,) to the city
- New Jersey Performing Arts Center (NJPAC) "The impossible dream."
- Prudential Center for the New Jersey Devils and Seton Hall University Basketball Team (City gave $185 Million, NHL New Jersey Devils $200 Million)
- Bears/Eagles Riverfront Baseball Stadium

- Downtown to airport rail link & new station
- 10,000 units of new housing
- Hope Six Program changed the landscape of the Central Ward (new townhouses, recreation centers and commercial development)
- Brought IDT to Newark
- Brought MBNA to Newark
- Newark Legal Center & Seton Hall Law School
- Rutgers Law School
- Home Depot
- Applebee's Restaurant, Starbucks, IHOP & KFC
- New neighborhood Pathmark Shopping Centers
- Ten (10)new hotels and occupancy tax
- Branch Brook Park Roller Skating Rink
- Malcolm X Shabazz Athletic Stadium & Recreation
- Ironbound B Athletic Field
- New Sharpe James/Kenneth Gibson Aquatic Center
- New Rotunda & Hayes Park East Swimming pools
- Congressman Joseph Minish waterfront project
- Newark Legal Center
- Gateway office buildings 2 and 3
- Newark Urban Screens (movie theater)
- University Housing on Central Avenue
- Berkeley College
- Brought Blue Cross/Blue Shield back to Newark after having moved ten years prior
- New FBI Headquarters (against the wishes of NJPAC officials)
- New Dr. Martin Luther King Federal Court House (negotiated with Mr. Diamond of the GSA)

The $64,000 Question

People keep asking me what things or one thing stand out in my mind after having been mayor for twenty years? What do you think your legacy should be? Well, of course, I have no control over what and how the bias media and history will treat Sharpe James.

So far they have done an excellent job in portraying me as a monster because of my fierce independence, always fighting for Newark and its citizens and kicking The Star-*Ledger* out of office space they occupied at Newark City Hall for a lack of balance in media coverage. When I vigorously and vociferously complained about their negative coverage, Mort Pye, who was the editor at the time, told me, "We cover plane crashes not plane landings."

They refused my offer to relocate them to another municipal building, instead opting to rent space across from City Hall from which they could launch daily attacks on me. I respected their right to do so. We were seeking parity not charity. Sometimes a divorce is necessary.

However, as for my legacy I was guided by one principle that I learned in church very early, the biblical quote, "Whatever you do for the least of my people, you do for me."

With that in mind I will always remember my two year fight with the members of the City Council to have my Newark Housing Authority appointed commissioners and director, Harold Lucas, introduce an implosion program to demolish Newark's failed public high-rises, which I affectionately called "Reservations for the poor."

The City Council did not want me to tear down empty ghost-like standing high-rises. Councilman-at-large Donald Tucker wanted to fight me over the issue of tearing down abandoned buildings, a mirror of hopelessness, decadence and a failed society, Columbus Homes. I kept saying to Donald, "They have been empty for over ten years, what plan do you have?"

So I would like to believe that the two year fight and victory against the City Council and the Newark Coalition for low-income housing to institute my "NHA implosion program," with Federal Judge Dickinson Debevoise becoming the monitor and demanding a "One for one unit replacement," changed the image, and quality of life in Newark forever. Thus, I would like my tombstone to read:

Here lies the mayor who had the conviction and courage to tear down high-rise structures (formerly reservations for the poor) and replace them with state-of-the-art low-rise townhouses where citizens are fighting to get in and not out.

No more Columbus Homes Projects

No more Archbishop Walsh Projects

No more Stella Wright Projects

No more Hayes Home Projects

No more Otto E. Kretchmer Home Projects

No more Scudder Home Projects

No more Hill Manor

So, clearly my best response to any question about my legacy would be "Let the work I've done speak for me." Or, in the words of the old Negro spiritual, "We are not what we want to be, we are not what we ought to be, but thank God we are not what we used to be;"

FOR NEWARK HAS EXPERIENCED

A SHARPE CHANGE.

Index

Index

Index

Index

Index

Questions

white suburban jury?

1. Jury - not of peers or constituents.
   Why were they chosen?

2. From the beginning you had detractors, people with grudges, investigating you, trying to find something to accuse you of —

   they saw you as a strong articulate Black man who could rise to higher positions in the state or basic revenge for taking successful Recalling Lee B

   Do you feel that was a carry over caused have been a revenge for taking over the South Ward successful Recalling Lee Bernstein? Even though the South Ward was predominantly Black.

3. Incident with Wally Choice, the all American athlete, and McClain, Dr. Alloway, and the kids with you + the baseball bats. pp 73-4

   U.S. Atty in Florida
   "U.S" under Congine

4. Kept the name Newark for the Airport!

5. James "Kicked the Star Ledger" out of City Hall. Now the S.L. wanted to Kick James out?

p. 259
"Christie' wrong doings
no prosecutions

Mr. Annette Gautier
Supr - the Pre Sentencing
Office

Ruthless Ambition